DANUBE CANAL

PAGES 106–111
*Street Finder maps
1, 2 & 5*

PAGES 68–87
*Street Finder maps
2, 4, 5 & 6*

PAGES 88–105
*Street Finder maps
3, 4 & 5*

PAGES 142–157
*Street Finder
map 4*

*Stephansdom
Quarter*

*Hofburg
Quarter*

*Belvedere
Quarter*

D0977924

EYEWITNESS TRAVEL GUIDES

VIENNA

Main contributor: STEPHEN BROOK

DK

LONDON, NEW YORK,
MELBOURNE, MUNICH AND DELHI
www.dk.com

PROJECT EDITOR Carolyn Pyrah
ART EDITOR Sally Ann Hibbard
EDITORS Marcus Hardy, Kim Inglis
US EDITOR Mary Ann Lynch
DESIGNERS Vanessa Hamilton, Andy Wilkinson
DESIGN ASSISTANT Elly King

PRODUCTION Hilary Stephens
PICTURE RESEARCH Ellen Root
DTP DESIGNER Adam Moore

CONTRIBUTORS
Gretel Beer, Caroline Bugler, Deirdre Coffey, Fred Mawer

PHOTOGRAPHER
Peter Wilson

ILLUSTRATORS
Richard Draper, Stephen Gyapay, Chris Orr,
Robbie Polley, Ann Winterbotham

Reproduced by Colourscan, Singapore
Printed and bound by L. Rex Printing Company Limited, China

First American Edition, 1994
06 07 08 09 10 9 8 7 6 5 4 3 2

Published in the United States by DK Publishing, Inc.,
375 Hudson Street, New York, New York 10014
Reprinted with revisions 1996, 1997 (twice), 2000, 2001,
2002, 2003, 2004, 2006

Copyright © 1994, 2006 Dorling Kindersley Limited, London

Published in Great Britain by Dorling Kindersley Limited

ISSN 1542-1554
ISBN 0-7894-9575-9

THROUGHOUT THIS BOOK, FLOORS ARE REFERRED TO IN ACCORDANCE WITH
EUROPEAN USAGE, I.E., THE "FIRST FLOOR" IS THE FLOOR ABOVE GROUND LEVEL.

**The information in this
Dorling Kindersley Travel Guide is checked regularly**.
Every effort has been made to ensure that this book is as up-to-date
as possible at the time of going to press. Some details, however,
such as telephone numbers, opening hours, prices, gallery hanging
arrangements and travel information are liable to change. The
publishers cannot accept responsibility for any consequences arising
from the use of this book, nor for any material on third party
websites, and cannot guarantee that any website address in this
book will be a suitable source of travel information. We value the
views and suggestions of our readers very highly. Please write to:
Publisher, DK Eyewitness Travel Guides,
Dorling Kindersley, 80 Strand, London WC2R 0RL, Great Britain.

CONTENTS

HOW TO USE
THIS GUIDE 6

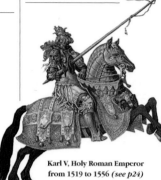

Karl V, Holy Roman Emperor
from 1519 to 1556 *(see p24)*

INTRODUCING
VIENNA

PUTTING VIENNA ON
THE MAP *10*

THE HISTORY OF
VIENNA *16*

VIENNA AT A
GLANCE *40*

VIENNA THROUGH THE
YEAR *62*

Bronze and copper Anker Clock
in Hoher Markt *(see p84)*

EYEWITNESS TRAVEL GUIDES

VIENNA

Façade of Schönbrunn Palace *(see pp172–75)*

Grinzing restaurant *(see pp215–17)*

TRAVELLERS' NEEDS

Sachertorte *(see p209)*

SURVIVAL GUIDE

The Vienna Boys' Choir *(see p39)*

Karlskirche in the Belvedere Quarter *(see pp148–9)*

HOW TO USE THIS GUIDE

THIS EYEWITNESS travel guide helps you get the most from your stay in Vienna with the minimum of difficulty. The opening section, *Introducing Vienna*, locates the city geographically, sets modern Vienna in its historical context and describes events through the entire year. *Vienna at a Glance* is an overview of the city's main attractions. *Vienna Area by Area* starts on page 66. This is the main sightseeing section,

Plotting the route

which covers all the important sights, with photographs, maps and illustrations. It also includes day trips from Vienna, a river trip and four walks around the city. Carefully researched tips for hotels, restaurants, cafés and bars, markets and shops, entertainment and sports are found in *Travellers' Needs*. The *Survival Guide* has advice from how to make a telephone call to using the transport system and its ticket machines.

FINDING YOUR WAY AROUND THE SIGHTSEEING SECTION

Each of the six sightseeing areas in the city is colour-coded for easy reference. Every chapter opens with an introduction to the part of Vienna it covers, describing its history and character, followed by a Street-by-Street

map illustrating a typical part of the area. Finding your way around each chapter is made simple by the numbering system used throughout. The most important sights are covered in detail in two or more full pages.

Each area has colour-coded thumb tabs.

A locator map shows where you are in relation to other areas in the city centre.

Locator map

A suggested route takes in some of the most interesting and attractive streets in the area.

1 Introduction to the area
For easy reference, the sights in each area are numbered and plotted on an area map. To help the visitor, this map also shows underground stations, train stations and parking areas. The area's key sights are listed by category: Churches and Cathedrals; Museums and Galleries; Streets and Squares; Markets; Historic Buildings and Parks and Gardens.

The area shaded pink is shown in greater detail on the Street-by-Street map on the following pages.

2 Street-by-Street map
This gives a bird's eye view of interesting and important parts of each sightseeing area. The numbering of the sights ties in with the area map and the fuller descriptions on the pages that follow.

The list of star sights recommends the places that no visitor should miss.

VIENNA AREA MAP

THE COLOURED AREAS shown on this map *(see inside front cover)* are the six main sightseeing areas used in this guide. Each is covered in a full chapter in *Vienna Area by Area (pp66–177)*. They are highlighted on other maps throughout the book. In *Vienna at a Glance (pp40–61)*, for example, they help you locate the top sights. They are also used to help you find the position of the four guided walks *(pp178–87)*.

Numbers refer to each sight's position on the area map and its place in the chapter.

Practical information provides all the information you need to visit every sight. Map references pinpoint each sight's location on the *Street Finder* map *(pp262–7)*.

The visitors' checklist provides all the practical information needed to plan your visit.

3 Detailed information on each sight

All the important sights in Vienna are described individually. They are listed in order, following the numbering on the area map at the start of the section. Practical information includes a map reference, opening hours, telephone numbers, admission charges and facilities available for each sight. The key to the symbols used is on the back flap.

Stars indicate the features no visitor should miss.

4 Vienna's major sights
Historic buildings are dissected to reveal their interiors; museums and galleries have colour-coded floorplans to help you find important exhibits.

A timeline charts the key events in the history of the building.

INTRODUCING VIENNA

VIENNE

Putting Vienna on the Map

Vienna has a population of just over 1.5 million and covers an area of 415 sq km (160 sq miles). The River Danube flows through it and the Danube Canal flows through the city centre. It is the capital of the Republic of Austria, of which it is also a federal state, and is the country's political, economic, cultural and administrative centre. At the heart of Central Europe, it makes a good base from which to explore cities such as Bratislava, Prague, Budapest, Zagreb, Salzburg and Munich, as well as many Austrian towns.

Satellite view of Greater Vienna

Europe
Vienna is served by Schwechat International Airport, and road and rail routes link it to cities throughout Europe. Prague is five hours away by road.

Vienna and Environs

The inner Ringstrasse and the outer Gürtel circle the city. The Gürtel links with major roads to other Austrian and European cities. For sights outside the centre see pp156–77.

VIENNA AND ENVIRONS

Korneuburg

Danube

Tulln
Klosterneuburg
Langenzersdorf
Deutsch-Wagram

Grossenzersdorf

Purkersdorf

See next page
Danube

Schwechat

Perchtoldsdorf

Mödling
Laxenburg

Heiligenkreuz
Mayerling
Gumpoldskirchen
Ebergassing

Baden
Traiskirchen
Mannersdorf

AGUE

Vltava

CZECH REPUBLIC

Melk
Abbey

Linz
Danube
Melk

A
VIENNA
BRATISLAVA

SLOVAKIA

Vah

Schwechat
Eisenstadt
L. Neusiedl

Bucharest

Schloss Esterházy
Eisenstadt

BUDAPEST

Houses on
Hauptplatz,
Graz

HUNGARY

Graz

KEY

Klagenfurt

L. Balaton

SLOVENIA

	Greater Vienna
✈	Airport
⚓	Ferry port
	Motorway
	Major road
	Railway
	Country boundary

Drava

Danube

Belgrade

0 kilometres 100
0 miles 50

Aerial view of central Vienna

Greater Vienna

THE CITY OF VIENNA IS SITUATED on the site of a Roman garrison *(see p20).* The Danube, or Donau, flows to the east of the city, and the Canal runs through the centre. The Greater Vienna area is divided into 23 districts *(see p245)* with districts 1–9 comprising the centre.

Kahlenberg

Klosterneuburg Krems Melk

Grinzing

SANDGASSE

Heiligenstadt

GRINZINGER ALLEE

Unterdöbling
222

Ober-
döbling

Pötzleinsdorf

WÄHRING

Tulln

DORNBACHER STRASSE

Gersthof

Neuwaldegg

222

221

BRIGIT

BRIGITTENAUER LÄNDE

Franz-Josefs-
Bahnhof

WÄHRINGER GÜRTEL

ALSERGRUND

HERNALS

Dornbach

OTTAKRING

WATTGASSE

221

JOSEFSTADT

INNERES

BURGGARTE

PENZING

223

FLÖTZERSTEIG

223

223

RUDOLFSHEIM

221

NEUBAU

1

*St Pölten
Linz*

Westbahnhof

FÜNFHAUS

MARIAHILF

Penzing

HADIKGASSE

HIETZINGER KAI

221

MARGARETEN

*St Pölten
Linz
Mariazell
Salzburg*

17

Unter-
St-Veit

1

221

SCHÖNBRUNN

HIETZING

224

MEIDLING

12

225

ALTMANNSDORFER STRASSE

TRIESTER STR.

225

Lainz

Siedlung
Wienerfel

KEY

Central Vienna
(see pp14–15)

Greater Vienna

Hetzendorf

A23

SÜDAUTOBAHN

Main line train station

Coach and bus station

Motorway

Motorway tunnel

Alterlaa

A2

230

Major road

Minor road

Railway

Perchtoldsdorf // Atzgersdorf

*Wiener Neustadt
Mayerling
Baden* ↓

224

↙ *Graz*

Inzersdorf

Praha
Brno
DONAUFERAUTOBAHN
idsdorfer
ke
STIFTER-STR.
A22
A22
A22
Brigittenauer
Brücke

FLORIDSDORF
3
Mühlschüttel
Alte Donau

Kagran
Raasdorf

WAGRAMER STR
8

DONAUSTADT

DONAU PARK

KAISERMÜHLEN

3
Neukagran

3B

ERZHERZOG - KARL - STRASSE
3

Reichs-
brücke

Stadlau

Hainburg
an der Donau

See next page

Donau

LEOPOLD-
STADT
8

Praterstern-
Wien Nord

HANDELSKAI

Prater-
brücke

227

Wien Mitte

PRATER

STADTPARK
1

GÜRTELAUTOBAHN
A23

227

10

LANDSTRASSE

221

227

BELVEDERE-
GARTEN

221

SIMMERINGER LÄNDE
A4

Südbahnhof

A4

A20

OSTAUTOBAHN

A23

SIMMERING

Flughafen
Schwechat

Bratislava

SIMMERINGER HAUPTSTRASSE

A4

FAVORITEN

Kaiser-Ebersdorf

A23

16

KURPARK

Neulaa

0 kilometres   1

Bruck
Budapest

Flughafen
Schwechat

Rust
Eisenstadt

Oberlaa

0 miles   0.5

Central Vienna

THIS BOOK DIVIDES VIENNA into six areas in the centre of town, and has further sections for sights on the outskirts of the city, suggested walks and day trips, as well as practical information. Each of the six main areas has its own chapter, and contains a selection of sights that convey some of that area's history and distinctive character, such as the Stephansdom in the Stephansdom Quarter and the imperial buildings in the Hofburg Quarter. Most of the city's famous sights are in or close to the city centre and are easy to reach on foot or by public transport.

Detail on the door of the Pallavicini Palace (1784) in Josefsplatz

Bars in Sterngasse
Sterngasse, in the Jewish Quarter (see p84), is packed with lively bars like these spilling out into the street (see Restaurants, Cafés and Bars on p217).

KEY

▨	Major sight
Ⓤ	U-Bahn station
⑤	Badner Bahn stop
Ⓟ	Parking
ⓘ	Tourist information office
⌨	Police station
✝	Church

0 metres   500

0 yards   500

View over the Rooftops from Am Hof
Am Hof, the largest enclosed square in Vienna, is circled by a number of interesting houses, some with statuary on their roofs and pediments (see p87).

Rathauskeller Façade
The city has plenty of wine cellars – many associated with old vineyards – where wine, beer and simple food is served. This one is located beneath the city hall (see pp128 and 213).

Pallas Athene Fountain
The figure of Pallas Athene by Karl Kundmann was placed on the fountain in front of the Parliament building in 1902 (see p125).

THE HISTORY OF VIENNA

VIENNA WAS ORIGINALLY a Celtic settlement on the site of the present-day city. Under the Romans it became the garrison of Vindobona, supporting the nearby town of Carnuntum. Its location on the edge of the Hungarian plains, however, made it vulnerable to attack, and Barbarian invasions reduced the town to ruins by the early 5th century. In the 10th century, the German Babenberg dynasty acquired Vienna, and during their reign of almost three centuries the city became a major trading centre. Later, in the 13th century, Vienna came under the control of the Habsburgs. In the 16th century, Turkish invasions threatened Vienna and devastated its outskirts. Only in 1683 were the Turks finally defeated, allowing Vienna to flourish. Immense palaces were built around the court within the city, and in the liberated outskirts, and by the 18th century Vienna was a major imperial and cultural centre. Napoleon's occupation of Vienna in 1809 shook the Habsburgs' confidence, as did the revolution of 1848 – the year Franz Joseph came to the throne. By 1914, Vienna's population had expanded to two million, as people from all over the Habsburg Empire flocked to this vibrant centre. After World War I, the Habsburg Empire collapsed and Vienna's role as the Imperial capital ended. In the following years a strong municipal government – "Red Vienna"– tried to solve the social problems of the city. Austria was annexed by Nazi Germany in the Anschluss of 1938 and then, following Hitler's defeat in 1945, came under Allied control. Vienna regained its independence in 1955, when Austria became a sovereign state.

Maximilian I shield

Circular plan of Turkish siege, from 1529

◁ Detail from *The Marriage of Joseph II to Isabella of Parma* (1760) by the Martin van Meytens School

Vienna's Rulers

VIENNA EMERGED from the Dark Ages as a German outpost controlled by Babenberg dukes, who brought great prosperity to the city by the 12th century. There followed a period of social disorder, and intermittent Bohemian rule known as the Interregnum. Vienna fell into Habsburg hands in the 13th century and remained the cornerstone of their domains until the dynasty's downfall in 1918. From 1452 until 1806, Habsburg rulers were almost invariably elected as Holy Roman Emperor, enabling Vienna to develop as an Imperial capital on the grandest scale.

Duke Friedrich II with falconer

1278–82 Rudolf I of Germany is regent of Austria.

1246–50 Interregnum under Margrave Hermann of Baden after death of Duke Friedrich II

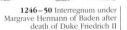

900	1000	1100	1200		1300	1400
BABENBERG RULERS					**HABSBURG RULERS**	
900	1000	1100	1200		1300	1400

976 Leopold of Babenberg

1198–1230 Duke Leopold VI

1177–1194 Duke Leopold V

1358–65 Duke Rudolf IV

1141–77 Duke Heinrich II Jasomirgott

1251–76 Interregnum under Přemysl Ottakar II

1637–57 Emperor
Ferdinand III

452–93 Friedrich V
crowned as Holy Roman
Emperor Friedrich III)

1485–90 King Matthias
Corvinus of Hungary
occupies Vienna

1493–1519 Emperor
Maximilian I

*Emperor
Franz
Joseph I*

1612–19
Emperor Matthias

1657–1705 Emperor Leopold I

1835–48
Emperor
Ferdinand I
of Austria

1576–1612
Emperor
Rudolf II

1705–11 Emperor
Joseph I

1848–1916 Emperor
Franz Joseph I

1711–40
Emperor Karl VI

1500	1600	1700	1800	1900

1500	1600	1700	1800	1900

1619–37 Emperor
Ferdinand II

1792–1835 Emperor
Franz II (becomes
Franz I of Austria
in 1806)

1918
Habsburgs
exiled

1564–76 Emperor Maximilian II

1916–18 Emperor
Karl I

1556–64 Emperor
Ferdinand I

1790–92 Emperor
Leopold II

1780–90 Emperor
Joseph II

1519–1556
Emperor Karl V

1740–80 Empress Maria Theresa

Early Vienna

THE REGION AROUND VIENNA was first inhabited in the late Stone Age, and Vienna itself was founded as a Bronze Age settlement in about 800 BC. Settled by Celts from about 400 BC, the Romans incorporated it into the province of Pannonia in 15 BC, establishing the garrison of Vindobona by the 1st century AD. Later overrun by Barbarian tribes, Vindobona diminished in importance until the 8th century, when the Frankish Emperor Charlemagne made it part of his Eastern March and part of the Holy Roman Empire.

Roman urn

EXTENT OF THE CITY

☐ *150 AD*   ☐ *Today*

Hallstatt Idol
The Iron-Age Hallstatt culture flourished around Vienna from 750 to 400 BC.

Main defensive wall

VINDOBONA
Established around 100 AD, the garrison of Vindobona was allied to the town of Carnuntum.

Vindobona   Carnuntum

Venus of Willendorf
Now in the Natural History Museum (see p126), this late Stone Age figurine was found at Willendorf, close to Vienna, in 1906.

Roman Map
This map of Pannonia shows the position of Roman towns and forts along the Danube.

TIMELINE

5000	2000	800	0	100	200
	2000 BC Indo-Germanic settlements on northwest wooded slopes	**800 BC** Bronze Age settlements on what is now Hoher Markt	**750 BC** Hallstatt culture **400 BC** Celtic culture	*Marcus Aurelius* **180** Roman Emperor Marcus Aurelius dies in Vindobona	**280** Rom Emperor Prob authorizes win growing in ▮ Danube a

5000 BC Late Stone Age culture		**15 BC** Celtic region of Noricum occupied by Romans	
	Preserved shoe from the Hallstatt culture		**250** Vindobona, developed as a garrison town, has a population of 20,000

☐ **Early Vienna**

Marcus Aurelius
This great Roman emperor and philosopher came to Carnuntum to fight the Germanic tribes; he died in Vindobona in 180 AD.

Gold Jewellery
The Romans were first attracted to the region around Vindobona for its valuable resources, among them gold.

Stables

Soldiers' quarters

Soldier's Tomb
This tomb, excavated at Carnuntum, dates from around the 1st century AD.

WHERE TO SEE EARLY VIENNA

Many of the Roman walls and ditches have left their mark on the layout of Vienna, but excavations have not been numerous. The most impressive are at Hoher Markt *(see p84)*, at No. 10 Am Hof *(p87)*, and in the Michaelerplatz *(p92)*. The most extensive remains are not in Vienna itself but at Carnuntum, about 25 miles (40 km) east of Vienna, where two amphitheatres and other ruins survive.

The Hoher Markt, *in the very heart of Vienna, is the site of excavations of the Roman garrison of Vindobona.*

This Gorgon's Head, *a large Roman relief of the mythical Medusa, is from Hoher Markt.*

395 First Barbarian invasions approach Vindobona

405 Romans withdraw from Vindobona

500–650 Repeated invasions by Langobards, Goths, Avars and Slav tribes

300 400 500 600 700 800

433 Vindobona destroyed by Huns

Barbarian horseman

883 First mention of Wenia (Vienna) on the borders of the Eastern March founded by Charlemagne

Medieval Vienna

I**N 955 THE HOLY ROMAN EMPEROR** Otto I expelled Hungarian tribes from the Eastern March *(see p20)*. In 976 he made a gift of Vienna to the German Babenbergs, who, despite further incursions by the Hungarians, restored the city's importance as a centre of trade and culture. Following Friedrich II's death in 1246 and the ensuing Interregnum *(see p18)*, the Habsburgs began centuries of rule over Austria. Vienna became a major European city and hub of the Holy Roman Empire.

EXTENT OF THE CITY
☐ *1400*   ☐ *Today*

St Ruprecht
St Ruprecht was the patron saint of salt merchants, who brought this precious commodity along the Danube from salt mines in western Austria. Today his statue overlooks the Danube canal.

DEATH OF FRIEDRICH II
Duke Friedrich II was the last of the Babenbergs to rule Vienna. He died in battle against invading Hungarian forces in 1246.

Stephansdom

The Nobility
Often elected as Holy Roman Emperors, the Habsburgs attracted nobility from all over their huge empire.

Duke
Friedrich II

Coronation Robe
This magnificent medieval robe (1133), originally from Palermo, formed part of the Habsburg's imperial regalia.

TIMELINE

900	1000	1100
955 Otto I of Germany defeats the Hungarians, restoring Christianity and re-establishing the Eastern March ("Ostmark", later renamed Ostarrichi)	**1030** The Hungarians besiege Vienna	**1147** Stephansdom consecrated
		1136 Death of Margave Leopold III
909 Eastern March invaded by Hungarian forces	**976** Otto I makes Leopold of Babenberg Margrave of the Eastern March, initiating Babenberg rule	**1137** Vienna becomes a fortified city
		1156 Heinrich II Jasomirgott moves his court to Vienna; builds Am Hof *(see p87)*

☐ **Medieval Vienna**

Richard the Lionheart
In 1192, Richard I of England, returning from the crusades in the Holy Land, was captured and held to ransom by Duke Leopold V.

WHERE TO SEE MEDIEVAL VIENNA

Gothic churches include the Stephansdom *(see pp76–9)*, Maria am Gestade *(p85)*, the Burgkapelle, Minoritenkirche *(p103)*, Ruprechtskirche *(p81)* and Augustinerkirche *(p102)*. The Michaelerkirche *(p92)* includes some Gothic sculptures and the Schottenkirche medieval art *(p110)*. Surviving medieval houses include the Basiliskenhaus in Schönlaterngasse *(p74)*.

Tributary of the River Danube

Medieval city wall

Verduner Altar
This masterpiece forms part of the treasury of the huge abbey at Kloster-neuburg (see p161). *Its 51 panels were completed in 1181 by Nikolaus of Verdun. The abbey itself was consecrated in 1136.*

Stained glass *(about 1340) in the Cathedral Museum (p74).*

Hungarian encampment

University
Vienna's University was founded in 1365 by Duke Rudolf IV. This miniature (about 1400) shows the medieval university building and some of the tutors and their students.

Seal of Přzemysl Ottakar II

1200	1300	1400

1278–82 Rudolf I becomes ruler of Austria after defeating Ottakar II; 640 years of Habsburg rule follow

1288 Viennese uprising against Habsburgs crushed

1359 Rudolf IV lays foundation stone of the Stephansdom tower

1365 University founded

1477 Friedrich III's son Maximilian I marries Mary of Burgundy, heiress to the Low Countries

1246 Death of Friedrich II followed by Interregnum, during which Přzemysl Ottakar II rules Vienna

1273 Count Rudolf of Habsburg crowned Rudolf I of Germany

1278 Vienna granted a city charter

1330 The first Gothic section of Maria am Gestade built

1438 Albrecht V elected Holy Roman Emperor; Vienna made seat of Empire

1452 Friedrich V crowned as Holy Roman Emperor Friedrich III

1485 Vienna occupied by King Matthias Corvinus of Hungary

Renaissance Vienna

U NDER MAXIMILIAN I, Vienna was transformed into a centre for the arts. The Habsburgs were invariably elected Holy Roman Emperor, and by the 16th century their mighty empire had expanded into Spain, Holland, Burgundy, Bohemia and Hungary. But it was under constant threat: from Turkish attacks, the plague, and disputes between Protestants and Catholics that destabilized the city until 1576, when the Jesuits spearheaded the Counter-Reformation.

EXTENT OF THE CITY

☐ *1600*　　☐ *Today*

Book Illustration
This Renaissance war wagon (1512) is from Maximilian I's collection of books of engravings and illustrations.

Viennese Enamel Casket
This ornate enamel and crystal casket is typical of the skilful craftsmanship practised in Vienna in the 16th century.

Maximilian I married Mary of Burgundy in 1477 and acquired the Burgundian domains.

Imperial Crown
This beautiful crown was made by Bohemian craftsmen in 1610 for Rudolf II and can now be seen in the Hofburg Treasuries (see pp100–1).

Ferdinand I married Anna of Bohemia and Hungary, and inherited Bohemia in 1526. It was a Habsburg domain until 1918.

TIMELINE

	1519 Karl V inherits Burgundy titles and is elected Holy Roman Emperor; his brother Ferdinand I becomes Austria's archduke		**1556** Karl V's son, Philip II, inherits Spain; Ferdinand I takes Bohemia, Austria, Hungary, and imperial title	**1571** Protestant Maximilian II allows religious freedom; 80% of city is Protestant
1516 Maximilian's grandson, Karl V, inherits Spain		**1533** Ferdinand I moves his court to the Hofburg in Vienna		

1500	**1520**	**1540**	**1560**	**158**

| | **1498** Emperor Maximilian I founds Vienna Boys' Choir | *Suleiman the Magnificent* | **1541** Plague | **1572** Spanish Riding School founded | |
| **1493** Maximilian I expels Hungarians from Vienna | | | **1529** Graf Niklas Salm vanquishes Turkish army besieging Vienna | **1551** Jesuits start Counter-Reformation | **1577** Protestant services forbidden by Rudolf II |

☐ **Renaissance Vienna**

Triumphal Arch of Maximilian I

The German artist Albrecht Dürer (1471–1528) paid homage to Maximilian I in a famous volume of engravings, which included this design for a triumphal arch.

Philip I married Juana of Castile and Aragon in 1496 and acquired Spain.

Karl V inherited Spain from his mother, Juana of Castile and Aragon, in 1516.

THE FAMILY OF MAXIMILIAN I

Painted by Bernhard Strigel (around 1520), this portrait can be read as a document of how, by marrying into prominent European families, the Habsburg family was able to gain control of almost half of Europe.

Mary of Burgundy was married to Maximilian I and was Duchess of the Burgundian domains.

Alte Burg
The medieval core of the Hofburg was constantly being rebuilt. This engraving shows its appearance in the late 15th century, before Ferdinand I had it rebuilt in the 1550s.

WHERE TO SEE RENAISSANCE VIENNA

The Schweizertor (see p97) in the Hofburg is the most colourful surviving remnant of Renaissance Vienna, though the Salvatorkapelle portal (p85) surpasses it in elegance. Also in the Hofburg is the Renaissance Stallburg (p93). Some courtyards, such as those at No. 7 Bäckerstrasse (p75) and the Mollard-Clary Palace (p94), preserve a few Renaissance features.

The Schweizertor, built in the 16th century, forms the entrance to the Schweizerhof of the Hofburg (p97).

medallion commemorating Maximilian II

1618 Bohemian rebellion starts Thirty Year's War	**1629** Plague claims 30,000 lives	**1643** Swedish forces threaten Vienna	**1673–9** War with France over the Low Countries	
1600	**1620**	**1640**	**1660**	
1598–1618 Protestantism is banned	**1621** Jews expelled from Inner City			
1620 Ferdinand II defeats Protestant Bohemian aristocracy; Counter-Reformation spreads throughout Habsburg domains	*17th-century French infantry*			

Baroque Vienna

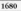

J B Fischer von Erlach

THE TURKISH THREAT TO VIENNA ended in 1683 when Kara Mustapha's forces were repelled. Under Karl VI the city expanded and the Karlskirche and the Belvedere palaces were constructed. Around the Hofburg, mansions for noble families sprang up, built by architects such as Johann Bernhard Fischer von Erlach *(see p149)* and Johann Lukas von Hildebrandt *(see p152)*. Vienna was transformed into a resplendent Imperial capital.

EXTENT OF THE CITY
☐ *1700*   ☐ *Today*

WINTER PALACE OF PRINCE EUGENE

J B Fischer von Erlach and Johann Lukas von Hildebrandt designed the Winter Palace *(see p80)* for Prince Eugene, hero of the Turkish campaign.

Plague
This lithograph depicts the plague of 1679, which killed around 30,000 Viennese.

Turkish Bed
Ornamented with martial emblems, this bed was designed for Prince Eugene in 1707.

Coffee Houses
The first coffee houses opened in Vienna in the mid-17th century and they have been a prized institution ever since.

Baroque Architecture
Baroque architecture was at its most prolific in Vienna in the early 18th century. **Trautson Palace *(see p117)***

TIMELINE

1683 Turkish siege of Vienna by 200,000 soldiers, under Kara Mustapha, from 14 July to 12 September

1700–14 The war of the Spanish Succession

1680	1690	1700

1679 Plague in Vienna

1683–1736 Prince Eugene of Savoy wins more victories over Turks and French, restoring Austria's fortunes

Kara Mustapha

The war of the Spanish Succession: Battle of Blenheim

☐ **Baroque Vienna**

THE HISTORY OF VIENNA

Turkish Siege
The defeat of the Turks in 1683 was crucial, not only for Vienna, but for Central Europe, which was spared the prospect of Ottoman rule.

Baroque statues

Elaborate window hoods

Baroque porticos

Prince Eugene's entourage

Dome ornamentation on the Karlskirche *(pp146–7)*

Window hood on the Zwölf Apostelkeller *(p74)*

WHERE TO SEE BAROQUE VIENNA

The Baroque is everywhere in Vienna. Hardly a street in the old city or inner suburbs is without a Baroque mansion or church. Fine examples of Baroque architecture include the Belvedere Palaces *(see pp152–57)*, the Prunksaal *(p102)*, the Karlskirche *(pp148–9)*, the Leopoldinischer Trakt in the Hofburg *(pp96–7)*, the Winter Riding School *(pp98–9)* and the Bohemian Court Chancery *(p84–5)*. Beautiful Baroque houses line many streets, including Naglergasse *(p94)* and Kurrentgasse *(p86)*.

The Prunksaal (1721–6) was built by J B Fischer von Erlach.

Prince Eugene
Best remembered for his role in defeating the Turks, Prince Eugene showed great military prowess in the ensuing decades, and died in 1736 laden with honours.

1713 Karl VI proclaims Pragmatic Sanction, allowing succession through the female line

1719 Karlskirche begun

Statue of Maria Theresa holding Pragmatic Sanction

10	1720	1730

1716 Lower Belvedere completed

1722 Vienna becomes an archbishopric

1724–6 Prunksaal and Upper Belvedere completed

Upper Belvedere

1713–14 Last plague in Vienna

Vienna under Maria Theresa

THE LONG REIGN OF MARIA THERESA was a time of serenity, wealth and sensible administration, despite a background of frequent wars. The vast palace of Schönbrunn was completed by the Empress, who also presided over Vienna's development as the musical capital of Europe. She was succeeded by Joseph II, who introduced many reforms, including religious freedom and public health measures. However, these reforms made him unpopular with his subjects, including the nobility who were angered by the way he handed out titles to bankers and industrialists.

Empress Maria Theresa

EXTENT OF THE CITY
☐ *1775*   ☐ *Today*

Rococo Table
Wilhelm Martitz designed this Rococo table in 1769 for Maria Theresa, who employed artists committed to the elaborate Rococo style.

Karlskirche   Stephansdom

Young Mozart
Mozart often performed for the Habsburgs, who were highly receptive to his genius.

Burgtheater Programme
This programme was printed for the first performance of Mozart's The Marriage of Figaro *in 1786, which took place in the original Burgtheater on Michaelerplatz.*

TIMELINE

Christoph von Gluck

1744–9 Schönbrunn Palace is extensively altered by Maria Theresa's court architect, Nikolaus Pacassi

1754 Vienna's first census records a population of 175,000

1740	1750	1760

1740 Maria Theresa comes to the throne; war of the Austrian Succession

Schönbrunn Palace

1762 First performance of Christoph von Gluck's *(see p38)* Orpheus and Eurydice *in the Burgtheater*

1766 Prater, formerly an imperial game reserve, opened to the public by Joseph II

☐ Vienna under Maria Theresa

Damenkarussell
This painting by Martin van Meytens depicts the Damenkarussell (1743), which was held at the Winter Riding School (see pp98–9) to celebrate the defeat of the French army at Prague.

WHERE TO SEE MARIA THERESA'S VIENNA

Schönbrunn Palace (*see pp174–5*) and the Theresianum (*p149*) date from the reign of Maria Theresa. Joseph II later commissioned the Josephinum (*p111*) and the Narrenturm (*p111*), and opened the Augarten (*p164*) and Prater (*pp162–63*) to the public. A Rococo organ is in the Michaelerkirche (*p92*), and some of Maria Theresa's tableware is in the Hofburg Treasuries (*pp100–1*).

VIEW FROM THE BELVEDERE
Under Maria Theresa, the Viennese were able to enjoy a prosperous city. This townscape by Bernardo Bellotto (1759–61) shows them sauntering through the gardens of the Belvedere, with the palaces and churches of the city in the distance.

Belvedere Gardens

Schönbrunn Palace is filled with Rococo interiors commissioned by Maria Theresa.

The Pope
In 1782 Pope Pius VI came to Vienna in an attempt to undo the religious reforms of Joseph II.

The Rococo high altar which is in the Michaelerkirche dates from around 1750.

1781 Joseph II's Edict of Toleration   *Allgemeine Krankenhaus*

1784 Joseph II founds the Allgemeine Krankenhaus and Narrenturm (*see p111*)

1770	1780		1790

1775 Augarten opened to the public by Joseph II

1782 Pope Pius VI in Vienna

1786 First performance of Mozart's *The Marriage of Figaro* in the Burgtheater

1790–2 Emperor Leopold II

1791 First performance of Mozart's *The Magic Flute*

Biedermeier Vienna

EXTENT OF THE CITY

☐ *1830*   ☐ *Today*

N APOLEON'S DEFEAT OF AUSTRIA was a humiliation for Emperor Franz I. The French conqueror briefly occupied Schönbrunn Palace, demolished part of the city walls, and married Franz I's daughter. After the Congress of Vienna, Franz I and his minister, Prince Metternich, imposed autocratic rule in Austria. The middle classes, excluded from political life, retreated into the artistic and domestic pursuits that characterized the Biedermeier age. Revolution in 1848 drove Metternich from power but led to a new period of conservative rule under Franz Joseph.

Early 19th-century dress

Prince Metternich
The architect of the Congress of Vienna, Metternich gained political supremacy of Austria over four decades. In 1848 revolutionary mobs drove him from Vienna.

THE CONGRESS OF VIENNA

After the defeat of Napoleon in 1814, the victorious European powers gathered in Vienna to restore the established order that had been severely disrupted by the French emperor. The crowned heads and elected rulers of Europe spent a year in the city, where the court and nobility entertained them with a succession of balls and other diversions. The outcome was the restoration of reactionary rule across Europe that, although repressive in many countries, managed to maintain the peace until a series of revolutions swept across Europe in 1848.

The singer Michael Vogl

Franz Schubert playing the piano

TIMELINE

Franz Grillparzer

1800 Vienna's population 232,000	**1811** Austria suffers economic collapse and state bankruptcy	
1806 The Holy Roman Empire ends after Franz II abdicates and becomes Emperor Franz I of Austria	**1812–14** Napoleon defeated by Russia, Prussia, England and Austria	

1800	**1810**	**1820**

1805 First performance of Beethoven's Eroica Symphony and *Fidelio* in Theater an der Wien. Napoleon wins victory at Austerlitz	**1809** Napoleon moves into Schönbrunn Palace and marries Franz I's daughter Maria-Louisa	**1815–48** Period of political suppression known as the Vormärz
	Napoleon Bonaparte	**1814–15** Congress of Vienna held under Presidency of Metternich; Austria loses Belgium but gains parts of Northern Italy
		1825 Johann Strauss the Elder forms first waltz orchestra

☐ **Biedermeier Vienna**

The 1848 Revolution
This painting from 1848 by Anton Ziegler shows the revolution in Vienna, when the middle classes and workers fought together against Metternich.

Biedermeier Chair
This style of furniture characterized the domestic aspirations of Vienna's middle classes in the 1820s.

WHERE TO SEE BIEDERMEIER VIENNA

Napoleon's partial demolition of the city walls led to the creation of the Burggarten *(p102)* and the Volksgarten *(p104)*. Domestic architecture flourished – Biedermeier houses include the Geymüller Schlössl *(p160)* and the Dreimäderlhaus *(p131)* – as did the applied arts *(pp82-3)*.

The Geymüller Schlössl, dating from 1802, is home to Vienna's Biedermeier museum.

SCHUBERTIADE

Franz Schubert *(see p38)* wrote over 600 songs. These were often performed at musical evenings such as the one shown in this painting, *An Evening at Baron von Spaun's*, by Moritz von Schwind (1804–71).

The Grand Gallop
Waltzes, popularized by Johann Strauss I (the Elder) (see p38), were extremely popular in the 1820s.

1827 Death of Beethoven	**1830** Vienna's population reaches 318,000	**1837** First railway constructed	**1846** Johann Strauss the Younger becomes music director of the court balls until 1870
	1831–2 Cholera epidemic		**1850** City population reaches 431,000

1830   **1840**

1828 Death of Schubert

1831 The dramatist Franz Grillparzer completes *Des Meeres und der Liebe Wellen*

1845 Gas lighting introduced

1848 Revolution in Vienna; Metternich forced from office, and Emperor Ferdinand I abdicates to be replaced by Franz Joseph

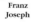

Ringstrasse Vienna

THE EMPEROR FRANZ JOSEPH ushered in a new age of grandeur, despite the dwindling power of the Habsburgs. The city's defences were demolished and a circular boulevard, the Ringstrasse, was built, linking new cultural and political institutions. Vienna attracted gifted men and women from all over the empire, as well as traders from Eastern Europe. However, the resulting ethnic brew often resulted in over-crowding and social tension.

Franz Joseph

EXTENT OF THE CITY

☐ *1885*   ☐ *Today*

Votivkirche (1856–79) p111
Heinrich Ferstel

Neues Rathaus (1872–83) p128
Friedrich von Schmidt

Parliament (1874–84) p125
Theophil Hansen

The Natural History Museum (1871–1890)
pp126–7, Gottfried Semper

Kunsthistorisches Museum (1871–1890) pp118–23
Gottfried Semper

THE SUICIDE OF ARCHDUKE RUDOLF AT MAYERLING

In 1889 the 30-year-old heir to the throne was found dead with his mistress Mary Vetsera. The Archduke's suicide was more than a social scandal. It was a blow to the Habsburg regime, since he was a progressive and intelligent man. His despair may have been aggravated by court protocol that offered no outlet for his ideas.

Theophil Hansen
This Danish-born architect (1813–91) studied in Athens before settling in Vienna. The Greek influence is most evident in his Parliament building on the Ringstrasse.

TIMELINE

Excavation for the Ringstrasse

1867 First performance of *The Blue Danube* by Strauss in Vienna. Hungary granted autonomy, leading to Dual Monarchy with separate governments

1850	1855	1860	1865

Anton Bruckner

1868 Anton Bruckner (*see p39*) moves from Linz to Vienna

1869 Johannes Brahms settles in Vienna as conductor of the Gesellschaft der Musikfreunde. Opera House opens on Ringstrasse

1857–65 Demolition of fortifications and the building of the Ringstrasse

☐ **Ringstrasse Vienna**

The Danube
The River Danube often flooded its banks, so its course was altered and regulated in the 1890s by a system of canals and locks.

Vienna Café Society
In the 19th century, Vienna's cafés became the haunts of literary and political cliques.

Museum of Applied Arts (1867–71)
pp82–3, Heinrich Ferstel

Horse-drawn Trams
Trams appeared on the Ringstrasse in the 1860s. Horseless trams ran along it by the end of the 19th century.

Stadtpark

Opera House (1861–69) pp138–9
Eduard van der Nüll and August Siccardsburg

RINGSTRASSE
This great boulevard, built on the orders of Franz Joseph, separates the Stephansdom and Hofburg Quarters from the suburbs. Completed in the 1880s, the Ringstrasse is as grand now as it was then.

The Opening of the Stadtpark
Laid out on either side of the River Wien, the Stadtpark was inaugurated in 1862.

1874 First performance of Strauss's *Die Fledermaus* at the Theater an der Wien. Opening of Central Cemetery

1889 Suicide of Archduke Rudolf at Mayerling

70	1875	1880	1885

1873 Stock market crash

1872 Death of Austrian poet and dramatist Franz Grillparzer

1879 Lavish historical parade along the Ringstrasse celebrates Franz Joseph's silver wedding

1890 The suburbs are incorporated into the city

Vienna in the 1900s

THE TURN OF THE CENTURY was a time of intellectual ferment in Vienna. This was the age of Freud, of the writers Karl Kraus and Arthur Schnitzler, and of the Secession and Jugendstil *(see pp54–7)*. At this time artists such as Gustav Klimt and the architects Otto Wagner and Adolf Loos *(see p92)* created revolutionary new styles. This was all set against a decaying Habsburg empire, which Karl I's abdication in 1918 brought to an end. After World War I Austria became a republic.

Engel Apotheke sign

EXTENT OF THE CITY

☐ *1912*   ☐ *Today*

Wiener Werkstätte
Josef Hoffmann (see p56), designer of this chair, was the principal artist and founder of this Viennese arts workshop (see p83).

KIRCHE AM STEINHOF
This stupendous church was designed by Otto Wagner and decorated by Kolo Moser *(see p57)*.

Loos Haus
The restrained elegance of this former tailoring firm is typical of Loos's style (see p92).

The Secession
This poster by Kolo Moser (see p57) was used to publicize the Secession's exhibitions.

Angels by Othmar Schimkowitz

TIMELINE

1895	1900	1905

1899 First issue of Karl Kraus's periodical *Die Fackel*

1903 Wiener Werkstätte founded

1906 Arnold Schönberg's *Chamber Symphony* and works by Anton von Webern and Alban Berg performed at the Musikverein, provoking a riot

1897 Secession established when 19 painters and architects break with the Künstlerhaus. Karl Lueger becomes mayor

1902 Gustav Klimt paints the *Beethoven Frieze*. Tramways are electrified

1905 Franz Lehar's operetta *The Merry Widow* first performed. Anti-Semitic riots at the university

1896 Death of the composer Anton Bruckner

Gustav Klimt

☐ **Vienna in the 1900s**

Reigen (*1903*)
Arthur Schnitzler's play
Reigen *shocked the Viennese
with its explicit sexuality.*

Altar by
Remigius
Geyling

The Kiss (*1907–8*)
*In paintings like
this, Gustav Klimt
developed the
glittering, erotic style
that characterized
much of his work.*

Kolo Moser
window

Sigmund Freud
*Freud developed
his theory of psycho-
analysis in Vienna for
almost 50 years* (see p110).

WHERE TO SEE 1900s VIENNA

Otto Wagner designed
the Karlsplatz Pavilions
(*see p146*), the Wagner
Apartments (*p139*), and the
Kirche am Steinhof (*p160*).
Adolf Loos (*p92*) designed
Loos Haus (*p92*) and the
American Bar (*p105*). Subur-
ban architecture includes
the Wagner Villas (*p160*).
Paintings by Klimt, Schiele,
and Kokoschka are displayed
at the Upper Belvedere
(*pp154–5*) and the Museum
of Modern Art (*p111*).

***The Secession Building** is
where Gustav Klimt's Beethoven Frieze is exhibited* (p55).

***The Wagner Apartments** are
decorated with Jugendstil motifs
(p56) by Kolo Moser* (p57).

1907 Gustav Mahler resigns as director of Court Opera. Hitler studies art in Vienna	1911 Death of Gustav Mahler	1914 Archduke Ferdinand assassinated in Sarajevo; international crisis follows resulting in World War I
1910		1915
1910 Death of Karl Lueger		1916 Death of Franz Joseph
1908 *The Kiss* by Klimt is first exhibited		1918 Declaration of Austrian Republic after abdication of Emperor Karl I. Austria shrinks from an empire of 50 million to a state of 6.5 million

Modern Vienna

Two DECADES OF STRUGGLE between the left and right political parties followed World War I, ending with the union of Austria with Germany – the Anschluss – in 1938. After World War II Vienna was split among the Allies until 1955, when Austria regained its independence.

1929 Ludwig Wittgenstein, a prominent member of the Vienna circle, leaves Vienna for England

1955 On 15 May the Austrian State Treaty brings to an end the Allied occupation. Austria granted independence and declares itself to be permanently neutral

1927 Workers, angered by deaths of bystanders during political violence, storm the Palace of Justice

1922 Karl Kraus publishes his immense drama *The Last Days of Mankind*

1944 Allied bombing of Vienna begins

1951 The First Festival of Vienna

1920	1930	1940	1950

1920	1930	1940	1950

1922 Death in Madeira of exiled Karl I, last Habsburg emperor

1939 Death of novelist Joseph Roth

1945 World War II ends. The second Austrian republic is declared, but Vienna remains divided between the four Allied powers

1918–20 Severe food shortages and an influenza epidemic afflict the Viennese

1933 Chancellor Dollfuss dissolves Parliament and forms a fascist regime, but refuses to accommodate Hitler

1934 Street fighting in Vienna between socialists and government troops; socialists banned. Murder of Chancellor Dollfuss by the Nazis

1919 Richard Strauss appointed joint director of the State Opera

1920–34 Socialism prevails in so-called "Red Vienna", despite conservative Catholic rule in Austria

1938 Chancellor Schuschnigg resigns. Hitler enters Vienna and pronounces Anschluss

1955 Reopening of Opera House and Burgtheater

1956 Atomic Energy Agency located in Vienna

1959 Ernst Fuchs and Arik Brauer establish the school of fantastic realism

1989 Death of Empress Zita, the last Habsburg to have ruled Austria

1988 Irmgard Seefried, star of the Vienna Opera House, dies

1986 The controversial Kurt Waldheim elected president; Franz Vranitzky elected Chancellor

1979 East-West summit held between Leonid Brezhnev and Jimmy Carter

1983 Pope John Paul visits Vienna

1970–83 Socialist Bruno Kreisky is Chancellor

1978 U-Bahn system opened

1992 Fire in the Hofburg Palace

960	1970	1980	1990	2000
960	1970	1980	1990	2000

1967 UN Industrial Development Organization (UNIDO) comes to Vienna

1995 Austria joins the European Union

1989 Velvet Revolution in Czechoslovakia heralds Austria's growing economic influence in the new democratic central Europe. Completion of Hans Hollein's Haas Haus in Stephansplatz

1985 Hundertwasser Haus by Friedensreich Hundertwasser completed

1979 UNO city opened

1961 John F Kennedy meets Nikita Khrushchev at East-West summit in Vienna

Music in Vienna

FROM THE LATE 18TH to the mid 19th centuries Vienna was the music capital of Europe. At first the Habsburg family and the aristocracy were the city's musical paymasters, but with the rise of the middle classes during the Biedermeier period *(see pp30–31)* music became an important part of bourgeois life. Popular music also flourished as migration from all parts of the Habsburg Empire brought in richly diverse styles of music and dance.

The Waltz became popular following the Congress of Vienna in 1814

a state occasion. The music of Franz Schubert (1797–1828) was little known in his short lifetime. He mostly performed chamber works, piano music and songs at Biedermeier *Schubertiaden* – evenings of music with friends. His music became more popular following his death. After this, "serious" music went through a

CLASSICISM

IN THE 18TH century, Vienna's musical life was dominated by the Imperial Court. Christoph Willibald Gluck (1714–87) was Court *Kapellmeister* (in charge of the court orchestra) to Maria Theresa until 1770, and wrote 10 operas specially for Vienna, including *Orpheus and Eurydice* (1762). His contemporary Wolfgang Amadeus Mozart (1756–91) later built on these foundations. Joseph Haydn (1732–1809) moved to Vienna in the 1790s from Prince Esterházy's palace in Eisenstadt *(see pp176–7)*, and wrote masterpieces such as *The Creation*.

Performance of *The Creation* (1808) on Haydn's birthday

ROMANTICISM

WITH THE arrival of Ludwig van Beethoven (1770–1827) in Vienna in the mid-1790s, the age of the composer as romantic hero was born. Beethoven was a controversial figure in his time, and many of his most innovative works were only successful outside Vienna. His funeral, however, attended by more than 10,000 people, was

Biedermeier *Schubertiade* evening

fallow period in Vienna, but Johann Strauss I (1804–49) and Joseph Lanner (1801–43) began creating dance music, centred on the waltz.

Performance of *The Magic Flute* (1791) by Mozart

TIMELINE

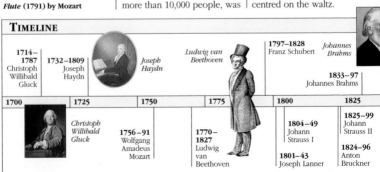

1714–1787 Christoph Willibald Gluck	1732–1809 Joseph Haydn	*Joseph Haydn*	*Ludwig van Beethoven*	1797–1828 Franz Schubert	*Johannes Brahms*
					1833–97 Johannes Brahms

1700	1725	1750	1775	1800	1825

	Christoph Willibald Gluck	1756–91 Wolfgang Amadeus Mozart	1770–1827 Ludwig van Beethoven	1804–49 Johann Strauss I	1825–99 Johann Strauss II
				1801–43 Joseph Lanner	1824–96 Anton Bruckner

AGE OF FRANZ JOSEPH

A NEW ERA of high musical art began in the 1860s. Johannes Brahms (1833–97) came to Vienna in 1862, and incorporated popular musical styles into works such as his Liebeslieder waltzes and Hungarian Dances. The Romantic composer Anton Bruckner (1824–96) came to the city from Upper Austria in 1868. Johann Strauss II (1825–99) rose to the status of civic hero, composing nearly 400 waltzes, including his famous operetta *Die Fledermaus*. One popular offshoot of the period was *Schrammel* music, named after Joseph Schrammel (1850–

Jugendstil poster (1901) for the Waltz depicting Johann Strauss II

93) and characterized by an ensemble of guitars, violins and accordion. Popular music also influenced Gustav Mahler (1860–1911), director of the Vienna Opera for 10 years.

THE MODERNS

T HE EARLY YEARS of the 20th century saw the rise of the Second Viennese School: Alban Berg (1885–1935), Arnold Schönberg (1874–1951) and Anton von Webern (1883–1945). These composers were not well received in Vienna, and Schönberg found he had to start his own society to get his works, and those of his colleagues, heard. In 1933 he emigrated to the USA. Since World War II no composers of comparable stature have arisen, though Kurt Schwertsik (born 1935) and H K Gruber (born 1943) now attract international attention. However, the Vienna Philharmonic, established in 1842, is still one of the finest orchestras in the world. The State Opera continues to enjoy a strong reputation, while the Vienna-based Alban Berg Quartet is one of the world's most sought-after chamber ensembles.

The Johann Strauss II orchestra at a Court ball

Concert poster (1913) for Arnold Schönberg

1860–1911 Gustav Mahler	1874–1951 Arnold Schönberg	
	1875	
1883–1945 Anton von Webern	1885–1935 Alban Berg	
1850–93 Joseph Schrammel		

VIENNA BOYS' CHOIR

The world-famous Vienna Boys' Choir, the Wiener Sängerknaben, was founded in 1498 by that great patron of the arts, Maximilian I. Today the boys perform masses by Mozart, Schubert or Haydn on Sundays and church holidays at the Burgkapelle *(see p103)*. To obtain a seat you need to book at least eight weeks in advance.

VIENNA AT A GLANCE

IENNA IS A COMPACT city and most of its sights are contained within a small area. However, the city boasts an astonishing array of monuments, palaces, parks and museums, which themselves house an impressive array of art and artefacts from all over the world and from all periods of history. Nearly 150 sights are listed in the *Area by Area* section of this book, but to help make the most of your stay, the next 20 pages offer a guide to the very best that Vienna has to offer. As well as churches, palaces, museums and galleries, there are sections on Jugendstil art and coffee houses. Many of the sights listed have a cross-reference to their own full entry. To start with, some of Vienna's top tourist attractions are listed below.

VIENNA'S TOP TOURIST ATTRACTIONS

Opera House
See pp140–41.

Burgtheater
See pp132–33.

Prater
See pp162–63.

Karlskirche
See pp148–49.

Schönbrunn See pp172–75.

Winter Riding School
See pp98–9.

Kunsthistorisches Museum
See pp122–27.

Stephansdom See pp76–9.

Belvedere
See pp152–57.

Café Central
See p61.

MuseumsQuartier
See p118–20.

◁ The façade of Otto Wagner's Majolikahaus *(see p139)* on the Linke Wienzeile

Vienna's Best: Historic Houses and Palaces

Baroque mansions dominate the streets of the Stephansdom Quarter, while outside the centre of Vienna are the grand summer palaces where the Habsburg emperors and aristocracy lived during warm Middle European summers. The interiors of several of the houses can be visited, while others can only be admired from the outside or from their inner courtyards and staircases. Further details can be found on pages 44–5.

Sigmund Freud's House
This waiting room in the house on Berggasse, where Sigmund Freud lived from 1891 to 1938, has been lovingly restored.

Kinsky Palace
This mansion (1713–16) by Johann Lukas von Hildebrandt (see p152), was built for the Daun family, and is sometimes called the Daun Kinsky Palace. Wirch Philip Daun was commander of the city garrison, and his son Leopold Joseph Daun was Maria Theresa's field marshal.

Schottenring and Alsergrund

Museum and Townhall Quarter

Hofburg
The apartments here are made up of over 20 rooms; among them are ceremonial balls and living quarters which were once occupied by Franz Joseph (see pp32–3) and the Empress Elisabeth.

| 0 kilometres | 0.5 |
| 0 miles | 0.25 |

Opera and Naschmarkt

Schönbrunn Palace
This palace, by J B Fischer von Erlach, was built on a scale to rival the palace of Versailles outside Paris. Parts of it were later redesigned by Maria Theresa's architect Nikolaus Pacassi (see p172).

Neidhart Fresco House
*Frescoes dating from 1400,
depicting the songs of the
medieval minnesinger
Neidhart van Reuenthal,
decorate the dining room of
this former house of a
wealthy clockmaker.*

Figarohaus
*Mozart lived in this
Baroque building for three
years between 1784 and
1787, and composed one of
his most famous works,* The
Marriage of Figaro, *here.*

**Winter Palace
of Prince Eugene**
*J B Fischer von Erlach and Johann
Lukas von Hildebrandt designed
this Baroque palace, with its
spectacular staircase, for the war
hero Prince Eugene (see pp26–7).*

**Zum Blauen
Karpfen**
*A stucco relief of a
blue carp and a
frieze of* putti *adorn
the façade of this
17th-century house
on Annagasse.*

Belvedere Quarter

Belvedere
*Designed by Johann Lukas von
Hildebrandt, Prince Eugene's
summer palaces, built on what were
originally the southern outskirts of
Vienna, now house important
museums of Austrian art.*

Danube Canal

*Johannsdom
Quarter*

*burg
arter*

Exploring Vienna's Historic Houses and Palaces

A STROLL AROUND VIENNA'S streets offers the visitor an unparalleled choice of beautifully-preserved historic buildings, from former imperial residences to humbler burgher's dwellings. The majority date from the 17th and 18th centuries, and illustrate the various phases of Baroque architecture. In most cases their original function as residences of the rich and famous has been superseded; a number have now been turned into museums, and their interiors are open to the public.

Façade of the Schönborn-Batthyány Palace

Frescoed ceiling of the Liechtenstein Museum

TOWN PALACES

THE MOST EXTENSIVE town palace is the **Hofburg**, with its museums and imperial apartments. The staircase of the magnificent **Winter Palace of Prince Eugene** is on view to the public, and the 19th-century Neo-Gothic **Ferstel Palace** (1860) houses the Café Central *(see p58)*. The **Obizzi Palace** is home to the Clock Museum *(see p86)*. Town palaces which can be admired from the outside only are the **Kinsky Palace** (1713–16), **Trautson Palace**, **Schönborn-Batthyány Palace**, **Lobkowitz Palace**, and **Liechtenstein Palace** (1694–1706), the winter home of the Liechtenstein family.

GARDEN PALACES

ALTHOUGH IT SEEMS strange that palaces within the city limits should be termed garden palaces, when they were built they were outside the city boundaries, and offered a cool refuge during the hot summer months. The most famous example is **Schönbrunn Palace**, where the state apartments can be seen as part of a guided tour. The **Belvedere**, to the south of the city, houses museums of Austrian art, and many of the rooms retain their original splendid decoration. The nearby **Schwarzenberg Palace** is now a luxury hotel open to hotel guests only. The **Hermes Villa** (1884), a cross between a hunting lodge and a villa, was commissioned by Franz Joseph for his wife Elisabeth. The interior of the Neo-Classical **Rasumofsky Palace** (1806–7), occupied by the Institute of Geology, can sometimes be seen on special occasions. The **Liechtenstein Museum** houses the private art collection of the Liechtenstein family *(see p111)*.

SUBURBAN VILLAS

THE DÖBLING regional museum is housed in the Biedermeier **Villa Wertheimstein** (1834–5), where the interior is furnished in its original flamboyant and overcrowded manner. By contrast, the **Geymüller Schlössl**, containing the Sobek Collection of clocks and watches, is a model of taste and restraint. In Hietzing, the **Villa Primavesi** (1913–15) is a small Jugendstil masterpiece designed by Josef Hoffmann *(see p56)* for the banker Robert Primavesi.

BURGHERS' HOUSES

ON TUCHLAUBEN, the **Neidhart Fresco House** is decorated with secular frescoes from around 1400. Charming Baroque houses of modest dimensions can be seen on **Naglergasse** and **Kurrentgasse** and in inner districts such as **Spittelberg** and **Josefstadt**. A particularly fine example of external decoration can be seen on the Baroque inn **Zum Blauen Karpfen** in Annagasse *(see p80)*. The **Dreimäderlhaus** in Schreyvogelgasse, built in an intermediate style between Rococo and Neo-Classicism, is also worth visiting.

Façade and gardens of the Hermes Villa

MEMORIAL HOUSES

VIENNA ABOUNDS in the former residences of famous composers. They are not all of great architectural merit, and their interest tends to reside mainly in the exhibits they contain. The **Pasqualati Haus** was one of Beethoven's many Viennese residences – it was here that he composed the opera *Fidelio* – and the museum here houses portraits and other mementoes of the great composer. The rooms of the **Heiligenstadt Testament House**, where Beethoven stayed in an attempt to cure his deafness, are now a memorial. The first-floor apartment of the **Haydn Museum** in Haydngasse is

Courtyard of the Heiligenstadt Testament House

pleasantly furnished and filled with letters, manuscripts, personal possessions and the composer's two pianos. Mozart and his family lived from 1784–7 in the **Figarohaus**. This is where Mozart wrote

The Marriage of Figaro.
The **Freud Museum** houses furnishings, documents and photographs, and the waiting room is as it looked when Freud used to see his patients. It is also a study centre.

DECORATIVE DETAILS

Many of the historic houses and palaces of Vienna were built during a period corresponding to the Baroque and late Baroque styles of architecture. Details such as window hoods and pediments over doorways were often extremely ornate.

Caryatid on the doorway of the Liechtenstein Palace

Decorative window hood on the façade of the Trautson Palace

Decorative urns on the Lobkowitz Palace

Decorative pediment with shield on the Schönborn-Batthyány Palace.

Stucco *putti* on the façade of Zum Blauen Karpfen

WHERE TO FIND THE PALACES AND HOUSES

Vienna's Best: Museums and Galleries

VIENNA BOASTS an astonishing number of museums, and many of the collections are housed in elegant former palaces or handsome buildings specially commissioned for the purpose. Some of the museums are of international importance, while others are of more local or specialist interest. Further details can be found on pages 48–9.

Natural History Museum
This museum has displays of fossils, ethnography, mineralogy and a much-visited dinosaur hall.

Sacred and Secular Treasuries
The Ainkurn sword (around 1450) can be seen in the Imperial Treasuries in the former imperial palace of the Hofburg.

Schottenring and Alsergrund

Kunsthistorisches Museum
Hans Holbein's portrait of Jane Seymour (1536) is one of hundreds of Old Master paintings displayed in this fine art museum.

Museum and Townhall Quarter

Hofburg Quarter

Opera and Naschmarkt

MuseumsQuartier
This vast cultural centre contains the largest Egon Schiele collection in the world, including this Self-portrait with Lowered Head *(1912).*

Albertina
This museum houses temporary exhibitions, mainly based on the Albertina's celebrated collection of prints and drawings (here, Albrecht Dürer's The Hare *dated 1502).*

**Historical Museum
of the City of Vienna**
*Stained-glass windows from the
Stephansdom (around 1390)
are among the many items here
documenting Vienna's history.*

Austrian Museum of Applied Arts
*The applied arts of Vienna, such as
this early 19th-century beaker and
Wiener Werkstätte furniture (see
pp54–7), are among the varied
artefacts on display in this museum.*

Cathedral Museum
*This St Andrew's cross
reliquary (about 1440) is
one of many medieval
religious treasures
on display here.*

**Museums of
Baroque and
Medieval Art**
*The Lower Belvedere
houses two museums
devoted to Austrian art
up to the 18th century.
Among the collections is
the medieval Schotten-
altar, which dates
from around 1470.*

DANUBE CANAL

Stephansdom
Quarter

**Museum of 19th-
and 20th-Century Art**
*Ferdinand Waldmüller's Roses in
the Window (1832) is one of
several Biedermeier canvases on
show here. There are also works
by Klimt, Schiele and Kokoschka.*

Belvedere Quarter

**Heeresgeschichtliches
Museum**
*Paintings of battles and
military commanders, such
as Sigmund L'Allemand's
portrait of Field Marshal
Gideon-Ernst Freiherr von
Laudon (1878), are part of
this museum's collection.*

0 kilometres   0.5

0 miles   0.25

Exploring Vienna's Museums and Galleries

VIENNA'S MUSEUMS EXHIBIT an amazing variety of fine, decorative and ethnic art from all periods of history and from different regions of the world. The visitor can see artefacts from all over the ancient world as well as more recent collections, from medieval religious art to 19th- and 20th-century paintings. Silverware is displayed in the city's imperial collections, and Vienna is also unrivalled for its turn-of-the-century exhibits.

Interior of Friedensreich Hundertwasser's Kunsthaus Wien

ANCIENT AND MEDIEVAL ART

VIENNA HAS marvellous collections of medieval art. The **Neidhart Fresco House** contains medieval secular frescoes, while a number of superb Gothic altarpieces can be seen in the **Museum of Medieval Art**. Displayed in the **Cathedral Museum** are outstanding Gothic sculptures as well as masterpieces of applied art; the highlight is a 9th-century Carolingian Gospel. The **Sacred and Secular Treasuries** in the Hofburg are awash with precious medieval objects, including the insignia and crown of the Holy Roman Empire, and a unique collection of medieval objects and Gothic paintings is on display in the treasury of the **Deutschordenskirche**. The splendours of the Verduner Altar at **Klosterneuberg**

await those prepared to make a short journey out of the centre of Vienna. The **Ephesos Museum** of the Hofburg houses ancient Roman and Greek antiquities unearthed at the turn of the century.

OLD MASTERS

THE PICTURE GALLERY in the **Kunsthistorisches Museum** has one of the best collections of Old Masters in the world, reflecting the tastes of the many generations of Habsburg collectors who formed it. There are works by Flemish and Venetian artists, and the best collection of Bruegels on display in any art gallery, as well as Giuseppe Arcimboldo's (1527–93) curious portraits composed of fruit and vegetables. The **Academy of Fine Arts** houses some fine examples of Dutch and Flemish works, its prize exhibit being Hieronymos Bosch's triptych of the *Last Judgement*,

which contains some of the most horrifying images in Christan art. There are also paintings by Johannes Vermeer (1632–75) and Peter Paul Rubens (1577–1640). The **Museum of Baroque Art** focuses on Austrian paintings and sculptures from the 17th and 18th centuries. The building that the museum is housed in is a masterpiece of Baroque architecture.

19TH- AND 20TH-CENTURY ART

A PERMANENT display of 19th- and 20th-century Austrian art is housed in the **Museum of 19th- and 20th-Century Art**. The most famous exhibits are by Gustav Klimt, and his newly-restored *Beethoven Frieze* can be seen in the **Secession Building**. The **Museum of Modern Art** has recently moved from the Liechtenstein Garden Palace to the new MuseumsQuartier (*see p120*). It contains exhibits by 20th-century European artists, including recent works by the Viennese avant garde. The **Leopold Museum** has a huge Egon Schiele collection. The work of Friedensreich Hundertwasser, perhaps Vienna's best-known modern artist, is on show at his gallery, the **Kunsthaus Wien**. Prints, drawings and photographs are housed in the recently restored **Albertina**.

Parthian monument (around AD 170) in the Ephesos Museum

THE APPLIED ARTS AND INTERIORS

O N DISPLAY IN THE **Austrian Museum of Applied Arts** is a rich collection of the decorative arts, including Oriental carpets, medieval ecclesiastical garments, Biedermeier and Jugendstil furniture, and the archives of the Wiener Werkstätte. The **Historical Museum of the City of Vienna** houses a reconstructed version of the poet Franz Grillparzer's apartment as well as Adolf Loos's *(see p92)* drawing room. In the **Silberkammer** of the Hofburg is a dazzling array of dinner services collected by the Habsburgs. The **Lobmeyr Museum** exhibits glassware designed by Josef Hoffmann.

Glass by Josef Hoffmann in the Lobmeyr Museum

Picture clock in the Clock Museum

SPECIALIST MUSEUMS

C LOCK ENTHUSIASTS can visit the **Clock Museum** and the Sobek Clock and Watch Collection at the **Geymüller Schlössl**. Music is celebrated at the **Sammlung Alter Musikinstrumente**, while the darker side of life can be seen at the **Kriminal-museum**, and at the **Bestattungsmuseum** which houses exhibits to do with Viennese funeral rites. The **Heeresgeschichtliches Museum** houses reminders of Austria's military past. The **Hofjagd und Rüstkammer** exhibits historical weaponry. Other specialist museums include the **Österreichisches Filmmuseum** and the **Doll and Toy Museum**.

NATURAL HISTORY AND SCIENCE

S TILL OCCUPYING the building constructed for it in the 19th century is the **Natural History Museum**, which has displays of mineralogy, dinosaur skeletons and zoology. The **Josephinum** houses a range of wax anatomical models, while the **Technical Museum** documents the contribution Austria has made to developments in technology, ranging from home-made items such as an amateur wooden typewriter, to the invention of the car.

ETHNOLOGY AND FOLKLORE

V IENNA'S Museum of Ethnology in the Hofburg, the **Völkerkundemuseum**, contains objects from all over the world. There are artefacts from Mexico and a collection of musical instruments, masks and textiles from the Far East. The Benin collection from Africa is now back on display in the museum *(see p95)*. There is also a section on Eskimo culture. The **Museum für Volkskunde** in Josefstadt houses fascinating exhibits on Austrian folklore and rural life over the centuries.

Benin carving in the Völkerkundemuseum

Vienna's Best: Churches

VIENNA'S MOST POTENT SYMBOL is its cathedral – the Stephansdom – a masterpiece of Gothic architecture which stands out in a city where the overwhelming emphasis is on the Baroque. After the defeat of the Turks in 1683 (see pp26–7), many churches were built or remodelled in the Baroque style, although it is often possible to detect the vestiges of older buildings beneath later additions. Many church interiors are lavishly furnished, and several have fine frescoes. Churches are generally open during the day except when mass is being held. Stage concerts or organ recitals are given in the evenings in some churches. A more detailed overview of Vienna's churches is on pages 52–3.

Peterskirche
The tall dome of this late Baroque church dominates the view as you approach from the Graben.

Michaelerkirche
This church has one of the most impressive medieval interiors in Vienna. The Neo-Classical façade and this cascade of Baroque stucco angels over the high altar were later additions.

Schottenring and Alsergrund

Museum and Townhall Quarter

Hofburg Quarter

Maria Treu Kirche
A statue of Mary Immaculate graces the square in front of this Baroque church (1716). Its façade dates from 1860.

Opera and Naschmarkt

0 kilometres 0.5
0 miles 0.25

Augustinerkirche
Antonio Canova's (1753–1822) tomb for Archduchess Maria Christina is in the Gothic Augustinerkirche, which once served as the Habsburgs' parish church.

Ruprechtskirche
Vienna's oldest church has a Romanesque nave and bell tower, a Gothic aisle and choir, and stained-glass windows which date back to the turn of the 14th century.

Maria am Gestade
Dating from the 14th century, this church was restored in the 19th century. This 15th-century Gothic panel, shows The Annunciation.

Stephansdom
The richly-carved Wiener Neustädter Altar from 1447 was a gift from Friedrich III (see p19).

Stephansdom Quarter

Jesuitenkirche
A series of twisted columns rise up to support the vault of the Jesuitenkirche (1623–31), which also features a trompe l'oeil dome.

Belvedere Quarter

Karlskirche
J B Fischer von Erlach's eclectic Baroque masterpiece (1714–39) boasts a dome, minarets and two Chinese-inspired lateral pavilions.

Franziskanerkirche
The dramatic high altar (1707) by Andrea Pozzo features a Bohemian statue of the Virgin Mary as its centrepiece.

Exploring Vienna's Churches

MANY OF VIENNA'S CHURCHES have undergone modifications over the centuries, and they often present a fascinating mixture of styles, ranging from Romanesque to Baroque. The great era for church building in the city was in the 17th and 18th centuries, when the triumphant Catholic church, in a spate of Counter-Reformation fervour, remodelled several early churches and built new ones. A number of churches were also constructed after the Turks were defeated in 1683 *(see pp26–7)*, and the city as a whole was able to spread out beyond its earlier confines.

MEDIEVAL CHURCHES

AT THE HEART OF THE CITY is the **Stephansdom**. Parts date from Romanesque times but most of the cathedral is Gothic; it contains a collection of Gothic sculpture, including a pulpit by Anton Pilgram *(see p78)*. Vienna's oldest church is the **Ruprechtskirche**, which stands in its own square in the Bermuda Triangle *(see p84)*; its plain façade contrasts with the delicate Gothic tracery of **Maria am Gestade**, which has a filigree spire and a lofty, vaulted interior. The early interior of the **Deutschordens-kirche** contains a number of heraldic blazons. A late Romanesque basilica with Gothic modifications lurks behind the façade of the **Michaelerkirche**. The 14th-century

Madonna and Child in the Minoritenkirche

Augustinerkirche contains the hearts of the Habsburg families *(see pp24–5)* down the centuries as well as Antonio Canova's tomb for Maria Christina *(see p102)*. Behind the façade of the **Minoritenkirche** is a newly-restored Gothic interior; the same is true of the **Burgkapelle**.

17TH-CENTURY CHURCHES

THERE IS LITTLE Renaissance architecture in Vienna, but a number of churches built before the Turkish siege survive. The **Franziskaner-kirche**, with its gabled façade and theatrical high altar, and the **Jesuitenkirche** are fine examples of the architecture inspired by the Counter-Reformation *(see p24)*. The **Ursulinenkirche**, built between 1665 and 1675, has a high-galleried interior and **Annakirche** is notable for its beautiful Baroque tower. The **Dominikanerkirche** has a majestic early Baroque façade built in the 1630s by Antonio Caneval. Although it dates back to Romanesque times,

the bulk of the rather squat **Schottenkirche** was built between 1638 and 1648. In the middle of the Baroque square of Am Hof is the impressive façade of the **Kirche am Hof**. It was founded by the Carmelites and is also known as "Church of the Nine Choir Angels".

Carving of St Anne (about 1505) in Annakirche, attributed to Veit Stoss

LATE BAROQUE AND NEO-CLASSICAL CHURCHES

AFTER THE Turkish defeat *(see pp26–7)*, a number of Viennese High Baroque churches were built. The most exotic is the **Karlskirche**, and just off the Graben is the great **Peterskirche**. The tiny, ornate **Stanislaus-Kostka Chapel** was once the home of a Polish saint. Two graceful 18th-century churches are to be found on the edge of the inner city: the majestic **Maria Treu Kirche** and the **Ulrichskirche**. Joseph Korn-häusel's **Stadttempel** has a Neo-Classical interior.

TOWERS, DOMES AND SPIRES

Vienna's skyline is punctuated by the domes, spires and towers of its fine churches. Topping **Maria am Gestade** is a delicate openwork lantern, while the **Ruprechtskirche** tower is characteristically squat. The towers of the **Jesuitenkirche** are Baroque and bulbous, and **Karls-kirche** has freestanding columns. **Peterskirche** has an oval dome and small towers.

Ruprechts-kirche

Maria am Gestade

Jesuitenkirche

The frescoed interior of the late Baroque Stanislaus-Kostka Chapel

19TH-CENTURY CHURCHES

DURING THE 19TH century the prevailing mood of Viennese architecture was one of Romantic historicism. Elements of past styles were adopted and re-created, for churches and for many other municipal buildings, specifically on the Ringstrasse *(see pp32–3)*. The **Griechische Kirche** on Fleischmarkt, took its inspiration from Byzantine architecture, and the inside is replete with iconostases and

frescoes. The **Votivkirche**, built just off the Ringstrasse as an expression of gratitude for Franz Joseph's escape from assassination, is based on French Gothic architecture; its richly-coloured interior contains the marble tomb of Count Niklas Salm, who defended Vienna from the Turks during the siege of 1529 *(see p24)*. On Lerchenfelder Strasse the red-brick **Altlerchenfelder Kirche** is a 19th-century architectural hodge-podge of Gothic and Italian Renaissance styles.

20TH-CENTURY CHURCHES

A MASTERPIECE of early 20th-century church architecture is Otto Wagner's *(see p57)* massive **Kirche am Steinhof**, built to serve a psychiatric hospital. The interior has a slightly clinical air, since it is tiled in white, but the austerity is relieved by Kolo Moser's *(see p57)* stained-glass windows and

The haphazard, sculpted blocks of the modern Wotruba Kirche.

mosaics. The **Dr-Karl-Lueger-Kirche**, located in the Central Cemetery, was built by a protégé of Otto Wagner, Max Hegele, and has the same monumental feel about it. For true devotees of the modern, there is the **Wotruba Kirche** on Georgsgasse in the suburb of Mauer, designed by the sculptor Fritz Wotruba. Not universally liked, this looks as if it is a haphazard assembly of concrete blocks.

19th-century interior of the Altlerchenfelder Kirche

Peterskirche

Karlskirche

Vienna's Best: Jugendstil

A STROLL AROUND Vienna's streets will reveal the
richness of the city's turn-of-the-century
architecture. Some of the buildings are well
known and instantly recognizable, and a few
of the public ones, such as the Secession building,
can be seen inside. However, it can be just as
rewarding to discover the lesser-known buildings
and monuments of the period and to savour the
variety of finely-crafted architectural
details. Further details
can be found on
pages 56–7.

Strudelhof Steps
*The setting for a famous novel
of the same name by Heimato
von Doderer (1896–1966),
these magnificent steps were
built by Theodore Jäger in 1910.*

Schottenr
and
Alsergrun

Kirche am Steinhof
*Commissioned for the grounds of a
lunatic asylum on the outskirts of
the city, this church with its grand
copper dome was designed by Otto
Wagner in 1905. The stained-glass
windows are by Kolo Moser.*

Museum an
Townhall
Quarter

Opera and
Naschmarkt

Kaiser Pavilion
*Otto Wagner's imperial station
pavilion (1899) was built as
a showcase for his work.*

**Wagner
Apartments**
*Otto Wagner's two
apartment blocks
(1899) overlook the
River Wien. No. 40,
the Majolikahaus,
is covered with
ceramic decoration.
No. 38 has gold
Jugendstil motifs.*

Anker Clock
*This clock, created by the
artist Franz Matsch in 1911,
sits on a bridge spanning
two buildings on the Hoher
Markt. Every hour, on the
hour, moving figures parade
across the clock face.*

Postsparkasse
*One of Otto Wagner's masterpieces, this post
office savings bank exhibits the finest
workmanship outside, and inside. Even the
interior ventilator shafts are by Wagner.*

Stadtpark Portals
*The city's municipal
park is adorned with
magnificent portals
(1903–7), designed
by Friedrich Ohmann
as part of a project to
regulate the flow of
the River Wien.*

Danube Canal

*Stephansdom
Quarter*

*Hofburg
Quarter*

Karlsplatz Pavilions
*Two recently-restored
pavilions standing in
Karlsplatz were built as
part of Otto Wagner's
scheme for Vienna's
turn-of-the-century
underground system.*

*Belvedere
Quarter*

| 0 kilometres | | 1 |
| 0 miles | 0.5 | |

Secession Building
*Nicknamed the Golden
Cabbage because of its
golden filigree dome, the
Secession Building was
designed at the turn of the
century by Joseph Maria
Olbrich for exhibitions of
avant-garde art. In the
basement is Gustav Klimt's*
Beethoven Frieze.

Exploring Viennese Jugendstil

THE TURN OF THE CENTURY saw a flowering of the visual arts in Vienna. A new generation of avant-garde artists formed the Secession in 1896 and, together with architects and designers, forged close ties between the fine and decorative arts, and created new architectural styles.

Hoffman tea service (1903) in the Austrian Museum of Applied Arts

PAINTING AND DRAWING

VIENNESE ART at the turn of the century did not conform to one particular style, but there were common elements: an obsession with line and rich surface pattern, as well as themes such as the *femme fatale*, love, sex and death. The finest collection of paintings from this period is in the **Museum of 19th- and 20th-Century Art** where pictures by Gustav Klimt (1862–1918) and Egon Schiele (1890–1918) feature prominently. Paintings by both artists and their contemporaries also form part of the permanent display at the **Historical Museum of the City of Vienna**. Further examples are at the **Museum of Modern Art** in the new MuseumsQuartier. The **Albertina** sometimes shows Schiele drawings. Klimt's *Beethoven Frieze* is in the **Secession Building**, and the decorative schemes he produced for the **Burgtheater** and **Kunsthistorisches Museum** are still in situ.

Decoration (1891) by Gustav Klimt in the Kunsthistorisches Museum

APPLIED ARTS

THE WIENER WERKSTÄTTE – an arts and crafts studio – was founded by Josef Hoffmann (1870–1956) in 1903, and produced jewellery, fabrics, ceramics, metalwork, cutlery, bookbinding and fashion accessories with the same artistic consideration normally given to painting or sculpture. An outstanding collection is in the **Austrian Museum of Applied Arts**, which also houses a document archive open to researchers. Glass designed by Hoffmann for the Viennese firm of Lobmeyr is displayed in the **Lobmeyr Museum**.

FAVOURITE JUGENDSTIL MOTIFS

Jugendstil motifs were similar to those employed by the French Art Nouveau movement, but were generally made up of a more rigorous, geometric framework. Decorations based on organic plant forms such as sunflowers were very popular, as were female figures, heads and masks. Abstract designs made up of squares and triangles were also used to great effect.

Sunflower motif from the Karlsplatz Pavilions by Otto Wagner

Postcard designed by Joseph Maria Olbrich from *Ver Sacrum*

FURNITURE

THE LEADING Secession designers, such as Hoffmann and Kolo Moser (1868–1918), wanted interior design to return to the simple lines of Biedermeier style *(see pp30–1)* after the excesses of the Ringstrasse era. The **Austrian Museum of Applied Arts** has several interesting displays of their work, as well as that of the Thonet firm, which made the bentwood furniture admired by the Wiener Werkstätte. Furniture was often conceived as just one element of interior design. Unfortunately, many interiors have disappeared or are not open to the public, but the **Historical Museum of the City of Vienna**, which also has some pieces of Jugendstil furniture, has a re-creation of Adolf Loos's *(see p92)* living room. This is a rare example of a progressive Viennese interior from the turn of the century, created before the architect finally broke with the Secession.

Writing desk and chair by Kolo Moser (1903) in the Austrian Museum of Applied Arts

Altar in the Kirche am Steinhof (1905–7)

ARCHITECTURE

ANYONE WALKING around Vienna will notice several buildings with charming Jugendstil details. By the 1890s young architects were beginning to react against buildings of the Ringstrasse era, many of which were pastiches of earlier historical styles. The leading architects at this time were Otto Wagner (1841–1918) and Joseph Maria Olbrich (1867–1908), who collaborated on a number of projects, notably the design and installation of a new city railway and its stations, the most famous examples of which are the **Kaiser Pavilion** at Hietzing and the **Karlsplatz Pavilions**, as well as the **Wagner Apartments** on the Linke Wienzeile. Working independently, Wagner produced the extraordinary **Kirche am Steinhof** as well as the **Postsparkasse**, while Olbrich designed the

Secession Building as an exhibition space for radical artists and designers. Hoffmann created a number of houses for Secession artists in **Steinfeldgasse**. There are also some Jugendstil houses in **Hietzing**, while the **Anker Clock** by Franz Matsch (1861–1942) is an example of the late flowering of the style. Other examples of street architecture are the **Strudelhof Steps** (1910) by Theodore Jäger and the **Stadtpark Portals** by Friedrich Ohmann (1858–1927) and Joseph Hackhofer (1868–1917).

Postcard design by Joseph Maria Olbrich from *Ver Sacrum*

Gold leaf detail from the Wagner Apartments

Lettering by Alfred Roller from *Ver Sacrum*

Abstract fabric design by Josef Hoffmann

Vienna's Best: Coffee Houses

OFFEE HOUSES HAVE BEEN an essential part of
Viennese life for centuries. The coffee
house is more than just a place to go to drink
coffee. It is a meeting place, somewhere to
linger over a snack or a light lunch, and a
refuge from city life. Each coffee house attracts
its own particular clientele and has its own
unique atmosphere. Most of them also serve
alcohol. Further details of what coffee houses
have to offer can be found on pages 60–61.

Landtmann
*This comfortable and formal
coffee house used to be frequented
by Sigmund Freud. Today it is
visited by theatregoers and actors
from the nearby Burgtheater, and
by journalists and politicians.*

*Schottenring and
Alsergrund*

*Museum and
Townhall
Quarter*

Central
*Once the meeting place of writers and
free thinkers, the most splendid of all the
coffee houses in Vienna has now been
restored to its former grandeur.*

*Hofburg
Quarter*

Sperl
*Just outside the city
centre, the Sperl has a
faithful clientele,
including many
young people who
come here for the
billiard tables and
hot strudels.*

Eiles
*Its location near
various government
offices has made the
Eiles a favourite haunt
of officials and lawyers.*

*Opera and
Naschmarkt*

Café Museum
*The Café Museum was built in 1899
to designs by Adolf Loos (see p92),
but was remodelled in the 1930s. It
has now been restored in accordance
with Loos's original design.*

Hawelka

This famous coffee house has long cultivated its bohemian image. The atmosphere is warm and theatrical, and no visit to Vienna is complete without a late-night cup of coffee or a drink here.

0 kilometres 0.5

0 miles 0.25

tephansdom Quarter

Prückel

The Prückel has been shabby and run down for as long as anyone can remember, but it has become a mecca for bridge players and locals who crowd into its back room.

Kleines

One of the smallest, quaintest coffee houses in Vienna, the Kleines still attracts a loyal clientele of actors.

Belvedere Quarter

Frauenhuber

The oldest coffee house in Vienna, this is where Mozart once performed. Its location off Kärntner Strasse makes it handy for shoppers and for tourists visiting the nearby Stephansdom.

Exploring Vienna's Coffee Houses

THE VIENNESE COFFEE HOUSE serves many functions and to make the best of the institution it helps to understand the many roles it plays in the lives of local people. In a coffee house you can read the newspapers, share a simple lunch with a friend, or in some play a game of bridge or billiards. Most places serve wines, beers and spirits as well as coffee. The coffee house is a priceless urban resource and, though no longer unique to Vienna, it is here that it has flourished in its most satisfying form. Vienna also has many Café-Konditoreien *(see p215)*.

Waiter at the Dommayer café

THE HISTORY OF THE COFFEE HOUSE

LEGEND MAINTAINS that the first coffee house opened its doors after the defeat of the Turks in 1683 *(see p26)*. However, historians insist that coffee was known in the city long before this date. Coffee houses took the form we know today in the late 18th century. They reached their heyday in the late 19th century, when they were patronized by cliques of like-minded politicians, artists, writers, composers, doctors or civil servants. In 1890, for instance, the controversial literary

18th-century Viennese girl holding a coffee grinder

group Jung Wien met regularly at the **Griensteidl**, while the essayist Peter Altenberg was reputed to have never been seen outside his favourite café, the **Central**.
Today, as in the past, the **Ministerium**, **Museum**, **Frauenhuber**, **Raimund**, **Eiles**, **Schwarzenberg** and **Zartl** continue to attract their own specific clientele.

COFFEE HOUSE ETIQUETTE

THERE IS A SIMPLE but formal etiquette attached to a coffee house. A waiter, almost certainly dressed in a tuxedo, however shabby the coffee house, will take your order, which will often be served with a plain glass of water. Once

you have ordered you are free to occupy your table for as long as you like. A cup of coffee is not cheap, but entitles you to linger for an hour or two and to read the newspapers which are freely available. The grander coffee houses, such as the **Landtmann** and **Central**, will also have a selection of foreign newspapers and periodicals.

WHAT COFFEE HOUSES HAVE TO OFFER

COFFEE HOUSES often function as local clubhouses. At the **Sperl** you can play billiards, at the **Prückel** there are bridge tables, and at the

TYPES OF COFFEE

Just as the coffee house is a Viennese institution, so too are the extraordinary varieties of coffee that are available. Just asking for a cup of coffee in Vienna will not always guarantee a result, as the Viennese are exceedingly particular about how they take their coffee; over the centuries they have devised their own specific vocabulary to convey to the waiter precisely how they like their beverage served. The list that follows will cover most variations of the Viennese cup of coffee, although you may well find local ones.

Türkischer: plain, strong black Turkish coffee served in the traditional manner.

Brauner:
coffee with milk (small or large).
Melange:
a blend of coffee and hot milk.
Kurz:
extra strong.
Obers:
with cream.
Mokka:
strong black coffee.

Kapuziner:
black coffee with a dash of milk, usually frothed.
Schwarzer:
black coffee (small or large).
Konsul:
black coffee with a dash of cream.
Kaffeinfreier Kaffee:
decaffeinated coffee.

Espresso: strong black coffee made by machine. Ask for it *gestreckt* for a weak one.

Dommayer you can attend literary readings. The **Central** and **Bräunerhof** both offer live piano music with your coffee. The **Kleines** is, as its name suggests, too tiny to offer entertainment, but still draws a regular crowd. The **Imperial** is part of the hotel of the same name. Coffee houses outside the city centre include the excellent **Westend**.

Coffee house sign

WHAT TO EAT

MOST COFFEE HOUSES offer snack foods throughout the day, simple lunches and occasional specialities, such as pastries, which are served at particular times. The **Hawelka** serves hot jam-filled buns (*Buchteln*) late at night, and the **Sperl** often has fresh strudel late morning. Larger coffee houses, such as **Diglas** and **Landtmann**, offer extensive lunchtime menus as well as a range of excellent pastries made on the premises.

COFFEE PLAIN AND SIMPLE

THERE ARE times when you quite simply want a good cup of coffee – when newspapers or a table of your own are luxuries you can dispense with. On such occasions you should keep an eye out for an Espresso bar, where you can lean informally against a counter and order coffee at a half or a third of the price you would normally expect to pay at a coffee house. The Café-Konditoreien belonging to the Aida chain (*see p217*), apart from serving delicious cakes and pastries, also function as Espresso bars.

Old Viennese coffee machine in Diglas

WHERE TO FIND THE COFFEE HOUSES

Bräunerhof
Stallburggasse 2. Map 5 C3.
🎵 Sat & Sun afternoons.

Central
Palais Ferstel, Herrengasse 14.
Map 2 D5 & 5 B2. 🎵

Diglas
Wollzeile 10. Map 6 D3. 🍴

Dommayer
Dommayergasse 1, Hietzing.
🍴 🎵 first Sat of month.

Eiles
Josefstädter Strasse 2. Map 1 B5.

Frauenhuber
Himmelpfortgasse 6.
Map 4 E1 & 6 D4.

Griensteidl
Michaelerplatz 2.
Map 2 D5 & 5 B3.

Hawelka
Dorotheergasse 6.
Map 2 D5 & 5 C3.

Imperial
Hotel Imperial,
Kärntner Ring 16.
Map 4 E2 & 6 D5. 🍴 🎵

Kleines
Franziskanerplatz 3. Map 6 D4.

Café Landtmann
See p131. 🍴

Ministerium
Georg-Coch-Platz 4.
Map 2 F5 & 6 F3. 🍴

Museum
Friedrichstrasse 6.
Map 4 D2. 🍴

Prückel
Stubenring 24. Map 6 F3.
🍴 🎵 evenings.

Raimund
Museumstrasse 6.
Map 3 B1. 🍴

Schwarzenberg
Kärntner Ring 17.
Map 6 D5. 🍴

Sperl
Gumpendorfer Strasse 11.
Map 3 A4. 🍴

Westend
Mariahilfer Strasse 128.
Map 3 A3.

Zartl
Rasumofskygasse 7,
Landstrasse. 🎵

Pharisäer: strong black, with whipped cream on top, served with a small liqueur glass of rum.

Schlagobers: strong black coffee served with either plain or whipped cream.

Einspänner: large glass of coffee with whipped cream on top.

Kaisermelange: black coffee with an egg yolk and brandy.

Vienna Through the Year

SPRING OFTEN ARRIVES unexpectedly, with a few days of sunshine and warmth. The climax of spring is the Wiener Festwochen in May. Summers are long and hot, and ideal for swimming and for river trips on the Danube (see pp178–9) during July and August, when some venues officially close. Vienna comes alive again in September when the most important theatres reopen. More often than not,

there is an Indian summer at this time, and it is still warm enough to sit in the Stadtpark. As autumn turns to winter, the streets fill with stalls selling chestnuts and by the feast of St Nicholas on 6 December, snow has often fallen. Christmas is a family occasion, but the New Year is celebrated in style as it heralds the start of the carnival season. The Wiener Fremdenverkehrsamt (see p239) has details of important events.

SPRING

VIENNA IS beautiful in spring and is the time for the **Wiener Festwochen** (see May). It is also a season that brings a few days of balmy weather, and when beautiful colours appear in the parks and the Prater woods (see pp162–63). This is the best time of the year to visit the Stadtpark (see p98) with its open-air bandstand and much-photographed resident peacock. The Volksgarten, Burggarten and the great parks of the Belvedere and Schönbrunn also come into their own and there are some splendid views of the city from the Stephansdom tower.

A collection of life-sized dolls on display during the Wiener Festwochen

MARCH

Easter Market (two weeks before Easter), held at the Freyung. Items on sale include arts, crafts and traditional food.
Schönbrunner Schlosskonzerte (until end Oct), at the Orangery, Schönbrunn Palace (see p172). Performances of the popular melodies of Johann Strauss.

Runners taking part in the annual Spring Marathon

APRIL

Volksprater Funfair (1 Apr–31 Sep), held in the Prater woods (pp162–63).
Spring Marathon (1st Sun Apr) starts from Schönbrunn Palace (see pp172–3), passing the Hofburg, Ringstrasse and Opera House, and ends at the Neues Rathaus (Town Hall).
Frühlingsfestival (2nd week Apr to mid-May). Classical music festival alternating between the Musikverein (p146) and the Konzerthaus (p229).
Spanish Riding School (until Jun). Performances of the Lipizzaner horses start again in the Winter Riding School (pp98–9).
Hofburg Orchestra (until Oct). Concerts at Musikverein (p146) and Hofburg (pp96–7).
Kursalon (until end Oct). Open-air concerts (p229).

MAY

Tag der Arbeit (1 May). Public holiday. Every year, Labour Day is celebrated with parades on Rathausplatz and Ringstrasse.
Maifest (1 May), in the Prater (pp162–63) with music and children's programmes.
Vienna Music Festival (6 May–12 Jun), part of the Wiener Festwochen programme, which begins a few days earlier at the Theater an der Wien (p138) and the Messepalast (p120).
Dancing on the Vindobona (15 May to end Sep). Board the boat at Schwedenplatz for a cruise on the Danube.
Wiener Festwochen (mid-May to mid-Jun). Vienna's greatest festival features operas, plays and performing arts.

Average Daily Hours of Sunshine

Hours
10
8
6
4
2
0

Jan Feb Mar Apr May Jun Jul Aug Sep Oct Nov Dec

Sunshine Chart
June, July and August are the hottest months in Vienna, with between six and eight hours of sunshine each day, but summer can also be quite damp and humid. Although the city cools down in September, Indian summers are quite common.

SUMMER

Summer can be both the busiest and most relaxing time in Vienna. The great theatres may be closed officially, but the Jazz Festival is on at the Opera House and the Volkstheater in July, and Mozart operas are performed in Schönbrunn Park until mid-August. The Danube beaches are ideal for sunbathing, swimming and other watersports on sunny days.

Summer outside the Votivkirche

JUNE

Corpus Christi *(2 Jun)*. Public holiday. Catholic festival held in honour of the Eucharist.
Vinova *(2nd week Jun)*, wine fair in the Prater *(pp162–63)*.

The Concordia Ball *(2nd Fri in Jun)* takes place at the Neues Rathaus *(p130)*.
Ball der Universität *(18 Jun)* held at the University *(p130)*.
Donauinselfest *(last weekend in Jun)*, three-day pop concert on Danube island.

JULY

Outdoor films, operas and concerts *(until Sep)* shown on a giant screen in Rathausplatz. Seating is provided free.
Klangbogen Wien *(Jul–Aug)*. Music festival with concerts in some of Vienna's most famous venues. Opera performances and chamber and symphony concerts are held at Theater an der Wien *(p138)*.
Jazzfest *(1st two weeks Jul)*, part of Klangbogen Wien music festival. Venues include the Opera House *(pp140–41)*, the Volkstheater *(p230)* and the arcaded courtyard of the Neues Rathaus *(p130)*.
International Dance Weeks *(mid-Jul to 3rd week Aug)* at the Universitäts Sportzentrum, Schmelz; Volkstheater *(p230)*.
Summer Dance Festival

Bathing beside the Danube

(Im Puls) *(end-Jul to 3rd week Aug)* is held at the Volkstheater *(p230)* and Universitäts Sportzentrum at Schmelz.
Soirée bei Prinz Orlofsky *(until mid-Aug)* held at the Schönbrunner Schlosstheater. Operetta by the Kammeroper.
Seefestspiele Mörbisch *(weekends mid-Jul to end Aug)*. An operetta festival which takes place in Mörbisch, some 40 km (25 miles) away.

AUGUST

Maria Himmelfahrt *(15 Aug)*, public holiday. A Catholic festival which celebrates the assumption of the Madonna.

Seefestspiele Mörbisch, an annual operetta festival performed against the backdrop of Lake Neusiedl

Rainfall Chart
The summer months are not only the hottest but also the wettest, helping to keep the city cool. During spring and autumn, days can be mild, with some drizzle, until November, which can be very wet. Around 600 mm (23 inches) of rain falls annually.

AUTUMN

IN VIENNA, AUTUMN means a new start. The theatres, and particularly Vienna's great opera houses, reopen once again. Shops get ready to tempt buyers with their range of autumn fashions. Then, almost overnight, all the shop windows seem to be filled with figures of St Nicholas and his wicked companion Krampus. This cute little furry devil appears everywhere. It is only after 6 December that the shop windows are finally cleared for Christmas displays.

SEPTEMBER

Spanish Riding School performances *(until end Oct)* and training sessions of the Lipizzaner horses *(pp98–9)*.
Vienna Boys' Choir *(mid-Sep to Dec)* perform at Mass at the Burgkapelle *(p103)* on Sundays.
Trotting in the Krieau *(until Jun)*. Trotting races at the Prater *(pp162–63)*.

OCTOBER

Küche und Keller *(1st week Oct)*. Hotel and food fair, at the Messegelände *(pp162–63)*.

The Vienna Boys' Choir performing at the Konzerthaus

Krampus, the wicked furry devil who accompanies St Nicholas

National Holiday *(26 Oct)*. Celebrations to mark the passing of the Neutrality Act in 1955.
Viennale *(end Oct)*, film festival at Gartenbau, Parkring 12; Metro, Johannesgasse 4; Künstlerhaus, Akademiestrasse 13; and Stadtkino, Schwarzenbergplatz 7–8.
Wien Modern *(until end Nov)*. Modern music festival at the Konzerthaus *(p229)*.

NOVEMBER

Allerheiligen *(1 Nov)*. Public holiday. Catholic festival celebrating All Saints' Day.

Antik-Aktuell *(2nd week Nov)*, art and antiques fair held at the Hofburg.
Schubertiade *(3rd week Nov)* at the Musikverein *(p146)*.
Krippenschau *(until mid-Dec)*, display of historic mangers at Peterskirche *(p87)*.
Christkindlmarkt *(2nd Sat Nov to end Dec)*, Christmas market and children's workshop by the Rathaus *(p130)*.
Christmas markets *(from last Sat Nov)* held at the Freyung, Heiligenkreuzerhof, Schönbrunn, Karlsplatz and Spittelberg.
International choirs *(last Sat Nov)* at the Town Hall, or Rathaus *(p130)*.

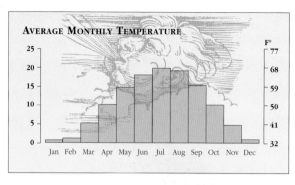

Temperature Chart
The chart shows the average temperatures each month. Top temperatures in July and August can reach 25˚ C (77˚ F) although May and September are also quite warm. Winters are icy, and temperatures can be as low as −1.4˚ C (29.5˚ F) in January.

WINTER

ROASTING CHESTNUTS over hot coals is a regular winter sight on Vienna's streets. As Christmas draws near, stalls offer mulled wine and hot snacks and shops enter into the festive spirit putting up lights and decorations.

The Viennese celebrate Christmas Eve with a traditional meal consisting of *Fisch-beuschelsuppe*, a creamy fish soup, followed by fresh fried carp. The usual dish which is eaten on Christmas Day is goose, although turkey is becoming more popular.

New Year also marks the start of Fasching, Vienna's famous Carnival season.

DECEMBER

Christmas markets *(continue from November).*

Chestnut-roasting in winter

Maria Empfängnis *(8 Dec).* Public holiday. Catholic festival celebrating the Immaculate Conception.
Midnight Mass *(Christmas Eve)* held in the Stephansdom *(pp76–7).* No tickets needed but arrive early for seats.
Stefanitag *(26 Dec).* Public holiday for Boxing Day.
New Year's Eve performance of *Die Fledermaus* *(31 Dec)* at the Opera House *(pp140–41)* and Volksoper *(p229).* The performance is shown on a large screen in Stephansplatz *(p70).*
New Year's Eve concerts at the Konzerthaus *(p229)* and Musikvereinsaal *(p146).*
Kaiserball *(31 Dec)* at the Hofburg *(pp96–7).*
New Year's Eve in the city centre: a street party with snacks and drink. Marquees provide music and cabaret.

JANUARY

New Year's Concert *(31 Dec & 1 Jan)* by the great Vienna Philharmonic at the Musik-verein *(p146).* Tickets are very difficult to obtain, and requests should be received on precisely 2 January for next year's concert *(p228).* Or you may watch it live on television.
Beethoven's Ninth Symphony *(31 Dec & 1 Jan)* is performed at the Konzert-haus *(p229).*
Fasching *(6 Jan to Ash Wed),* the Vienna Carnival includes the **Heringschmaus** *(Ash Wed),* a hot and cold buffet.
Holiday on Ice *(mid- to end Jan).* This is held at the Stadthalle, Vogelweidplatz.
Resonanzen *(2nd to 3rd week Jan).* Festival of ancient music at the Konzerthaus *(p229).*

FEBRUARY

Opera Ball *(last Thu before Shrove Tue),* one of the grand-est balls of Fasching *(p141).*
Wintertanzwoche *(5–13 Feb).* Part of the Dance Festival *(see below).* Events are held in the MuseumsQuartier *(p118).*
Dance Festival *(17 Feb to 27 Mar),* includes classic and jazz dance at the Universitäts Sportzentrum at Schmelz.
Haydn Tage *(3rd week Feb to 1st week Mar).* Haydn's music at the Konzerthaus *(see p229).*

The Christkindlmarkt, in front of the Neues Rathaus

VIENNA AREA BY AREA

STEPHANSDOM QUARTER

THE WINDING STREETS and spacious squares of this area form the ancient core of Vienna. Following World War II, subterranean excavations uncovered the remains of a Roman garrison from 2,000 years ago, and every succeeding age is represented here, from the Romanesque arches of the Ruprechts-kirche to the steel and glass of the spectacular Haas Haus in Stephansplatz. Many of the buildings in the area house government offices, businesses, taverns and stylish shops. Dominating the skyline is the Stephansdom, the focus of the city at its geographical centre.

Plaque on No. 19
Sonnenfelsgasse, once
part of the university

SIGHTS AT A GLANCE

Streets and Squares
Am Hof **36**
Annagasse **18**
Bäckerstrasse **14**
Blutgasse **3**
Domgasse **4**
Fleischmarkt **23**
Griechengasse **24**
Grünangergasse **6**
Hoher Markt **27**
Jewish District **26**
Judenplatz **31**
Kurrentgasse **33**
Schönlaterngasse **10**
Sonnenfelsgasse **12**

Historic Buildings
Academy of
  Sciences **9**
Altes Rathaus **29**
Bohemian Court
  Chancery **28**
Haas Haus **15**
Heiligen-
  kreuzerhof **13**
Postsparkasse **22**
Winter Palace of
  Prince Eugene **17**

Churches and Cathedrals
Annakirche **19**
Deutschordenskirche **2**
Dominikanerkirche **7**
Franziskanerkirche **16**
Jesuitenkirche **8**
Kirche am Hof **35**
Maria am Gestade **30**
Peterskirche **37**
Ruprechtskirche **25**
Stephansdom pp76–9 **1**

Museums and Galleries
Austrian Museum of Applied
  Arts pp82–3 **21**
Cathedral Museum **11**
Clock Museum **32**
Doll and Toy Museum **34**
Figarohaus **5**
Haus der Musik **20**
Museum Judenplatz **31**

GETTING THERE
This area is served by the Steph-ansplatz (lines U1, U3), Stuben-tor (line U3) and Schwedenplatz (lines U1, U4) U-Bahn stations. Trams 1 and 2 go along Franz-Josefs-Kai and the Ringstrasse. Buses 1A, 2A and 3A stop at the junction of Hoher Markt and Marc-Aurel-Strasse.

KEY

▨	Street-by-Street map *See pp70–71*
Ⓤ	U-Bahn station
Ⓟ	Parking

◁ **Sculpture in the Peterskirche by Lorenzo Mattielli (1729) of** **St John Nepomuk's martyrdom**

Street-by-Street: Old Vienna

THIS PART OF THE INNER CITY retains its medieval layout, offering a complex of lanes, alleys and spacious courtyards. The influence of the church is particularly evident. You can find remains of monastic orders such as the Dominicans and feudal orders such as the Teutonic Knights, as well as ideological orders, for example the Jesuits. Yet there is nothing ossified about the area: at night the bars and restaurants on Bäckerstrasse and Schönlaterngasse are thronged with people until the early hours of the morning. Dominating everything is the 137-m high (450-ft) spire of the Stephansdom cathedral in the very heart of Vienna.

★ Cathedral Museum
Much of this collection was donated by Duke Rudolf IV who is shown here ⓫

To Rotenturm-strasse

★ Stephansdom
The cathedral took centuries to build and is rich in medieval and Renaissance monuments ❶

To Kärntner Strasse STEPHANS-PLATZ

Deutschordenskirche
A remarkable Treasury, with objects collected by German aristocrats, lies alongside this Gothic church ❷

The Haas & Haas Tea Garden is a charming, informal café and tea house.

Figarohaus
Mozart lived here from 1784 to 1787. He had a suite of rooms where he wrote many of his great works ❺

Domgasse
This pretty street includes a bookshop at No. 8, Buchhandlung 777 ❹

Blutgasse
Courtyards like this are typical of the tenement houses on Blutgasse ❸

Dominikaner-kirche
Originally consecrated on this site in 1237, the present Baroque church dates from the 1630s **7**

LOCATOR MAP
See Street Finder, maps 2 & 6

Schönlaterngasse
The lantern at No. 6 gave this charming street its name **10**

Jesuitenkirche
This pulpit detail of the apostle Matthew is from the Baroque Jesuitenkirche. One of Vienna's most ornate churches, it was built by the Jesuits in the 1620s **8**

★ Academy of Sciences
The great hall (Aula) of the Academy is one of the noblest salons in Vienna **9**

Grünanger-gasse
This quiet lane is full of bookshops and art galleries **6**

KEY

- – – Suggested route

0 metres 50
0 yards 50

STAR SIGHTS

★ Stephansdom

★ Cathedral Museum

★ Academy of Sciences

Stephansdom ❶

See pp76–9.

Deutschordens-kirche ❷

Singerstrasse 7. **Map** 2 E5 & 6 D3. [C]
5121065. [U] *Stephansplatz.* **Church**
[] *7am–6pm daily.* [o] **Treasury**
[] *10am–noon Mon & Thu, 3–5pm*
Wed & Fri, 10am–noon & 3–5pm Sat.
[●] *Tue & Sun, public hols.* [∅]

Inner courtyard of No. 9 Blutgasse, the Fähnrichshof

THIS CHURCH belongs to the
Order of Teutonic Knights,
a chivalric order which was
established in the 12th century.
It is 14th-century Gothic, but
was restored in the 1720s by
Anton Erhard Martinelli.
Numerous coats of arms of
teutonic knights and memorial
slabs are displayed on the
walls. The altarpiece from
1520 is Flemish and
incorporates panel paintings
and carvings of scenes from
the Passion beneath some very
delicate traceried canopies.

The Order's Treasury is
situated off the church's
courtyard and now serves as
a museum, displaying various
collections acquired by its
Grand Masters over the
centuries. The starting point is
a room which houses a large
collection of coins, medals and
a 13th-century enthronement
ring. This leads into the second
room which contains chalices
and Mass vessels worked
with silver filigree. Following
this is a display of
maces, daggers
and ceremonial
garb. The final exhibits show
some Gothic paintings and a
Carinthian carving of *St George
and the Dragon* (1457).

Blutgasse ❸

Map 2 E5 & 6 D3. [U] *Stephansplatz.*

A LOCAL LEGEND relates that
this street acquired its
gruesome name – Blood Lane
– after a massacre in 1312
of the Knights Templar (a
military and religious order)
in a skirmish so violent that
the streets flowed with blood.
But there is no evidence to
support this story and the
street's name belies its charm.

Its tall apartment buildings
date mostly from the 18th
century. Walk into No. 3 and
see how the city's restorers
have linked up the buildings
and their courtyards. No. 9,
the Fähnrichshof,
is particularly
impressive.

Domgasse ❹

Map 2 E5 & 6 D3. [U] *Stephansplatz.*

IN ADDITION TO the Figarohaus,
Domgasse boasts some
interesting buildings, including
the Trienter Hof, with its airy
courtyard. No. 6 is a house of
medieval origin called the
Kleiner Bischofshof or small
bishop's house: it has a 1761
Matthias Gerl façade. Next
door is the site of the house
where Franz Georg Kolschitzky
lived and, in 1694, died. It is
said that he claimed some
Turkish coffee beans as a
reward for his bravery in the
1683 Turkish siege, and later
opened Vienna's first coffee
house. The truth of this story,
however, is doubtful.

Figarohaus ❺

Domgasse 5. **Map** 2 E5 & 6 D3.
[C] *5136294.* [U] *Stephansplatz.*
[] *9am–6pm Tue–Sun.* [📷][o]

MOZART and his family
occupied a flat on the
first floor of the Figarohaus
from 1784 to 1787. Of Mozart's
11 Viennese residences, this is
the one where he is said to
have been happiest, and
where he composed some of
his masterworks: the exquisite
Haydn quartets, a handful of
piano concerti, and *The
Marriage of Figaro* – after
which the building was named.
Since Mozart died impover-
ished and left few effects, the
museum is spartan, displaying
a small number of prints on the
walls, and a few documents
and photocopies of scores.

Winged altar-
piece in the
Deutschordens-
kirche (1520)

Elaborate nave of the Dominikanerkirche

Grünangergasse ❻

Map 4 E1 & 6 D3. **U** *Stephansplatz.*

THIS QUIET LANE takes its name from the creperie Zum Grünen Anker at No. 10, a tavern frequented by Franz Schubert in the 19th century.

No. 8's portal has crude carvings of rolls, croissants and pretzels. It is known as the Kipferlhaus after a Viennese crescent-shaped roll. The former Fürstenberg Palace, from 1720, has a Baroque portal with carved hounds racing to the top of the keystone.

Dominikaner-kirche ❼

Postgasse 4. **Map** 2 E5 & 6 E3. **C** 5129174. **U** *Stephansplatz, Schwedenplatz.* ◯ *7am–7pm Mon–Sat, 7am–9pm Sun.* 📷

THE DOMINICAN order of monks came to Vienna in 1226, and by 1237 they had consecrated a church here. In the 1630s Antonio Canevale designed their present church, which boasts a majestic and really rather handsome Baroque façade. The interior is equally imposing. The central chapel on the right has swirling Rococo grilles and candelabra, and there is a very beautiful gilt organ above the west door. Its casing dates from the mid-18th century. The frescoes by Tencala and Rauchmiller are especially noteworthy, as is the high altar.

Jesuitenkirche ❽

Dr-Ignaz-Seipel-Platz 1. **Map** 2 E5 & 6 E3. **C** 5125232. **U** *Stubentor, Stephansplatz, Schwedenplatz.* ◯ *7am–6:30pm daily.* 📷

ANDREA POZZO, an Italian architect, redesigned the Jesuitenkirche between 1703 and 1705 and its broad, high façade dominates the Dr-Ignaz-Seipel-Platz. In the 1620s the Jesuits decided to move their headquarters here in order to be near the Old University, which they controlled. The Jesuit order was the dominant force behind the Counter-Reformation. The Jesuits were not afraid of making a statement, and the church's grand design and high façade reflects this dominance.

The interior is gaudy, with plump marble columns screening the side chapels. Pozzo's ceiling frescoes are cleverly executed using a *trompe l'oeil* effect and the pews are richly carved.

Academy of Sciences ❾

Dr-Ignaz-Seipel-Platz 2. **Map** 2 E5 & 6 E3. **U** *Schwedenplatz, Stubentor.* **C** 515810. ◯ *8am–5pm Mon–Fri.*

ONCE THE CENTREPIECE of the Old University, the Akademie der Wissenschaften has an impressive Baroque façade. Designed in 1753 by Jean Nicolas Jadot de Ville-Issey as the *Aula,* or great hall, it has recently been restored. A double staircase leads up to a huge salon that, despite its reconstruction after a fire in 1961, is still one of the great rooms of Vienna.

Elaborate frescoes adorn the ceilings of the Ceremonial Hall and the walls are composed of marble embellished with Rococo plasterwork. Haydn's *Creation* was performed here in 1808 in the presence of the composer: it was the eve of his 76th birthday and his last public appearance.

Fountain by Salomon Kleiner on the Academy of Sciences (about 1755)

The Baroque Bernhardskapelle *(left)*, seen from Schönlaterngasse

Schönlaterngasse ⑩

Map 2 E5 & 6 E3. 🚇 *Stephansplatz, Schwedenplatz.* **Alte Schmiede**
📞 5128329. ⏰ *10am–3pm Mon–Fri.*

THE ATTRACTIVE CURVING lane derives its name (Pretty Lantern Lane) from the handsome wrought-iron lantern which is clamped to No. 6. This is a copy of the 1610 original which is now in the Historical Museum of the City of Vienna *(see p146).* At No. 4, a solid early 17th-century house guards the curve of the street. No. 7, the Basilisken-haus, which is of medieval origin, displays on its façade an artist's impression of a mythical serpent, dating from 1740. A serpent is reputed to have been discovered in 1212 in a well by the house.

The composer Robert Schumann lived at No. 7a from 1838 to 1839. No. 9 is the Alte Schmiede – the large smithy from which it takes its name has been reassembled in the basement. This complex also contains an art gallery and a hall used for poetry readings and musical workshops.

Cathedral Museum ⑪

Stephansplatz 6. **Map** 2 E5 & 6 D3.
📞 515523560. 🚇 *Stephansplatz.*
⏰ *10am–5pm Tue–Sat.* ● *24 & 31 Dec, Maundy Thu & Easter Mon.* 🏛 📷 ♿

KNOWN IN GERMAN as the Dom und Diözesan-museum, its exhibits include 18th-century religious paintings by important Austrian artists such as Franz Anton Maulbertsch, and some 16th- and 17th-century rustic carvings. There are also works by the Dutch painter Jan van

Hemessen. Not to be missed is the display of medieval carvings, many of which are of the Madonna and Child.

The Treasury is spectacular as many of the items were the personal gift of Duke Rudolf IV to the Cathedral. His shroud is housed here as well as a famous portrait of him by a Bohemian master dating from the 1360s *(see p70)*. Other items include the St Leopold reliquary from 1592, which is encrusted with figures of saints and coats of arms, and some outstanding enamels from the 12th-century.

Sonnenfelsgasse ⑫

Map 2 E5 & 6 E3. 🚇 *Stephansplatz, Schwedenplatz.*

FINE HOUSES line this pleasant street. Though by no means uniform in style, most of the dwellings on the north side of the street are solid merchant and patrician houses dating from the late 16th century. No. 19, which was built in 1628 and renovated in 1721, was once part of the Old University *(see p73)*. No. 11 has an impressive courtyard. Many of the balconies over-looking the courtyard have been glassed in to their full height so as to provide extra living space. No. 3 has the most elaborate façade, and contains a *Stadtheuriger* called the Zwölf Apostelkeller *(see p219)*. This is an urban equivalent of the *Heurige*, the wine growers' inns found in the villages outside Vienna *(see p218)*. The street was named after a soldier called Joseph von Sonnenfels. He became Maria Theresa's legal adviser and under his guidance, she totally reformed the penal code and abolished torture.

Gothic Madonna (1325) in the Cathedral Museum

Heiligen-kreuzerhof ⑬

Schönlaterngasse 5. **Map** 2 E5 & 6 E3.
📞 *5125896.* 🚇 *Schwedenplatz.*
⬜ *6am–9pm Mon–Sat.* ⬛ *Sun.*
📷 ♿ *Bernhardskapelle*
⬜ *on request*

I N THE MIDDLE AGES, the rural
monasteries expanded by
establishing a presence in the
cities. Secularization in the
1780s diminished such hold-
ings, but this one, belonging
to the abbey of Heiligenkreuz
(see p176), survived.

The buildings around the
courtyard housing the city's
Applied Arts College present
a serene 18th-century face. On
the south side of the courtyard is the Bernhardskapelle.
Dating from 1662, but altered
in the 1730s, the chapel is a
Baroque gem. Across from the
chapel a patch of wall from
Babenberg times *(see pp22–3)*
has been exposed to remind
you that, as so often in Vienna,
the building is much older in
origin than it at first appears.

Fresco at No. 12 Bäckerstrasse

Bäckerstrasse ⑭

Map 2 E5 & 6 D3. 🚇 *Stephansplatz.*

N OWADAYS PEOPLE VISIT this
street, which used to
house the city's bakers in
medieval times, to sample its
nightlife rather than its bread.
The architecture is also of
considerable interest: No. 2
sits beneath a 17th-century
tower, and has a pretty
courtyard. Opposite, at No. 1,
is the site of the Alte Regens-
burgerhof, the outpost of
Bavarian merchants who were
given incentives to work in
Vienna in the 15th century.
No. 8 is the former palace of
Count Seilern dating from
1722, and No. 7 is famous for
its arcaded Renaissance

courtyard and stables, which
is the only surviving example
in Vienna. Two other houses
of Renaissance origin are
located at Nos. 12 and 14.

Haas Haus ⑮

Stephansplatz 12. **Map** 2 E5 & 6 D3.
📞 *5356083.* 🚇 *Stephansplatz.*
⬜ *6am–2am daily.* 📷 ♿

C OMMISSIONING a modern
building directly opposite
the Stephansdom was a
sensitive task, and the city
entrusted its design to one of
Austria's leading architects,
Hans Hollein. The result is
the 1990 Haas Haus, a shining
structure of glass and blue-
green marble that curves
elegantly round right into the
Graben. The building has a
very pleasing asymmetrical
appearance, with decorative
elements such as lopsided
cubes of marble attached to
the façade, a protruding
structure high up resembling
a diving board and a Japanese
bridge inside. The atrium
within is surrounded by cafés,
shops, a restaurant, Do & Co
(see p214) and offices.

Franziskaner-kirche ⑯

Franziskanerplatz 4. **Map** 4 E1 & 6 D4.
📞 *5124578.* 🚇 *Stephansplatz.*
⬜ *6:30am–noon & 2–5:30pm
Mon–Sat, 7am–5:30pm Sun.* 📷 ♿

T HE FRANCISCANS were fairly
late arrivals in Vienna and
one of their first tasks was
to build a church on
the site of a former
medieval convent.
Dating from 1603,
the church totally
dominates the
Franziskanerplatz.

The façade is in
South German
Renaissance
style, and is
topped by
an elaborate
scrolled gable
with obelisks.

**Gleaming
façade of Haas
Haus (1990)**

**Detail from Andrea Pozzo's altar
(1707) in the Franziskanerkirche**

The Moses Fountain in front
of the church was designed
by the Neo-Classicist Johann
Martin Fischer in 1798.

The interior is in full-blown
Baroque style and includes a
finely-modelled pulpit dating
from 1726, and richly-carved
pews. A dramatic high altar
by Andrea Pozzo rises to the
full height of the church. Only
the front part of the structure
is three-dimensional – the
rest is *trompe l'oeil.* Look out
for a 1725 *Crucifixion* by
Carlo Carlone among the
paintings in the side altars.

You usually have to ask a
passing monk for permission
to see the church organ. It is
worth being persistent, as this
is the oldest organ in Vienna
(1642), designed by Johann
Wöckerl. It has statues of
angel musicians and beauti-
fully painted
doors on
religious
themes.

Stephansdom ❶

Ｓ ITUATED IN THE CENTRE of Vienna, the Stephansdom is the soul of the city itself; it is no mere coincidence that the urns containing the entrails of some of the Habsburgs lie in a vault beneath its main altar. A church has stood on the site for over 800 years, but all that remains of the original 13th-century Romanesque church are the Giants' Doorway and Heathen Towers. The Gothic nave, choir and side chapels are the result of a rebuilding programme in the 14th and 15th centuries, while some of the outbuildings, such as the Lower Vestry, are Baroque additions.

Carving of Rudolf IV

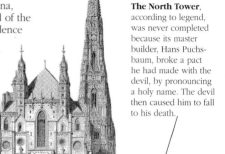

The North Tower, according to legend, was never completed because its master builder, Hans Puchsbaum, broke a pact he had made with the devil, by pronouncing a holy name. The devil then caused him to fall to his death.

★ Giants' Doorway and Heathen Towers
The entrance and twin towers apparently stand on the site of an earlier heathen shrine.

Entrance to the catacombs

Pilgram's Pulpit
(see p78)

STAR FEATURES

★ Giants' Doorway and Heathen Towers

★ *Steffl* or Spire

★ Tiled Roof

★ Singer Gate

The symbolic number "O5" of the Austrian Resistance Movement was carved here in 1945.

Main entrance

★ Singer Gate
This was once the entrance for male visitors. A sculpted relief above the door depicts scenes from the life of St Paul.

Lower Vestry

★ **Steffl or Spire**
The 137-m high (450-ft) Gothic spire is a famous landmark. From the Sexton's Lodge (see p79), visitors can climb the stairs as far as a viewing platform.

VISITORS' CHECKLIST

Stephansplatz 3, A-1010.
Map 2 E5 & 6 D3. 51553135.
Stephansplatz. 1A.
6am–10pm daily. 6:30am, 7:15am, 8am, noon, 6pm, 7pm Mon–Sat; 9am, 10:15am, 11:15am, noon, 6pm, 7pm, 9pm Sun. Jul & Aug: 7:30am, noon, 7pm Mon–Sat; 7:30am, 9:30am, noon, 6pm, 7pm, 9pm Sun; 7pm Sat in English.
organ concerts May–Nov: Wed.

★ **Tiled Roof**
Almost a quarter of a million glazed tiles cover the roof; they were meticulously restored after the damage caused in the last days of World War II.

JOHANNES CAPISTRANO

On the exterior north-eastern wall of the choir is a pulpit built after the victory over the Turks at Belgrade in 1456. It was from here that the Italian Franciscan, Johannes Capistrano, (1386–1456) is said to have preached against the Turkish invasion in 1451. The 18th-century Baroque statue above it depicts the triumphant saint trampling on a defeated Turkish invader.

South-eastern entrance

TIMELINE

1147 The first Romanesque building on the site consecrated by the Bishop of Passau

1304 Duke Rudolf IV initiates work on High Gothic Albertine Choir

1515 Anton Pilgram carves his pulpit

1711 Pummerin bell cast from remains of guns left by Turks on their retreat from Vienna

1948 Reconstruction and restoration carried out

1100	1200	1300	1400	1500	1600	1700	1800	1900	2000

1230 Second Romanesque building erected on the same ground

1359–1440 Main aisle, southern arches and southern tower built

1515 Double wedding of grandchildren of Maximilian with children of the King of Hungary takes place

1556 North Tower is roofed over

1783 Stephansdom churchyard closed after plague

1916 Emperor Franz Joseph's funeral

1945 Cathedral catches fire during bombing

Inside the Stephansdom

THE LOFTY VAULTED INTERIOR of the Stephansdom contains an impressive collection of works of art spanning several centuries. Masterpieces of Gothic sculpture include the fabulously intricate pulpit, several of the figures of saints adorning the piers, and the canopies or baldachins over many of the side altars. To the left of the High Altar is the early 15th-century winged Wiener Neustädter Altar bearing the painted images of 72 saints. The altar panels open out to reveal delicate sculpture groups. The most spectacular Renaissance work is the tomb of Friedrich III, while the High Altar adds a flamboyant Baroque note.

The Catacombs
A flight of steps leads down to the catacombs, which extend under the cathedral square.

Christ with Toothache (1420) is the irreverent name of this figure; an old legend has it that Christ afflicts mockers with toothache.

Lift to the Pummerin Bell

Bishop's Gate

The Tirna Chapel houses the grave of the military hero Prince Eugene.

The Statue of Crucified Christ above the altar has, according to legend, a beard of human hair that is still growing.

Main entrance

Portrait of Pilgram
Master craftsman Anton Pilgram left a portrait of himself, holding a square and compass, below the corbel of the original organ.

★ Pilgram's Pulpit
Pilgram's intricate Gothic pulpit is decorated with portraits of the Four Fathers of the Church (theologians representing four physiognomic temperaments), while Pilgram himself looks out from a "window" below.

Organ Gallery and Case
In 1960 this modern organ was installed in the loft above the entrance. A more recent organ is in the south choir area.

The Canopy with Pötschen Madonna is a 16th-century canopy that shelters a 1697 icon of the Madonna, to which Prince Eugene's victory over the Turks at Zenta was attributed. It comes from Pecs, a village in Hungary.

★ **Wiener Neustädter Altar**
Friedrich III commissioned the elaborate altarpiece in 1447. Painted panels open out to reveal an earlier carved interior showing scenes from the life of the Virgin Mary and Christ. This panel portrays the Adoration of the Magi *(1420).*

Albertine Choir

Exit from crypt

Emperor Friedrich III's tomb is made from ornate red marble and has a lid bearing a life-like carved portrait of the Emperor. It dates from the 15th century.

The Sexton's Lodge houses the stairs that lead up the steeple.

Chapel of St Catherine

The Madonna of the Servants

The Füchsel Baldachin is a fine Gothic canopy.

The Trinity Altar probably dates from around 1740.

★ **High Altar**
Tobias Pock's altarpiece shows the martyrdom of St Stephen. The sculptures were fashioned by Johann Jakob Pock in 1647.

STAR SIGHTS

★ **Pilgram's Pulpit**

★ **Wiener Neustädter Altar**

★ **High Altar**

THE PUMMERIN BELL

The bell that hangs in the North Tower, known as the *Pummerin* or "Boomer", is a potent symbol for the city reflecting Vienna's turbulent past. The original bell was made from melted-down cannons abandoned when the Turks fled Vienna in 1683. The bell crashed down through the roof in 1945 when fire swept through the Stephansdom, so a new and even larger bell was cast using the remains of the old.

Statuary in the hall of the Winter Palace of Prince Eugene

Winter Palace of Prince Eugene ⑰

Himmelpfortgasse 4–8. **Map** 4 E1 & 6 D4. ⚡ *51433.* Ⓤ *Stephansplatz.* **Vestibule** ◯ *8am–4pm Mon–Fri.* 📷

N OW THE Ministry of Finance (Bundesministerium für Finanzen), the Winter Palace was commissioned in 1694 by Prince Eugene of Savoy *(see p27)*, hero of the 1683 Turkish siege. It was begun by Johann Bernhard Fischer von Erlach *(see p149)* and taken over by Johann Lukas von Hildebrandt *(see p152)* in 1702. The result is an imposing town mansion, considered one of the most magnificent Baroque edifices in Vienna. Maria Theresa bought it for the state in 1752. Access is limited, but you can view the Baroque staircase *(see p43)* and glance into the courtyard with its lovely Rococo fountain.

Annagasse ⑱

Map 4 E1 & 6 D4. Ⓤ *Stephansplatz.* **Zum Blauen Karpfen** ◯ *to the public.*

N OW SPLENDIDLY Baroque, Annagasse dates from medieval times. It is pedestrianized and a pleasant place to browse in the bookshops.

Of note are the luxurious Mailberger Hof and the stuccodecorated Römischer Kaiser hotels *(see p199)*. No. 14's lintel has a Baroque carving of babes making merry, while above this is a relief of the blue carp that gives the house, once a pub, its name: Zum Blauen Karpfen. No. 2 is the 17th-century Esterházy Palace, which is now a casino. Until a few years ago you could see the Countess Esterházy sweeping her front doorstep!

Annakirche ⑲

Annagasse 3b. **Map** 4 E1 & 6 D4. ⚡ *5124797.* Ⓤ *Stephansplatz.* ◯ *7am–7pm daily.* 📷

T HERE HAS BEEN a chapel in Annagasse since 1320, but the present Annakirche dates from 1629 to 1634, and it was renovated by the Jesuits during the early 18th century. Devotion to St Anne has deep roots in Vienna and this very intimate church is often full of quiet worshippers.

The finest exterior feature of the church is the moulded copper cupola over the tower. Daniel Gran's ceiling frescoes are now fading and his richly-coloured painting glorifying St Anne on the High Altar is more striking. Gran, together with Franz Anton Maulbertsch, was a leading painter of the Austrian Baroque period. The first chapel on the left houses a copy of a carving of St Anne from about 1505 – the original is in the cathedral museum *(see p74)*. St Anne is portrayed as a powerfully maternal figure and shown with her daughter, the Virgin Mary, who in turn has the baby Jesus on her knee. The carving is attributed to the sculptor Veit Stoss.

Haus der Musik ⑳

Seilerstätte 30. **Map** 4 E1. ⚡ *51648.* ◯ *10am–10pm daily.* 📷 ✎ *on request.* 🖥 📷 Ⓦ www.hdm.at

T HE HOUSE OF MUSIC opened in 2000 and makes the most of the latest audio-visual and interactive technologies to explain and demonstrate all aspects of music. Visitors move through "experience zones" such as the Instrumentarium, with its giant instruments, and the Polyphonium, which is a collection of different sounds.

Moulded copper cupola over the tower of the Annakirche

Detail on the façade of the Griechische Kirche on Griechengasse

Austrian Museum of Applied Arts ㉑

See pp82–3.

Postsparkasse ㉒

Georg-Coch-Platz 2. **Map** 2 F5 & 6 F3.
📞 514000. Ⓤ *Schwedenplatz.*
🕐 *8am–3pm Mon–Wed & Fri,*
8am–5:30pm Thu. 📷

THIS BUILDING IS the Austrian
Post Office Savings Bank
and is a wonderful example
of Secession architecture *(see
pp54–57)*. Designed between
1904 and 1906 by Otto Wagner,
it still looks unashamedly
modern. The building features
the architect's characteristic
overhanging eaves, spindly
aluminium columns supporting
a canopy, heroic sculptures
of angels and ornament-like
nailheads protruding from the
surface of the building.

Wagner was a pioneer in
incorporating many functional
elements into his decorative
schemes. Inside the banking
hall the metal columns are clad
in aluminium, and tubular
heating ducts encircle the hall.

Fleischmarkt ㉓

Map 2 E5 & 6 D2–E3. Ⓤ *Schwedenplatz.* **Griechische Kirche**
📞 5122133. 🕐 *9am–4pm Mon–Fri.*

FLEISCHMARKT, THE FORMER meat
market, dates from 1220.

The small cosy inn called the
Griechenbeisl *(see p213)* is its
best-known landmark. On its
façade is a woodcarving of a
bagpiper known as *Der liebe
Augustin* (Dear old Augustin).
Rumour has it that during the
1679 plague, this bagpiper
slumped drunk into the
gutter one night and, taken
for dead, was put in the
plague pit. He woke,
attracted attention by playing
his pipes and was rescued.
Miraculously, he did not
catch the plague.

Next to the Griechenbeisl is
the Neo-Byzantine Griechische
Kirche (Greek church of the
Holy Trinity). The versatile
architect Theophil Hansen
(see p32) created its rich, gilt
appearance in the 1850s.

A passage links the Griechenbeisl to Griechengasse.

Griechengasse ㉔

Map 2 E5 & 6 E2. Ⓤ *Schwedenplatz.*
Griechische Kirche. 📞 5122133.
🕐 *by appt, 9am–4pm Mon–Fri,*
10am–1pm for mass only Sat & Sun.

THIS STREET NAME refers to
the Greek merchants who
settled here in the 18th
century and it leads up from
Rotenturmstrasse. The house
on the right dates from 1611
but has since been altered.
Opposite is the Griechische
Kirche (St George's), not to be
confused with the Griechische
Kirche in Fleischmarkt. This
one was built in 1803 but the
gable was added later, in 1898.
No. 7 is a 17th-century house.
The façade was rebuilt in the
late 18th century.

Ruprechtskirche ㉕

Ruprechtsplatz. **Map** 2 E5 & 6 D2.
📞 5356003. Ⓤ *Schwedenplatz.*
🕐 *9:30–11:30am Mon–Fri & for
mass 5pm Sat & 10:30am Sun; Jul–Aug:
for mass 6pm Sat only.* 📷 ♿
Donation expected.

Ivy-clad façade of Ruprechtskirche

ST RUPRECHT *(see p22)* was
the patron saint of Vienna's
salt merchants and the church
that takes his name overlooks
the merchants' landing stage
on the Danube canal. There is
a statue of the saint holding a
tub of salt at the foot of the
Romanesque tower. Salt was a
valuable commodity in the
Middle Ages, and evidence
suggests that the church dates
back to the 11th century,
making it the oldest church in
Vienna. The interior is less
interesting, having been
restored at various times, but
the chancel has two panes of
Romanesque stained glass. The
choir is 13th century, the vaulted south aisle 15th century.

Carving of the bagpiper on the façade of the Griechenbeisl, Fleischmarkt

Austrian Museum of Applied Arts ㉑

THE RENOVATED MAK (Museum für angewandte Kunst) acts both as a showcase for Austrian decorative arts and as a repository for fine objects from around the world. Originally founded in 1864 as a museum for art and industry, it expanded and diversified over the years to include objects representing new artistic movements. The museum has a fine collection of furniture, including some classical works of the German cabinet-maker David Roentgen, textiles, glass, Islamic and East Asian art and fine Renaissance jewellery. In 1993 the museum was completely renovated and each room was re-designed by a different leading artist. The result is a series of displays that lend the exhibits a unique, unusual flavour.

★ Wiener Werkstätte Collection
Kolo Moser created this brass vase, inlaid with citrines (false topaz), for the Wiener Werkstätte in 1903.

Stairs to second floor

★ Dubsky Porcelain Room
A reassembly of a room (around 1724) in the Dubsky Palace at Brno, Czech Republic.

First floor

First floor mezzanine

Romanesque, Gothic and Renaissance Room
Blue walls set off the furniture and ceramics in display cases designed by Matthias Esterházy in 1993.

Entrance to MAK Café *(see p213)*

Entrance hall

Stubenring entrance

MUSEUM GUIDE
The basement houses the individual collections, and the extension is used for special exhibitions. Most of the permanent collection is displayed in the ground-floor galleries, although the Wiener Werkstätte collection is on the first floor. A flight of stairs in the west wing leads to the contemporary architecture and design rooms on the second floor.

KEY
- ☐ Romanesque, Gothic, Renaissance
- ☐ Baroque, Rococo
- ☐ Wiener Werkstätte
- ☐ Art Nouveau, Art Deco
- ☐ Islamic Art
- ☐ Biedermeier
- ☐ 20th-century design
- ☐ Individual collections
- ☐ Temporary exhibition space
- ☐ Non-exhibition space

Basement

Monk of the Nichiren Sect
This Japanese wooden sculpture of a praying monk dates from the Muromachi Period (around 1500).

THE WIENER WERKSTÄTTE

In 1903 Josef Hoffman (pictured) and Kolo Moser founded a co-operative arts and crafts workshop, the Wiener Werkstätte. This promoted all aspects of design from postage stamps and book illustrations to fabric, furniture, jewellery and interiors. The museum houses its archives, which include sketches, fabric patterns and fine pieces.

VISITORS' CHECKLIST

Stubenring 5. **Map** 2 F5 & 6 F3.
711360. Stubentor. 1A, 74A. 1, 2. Landstrasse. 10am–midnight Tue, 10am–6pm Wed–Sun. 1 Jan, 1 May, 1 Nov, 25 Dec (24 & 31 Dec: 10am–3pm). www.MAK.at

Lecture Hall

Library

Ground floor

Mundus Chair

Bentwood furniture was made popular by the 19th-century designer, Michael Thonet (1796–1871), who pioneered bentwood furniture techniques in the 1830s. This example was manufactured by Mundus in 1910.

Knotted Mameluke Carpet

This 16th-century Egyptian silk rug is the only known surviving example of its kind.

STAR FEATURES

★ Dubsky Porcelain Room

★ Wiener Werkstätte Collection

★ Biedermeier Room

★ Biedermeier Room

This cherrywood sofa (1825–30), designed and manufactured by Danhauser'sche Möbelfabrik, is an outstanding example of Viennese Empire-style Biedermeier design (see pp30–31). The original upholstery has been reproduced.

Jewish District 26

Map 2 F5 & 6 D2. **Ⓤ** *Schwedenplatz.*
***Stadttempel* Ⓒ** *531040.* **◯** *Mon–*
Thu (am) by appt or for tours at
11:30am and 3pm (take identification).

V IENNA'S JEWISH DISTRICT is
more famous today for its
area of bars and discos called
the Bermuda Triangle than
for its Jewish community.
Judengasse is now a bustling
lane lined with clothes shops
and bars. There are some
solid Biedermeier apartment
blocks and on Ruprechts-
platz, in the former town
hall, is a kosher restaurant, the
Arche Noah. Behind it is a
jutting tower, the Korn-
häuselturm. Named after Josef
Kornhäusel, an architect from
the Biedermeier period *(see*
pp30–31), it was apparently
built as a refuge from his wife.

Close to Arche Noah is
Sterngasse. This street has an
English-language bookshop
called Shakespeare & Co *(see*
p225) and the Neustädter-Hof,
a Baroque palace built by
Anton Ospel in 1734. A
Turkish cannonball, fired in
1683, is embedded in its façade.

Vienna's oldest surviving
synagogue, the Stadttempel,
designed by Kornhäusel in
the 1820s, is on Seitenstetten-
gasse. On the same street is
the headquarters of Vienna's

The Anker Clock in Hoher Markt

Jewish community. It used to
house the Jewish museum,
which is now located in
Dorotheergasse *(see p93).*

Hoher Markt 27

Map 2 E5 & 6 D2. **Ⓤ** *Stephansplatz,*
Schwedenplatz. **Roman ruins**
Ⓒ *5355606.* **◯** *9am–12:15pm,*
1–4:30pm Tue–Sun.

H OHER MARKT IS the oldest
square in Vienna. In
medieval times fish and cloth
markets were held here, and

so were executions. Today it
is possible to view the subterranean ruins of a former
Roman garrison beneath it *(see*
p21). Discovered after World
War II, the ancient foundations
show groups of houses bisec-
ted by straight roads leading
to the town gates. It seems
probable that they were 2nd-
and 3rd-century officers'
houses. The excavations are
well laid out and exhibits of
pottery, reliefs and tiles
supplement the ruins.

In the centre of the square is
the Vermählungsbrunnen
(Nuptial Fountain), or Josefs-
brunnen. Emperor Leopold I
vowed to commemorate the
safe return of his son Joseph
from the Siege of Landau
and commissioned Johann
Bernhard Fischer von Erlach
to design this monument,
which was built by von
Erlach's son Joseph Emanuel
between 1729 and 1732. The
fountain celebrates the
betrothal of Joseph and Mary
and bears figures of the high
priest and the couple, with gilt
urns, statues of angels, and
fluted columns supporting an
elaborate canopy.

Linking two office buildings
on the square is the bronze
and copper sculptural clock,
known as the Anker Clock.
Commissioned by the Anker
Insurance Company, and
designed by Franz Matsch, it
was completed in 1914. Every
hour a procession of cut-out
historical figures, ranging from
the Emperor Marcus Aurelius
and Duke Rudolf IV to Joseph
Haydn, glide from one side of
the clock to the other to the
sound of organ music. Noon
is the best time to see it, as all
the figures are on display then.

Bohemian Court Chancery 28

Judenplatz 11. **Map** 2 D5 & 5 C2.
Ⓒ *53122.* **Ⓤ** *Stephansplatz.*
◯ *8am–3:30pm Mon–Fri.*

H ABSBURG RULERS were also
kings of Bohemia, which
was governed from this magnificent palace (1709–14). Its
architect was the finest of the
day: Johann Bernhard Fischer
von Erlach *(see p148).*

VIENNA'S JEWS – PAST AND PRESENT

A Jewish community has thrived in Vienna since at least the
12th century, with Judenplatz and, later, the Stadttempel at
its core. Unfortunately, the Jews' commercial success caused
envy and in 1421, after a charge of ritual murder, almost the
entire Jewish population was burnt to death, forcibly baptised
or expelled. Thereafter Jewish fortunes fluctuated, with periods
of prosperity alternating with expulsions. The 1781 Edict of
Tolerance lifted legal constraints that had applied to Jews and
by the late 19th century the city's cultural and intellectual life
was dominated by Jews. Anti-Semitism spread in the early
20th century and burgeoning Nazism forced many Jews to
leave. Of those who remained, 65,000 were murdered. In

1938 170,000
Jews lived in the
city; 50 years
later there were
7,000. Now East-
ern European
Jews are adding
to the number.

The interior of
the Stadttempel

Matthias Gerl enlarged the Chancery between 1751 and 1754 to accommodate the Ministry of the Interior. Its glory is the huge Baroque portals, yet the building is as subtle as it is powerful. The elegantly-curved window frames on the first floor are particularly noteworthy.

The building's interior, now a courthouse, and its two courtyards, are less impressive, partly due to reconstruction undertaken after serious bomb damage in World War II.

Altes Rathaus ㉙

Wipplinger Strasse 8. **Map** 2 D5 & 6 D2. *Schwedenplatz*. ***Salvatorkapelle*** *5337133.* ☐ *9–11am Mon, Wed, Sat, or by appointment.* ***Austrian Resistance Archive*** *53436779.* ☐ *by appointment.*

A FTER THE GERMAN brothers Otto and Haymo of Neuburg conspired to overthrow the Habsburgs *(see p22)* in 1309, their property

Ironwork at the Rathaus entrance

was confiscated and donated to the city. Over the centuries the site was expanded to form the complex of buildings that until 1883 served as the city hall or *Rathaus.*

The entrance of the Altes Rathaus is festooned with ornamental ironwork. The building is now occupied by offices and shops. The District Museum, which deals with the first municipal district of Vienna (roughly covering the area within the Ring), is also here. Of much greater interest is the Austrian Resistance Archive on the first floor, where

Portal figure by Lorenzo Mattielli in the Bohemian Court Chancery

Austrian resistance to Nazism is documented. Although many Austrians welcomed Hitler's takeover in 1938, a distinguished minority fiercely resisted it, and this exhibition pays tribute to them.

In one corner of the Altes Rathaus is the Andromeda Fountain. Located in the main courtyard, it was the last work by sculptor Georg Raphael Donner who designed it in 1741. The relief shows Perseus rescuing Andromeda.

At No. 5 Salvatorplatz is a late 13th-century chapel, the Salvatorkapelle, the only surviving building of the original medieval town house. It has since been enlarged and renovated, but retains its fine Gothic vaults. The walls are lined with old marble tomb slabs, some from the 15th century. Its pretty organ dates from around 1740 and is sometimes used for recitals in the chapel. On the outside wall on Salvatorgasse is an exquisite Renaissance portal dating from 1520 to 1530 – a rare example of Italianate Renaissance style.

Maria am Gestade ㉚

Salvatorgasse 12. **Map** 2 D5 & 5 C2. *5339594.* *Schwedenplatz, Stephansplatz.* ☐ *7:30am–6pm daily & inside at rear by appointment only.*

O NE OF THE CITY'S oldest sights is this lofty, Gothic church with its 56-m high (180-ft) steeple and immense choir windows. Mentioned as early as 1158, the present building dates from the late 14th century. It was restored in the 19th century. The church has had a chequered history and during the occupation of Vienna by Napoleon in 1809 his troops used it as an arsenal.

Inside, the nave piers are enlivened with Gothic canopies sheltering statues from various periods: medieval, Baroque and modern. The choir contains two High Gothic panels (1460): they depict the Annunciation, the Crucifixion and the Coronation of the Virgin. Behind the high altar the windows contain medieval stained glass, which is patched with surviving fragments. Tucked away on the north side of the choir is a chapel with a beautiful painted stone altar from 1520. The main parts of the interior are visible from the front entrance, but to walk around inside you need to make an appointment.

Gothic canopies in the Maria am Gestade church

Holocaust memorial in Judenplatz

Judenplatz 🜳

Map 2 D5 & 5 C2. Ⓤ *Stephansplatz, Herrengasse.* **Museum Judenplatz**
Ⓒ 53504310. ⬤ *10am–6pm Sun–Thu, 10am–2pm Fri.*
⬤ *on main Jewish holidays.*
🖼 & *except to synagogue.* 📷
🎫 *free, 2pm & 5pm Thu & Sun. Take identification.* 🖥 *www.jmw.at*

JUDENPLATZ WAS THE SITE of the Jewish ghetto in medieval times. In the centre of the square stands a statue of the German playwright and critic Ephraim Lessing by Siegfried Charoux. The Nazis did not like a tribute to a writer whose works plead for toleration towards Jews, and they destroyed it in 1939. It was later redesigned by the same sculptor and reinstated in the square in 1982.

In 1996 British artist Rachel Whiteread was the controversial win-ner of a competition to design a monument for the Jewish victims of the Nazi regime, to be unveiled in the square on 9 Novem-ber 1999, the anniver-sary of Kristal Nacht. A heated public debate ensued and following many changes, including the repositioning of the monument by one metre, Judenplatz was reopened on 25 October 2000 as a place of remembrance. It now contains Whiteread's memorial, the new Museum Judenplatz at No. 8, and the excavated remains of the medieval synagogue that lie beneath the square. The museum celebrates the vibrant Jewish quarter that was centred on the square until the expulsion of the Jews in 1421, an event gleefully recorded in an inscription, *Zum Grossen Jordan*, on the façade of No. 2. The museum also houses a public database of the 65,000 Austrian Jews killed by the Nazis and, in the basement, the excavated synagogue.

Clock Museum 🜲

Schulhof 2. **Map** 2 D5 & 5 C2. Ⓒ 5332265. Ⓤ *Stephansplatz.* ⬤ *9am–4:30pm Tue–Sun.* ⬤ *1 Jan, 1 May, 25 Dec.* 📷 🖥 *www.wienmuseum.at*

YOU DON'T HAVE TO be a clock fanatic to enjoy a visit to this wonderful and fascinating museum. Located in the beautiful former Obizzi Palace (1690), the museum contains a fine collection of clocks which were accumulated by an earlier curator, Rudolf Kaftan, as well as those of the novelist Marie von Ebner-Eschenbach. The first floor displays the mechanisms of tower clocks from the 16th century onwards, painted clocks, grandfather clocks and pocket watches. On the floors above are huge astronomical clocks and various novelty ones. There are more than 3,000 exhibits.

Kurrentgasse 🜳

Map 2 D5 & 5 C2. Ⓤ *Stephansplatz.* **Grimm bakery** ⬤ *7am–6:30pm Mon–Fri, 7am–noon Sat.*

THIS NARROW street is shaded by elegant tall Baroque houses, their lower floors filled with cosy bars and pricey Italian restaurants. It's a pleasant place to while away an afternoon. The Grimm bakery at No. 10 is one of the best in Vienna and offers an astonishing variety of breads. No. 12, a house dating from 1730, has an attractive pink cobbled courtyard filled with numerous plants and trees.

Doll and Toy Museum 🜴

Schulhof 4. **Map** 2 D5 & 5 C2.
Ⓒ 5356860. Ⓤ *Stephansplatz, Herrengasse.* ⬤ *10am–6pm Tue–Sun.* 📷

ONE OF VIENNA'S more unexpected museums is housed in this fine Baroque building. Originally a private collection, it was opened to the public in 1989 and com-prises dolls and toys from the past two centuries. The dolls are mainly of French and German origin. Particularly intriguing are the early 20th-century "exotic" dolls or Südsee-Babies (South Sea babies); they are black, Poly-nesian and Oriental models.

Among the exhibits are some astonishingly opulent dolls' houses from the turn of the century, and some teddy bears. There is also a shop which sells historic dolls.

Musical doll from the Doll and Toy Museum

Statue on top of No. 10 Am Hof

Kirche am Hof �35

Schulhof 1. **Map** 2 D5 & 5 C2.
☎ 5338394. Ⓤ *Herrengasse.*
○ *7am–noon, 4–6pm daily.* ▣ &

THIS CATHOLIC CHURCH, which is picturesquely dedicated to the Nine Choirs of Angels, was founded by Carmelite friars in the late 14th century. The façade, at present being renovated, was redesigned by the Italian architect Carlo Carlone in 1662 to provide space for a large balustraded balcony. The church is now used for services by Vienna's large Croatian community.

It is also worth taking a walk behind the church into Schulhofplatz to look at the tiny restored shops which snuggle happily between the buttresses of the Gothic choir.

Am Hof �36

Map 2 D5 & 5 C2.
Ⓤ *Stephansplatz, Schottentor.*

THIS IS THE LARGEST enclosed square in Vienna. The Romans established a garrison here and, later, the Babenberg ruler Duke Heinrich II Jasomirgott built his castle close to where No. 2 Am Hof stands. In the centre of the square you can see the Mariensäule (Column of Our Lady), a monument that commemorates the end of

the threat of Swedish invasion during the Thirty Years War *(see p25)*. Dating from 1667, it was designed by Carlo Carlone and Carlo Canevale.

There are a number of interesting houses around the square. Opposite the church is the palatial Märkleinisches Haus which was designed by Johann Lukas von Hildebrandt *(see p152)* in 1727. Its elegant façade was wrecked by the insertion of a fire station on the ground floor in 1935. The 16th-century red house next door is the headquarters of Johann Kattus, a producer of sparkling wine. No. 10, designed by Anton Ospel, is the Bürgerliche Zeughaus, the citizens' armoury, where the city's fire services are now permanently based. The façade is dominated by the Habsburg coat of arms and military emblems. The allegorical statues above are by Lorenzo Mattielli.

At No. 12 the bay-windowed Urbanihaus dates from the 1730s, and its iron inn sign dates from the same period. Next door is the Collalto Palace – it was here, in 1762, that Mozart made his first public appearance aged just six *(see p38)*.

Peterskirche �37

Petersplatz 6. **Map** 2 D5 & 5 C3.
☎ 5336433. Ⓤ *Stephansplatz.*
○ *7am–6pm daily.* ▣

A CHURCH HAS STOOD here since the 12th century, but the oval structure you see today dates from the early 18th century. It was modelled on St Peter's in Rome and a number of architects collaborated on the design, notably Gabriele Montani. The interior is amazingly lavish, and there's an exuberant, eye-catching pulpit (1716) by the sculptor Matthias Steindl. The richly-clothed skeletons on the right and beneath the altar are the remains of early Christian martyrs originally deposited in the catacombs in Rome. The frescoes inside the huge dome, depicting the Assumption of the Virgin, are by J M Rottmayr.

In 1729 Lorenzo Mattielli designed the sculpture of St John Nepomuk to the right of the choir. This priest earned his sainthood by being thrown into the River Vltava in Prague in 1393 after he refused to reveal the secrets of the confessional to King Wenceslas IV; his martyrdom by drowning later became a favourite subject of artists.

18th-century engraving of Peterskirche

HOFBURG QUARTER

WHAT BEGAN AS a modest city fortress has grown over the centuries into a vast palace, the Hofburg. The palace was still expanding up until a few years before the Habsburgs fell from power in 1918. The presence of the court had a profound effect on the surrounding area. The former gardens of the palace are now **Portal detail in Josefsplatz** the Volksgarten and Burggarten, and some of the buildings are now splendid museums. Streets such as Herrengasse and Bankgasse are lined with the palaces that the nobility built in their eagerness to be as close as possible to the centre of imperial power. This area is bustling with tourists by day, but at night it is almost deserted.

SIGHTS AT A GLANCE

Streets and Squares
Bankgasse ③①
Dorotheergasse ⑦
Graben ⑧
Herrengasse ⑬
Josefsplatz ⑥
Kärntner Strasse ③⑥
Kohlmarkt ⑩
Michaelerplatz ①
Minoritenplatz ②⑨
Naglergasse ⑫
Neuer Markt ③⑤
Stock-im-Eisen-Platz ③⑧

Historic Buildings
American Bar ③⑦
Bundeskanzleramt ②⑧
Demel Konditorei ⑪
Grosses und Kleines
  Michaelerhaus ③
Hofburg Complex pp96–7 ⑮
Lobkowitz Palace ③③
Loos Haus ②
Mollard-Clary Palace ⑭
Prunksaal ②④
Stallburg ⑤
*Winter Riding School
  pp98–9* ②⑥

Churches and Cathedrals
Augustinerkirche ②③
Burgkapelle ②⑤
Kapuzinerkirche
  und Kaisergruft ③④
Michaelerkirche ④
Minoritenkirche ③⓪

Museums and Galleries
Albertina ②②
Ephesos Museum ⑰
Hofjagd und Rüstkammer ⑲
Neue Burg ⑯
Sammlung Alter
  Musikinstrumente ⑱
*State Apartments and
  Treasuries pp100–101* ②⑦
Völkerkundemuseum ②⓪

Parks and Gardens
Burggarten ②①
Volksgarten ③②

Monuments
Pestsäule ⑨

GETTING THERE
This area is served by the Herrengasse (line U3) U-Bahn station. Trams 1 and 2 run along the Burgring and Dr-Karl-Renner-Ring. Buses 2A and 3A run along Herrengasse and bus 1A goes from Stubentor to the Graben.

0 metres   250

0 yards   250

KEY

⬜ Street-by-Street map
  See pp90–91

Ⓤ U-Bahn station

🅿 Parking

◁ **Detail of Danubius fountain by Johann Meixner (1869)** **outside the Albertina**

Street-by-Street: Imperial Vienna

THE STREETS AROUND the Hofburg are no longer filled with the carriages of the nobility. Most of the palaces have become offices, embassies or apartments. Yet this district remains the most fashionable in Vienna, crammed with elegant shops, art galleries and coffee houses, which offer enjoyable interludes between visits to the many museums and churches in the area.

Herrengasse
This was a prime site for the palaces of the nobility ⓭

Herrengasse U-Bahn

Demel Konditorei
This Café-Konditorei offers delightful décor and exquisite pastries ⓫

Grosses und Kleines Michaelerhaus
Joseph Haydn (see p38) once lived in rooms overlooking the handsome courtyard of the Grosses Michaelerhaus ❸

Mollard-Clary Palace
This mansion, built at the end of the 17th-century, has a façade designed by J L Hildebrandt ⓮

Michaelerplatz
Roman remains were recently excavated here ❶

★ Loos Haus
Built in 1912, this unadorned design outraged the conservative sensibilities of the ornament-loving Archduke Franz Ferdinand (see p166) ❷

STAR SIGHTS

★ Loos Haus

★ Michaelerkirche

★ Pestsäule

KEY

– – – Suggested route

0 metres   50

0 yards   50

★ Michaelerkirche
The crypt of this church contains well-preserved corpses from the late 18th century ❹

Josefsplatz
An equestrian statue of Joseph II stands at the centre of this elegant square ❻

Naglergasse
This lane has some of the finest Baroque façades in the city ⓬

Graben
The Spar-Casse Bank, with its gilt bee on the pediment, is just one of many fine buildings on the pedestrianized Graben ⓼

LOCATOR MAP
See Street Finder, maps 2 & 5

Kohlmarkt
This street has a number of shops by Hans Hollein, one of Austria's finest architects ⓾

★ **Pestsäule**
Built after the plague of 1679, this is the most imposing of the Baroque plague columns ⓽

Dorotheergasse
Lining this narrow lane are art galleries and auction houses, and the much-loved Café Hawelka (see p58–61) ⓻

Stallburg
Once a royal residence, the Stallburg now houses the Spanish Riding School stables and the Lipizzaner Museum ⓹

The Palffy Palace, built in the 16th century, was later the venue for a private performance of Mozart's *The Marriage of Figaro*.

The Pallavicini Palace is a late 18th-century aristocrats' palace, strategically located opposite the Hofburg.

Michaelerplatz ❶

Map 2 D5 & 5 C3. Ⓤ *Herrengasse.*

MICHAELERPLATZ faces the grandiose entrance into the Hofburg, the Michaelertor. Opposite are the Michaelerkirche and Loos Haus. On one side of Michaelerplatz is the Michaelertrakt, commissioned by Franz Joseph in 1888 when the new Burgtheater *(see pp132–33)* on the Ringstrasse opened, and the original theatre dating from 1751, which occupied this site, was demolished. An old design by Joseph Emanuel Fischer von Erlach *(see p149)* was used as the basis for a new design by Ferdinand Kirschner (1821–96). It was finished in 1893, complete with gilt-tasselled cupolas and statuary representing Austria's land and sea power.

Recent excavations have uncovered remains of a Roman encampment, as well as some medieval foundations.

Loos Haus ❷

Michaelerplatz 3. **Map** 2 D5 & 5 C3. ☎ 53173455. Ⓤ *Herrengasse.* ◯ 8am–3pm Mon–Wed & Fri, 8am–5:30pm Thu. ♿

ERECTED opposite the Michaelertor in 1910–12, and designed by Adolf Loos, this building so outraged Franz Ferdinand *(see p166)* that he declared he

ADOLF LOOS

Unlike his contemporary Otto Wagner *(see p57)*, Adolf Loos (1870–1933) loathed ornament for its own sake. Instead, he used smooth lines and exquisite interior decoration; his buildings' lack of "eye-brows" (the window hoods on many of Vienna's buildings) scandalized Viennese society. Surviving interiors include Knize *(see p93)*, the American Bar *(see p105)* and the Café Museum *(see p137)*.

would never use the Michaelertor again. Today it's hard to understand why: the outside is unexceptional but the inside is a lesson in stylish elegance.

Grosses und Kleines Michaelerhaus ❸

Kohlmarkt 11 & Michaelerplatz 6. **Map** 2 D5 & 5 C3. Ⓤ *Herrengasse.* ● *to the public.*

Michaelerplatz fountain

AT NO. 6 Michaelerplatz a footpath leads to the Baroque Kleines Michaelerhaus (1735). Look out for a vivid painted relief of Christ on the Mount of Olives with a crucifixion in the background (1494) on the side of the Michaelerkirche. The Baroque façade of the Grosses Michaelerhaus is at No. 11 Kohlmarkt. It has a

handsome courtyard and coach house. From here there is a fine view of the older parts of the Michaelerkirche. The buildings around the courtyard were erected in about 1720, and the composer Joseph Haydn *(see p38)* is said to have lived in an unheated attic here in 1749.

Michaelerkirche ❹

Michaelerplatz 1. **Map** 2 D5 & 5 C3. ☎ 5338000. Ⓤ *Herrengasse.* ◯ 6:30am–6pm daily. ♿ ◉ ♿ ✦ May–Oct: 11am, 1pm, 2pm, 3pm, 4pm; Nov–Apr: 11am, 3pm.

THE MICHAELERKIRCHE was once the parish church of the court. Its earliest parts were built in the 13th century, and the choir dates from 1327–40. The Neo-Classical façade is from 1792. Its porch is topped by Baroque statues (1724–25) by Lorenzo Mattielli depicting the Fall of the Angels. Inside are Renaissance and 14th-century frescoes, and a glorious, vividly-carved organ from 1714 by Johann David Sieber. The main choir (1782), replete with tumbling cherubs and sunbursts, is by Karl Georg Merville. The altarpiece of the north choir (1755) is by Franz Anton Maulbertsch.

Off the north choir is the crypt entrance. In the 17th and 18th centuries parishioners were frequently buried beneath their church. Corpses clothed in their burial finery, well-preserved due to the constant temperature, can still be seen in open coffins.

Baroque organ (1714) in the Michaelerkirche

Stallburg ❺

Reitschulgasse 2. **Map** 4 D1 & 5 C3.
🚇 *Stephansplatz, Herrengasse.*
Lipizzaner Museum 📞 *5337811.*
🚪 *9am–6pm daily.* 🎫 📷

THE STALLBURG WAS BUILT in the mid-16th century for Archduke Maximilian. This former royal residence was later converted to stables for the Hofburg, these are ranged around a large courtyard with arcades on three storeys. The Stallburg today houses the Spanish Riding School *(see pp98–9)* and the Lipizzaner Museum which contains objects from the Imperial Collection, exhibits on the history of the Lipizzaner horses and works of art portraying the Spanish Riding School.

Josefsplatz ❻

Augustinerstrasse. **Map** 4 D1 & 5 C4.
🚇 *Stephansplatz, Herrengasse.*

IN THE CENTRE OF the Josefsplatz is an equestrian statue (1807) of Joseph II by Franz Anton Zauner. Despite his reforms, Joseph II was a true monarchist, and during the 1848 revolution *(see p31)* loyalists used the square as a gathering place.

Facing the Hofburg are two palaces. No. 5 is the Pallavicini Palace (1783–4), a blend of Baroque and Neo-Classical styles by Ferdinand von Hohenberg. No. 6 is the 16th-

century Palffy Palace. On the right of the Prunksaal *(see p102)* is the Redoutensaal. It was built from 1750–60 and was the venue for masked balls in imperial times. To the left is an extension to the library which was built a few years later. Both are by Nikolaus Pacassi, a favourite architect of Maria Theresa.

Dorotheergasse ❼

Map 4 D1 & 5 C4. 🚇 *Stephansplatz.*
Jewish Museum 📞 *5350431.*
🚪 *10am–6pm Mon–Wed, Fri & Sun, 10am–8pm Thu.* 🌐 *www.jmw.at*

AT NO. 11 OF THIS street is the Eskeles Palace, now home to the Jewish Museum (Jüdisches Museum) which, along with its new extension in Judenplatz *(see p86)*, chronicles the city's rich Jewish heritage. At No. 27 is the Dorotheum *(see pp224–5)*, from the 17th century. A pawnbrokers and, more importantly, an auction house, it has branches all over Vienna. Halfway along the street is the Evangelical church (1783–4), originally by Gottlieb Nigelli. Towards the top end, close to Graben, are two immensely popular Viennese gathering places, Café Hawelka at No. 6 *(see pp58–61)*, and the Buffet Trzesniewski at No. 1 *(see p219)*.

Baroque plague column (Pestsäule)

Graben ❽

Map 2 D5 & 5 C3. 🚇 *Stephansplatz.*
Neidhart Fresco House 🚪 *9am– 12:15pm, 1–4:30pm Tue–Sun.*

FACING NO. 16 of this pedestrianized street is the Joseph Fountain by Johann Martin Fischer. Further along is his identical Leopold Fountain (both 1804). No. 13, the clothing shop Knize *(see p223)*, is by Adolf Loos. No. 10, the Ankerhaus by Otto Wagner, is topped by a studio used by Wagner himself and, in the 1980s, by Friedensreich Hundertwasser *(see p164)*. No. 21 is Alois Pichl's Spar-Casse Bank from the 1830s. Just off the Graben at No. 19 Tuchlauben is the Neidhart Fresco House, containing medieval frescoes. *(See pp54–7)*.

Pestsäule ❾

Graben. **Map** 2 D5 & 5 C3.
🚇 *Stephansplatz.*

DURING THE PLAGUE of 1679, Emperor Leopold I vowed to commemorate Vienna's eventual deliverance. The plague over, he commissioned Matthias Rauchmiller, Lodovico Burnacini and the young Johann Bernhard Fischer von Erlach *(see p149)* to build this Baroque plague column. Devised by the Jesuits, its most striking image shows a saintly figure and an angel supervising the destruction of a hag representing the plague, while above the bewigged Emperor prays.

Statue in Josefsplatz of Joseph II by Franz Anton Zauner (1746–1822)

Exterior of Schullin shop *(see p223)*

Kohlmarkt ⑩

Map 2 D5 & 5 C3. Ⓤ *Herrengasse.*

Leading directly up to the Imperial Palace, the pedestrianized Kohlmarkt is lined with some of Vienna's most exclusive shops and remarkable shopfronts. No. 9, the Jugendstil Artaria Haus (1901), was the work of Max Fabiani (1865–1962), a protégé of Otto Wagner *(see p57)*. No.16, the book-shop and publishers Manz, boasts a characteristic portal from 1912 by Adolf Loos *(see p92)*. The striking abstract shopfront of jewel-lers Schullin (1982) was designed by the architect Hans Hollein *(see p91)*.

Demel Konditorei ⑪

Kohlmarkt 14. **Map** 2 D5 & 5 C3. 🕿 53517170. Ⓤ *Stephansplatz.* ◷ *10am–7pm daily.* 📷 ♿

This famous pastry shop at No. 14 Kohlmarkt still bears its imperial patent – K.u.k. Hof-Zuckerbäcker – proudly lettered above the shopfront.

The pastry shop was founded in Michaelerplatz in 1785 and acquired by the pâtissier Christoph Demel in 1857, before moving to its present site on Kohlmarkt in 1888. Its many small rooms are in an ornate late 19th-century style.

Naglergasse ⑫

Map 2 D5 & 5 C2. Ⓤ *Herrengasse.*

During the Middle Ages needle-makers had their shops here, which is how the street acquired its name. This narrow lane also follows the line of a wall that used to stand here in Roman times. Today Naglergasse is lined with a succession of gorgeous Baroque houses. The delight-ful Renaissance bay window of No. 19 is ornamented with carved cherubs. No. 13 dates from the 16th century but has been considerably altered since. No. 21 (1720) is now an inn with a particularly snug and cosy interior.

Herrengasse ⑬

Map 2 D5 & 5 B2. Ⓤ *Herrengasse.*

Flanking the hofburg, this street was the prime location for the palaces of the Habsburg nobility. In 1843 a visiting writer, J G Kohl, wrote of the street's "silent palaces", and today little has changed.
The base of the provincial government of Lower Austria, the Landhaus, is at No. 13; the façade of the present building dates from the 1830s.

In the courtyard a tablet from 1571 warns visitors not to carry weapons or to fight here. The injunction was famously ignored when the 1848 Revolution *(see p31)* was ignited on this very spot.
The long, low Neo-Classical façade of No. 7 received its present appearance from Ludwig Pichl and Giacomo Quarenghi in 1811. At No. 5 Anton Ospel (1677–1756) gave the Wilczek Palace (built before 1737) an original façade, with angled pilasters lending the central bays an illusion of perspective.

Coat of arms in the courtyard of the Mollard-Clary Palace

Mollard-Clary Palace ⑭

Herrengasse 9. **Map** 2 D5 & 5 B3. Ⓤ *Herrengasse.* ● *to the public.*

At no. 9 herrengasse is the former Mollard-Clary Palace, a mansion constructed by Domenico Martinelli in 1698. The façade, which also dates from 1698, was the first commission for Johann Lukas von Hildebrandt *(see p152)*.
From 1923 until 1997 the palace housed the Lower Austrian Provincial Museum, or Landesmuseum. Today the building houses offices.
Visible throught the court-yard gates are an elaborate, 16th-century wrought-iron well cover and a carved stone coat of arms (1454).

Hofburg Complex ⑮

See pp96–101.

Inside the ornately-decorated Demel Konditorei

Neue Burg 16

Burgring. **Map** 4 D1 & 5 B4.
[52524484. [V] Volkstheater,
Herrengasse. [🚊] 1, 2, D, J.
[○] 10am–6pm Mon, Wed–Sun.
[📷] [W] www.khm.at

THE NEUE BURG, a massive
curved building situated on
Heldenplatz, was added to the
Hofburg Complex in 1881–
1913. It embodies the last gasp
of the Habsburg Empire as it
strained under aspirations of independence from its domains,
when the personal prestige of
Emperor Franz Joseph was all
that seemed able to keep it
intact. It was not the perfect
moment to embark on an
extension to the Hofburg, but
the work was undertaken
nevertheless, and the Neue
Burg was built to designs by
the Ringstrasse architects Karl
von Hasenauer (1833–94) and
Gottfried Semper (1803–79).
Five years after its completion,
the Habsburg empire ended.
   In 1938, Adolf Hitler stood
on the terraced central bay to
proclaim the Anschluss – the
union of Austria and Germany
– to tens of thousands of
Viennese (see p36).
   Today the Neue Burg is
home to the reading room of
the National Library, as well
as a number of museums
(see following entries).

Ephesos Museum 17

As Neue Burg. [52524484.
[○] 10am–6pm Mon, Wed–Sun.

FOR DECADES Austrian archaeologists have been
excavating the
Greek and
Roman site of
Ephesus in
Turkey. Since
1978 their discov-
eries have been on
display in the main block of
the Neue Burg. Also on show
are finds from the Greek
island of Samothrace, excavated in the 1870s. The main
exhibits include a colossal
frieze commemorating Lucius
Verus's victory over
the Parthians in AD 165, as
well as a substantial number
of architectural fragments.

Armour at Hofjagd und Rüstkammer

Sammlung Alter Musikinstrumente 18

As Neue Burg.

PIANOS THAT belonged to
Beethoven, Schubert and
Haydn, among countless
other items, are housed in the
musical instrument museum.
More important, however, is
the collection of Renaissance
instruments, widely believed
to be the finest in the world.
The claviorgan (1596), the
oldest surviving example of
this instrument, is particularly
fascinating, and features stops
used to create special effects
such as birdsong.

**Renaissance cittern
from the Sammlung
Alter Musikinstrumente**

Hofjagd und Rüstkammer 19

As Neue Burg.

THE HOFBURG'S weapons
collection is impressive
both for its size and for the
workmanship of its finest
items: ivory and filigree inlay
on weapons, medieval ceremonial saddles and jewelled
Turkish and Syrian maces.
Particularly resplendent are
the 16th-century ceremonial
suits worn by the Habsburgs
for tournaments and military
parades, and the decorative
fighting and hunting weapons.
   The museum was based on
the personal armouries of the
Habsburg emperors and, not
surprisingly, houses one of the
finest collections in Europe.

Völkerkunde-museum 20

As Neue Burg. [534300.
[○] 10am–6pm Mon, Wed–Sun.

RANGED AROUND an arcaded
Italian Renaissance-style
courtyard is Vienna's ethno-
logical museum. It is situated
at the west end of the Neue
Burg. To one side are the
Oriental collections: lacquer
screens, clothes, furniture,
weapons, ceramics, farm tools,
masks and musical instruments.
In a neighbouring room are
African figurines and masks.
The artefacts from Benin are
the highlight of the African
collection. Australasia and
Polynesia dominate the
displays upstairs, with fabrics
from Bali, weapons from
Borneo and many musical
instruments from the Far East.
   The large pre-Columbian
collection from Mexico
includes an Aztec feather
headdress. A recent addition
to the permanent collection is
a section on Eskimo culture.

The Hofburg Complex ⑮

THE VAST HOFBURG COMPLEX contains the former imperial apartments, several museums, a chapel, a church, the Austrian National Library, the Winter Riding School and the President of Austria's offices. It was the seat of Austrian power for over six centuries, and successive rulers were all anxious to leave their mark. Seven centuries of architectural development can be seen in the 10 or so buildings, ranging from Gothic to late 19th-century historicism.

Burggarten
(see p102)

Albertina
(see p102)

Augustinerkirche *(see p102)*

★ **Prunksaal**
The showpiece of the Austrian National Library (1722–35) is the flamboyant, wood-panelled Prunksaal, or Hall of Honour.

Statue of Joseph II (1806) in Josefsplatz *(see p93)*

Burgkapelle *(see p103)*

Alte Burg

Redoute Wing

Stallburg (Stables) *(see p93)*

★ **Michaelertrakt** *(1893)*
The curved façade of the Michaelertrakt is surmounted by an imposing dome.

Winter Riding School *(see pp98–9)*

Michaelertor

Reichskanzleitrakt

TIMELINE

Statue of the angel Gabriel in the Burgkapelle

1275 First fort built on site of the Schweizerhof		**1558–65** Stallburg built – a Renaissance palace, later a mews	**1729–35** J E Fischer von Erlach's Winter Riding School built	**1938** Hitler proclaims annexation of Austria from the Neue Burg
		1575–1611 Amalienburg built	**1881–1913** Neue Burg built	
1300	**1500**		**1700**	**1900**
	1547–52 Ferdinand I reconstructs the Alte Burg	**1552–3** Schweizertor built	**1728** Work begun on J E Fischer von Erlach's Reichskanzleitrakt	**1992** The banqueting hall and ball-room in the Redoute Wing destroyed by fire
1447–9 Alterations carried out on the Burgkapelle under Friedrich III		**1660–80** Leopoldinischertrakt built under Leopold I	**1889–93** Construction of Michaelertrakt and Michaelertor	

Mozart Memorial *(1896)*
Viktor Tilgner's statue of the composer stands just inside the Ringstrasse entrance.

VISITORS' CHECKLIST

Michaelerplatz 1, A-1010.
Map 4 D1 & 5 B4.
Ⓤ *Stephansplatz, Herrengasse.*
🚌 *2A to Heldenplatz, 3A to Michaelerplatz.* 🚃 *D, J, 1. For opening times of individual museums, see pp92–105.*

Burgtor or outer gate was built to a design by Peter Nobile in 1821– 4.

Neue Burg
(see p95)

★ **Prince Eugene Statue**
Anton Dominik Fernkorn designed this monument of Prince Eugene (1865). The pedestal is by Eduard van der Nüll.

Heldenplatz

★ **Schweizertor**
This 16th-century Renaissance gateway leads to the Schweizerhof, the oldest part of the Hofburg, originally a stronghold with four towers.

Leopold-inischertrakt

Amalienburg
The oddly-shaped Amalienburg, built in 1575 for emperor Maximilian's son Rudolf, has a Renaissance façade and an attractive Baroque clock tower.

STAR SIGHTS

★ **Prunksaal**

★ **Prince Eugene Statue**

★ **Schweizertor**

★ **Michaelertrakt**

Winter Riding School ㉖

THE ORIGINS OF THE Spanish Riding School are obscure, but it is believed to have been founded in 1572 to cultivate the classic skills of *haute école* horsemanship. By breeding and training horses from Spain, the Habsburgs formed the Spanische Reitschule. Today, 80-minute shows take place in the building known as the Winter Riding School. Commissioned by Karl VI, it was built from 1729 to 1735 to a design by Josef Emanuel Fischer von Erlach. There are two entrances to the building – one from door 2, Josefsplatz, the other from the Michaelerkuppel.

Specially-bred Lipizzaner stallions are trained from the age of three.

The black bicorn hat has a gold braid stripe from the upper left to the lower centre.

Jackets are coffee-coloured – waisted, double-breasted and with two rows of brass buttons.

Buckskin jodhpurs are worn.

Pale leather gloves are worn.

Long boots covering the knees are part of the uniform.

Tack
The elegant saddle with embroidered cloth differs from modern versions and complements the historical dress of the riders; the curb rein is generally used.

Stables
The three storey-high Renaissance former palace of the Stallburg is across the road from the Winter Riding School. It is now home to the Lipizzaner Museum (see p93) as well as providing stabling for the horses.

THE HORSES' STEPS
The steps made by the horses and riders are part of a carefully orchestrated ballet. Many derive from exercises that were developed during the Renaissance period by cavalrymen, who needed agile horses capable of special manoeuvres.

The Croupade: the horse leaps into the air with hind legs and forelegs bent under its belly.

Levade: the horse stands on its hind legs with hocks almost touching the ground.

VISITORS' CHECKLIST

Michaelerplatz 1, A-1010. **Map** 5
C3. 📞 *5339031.* 🚇 *Herrengasse.*
🚌 *3A to Habsburgergasse, 2A to
Michaelerplatz.* 🚪 *for performances (see annual programme).* ⬤
*1 Jan, 6 Jan, 1 May, Ascension Day,
Corpus Christi, 15 Aug, 26 Oct, 1
Nov, 8 Dec, 25–26 Dec (dates do
vary).* 🖼 📷 🛍 ♿ *some areas.*

Portrait of Karl VI
*An equestrian portrait of
Emperor Karl VI who
commissioned the building,
hangs in the royal box.
Whenever a rider enters the
hall, he must express his
respect to the founder of the
school by raising his bicorn
hat to the portrait.*

THE LIPIZZANER HORSES

The stallions that perform their athletic feats on the sawdust
of the Winter Riding School take their name from the stud
at Lipizza near Trieste in Slovenia *(see below)*, which was
founded by Archduke Karl in 1580. Today the horses are
bred on the Austrian National Stud Farm at Piber near Graz.
The breed was originally produced by crossing Arab, Berber
and Spanish horses. The horses are renowned for their grace
and stamina. You may be able to obtain a ticket without a
reservation to see them at their morning training session.

**Interior of the Winter
Riding School**
*The gracious interior is lined
with 46 columns and adorned
with elaborate plasterwork,
chandeliers and a coffered
ceiling. At the head of the
arena is the court box.
Spectators sit here or watch
from upper galleries.*

Capriole: this is a
leap into the air with
a simultaneous kick
of the hind legs.

The Piaffe: the horse
trots on the spot, often
between two pillars.

State Apartments and Treasuries ㉗

THE STATE APARTMENTS in the Reichskanzleitrakt (1723–30) and the Amalienburg (1575) include the rooms occupied by Franz Joseph from 1857 to 1916, Empress Elisabeth's apartments from 1854 to 1898 and the rooms where Tsar Alexander I lived during the Congress of Vienna in 1815. The sacred and secular treasures amassed during centuries of Habsburg rule are displayed in 21 rooms. They include relics of the Holy Roman Empire, the crown jewels and liturgical objects of the imperial court.

Entrance to Treasuries

★ 10th-Century Crown
The insignia of the Holy Roman Empire includes this crown set with enamel plaques and cabochons.

Emperor Maximilian I
(around 1500)
This portrait by Bernhard Strigel hangs in the room containing Burgundian treasure. Emperor Maximilian married Mary, Duchess of Burgundy in 1477.

Cradle of the King of Rome
Designed by the French painter Prud'hon, Maria Louisa gave this cradle to her son, the King of Rome (see p175).

Entrance through the Michaelerkuppel to State Apartments and Silberkammer

Crucifix after Giambologna
(around 1590)
This type of crucifix, a Cristo Morto, *can be traced back to a similar model by Giambologna which is in Florence.*

KEY

☐	Franz Joseph's State Apartments
☐	Elisabeth's State Apartments
☐	Alexander's State Apartments
☐	Sacred Treasury
☐	Secular Treasury
☐	Sisi Museum
☐	Non-exhibition space

STAR FEATURES

★ **10th-Century Crown**

★ **Imperial Dining Hall**

★ **Empress Elisabeth by Franz Xaver Winterhalter**

THE SILBERKAMMER

On display in the ground-floor rooms of the court tableware and silver depot is a dazzling array of items – gold, silver and the finest porcelain – that were once used at the Habsburg state banquets. One of the highlights is a 33-m long (100-ft) gilded bronze centrepiece with accompanying candelabra from around 1800. Visitors can also admire the mid-18th-century Sèvres dinner service that was a diplomatic gift from Louis XV to Maria Theresa.

Goblet from the Laxenburg Service (around 1821)

VISITORS' CHECKLIST

Map 4 D1 & 5 B3. *State Apartments (Kaiserappartements), Sisi Museum & Silberkammer* Michaelerkuppel. ☏ 5337570. ☐ 9am–5pm daily. 🅿 🅾 🆚 Sat & Sun. 🅦 www.hofburg-wien.at *Secular & Sacred Treasuries (Schatzkammer)* Schweizerhof. ☏ 525240. ☐ 10am–6pm Wed–Mon; 24 Dec: to 1pm; 31 Dec: to 3pm. ⬤ 1 Jan, 1 May, 25 Dec. 🅿 🅾 🅰 🅾 🅾 🅦 www.khm.at

Elisabeth's Gymnastic Equipment
The Empress was a fitness enthusiast, and the bars at which she exercised are still in place in her dressing room.

Passage to Neue Burg and Heldenplatz

Ticket office

Entrance through the Kaisertor to State Apartments and Silberkammer

★ Imperial Dining Hall
The table is laid as it used to be in Emperor Franz Joseph's day (see p32–3), in the room where the Imperial family used to dine.

Exit from apartments

GUIDE TO TREASURIES
Entering the Secular Treasury, Rooms 1–8 contain items from the Austrian Empire (with Room 5 commemorating Napoleon). Rooms 9–12 exhibit treasures from the Holy Roman Empire, while the Burgundian Inheritance is displayed in Rooms 13–16. Rooms I–V, furthest from the entrance, house the Sacred Treasury. (There is one route through the State Apartments, starting with Franz Joseph's rooms.)

★ Empress Elisabeth
Winterhalter's portrait of the Empress (1865) with stars in her hair hangs in the large drawing room.

Greenhouses in the Burggarten by Friedrich Ohmann (1858–1927)

Burggarten ㉑

Burgring/Opernring. **Map** 4 D1 & 5 B4.
Ⓤ *Babenbergerstrasse.* ◯ *Apr–Sep: 6am–10pm; Oct–Mar: 6am–8pm daily.*

B EFORE LEAVING Vienna, Napoleon showed his contempt for the Viennese by razing part of the city walls which had proved so ineffective at preventing his entry. Some of the space left around the Hofburg was later transformed by the Habsburgs into a landscaped garden, planted with a variety of trees. It was opened to the public in 1918.

Overlooking the garden are greenhouses (1901–7) by the Jugendstil architect Friedrich Ohmann, and near the Hofburg entrance is a small equestrian statue (1780) of Emperor Franz I by the sculptor Balthasar Moll. Closer to the Ringstrasse is the Mozart Memorial (1896) by Viktor Tilgner.

Albertina ㉒

Augustinerstrasse 1. **Map** 4 D1 & 5 C4. 534830. Ⓤ *Karlsplatz, Stephansplatz.* ◯ *10am–6pm daily (to 9pm Wed).* Ⓦ www.albertina.at

O NCE HIDDEN AWAY at the Opera end of the Hofburg, the newly restored Albertina is now a distinctive landmark, its raised entrance boasting a controversial freestanding diving-board roof by architect Hans Hollein *(see p91)*. The palace once belonged to Maria Theresa's daughter, Maria Christina, and her husband Duke Albert of Sachsen-Teschen, after whom the gallery is named. Today the Albertina houses a collection of one million prints, over 65,000 watercolours and drawings, and some 70,000 photographs. The gems of the collections are by Dürer, with Michelangelo and Rubens also well represented. Picasso heads a fine 20th-century section.

Although there is no permanent exhibition, three halls house the Albertina's several annual temporary exhibitions, which display works from the home collection in combination with prints, drawings and paintings on loan. The new extension on the Burggarten side houses study facilities and the largest of the three exhibition halls. The recent renovation restored a number of features of the Albertina to their former glory, including the façades and the central courtyard. Most notably, the Habsburg State Rooms are now open to the public for the first time in 200 years. They represent a remarkable example of Neo-Classical architecture and interior decoration, inspired by the Archduchess Maria Christina herself.

Augustinerkirche ㉓

Augustinerstrasse 3. **Map** 4 D1 & 5 C4. 5337099. Ⓤ *Stephansplatz.* ◯ *8am–5pm daily.*

T HE AUGUSTINERKIRCHE has one of the best-preserved 14th-century Gothic interiors in Vienna; only the modern chandeliers strike a jarring note. The church also houses the Loreto Chapel, which is currently closed for restoration. The chapel contains the silver urns that preserve the hearts of the Habsburg family *(see pp24–5)*. Here too is one of the most powerful works by the Italian Neo-Classical sculptor Antonio Canova, the tomb of Maria Christina, favourite daughter of Maria Theresa. Like the tomb of Leopold II, which is also here, Maria Christina's tomb is empty; the royal remains lie in the Kaisergruft *(see p104)*.

The church is also celebrated for its music, including masses by Schubert or Haydn held here on Sundays.

Prunksaal ㉔

Josefsplatz 1. **Map** 4 D1 & 5 C4. 53410397. Ⓤ *Herrengasse.* ◯ *10am–2pm daily.* Ⓦ www.oub.ac.at

C OMMISSIONED AS the court library by Karl VI, the main hall, or Prunksaal, of the National Library was designed by Johann Bernhard Fischer von Erlach *(see p149)* in 1719. After his death in 1723, the building was completed by his son. The collection consists of approximately 2.6 million books, and includes the personal library of Prince Eugene *(see pp26–7)*, as well as books that were taken from monastic libraries closed during the religious reforms of Joseph II *(see p29)*.

The Prunksaal is 77 m (252 ft) long and is the largest Baroque library in Europe. Paired marble columns frame the domed main room, and bookcases line the walls. Spanning the vaults are frescoes by the Baroque painter Daniel Gran (1730), which were restored by Franz

Domed interior of the Prunksaal in the National Library building

Anton Maulbertsch (1769). The many fine statues, including the likeness of Karl VI in the centre of the hall, are the work of Paul Strudel (1648–1708) and his brother Peter (1660–1714).

Burgkapelle 🄫

Wiener Hofburg, Schweizerhof.
Map 4 D1 & 5 B4. 🄫 5339927.
🄫 *Herrengasse.* 🄫 *11am–3pm Mon–Thu, 11am–1pm Fri.*
🄫 *1 Nov, 8 Dec, 1 Jan.* 🄫 🄫
Vienna Boys' Choir 🄫 *Jan–Jun & Sep–Dec: 9:15am Sun (book by phone).* 🄫

F ROM THE SCHWEIZERHOF, steps lead up to the Burgkapelle, or Hofburg Chapel, originally constructed in 1296 but modified 150 years later on the orders of Friedrich III. On Sundays, visitors can hear the Wiener Sängerknaben, the Vienna Boys' Choir *(see p39)*. The chapel interior has Gothic statuary in canopied niches and Gothic carvings, and boasts a bronze crucifix (1720) by Johann Känischbauer.

Winter Riding School 🄫

See pp98–9.

State Apartments and Treasuries 🄫

See pp100–1.

Bundeskanzleramt 🄫

Ballhausplatz 2. **Map** 1 C5 & 5 B3.
🄫 531150. 🄫 *Herrengasse.*
🄫 *to the public.*

T HE BUNDESKANZLERAMT (1717–19), the Austrian Chancery and Foreign Ministry, was designed by Johann Lukas von Hildebrandt *(see p152)*. It was expanded to its present size in 1766 by Nikolaus Pacassi. Major events that shaped Austria's history have taken place here, including meetings of the Congress of Vienna *(see p30)* in 1814–15, the final deliberations in 1914 that led to

No. 4 Minoritenplatz

the outbreak of World War I, and the murder of Chancellor Dollfuss by Nazi terrorists in 1934 *(see p36)*.

Minoritenplatz 🄫

Map 2 D5 & 5 B3. 🄫 *Herrengasse.*

A T NO. 1 MINORITENPLATZ is the Baroque-style State Archives building (the archives are no longer housed here), built on to the back of the Bunderskanzleramt in 1902. There are a number of palaces around the square. No. 3 is the former Dietrichstein Palace of 1755, an early building by Franz Hillebrand. It now contains the offices of the Federal Chancellor and the Foreign Office. No. 4 is the side of the Liechtenstein Palace *(see p104)*. The mid-17th-century Starhemberg Palace is at No. 5. Now housing ministry offices, it was the residence of Count Ernst Rüdiger von Starhemberg, a hero of the 1683 Turkish siege *(see p27)* when he led the Austrian forces within the city.

Minoritenkirche 🄫

Minoritenplatz 2. **Map** 1 C5 & 5 B3.
🄫 5334162. 🄫 *Herrengasse.*
🄫 *9am–6pm daily.* 🄫

T HIS ANCIENT CHURCH was established here by the Minor Friars in around 1224, although the present structure dates from 1339. The tower was given its odd pyramidal

shape during the Turkish siege of 1529, when shells sliced the top off the steeple. In the 1780s the Minoritenkirche was restored to its original Gothic style, when Maria Theresa's son, Joseph II *(see p28)*, made a gift of the church to Vienna's Italian community. The church retains a fine west portal (1340) with statues beneath traceried canopies; the carvings above the doorway are modern.

The interior of the church is unexpectedly bright and large and contains a mosaic copy of Leonardo da Vinci's *Last Supper*. Napoleon Bonaparte commissioned Giacomo Raffaelli to execute this work as he proposed to substitute it for the original in Milan and remove the real painting to Paris. Following Napoleon's downfall at Waterloo in 1815, Raffaelli's version was bought by the Habsburgs. In the south aisle is a painted statue of the Madonna and Child (dating from around 1350), while at the same spot in the north aisle is a faded fragment of a 16th-century fresco of St Francis of Assisi.

Gothic statue (about 1400) of Leopold III in the Burgkapelle

Bankgasse ③

Map 1 C5 & 5 B3. Ⓤ *Herrengasse.*
Liechtenstein Palace ⬚ *10am–6pm Wed–Mon.*

FEW STREETS IN VIENNA are
more crammed with the
palaces of the nobility.

At Nos. 4–6 is the former
Strattmann-Windischgrätz
Palace (1692–1734), originally
designed by Johann Bernhard
Fischer von Erlach *(see p149)*.
The present façade (1783–4)
is by Franz Hillebrand, who
expanded the building by
incorporating the palace next
door. Today, it houses the
Hungarian Embassy.

Nos. 5–7 are the back of the
Starhemberg Palace. No. 9 is
the Liechtenstein Palace, built
as a town residence for the
Liechtenstein family by Dome-
nico Martinelli (1694–1706).
No. 2 is the Schönborn-
Batthyány Palace (1695).

Volksgarten ③

Dr-Karl-Renner-Ring. **Map** 1 C5 &
5 A3. ⚌ *5339083.* Ⓤ *Herrengasse.*
⬚ *Apr–Nov: 6am–10pm daily;
Dec–Mar: 6:30am–10pm daily.* 📷 ♿

LIKE THE BURGGARTEN land-
scaped garden *(see p102)*,
the Volksgarten was created
after the destruction of the

Statuary above the portal to the Lobkowitz Palace

city walls by Napoleon, and
opened up a space previously
occupied by fortifications.
Unlike the Burggarten, the
Volksgarten was opened to
the public soon after its completion in 1820. The formal
plantations, especially the
splendid rose gardens, are
matched in grandeur by the
garden's ornaments, notably
the Temple of Theseus (1823)
by Peter von Nobile. It was
built to house Canova's statue
of the Greek god, which now
graces the staircase of the
Kunsthistorisches Museum.
Other compositions include
Karl von Hasenauer's
monument to the poet Franz
Grillparzer *(see p33)* and the
fountain memorial to the
assassinated Empress Elisabeth
(1907) by Friedrich Ohmann
(see p57) and the sculptor
Hans Bitterlich.

Lobkowitz Palace ③

Lobkowitzplatz 2. **Map** 4 D1 &
5 C4. ⚌ *5128800.* Ⓤ *Karlsplatz,
Stephansplatz.* ⬚ *10am–5pm
Tue–Sun (to 8pm Wed).* 📷 📷 ♿
Ⓦ www.theatermuseum.at

THIS LARGE PALACE WAS built
for Count Dietrichstein in
1685–7 by Giovanni Pietro
Tencala and altered by Johann
Bernhard Fischer von Erlach
(see p149) in 1710. In 1753
it was acquired by the
Lobkowitz family. Balls were
held here during the Congress
of Vienna *(see p30)*.

Since 1991 the palace has
been the Austrian Theatre
Museum, which houses a
model of the first Hofburg
theatre and the Eroica-Saal
(1724–29) – where many first
performances of Beethoven's
work took place. The main
exhibits chronicle Austrian
theatre in the 1940s.

Kapuzinerkirche und Kaisergruft ③

Tegetthoffstrasse 2. **Map** 4 D1 & 5 C4.
⚌ *5126852.* Ⓤ *Stephansplatz.*
Kaisergruft ⬚ *9:30am–4pm daily.*
Kapuzinerkirche ⬚ *6am–6pm
daily.* 📷

BENEATH THE Kapuziner-
kirche are the vaults of
the Kaisergruft, the imperial
crypt founded in 1619 by the
Catholic Emperor Matthias.
Here lie the remains of 138
Habsburgs, including Maria
Theresa and her husband
Franz Stephan in a large tomb
by Balthasar Moll (1753). The
most poignant tomb is that of
Franz Joseph, flanked by his
assassinated wife Elisabeth
and their son Rudolf, who

Formal rose garden in the Volksgarten

Tomb of Karl VI by Balthasar Moll

committed suicide *(see p32)*. The last reigning Habsburg, Empress Zita, died in 1989 and her remains are also buried in the crypt.

Neuer Markt 🟤

Map 4 D1 & 5 C4. 🚇 *Stephansplatz.*

K NOWN AS THE Mehlmarkt or flour market until around 1210, the Neuer Markt was also used as a jousting area. Of these origins nothing is left, though a few 18th-century houses remain. In the middle of the Neuer Markt is a replica of the Donner Fountain (1737–9) by Georg Raphael Donner, a symbolic celebration of the role played by rivers in the economic life of the Habsburg Empire. The four figures denote tributaries of the Danube, while the central figure represents Providence. The original figures are in the Lower Belvedere *(see p157)*.

Kärntner Strasse 🟤

Map 4 D1 & 5 C5. ☎ 5127244. 🚇 *Stephansplatz.* **Malteserkirche** ☐ 8am–6pm daily. **Lobmeyr Museum** ☐ 9am–6pm Mon–Fri, 10am–5pm Sat.

T HIS PEDESTRIANIZED STREET was the main highway to Carinthia in medieval times. Now it is the old city's principal shopping street. Day and night, it is packed

with people shopping, buying fresh fruit juice from stands, pausing in cafés, or listening to the street musicians.

No. 37 is the Malteser-kirche. This church was founded by the Knights of Malta who were invited to Vienna early in the 13th century by Leopold VI. The interior retains lofty Gothic windows and vaults.

At No. 1 is the Lobmeyr Museum, which houses glass designed by Josef Hoffmann *(see p56)*, among others, for the Viennese firm of Lobmeyr.

Around the corner at No. 5 Johannesgasse is the superb Questenberg-Kaunitz Palace which dates from the early 18th century. Its design has been attributed to the architect Johann Lukas von Hildebrandt *(see p152)*.

American Bar 🟤

Kärntner Strasse 10. **Map** 4 D1 & 6 D3. 🚇 *Stephansplatz.*

B ENEATH A GARISH depiction of the Stars and Stripes is this bar designed by Adolf Loos *(see p92)* in 1908. The interior, restored in 1990, is a gem.

The Donner Fountain in Neuer Markt

The bar is tiny, with every detail worked out by Loos, such as the tables lit from below and the exquisite glass cabinets for storing glasses. One of his hallmarks is the use of mahogany panelling, and this bar is no exception. Mirrors give the impression that the interior is larger than it actually is, and onyx and marble panels reflect a soft light.

Façade of the American Bar

Stock-im-Eisen-Platz 🟤

Map 2 D5 & 5 C3. 🚇 *Stephansplatz.*

T HIS SQUARE is at the inter-section of Stephansplatz, Kärntner Strasse and Graben. Opposite Haas Haus *(see p75)* is the Equitable Palace (1891), once headquarters to the Equitable Life Insurance Company. There is also an old tree trunk with nails in it in the square. Passing locksmiths' apprentices would bang in a nail to ensure a safe passage home.

SCHOTTENRING AND ALSERGRUND

THIS PART OF THE CITY is dotted with sites of interest, such as the ornate Ferstel Palace and the glass-roofed Ferstel Passage that runs through it. The Schottenring and the Schottentor are named after the Benedictine monks who came here in Babenberg times to found the Schottenkirche Monastery. Later rulers of Austria were responsible for the

Relief on the façade of the Schottenkirche

area's other monuments: Joseph II built a huge public hospital, now the Josephinum, and Franz Joseph founded the Votivkirche as a way of giving thanks after escaping assassination in 1853. To the east, nearer the Danube Canal, quiet residential streets are broken only by the imposing Liechtenstein Museum, one of many summer palaces built beyond the city gates by Vienna's nobility.

SIGHTS AT A GLANCE

Streets and Squares
Freyung ❷
Freyung Passage ❶

Churches and Cathedrals
Schottenkirche ❸
Servitenkirche ❺
Votivkirche ❾

Museums and Galleries
Freud Museum ❹
Josephinum ❼
Liechtenstein Museum ❻
Narrenturm ❽

GETTING THERE
This area is served by the Schottentor (line U2) and Rossauer Lände (line U4) U-Bahn stations. Trams 37, 38, 40, 41 and 42 go along Währinger Strasse. Bus 40A runs the length of Liechtensteinstrasse.

KEY

Street-by-Street map
See pp108–9

Ⓤ U-Bahn station

P Parking

0 metres   250
0 yards   250

◁ **The impressive façade of the 19th-century Votivkirche**

Street-by-Street: Around the Freyung

A T THE CORE of this elegant part of the city is the former medieval complex of the Schottenkirche and its courtyards and school. On the other side of the Freyung square are some beautiful Baroque palaces, including Hildebrandt's Kinsky Palace (1713–16), and the Palais Ferstel. The Freyung Passage links the Freyung square with Herrengasse, which is lined with Baroque mansions as well as the city's first skyscraper. Backing onto the Schottenring is the Italianate Börse.

Statue of Turkish soldier, south of the Freyung

★ **Schottenkirche**
Founded in 1177 and redecorated in the Baroque period, this fine church has a museum and there is a famous boys' school alongside it ❸

Passageway leading from No. 2 Helferstorferstrasse to the Freyung

HELFERSTORFERSTRASSE

SCHOTTENGASSE

★ **Freyung**
This square is overlooked by fine buildings, including the former Schottenkirche priory, originally founded in 1155, then rebuilt in 1744 and, due to its appearance, known by the Viennese as the "chest of drawers house" ❷

★ **Freyung Passage**
The Freyung and Herrengasse are connected by a luxury shopping arcade ❶

FREYUNG

HERRENGASSE

The Café Central has a papier-mâché statue of the poet Peter Altenberg next to the main entrance. Altenberg spent a great deal of time in various coffee houses around the city (*see pp58–61*).

To Herrengasse U-Bahn

A central courtyard lies hidden within the stock exchange buildings.

LOCATOR MAP
See Street Finder, maps 2 & 5

The Börse, or stock exchange, was commissioned when the Ringstrasse was conceived *(see pp32–3)*. Designed by Theophil Hansen, it was completed in 1877 and today houses offices, a gardening centre and a restaurant.

The Schönborn-Batthyány Palace is a fine Baroque palace built from 1699 to 1706.

The Hermann Gmeiner Park includes a playground with wendy houses and open spaces and commemorates the life and work of Hermann Gmeiner (1919–86). He founded SOS Children's Villages, a worldwide organization that cares for orphans.

KEY

– – – Suggested route

0 metres   50
0 yards   50

STAR SIGHTS

★ **Schottenkirche**

★ **Freyung**

★ **Freyung Passage**

Freyung Passage ❶

Map 2 D5 & 5 B2. Ⓤ *Herrengasse.*

FACING THE FREYUNG is the Italian-style *palazzo* known as the Palais Ferstel, dating from 1860 and taking its name from the architect, Heinrich von Ferstel. Wander in and you will find yourself in the glass-roofed Freyung Passage: lined with elegant shops, it converges on a small courtyard of which the centrepiece is a many-tiered statue portraying the lissom water-sprite of the Danube holding a fish. It then emerges on Herrengasse. As an example of civilized urban amenities, the passage is a great success. It also has an entrance into one of Vienna's grandest coffee houses, the Café Central *(see pp59–61).*

Danube Mermaid's Fountain (1861) in Freyung Passage

Freyung ❷

Map 2 D5 & 5 B2. Ⓤ *Herrengasse.* **Kinsky Palace** 🕐 *10am–5pm Mon–Fri.*

THE FREYUNG is a curiously shaped "square". Its name derives from the right of sanctuary granted to the monks of the Schottenkirche that lasted until Maria Theresa abolished it. Fugitives from persecution who entered the area were safe from arrest. No. 4 is the Kinsky Palace (1713–16), by Johann Lukas von Hildebrandt *(see p152).* Next door is the Porcia Palace of 1546, one of the oldest in Vienna, though much altered. At No. 3 is the Harrach

Façade of the Schottenkirche

Palace; the interior has some fine Rococo doors. Opposite is the Austria Fountain: its four figures symbolize the major rivers of the Habsburgs' lands. Behind is the former Schottenkirche priory, unkindly known as the chest-of-drawers house.

Schottenkirche ❸

Schottenstift, Freyung 6. **Map** 2 D5 & 5 B2. ℂ *53498600.* Ⓤ *Schottentor.* **Museum** 🕐 *10am–5pm Mon–Sat, 10:30am–1pm Sun & hols.*

DESPITE ITS NAME (Scottish church) this 1177 monastic foundation was established by Irish Benedictines. The adjoining buildings have a fine medieval art collection that includes the famous Schotten altarpiece (1475). The church has been altered repeatedly and has recently undergone extensive renovation. Today it presents a rather drab Neo-Classical façade, with a rich Baroque interior.

Freud Museum ❹

Berggasse 19. **Map** 1 C3. ℂ *3191596.* Ⓤ *Schottentor.* 🕐 *9am–5pm daily.* w www.freud-museum.at

No. 19 BERGGASSE differs little from any other 19th-century apartment in Vienna, yet it is now one of the city's most famous addresses. The father of psychoanalysis, Sigmund Freud, lived, worked and received patients here from 1891 until his departure from Vienna in 1938.

The flat housed Freud's family as well as his practice. The catalogue lists 420 items of memorabilia on display, including letters and books, furnishings, photographs documenting Freud's long life, and various antiquities.

Although quickly abandoned when the Nazis forced Freud to leave the city where he had lived almost all his life, the flat still preserves an intimate domestic atmosphere. Even his hat and cane are on show.

Servitenkirche ❺

Servitengasse 9. **Map** 1 C3. ℂ *317 6195.* Ⓤ *Rossauer Lände.* 🕐 *7–9am, 6–7pm Mon–Fri, 7–9am, 5–8pm Sat, 7am–noon, 5–8pm Sun.*

ALTHOUGH OFF the beaten track, this Baroque church (1651–77) is well worth a visit. Inside, a riot of Baroque decoration includes elaborate stucco ornamentation, a fine wrought-iron screen near the entrance, and an exuberant pulpit (1739), partly by Balthasar Moll.

FREUD'S THEORIES

Sigmund Freud (1856–1939) was not only the founder of the techniques of psychoanalysis, but a theorist who wrote many essays and books expounding his contentious ideas. Modern concepts such as subconscious, ego, sublimation and Oedipus complex, evolved from Freudian theories. Freud posited different structural systems within the human psyche that, if seriously out of balance, result in emotional or mental disturbance.

Liechtenstein Museum ❻

Fürstengasse 1. **Map** 1 C2.
🕾 31957670. Ⓤ *Friedensbrücke.*
🚌 40A. 🚋 D. ◐ *9am–8pm Wed–Mon.* Ⓦ www.liechtensteinmuseum.at

DESIGNED BY Domenico Martinelli and completed in 1692, the Liechtenstein Palace was the summer home of the Liechtenstein family and now houses the art collection of Prince Hans-Adam II von und zu Liechtenstein. Behind the imposing Palladian exterior, notable features include the Neo-Classical library, and the Hercules Hall and grand staircase with their magnificent frescoes. The art collection centres on the Baroque, with a special focus on Rubens, and numerous paintings and sculptures by German, Dutch and Italian masters from the Renaissance through to the 19th century. The palace stands in an extensive English-style garden, designed in the 19th century.

Josephinum ❼

Währinger Strasse 25/1. **Map** 1 C4.
🕾 427763401. Ⓤ *Schottentor.* ◐ *9am–3pm Mon–Fri (10am–2pm 1st Sat of month).* ● *public hols.* 🖼 ♿

THE ARDENT REFORMER Joseph II *(see p28)* established this military surgical institute. Designed by Isidor Canevale in 1785, it is now a medical museum. Some rooms contain memorabilia from the 19th century, when Vienna was a leading centre for medical research, but the museum's main attraction is its unusual collection of wax anatomical models commissioned by the emperor from Tuscan artists.

Narrenturm ❽

Spitalgasse 2. **Map** 1 B3. 🕾 4068672. Ⓤ *Schottentor.* ◐ *3–6pm Wed, 8–11am Thu, 10am–1pm 1st Sat of month.* 🚫 ● *public hols.*

WHAT USED TO be the Allgemeines Krankenhaus, founded by Joseph II

Detail on the Votivkirche façade

(see p28) in 1784, has been renovated and now houses various faculties of the University of Vienna. At the far end of the complex is the Narrenturm Tower, a former lunatic asylum designed by Isidor Canevale. The tower now houses the Museum for Pathological Anatomy, which includes a reconstruction of an apothecary's shop and wax models. The few ground-floor rooms open to the public only show a small part of the collection, but serious students can enrol on a guided tour of the corridors upstairs.

Votivkirche ❾

Rooseveltplatz 8. **Map** 1 C4 & 5 A1.
🕾 4061192. Ⓤ *Schottentor.* ◐ *9am–1pm, 4–6:30pm Tue–Sat, 9am–1pm Sun.* 📷 ♿ *side entrance.*

AFTER A DERANGED tailor tried but failed to assassinate Emperor Franz Joseph on 18 February 1853, a collection was made to pay for a new church to be built opposite the Mölker-Bastei, where the attempt had been made. The architect was Heinrich von Ferstel, who began the church in 1856 though it was not dedicated until 1879. The lacy steeples and spire are very attractive. Many of the church's chapels are dedicated to Austrian regiments and military heroes. The finest monument is the Renaissance sarcophagus tomb of Niklas Salm in the chapel just west of the north transept. Salm commanded Austria's forces during the 1529 Turkish siege.

Wooden pietà in Gothic style (1470) in the Servitenkirche

MUSEUM AND TOWNHALL QUARTER

THE EMPEROR Franz Joseph commissioned the major institutional buildings of the Habsburg empire, and the city, along the Ringstrasse in the mid-19th century *(see pp32–3)*. Today these buildings remain a successful and imposing example of good urban planning. The districts to the west of the Ringstrasse are untouched, including

Der liebe Augustin, Sankt-Ulrichs-Platz

Josefstadt, which still retains an 18th-century atmosphere with its picturesque streets, modest palaces and Baroque churches. The area's cultural institutions are vibrant: the brilliant productions of the Burgtheater and the wide-ranging exhibits of the Natural History Museum and the Kunsthistorisches Museum are all popular today.

SIGHTS AT A GLANCE

Streets and Squares
Mölker-Bastei ⑰
Sankt-Ulrichs-Platz ❻
Spittelberg Pedestrian Area ❼

Historic Buildings
Alte Backstube ❷
Burgtheater pp132–33 ⑲
Café Landtmann ⑮
Dreimäderlhaus ⑯
Josefstadt Theater ❹
Neues Rathaus ⑫
Parliament ❾
Pasqualati Haus ⑱
Trautson Palace ❺
University ⑭

Churches and Cathedrals
Dreifaltigkeitskirche ⑬
Maria Treu Kirche ❸

Museums and Galleries
Kunsthistorisches Museum pp122–27 ❿
Museum für Volkskunde ❶
MuseumsQuartier ❽
Natural History Museum pp128–9 ⑪

GETTING THERE
This area is served by the Rathaus (line U2) and Volkstheater (lines U2, U3) U-Bahn stations. Tram 5 runs from Josefstädter Strasse to Lange Gasse, and 46 goes down Lerchenfelder Strasse. Bus 2A runs from Schwedenplatz to Volkstheater. 13A runs along Piaristengasse, and 48A along Burggasse.

KEY

🟦 Street-by-Street map
See pp114–15

Ⓤ U-Bahn station

🅿 Parking

◁ **Neues Rathaus façade by night**

Street-by-Street: Josefstadt

T UCKED BEHIND THE GRAND MUSEUMS of the Ringstrasse is the 18th-century district known as Josefstadt, named after Emperor Joseph II. Although outside the Inner City, Josefstadt has a vibrant cultural life of its own, with a popular theatre, many good restaurants, and handsome churches and museums. Students from the university and lawyers from the courthouses provide a constantly changing clientele for the district's varied establishments.

★ **Maria Treu Kirche**
Founded by the fathers of the Piarist order, this church was built from 1716 ❸

Josefstadt Theater
Founded in 1788, Vienna's oldest theatre has kept its doors open continuously since it was rebuilt by Josef Kornhäusel (see p84) in 1822 ❹

No. 29 Lange Gasse
Originally built for servants and workers in the 18th century, the cottages lining this courtyard have changed little over the years.

KEY

— — — Suggested route

STAR SIGHTS

★ **Maria Treu Kirche**

★ **Museum für Volkskunde**

PIARISTENGASSE

MARIA TREU GA

JOSEFSTÄDTER STRASSE

ZELTGASSE

The Plague Column here commemorates an epidemic that occurred in 1713.

To Lerchenfelder Strasse

LOCATOR MAP
See Street Finder, map 1

★ **Museum für Volkskunde**
The Schönborn Palace houses exhibits reflecting folklore and rural life in Austria ❶

Schönborn Park
is a secluded, leafy retreat. Among the sculptures is this bust (1974) of the composer Edmund Eysler by Leo Gruber.

No. 53 Lange Gasse has handsome statuary on its gates. It was built in the early 18th century when Vienna was expanding beyond the old city walls.

The Schnattl Restaurant,
occupying the spacious ground floor and courtyard of an old house on Lange Gasse, is one of Vienna's finest *(see p215)*.

Alte Backstube
A working bakery from 1701 to 1963, since 1965 it has been a museum and restaurant ❷

0 metres   50

0 yards   50

Museum für Volkskunde ❶

Laudongasse 15–19. **Map** 1 B4.
📞 4068905. 🚇 *Rathaus.*
🕐 10am–5pm Tue–Sun.
⬛ public hols. 📷 ♿
🌐 www.volkskundemuseum.at

The charming Museum of Austrian Folklore is a reminder that Vienna is not only full of imperial grandeur. Here you will find artifacts reflecting the culture of people in Austria and neighbouring countries. Exhibits include objects dating from the 17th to 19th centuries. The museum is housed in the 18th-century Schönborn Palace, designed by Johann Lukas von Hildebrandt as a homely two-storey mansion and altered in 1760 by Isidor Canevale. Today it has a rather imposing façade with statuary running along its top. There is a pleasant park behind the palace.

Alte Backstube ❷

Lange Gasse 34. **Map** 1 B5.
🚇 *Rathaus.* 📞 4061101.
🕐 11am–midnight Mon–Sat, 5pm–midnight Sun. ⬛ mid-Jul–mid-Aug and public hols. 📷 ♿

One of the finest middle-class houses in Vienna was built at No. 34 Lange Gasse in 1697 by the jeweller Hans Bernhard Leopold. The sandstone sculpture that is positioned above the doorway symbolizes the Holy Trinity. Inside is an old bakery, the Alte Backstube, that was in continuous use from 1701 to 1963. The baking ovens were never removed, and today the rooms have been sympathetically restored and incorporated into a traditional restaurant and café. They also contain a museum dedicated to the art of baking where 300-year-old equipment is on display.

A few doors away, at No. 29, it's worth glancing into the courtyard to see the rows of single-storey houses facing each other – a rare example of working-class Vienna that is probably about 200 years old.

Maria Treu Kirche ❸

Jodok-Fink-Platz. **Map** 1 B5.
【 *4061453*. 🚇 *Rathaus*. 🕐 *for services and by appointment.* 📷

O VERLOOKING Jodok-Fink-Platz and flanked by monastic buildings stands the Church of Maria Treu. It was founded in 1698 by the fathers of the Piarist order.

This outstanding church was originally designed by Johann Lukas von Hildebrandt in 1716 and altered by Matthias Gerl in the 1750s. The elegant twin towers were not completed until 1854. Inside, there is a splendid Baroque frescoed ceiling in vibrant colours from 1752–3 by the great Austrian painter Franz Anton Maulbertsch. A chapel immediately to the left of the choir contains an altarpiece of the Crucifixion dating from about 1774, also painted by Maulbertsch.

Directly in front of the church and rising up from the square is a fine Baroque pillar topped with a statue of the Madonna, attended beneath by statues of saints and angels. Like many such columns in Vienna, it was erected to commemorate an outbreak of plague, in this case the epidemic of 1713.

Ceiling frescoes above the altar in the Maria Treu Kirche

Josefstadt Theater ❹

Josefstädter Strasse 26. **Map** 1 B5.
【 *427000*. 🚇 *Rathaus*. 🕐 *by appointment only.* 🅦 www.josefstadt.org

T HIS INTIMATE theatre *(see p230)*, one of the oldest still standing in Vienna, has

The façade of the glorious Josefstadt Theater

enjoyed a glorious history. Founded in 1788, it was rebuilt by Joseph Kornhäusel *(see p84)* in 1822, and has been in operation ever since, accommodating ballet, opera and theatre performances. Beethoven composed and conducted his overture *The Consecration of the House* for the reopening of the theatre in 1822 after its renovation. The director Max Reinhardt supervised the restoration of this attractive theatre in 1924. Today, it puts on mostly light plays and comedies.

Trautson Palace ❺

Museumstrasse 7. **Map** 3 B1.
🚇 *Volkstheater.* ⬤ *to the public.*

S ET BACK FROM the street next to the Volkstheater is this elegant Baroque palace, designed in 1710 by Johann Bernhard Fischer von Erlach *(see p149)*. Most Viennese palaces have flat fronts but on this one the central bays of the façade jut out with real panache. Nor is there anything restrained about the ornamentation: above the cornice and pediment is one of the largest collections of statuary atop any palace in the whole of Vienna. This includes a large statue of Apollo playing the lyre. Passing beneath the tall portal you will see on the left an immense staircase, with carvings of bearded giants bearing its weight, by the Italian sculptor Giovanni Giuliani. This leads to the ceremonial hall.

Originally built for Count Johann Leopold Donat Trautson who was in the service of Joseph I, the palace was acquired in 1760 by Maria Theresa *(see pp28–9)*. She donated it to the Royal Hungarian Bodyguard that she had founded. It has housed the Ministry of Justice since 1961, so there is no public access to the interior.

Sankt-Ulrichs-Platz ❻

Between Neustiftgasse and Burggasse.
Map 3 B1. 🚇 *Volkstheater.* **Café Nepomuk** 【 *5263919*. 🕐 *8am–11pm Mon–Fri, 8am–11pm Sat & Sun.* **Ulrichskirche** 【 *5231246*. 🕐 *on request or for services only.*

T HIS TINY SLOPING SQUARE is an exquisite survival of early Vienna. The dainty Baroque house at No. 27 is now the Café Nepomuk, and adjoining it is a Renaissance house that escaped destruction by the Turks during the sieges of the city, most probably because the Turkish commander Kara Mustafa pitched his own tent nearby.

The house partly obscures the façade of the Baroque Ulrichskirche, built by Josef Reymund from 1721–4. Handsome patrician houses encircle it, of which the prettiest is No. 2, the Schulhaus. Elaborately decorated, it dates from the mid-18th century. In the church the composer Gluck was married and Johann Strauss the Younger was christened.

Spittelberg Pedestrian Area ❼

Map 3 B1. Ⓤ *Volkstheater.* **Amerlinghaus** ◻ 2–10pm Mon–Fri. **Market** ◻ Apr–Jun & Sep–Nov: 10am–6pm Sat; Jul & Aug: 2–9pm Sat. 🖸 ♿

A GROUP OF STREETS – the pedestrianized Spittelberggasse, Gutenberggasse and Schrankgasse – has been well restored to present a pretty group of 18th- and 19th-century houses. Traditionally the area was lower class and very lively, home to the actors, artists and strolling players of the day. The houses were mostly tenements, without gardens or courtyards.

The charm of the district was rediscovered in the 1970s and the city authorities set about restoring the buildings. Today, it is a district of restaurants, cafés

Façade detail at No. 20 Spittelberggasse

and boutiques. It hosts a Christmas and an Easter market, as well as a regular arts and crafts market from April to November. The Amerlinghaus theatre at No. 8 Stiftgasse is the area's cultural centre and provides a venue for exhibitions and events. The Spittelberg is a great success, and café life keeps the cobbled streets buzzing into the early hours of the morning.

The Amerlinghaus at No. 8 Stiftgasse was the birthplace of the painter Friedrich Amerling. Today it is a community centre, theatre and *Beisl (see p203).*

No. 10 Stiftgasse has a handsome façade, decorated with statues.

Nos. 18 and 20 Spittelberggasse are fine examples of Baroque houses.

No. 29 Gutenberggasse is a delightfully pretty Biedermeier building.

Spittelberggasse acts as the venue for an arts and crafts market that is held on every Saturday from April to November, and daily during Easter and Christmas.

The Witwe Bolte restaurant used to be an inn in the 18th century; legend has it that Emperor Joseph II was thrown out of here in 1778.

No. 9 Spittelberggasse is a beautifully-decorated house, with skilfully-painted *trompe l'oeil* windows, dating from the 18th century.

MuseumsQuartier Wien ❽

ONCE HOME TO the imperial stables and carriage houses, the MuseumsQuartier Wien is one of the largest cultural centres in the world. It houses a diverse range of facilities from classical art museums to venues for film, theatre, architecture, dance, new media and a children's creativity centre, as well as a variety of shops, cafés and restaurants. Blending the Baroque architecture of the imperial stables with bold modern buildings, such as the white limestone façade of the Leopold Museum and the dark grey basalt of the Museum of Modern Art Ludwig Foundation Vienna, this impressive and diverse complex aims to provide an almost unprecedented experience.

★ Leopold Museum
Self-portrait with Chinese Lantern (1912) by Egon Schiele is part of the world's largest collection of Schiele's works, housed in this museum.

math.space

Tabakmuseum
This ornate pipe is just one of the items on display in the Tobacco Museum, part of a mostly 19th-century exhibition. In 1784 Joseph II reorganized the Austrian tobacco industry into a state monopoly; this still survives as Austria Tabak.

Tanzquartier Wien

STAR SIGHTS

★ ZOOM Kindermuseum

★ Leopold Museum

★ Museum of Modern Art Ludwig Foundation Vienna (MUMOK)

★ ZOOM Kindermuseum
Providing an exciting place to learn, children are encouraged to explore in the ZOOM Lab, play in ZOOM Ocean, be creative in ZOOM Atelier and have fun exploring the ZOOM exhibitions.

Halls E + G
This foyer leads to the former Winter Riding Hall, now Halls E + G showing a variety of concert, theatre and dance performances. The foyer is also the entrance to the Kunsthalle Wien which exhibits international modern art.

Architekturzentrum Wien

Main entrance in the Fischer von Erlach Wing

Main Courtyard
Often called the largest open-air festival hall in Vienna, from here the diverse architecture of the complex can be appreciated.

★ Museum of Modern Art Ludwig Foundation Vienna
Homme accroupi (1907) by Andre Derain, is part of the collection of European contemporary and modern art in this museum, otherwise known as MUMOK.

Exploring the MuseumsQuartier Wien

O VER 20 DIFFERENT CULTURAL institutions are
gathered together in the MuseumsQuartier
Wien, together with a wide variety of restaurants,
cafés and shops. The sight is an ideal starting point
for any trip to Vienna, as many other attractions are
nearby. It is advisable to begin your visit by going
to the Visitor Centre in the Fischer von Erlach
Wing, to obtain a programme detailing the events
and the exhibitions happening in the complex.

Die Quelle (1923), Leopold Museum

Architekturzentrum Wien
523311530. ☐ 10am–7pm daily.
ⓦ www.azw.at
The permanent exhibition at
this venue is concerned with
thematic and structural diversity
in 20th-century architecture.
Committed to providing
access to architecture, the
venue introduces new
architectural work to the
public. The four to six
temporary exhibitions a year
aim to complement this by
linking modern architecture
with architectural history.

Museum of Modern Art Ludwig Foundation Vienna (MUMOK)
52500. ☐ 10am–6pm Tue–Sun
(to 9pm Thu). ⓦ www.mumok.at
This museum contains
one of the largest European
collections of modern and
contemporary art. MUMOK
comprises of a variety of
genres ranging from American
Pop Art, Photo Realism,
Fluxus and Nouveau Réalism
to Viennese Actionism, Arte
Povera, Conceptual and
Minimal Art, as well as other
contemporary art from Central
and Eastern Europe. The
galleries are split historically
and chronologically over five
levels, two underground.

Tabakmuseum
52617160. ☐ 10am–5pm
Tue–Fri (to 7pm Thu); 10am–
2pm Sat, Sun & hols.
ⓦ www.austriatabak.com
A permanent exhibition on
tobacco traces the development of the plant from its
discovery in 1492 to its
economic significance today.
It contains rare exhibits such
as smoking kits, snuffboxes,
pipes and cigarette boxes.

Leopold Museum
525700. ☐ 10am–7pm Mon,
Wed, Thu; 10am–9pm Fri;
10am–7pm Sat, Sun & hols.
ⓦ www.leopoldmuseum.org
Home to over 5,000 works of
art, the Leopold Collection
of Austrian art was compiled
over five decades by Rudolf
Leopold. The exhibition space
spans five floors. One of the
highlights is the world's largest
Egon Schiele collection (on
the second floor) along with
Expressionist paintings and
Austrian inter-war paintings.
    Paintings after 1945 and
works by Albin Egger-Lienz,
including *Die Quelle*, are
on the first floor, while an
exhibition on Secessionism and
Art Nouveau is on the ground
level, with major works by
Gustav Klimt, Richard Gerstl

and Oskar Kokoschka. The
lower two levels include art
from other 19th- and early
20th-century Austrian artists.

Tanzquartier Wien
581936. ⓦ www.tqw.at
The Tanzquartier Wien offers
facilities and training to dancers
and presents dance and other
performances to the public.

ZOOM Kindermuseum
5247908. ☐ 8:30am–5pm
Mon–Fri; 10am–5:30pm Sat, Sun,
school hols, public hols. Visits must be
pre-booked. ⓦ www.kindermuseum.at
This lively centre offers an
unconventional approach
to the world of the museum
for children from babies to
the age of 12. The aim is to
encourage learning about
exhibition subjects through
play and exploration, such
as the ZOOM Lab for older
children, while younger ones
can have a dip in the ZOOM
Ocean with their parents.

KUNSTHALLE wien
5218933. ☐ 10am–7pm daily
(to 10pm Thu).
ⓦ www.KUNSTHALLEwien.at
This striking red brick building
is a home for innovation and
creativity, showing exhibitions
of international and contemporary art. The exhibitions
emphasize cross-genre and
cross-border trends in the
arts. Highlights range from
experimental architecture,
video, photography and
film, to new media.

math.space
5235881/1730. ☐ varies, phone
to check. ⓦ http://math.space.or.at
Linking maths to the arts, this
centre for the popularization
of maths is aimed at people
of all ages, with interactive
workshops for children and
many programmes for adults.

The Red Horseman (1974) by Roy Lichtenstein in MUMOK

Parliament 🔮

Dr-Karl-Renner-Ring 3. **Map** 1 C5 &
5 A3. 🔲 4011002715. 🔘
Volkstheater. ◯ *for* 🔳 *11am, 3pm
Mon–Thu, 11am, 1pm, 2pm, 3pm Fri
(except when parliament is in session);
during summer break, mid-Jul–mid-
Sep: 9am, 10am, 11am, 1pm, 2pm,
3pm Mon–Fri.* ♿

T HE ARCHITECT Theophil
Hansen *(see p32)* chose a
strict Neo-Classical style when
he designed the immense
Parliament building (he also
designed the neighbouring
Palais Epstein). The Parliament
building was originally
constructed as part of the
Ringstrasse development to act
as the *Reichsrat* building (the
Parliament of the Austrian part
of the Habsburg empire).
Construction began in 1874
and finished in 1884.

The Parliament's entrance is
raised above street level and
approached up a broad ramp.
At the foot of the ramp are the
the bronze Horse Tamers
(1901) by sculptor Josef Lax;
the ramp itself is decorated
with marble figures of Greek
and Roman historians. On the
roof there are chariots and
impressive statues of ancient
scholars and statesmen.

In front of the central
portico is the Athenebrunnen,

Façade of the Parliament building and the Athenebrunnen fountain

a fountain dominated by the
figure of Pallas Athene, the
goddess of Wisdom. It was
designed by Karl Kundmann
and was placed here in 1902.
In this splendid, if chilly, setting
on 11 November 1918 after
the collapse of the Habsburg
empire, the parliamentary
deputies proclaimed the
formation of the republic of

Deutsch-Österreich. It was
renamed the Republic of
Austria in 1919.

During World War II, half of
the Parliament building was
completely destroyed.
Reconstruction was eventually
completed by June 1956, but
the restoration of some of the
damaged artwork, only began
in the 1990s.

THE AUSTRIAN PARLIAMENT

The Austrian parliament is composed of two houses
– the Lower House, or *Nationalrat*, and the Upper
House, or *Bundesrat*. The Lower House has 183
seats and its members are elected for a four-year
term by proportional representation. It comprises
the governing party and the opposition. The Upper
House is composed of elected representatives from
Austria's nine provinces, and its function is to
approve legislation passed by
the Lower House. Bills may
also be presented to
parliament by the general
public or by the Chambers of
Labour (representing
consumers and employees)
and the Chambers of the
Economy (representing
employers and industry). The
federal President is elected for
a six-year term and is largely
a figurehead. Theoretically, he
or she has the power to veto
bills and dissolve parliament,
though this has never occurred.

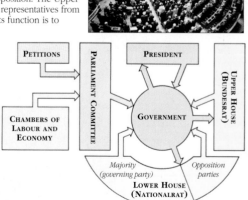

PETITIONS
PARLIAMENT COMMITTEE
PRESIDENT
UPPER HOUSE (BUNDESRAT)
CHAMBERS OF
LABOUR AND
ECONOMY
GOVERNMENT
*Majority
(governing party)*
*Opposition
parties*
LOWER HOUSE
(NATIONALRAT)

Kunsthistorisches Museum ⑩

MORE THAN ONE AND A HALF MILLION people visit the Museum of the History of Art every year. Its collections are based largely on those built up over the centuries by generations of Habsburg monarchs. Originally the works of art were housed in the Hofburg and the Belvedere, but when the Ringstrasse was built *(see pp32–3)* two magnificent buildings were erected to house the collections of imperial art and natural history. The former are on display in this museum where lavish internal decoration complements the exhibits.

Second floor

★ **Hunters in the Snow** *(1565)*
The last painting in Pieter Bruegel the Elder's series of the seasons shows hunters returning to the village on a winter's day.

First floor

★ **The Artist's Studio**
In this 1665 allegory of art, Johannes Vermeer shows an artist in decorative dress painting a model posing as Clio, the Muse of History.

★ **Salt Cellar** *(1540–3)*
Benvenuto Cellini's sumptuous gold Saliera (stolen in 2003) shows the sea and earth united, represented by a female earth goddess and the sea god Neptune.

KEY

☐ Egyptian and Near Eastern collection

☐ Collection of Greek and Roman Antiquities

☐ Collection of Sculpture and Decorative Arts

☐ Picture gallery

☐ Coin cabinets

☐ Non-exhibition space

Portrait of the Infanta Margarita Teresa (1659)
Diego Velázquez captures the fragility of the eight-year-old Spanish princess in all her finery in this official portrait.

Gemma Augustea
The Emperor Augustus dressed as Jupiter sits next to Roma, the personification of Rome, in this Roman cameo carved from onyx.

MUSEUM GUIDE
The ground floor, housing sculpture and the applied arts, is due to re-open in 2007. Until then, parts of this collection are on display in the picture gallery, on the first floor. Three rooms on the second floor house the impressive coin collection.

Ground floor

Rooms k1-k7

King Thutmosis III
Sculpted around 1460 BC, this royal portrait of King Thutmosis III is a remnant of a standing or kneeling figure.

Main entrance from Maria-Theresia-Platz

Rotunda

STAR EXHIBITS

★ **Hunters in the Snow by Bruegel**

★ **The Artist's Studio by Vermeer**

★ **Salt Cellar by Cellini**

THE APOTHEOSIS OF THE RENAISSANCE

Many prominent artists were employed to decorate the museum's interior. As part of an extravagant decorative scheme, the Hungarian painter Michael Munkácsy contributed a fabulous *trompe l'oeil* ceiling painting for the main staircase depicting *The Apotheosis of the Renaissance* (1890). It features Leonardo, Raphael, Veronese, Michelangelo and Titian and their models, presided over by Pope Julius II.

Exploring the Kunsthistorisches' Picture Collection

THE COLLECTION FOCUSES on Old Masters from the 15th to the 18th centuries, and largely reflects the personal tastes of its Habsburg founders. Venetian and 17th-century Flemish paintings are particularly well represented, and there is an excellent display of works by earlier Netherlandish and German artists. Broadly speaking, the pictures are hung following regional schools or styles of painting, although there is considerable overlap between the various categories.

Large Self-Portrait (1652) by Rembrandt van Rijn

The Fur (around 1635–40) by Peter Paul Rubens

Three rooms, XIII, XIV and XX, are devoted to Rubens and include large-scale religious works such as the *Ildefonso Altarpiece* (1630–32) and *The Fur*, an intimate portrait of his wife. Rubens' collaborator and pupil, Anthony Van Dyck, is also represented here by some outstanding works in which his sensitivity to human emotion is fully portrayed.

DUTCH PAINTING

PROTESTANT HOLLAND's newly-rich merchants of the 17th century delighted in pictures that reflected their own world rather than the hereafter. The Dutch genre scenes include works of great domestic charm such as Pieter de Hooch's lovely *Woman with Child at her Breast* (1663–5) and Gerard ter Borch's *Woman Peeling Apples* (1661) while Jacob van Ruisdael's *Great Forest* (1655–60) shows the advances made by Dutch painters in their observations of the natural world. All the

Rembrandts on show in Room XV are portraits; there is the picture of his mother as the prophetess Hannah (1639) and, in contrast to earlier works, the *Large Self-Portrait* shows the artist wearing a plain smock, with the emphasis on his face. The only painting by Johannes Vermeer is the enigmatic *The Artist's Studio* (Room 24). It is a complicated work with layers of symbolism; whether it is a self portrait or not has never been resolved.

ITALIAN PAINTING

THE ITALIAN GALLERIES have a strong collection of 16th-century paintings from Venice and the Veneto. In Room I the broad chronological and stylistic sweep of Titian's work, from his early *Gypsy Madonna*

FLEMISH PAINTING

BECAUSE OF THE historic links between the Habsburg monarchy and the Netherlands, there are several works from this part of Europe (present-day Belgium). The works of the early Flemish masters, who pioneered the development of oil painting, are characterized by their luminous colours and close attention to detail. This can be seen in the triptychs by Rogier van der Weyden and Hans Memling, and Jan van Eyck's *Cardinal Niccolo Albergati* (1435). The highlight for many is Room X, in which about half of all Pieter Bruegel the Elder's surviving works are displayed, including his *Tower of Babel* and most of the cycle of *The Seasons*, all from the mid-16th century.

Susanna and the Elders (1555) by Tintoretto

(1510) to the late *Nymph and Shepherd* (1570–5), can be seen. Other Venetian highlights include Giovanni Bellini's graceful *Young Woman at her Toilette* (1515) and Tintoretto's *Susanna and the Elders*. This is considered to be one of the major works of Venetian Mannerism. Giuseppe Arcimboldo's series of allegorical portrait heads representing the elements and the seasons are usually on show in Room 19, together with other works commissioned by Emperor Rudolf II. Italian Baroque painting includes works by Annibale Carracci and Michelangelo Merisi da Caravaggio, including the huge *Madonna of the Rosary*. Painted between 1606 and 1607, it depicts an intensely realistic Madonna advising St Dominic to distribute rosaries.

FRENCH PAINTING

ALTHOUGH THE number of French paintings on show is relatively small, there are some minor masterpieces. The minutely detailed and highly original portrait of *The Court Jester Gonella* (1440–45), is thought to be the work of Jean Fouquet. It depicts a wily old man, seemingly squeezed into the picture, believed to be a famous court jester of the time. A more formal court portrait from 1569 is that of the youthful Charles IX of France by François Clouet. *The Destruction of the Temple in Jerusalem*, a monumental work painted by Nicolas Poussin in 1638, depicts the Emperor Titus watching the Old Testament prophecy of the destruction of the Temple of Solomon come true. It combines agitated movement with thorough archaeological research. Joseph Duplessis' *Christopher Willibald Ritter von Gluck at the Spinet* shows the famous composer gazing into the heavens for inspiration.

Summer (1563) by Giuseppe Arcimboldo

BRITISH AND GERMAN PAINTING

THERE ARE FEW British works. Perhaps the most appealing is the *Landscape of Suffolk* (around 1750) by Thomas Gainsborough. There are also portraits by Gainsborough, Reynolds and Lawrence.

The German collection is rich in 16th-century paintings. There are several Albrecht Dürer works, including his *Madonna with the Pear* (1512). Other works include the *Stag Hunt of Elector Friedrich the Wise* (1529) by Lucas Cranach the Elder and seven portraits by Hans Holbein the Younger.

SPANISH PAINTING

ROOM 10 HOUSES several fine portraits of the Spanish royal family by the artist Diego Velázquez. He lived from 1599 to 1660 and was the court painter to Philip IV. His works include three portraits of Philip IV's daughter, the Infanta Margarita Teresa (in one aged three, another aged five and in a third aged eight), as well as a portrait of her sickly infant brother, Philip Prosper. Other Spanish works include paintings by Alonso Sánchez Coello and Antonio de Pereda.

Stag Hunt of Elector Friedrich the Wise (1529), by Lucas Cranach the Elder, in the German Collection

Exploring the Kunsthistorisches' Other Collections

APART FROM THE PICTURE GALLERY, the Kunsthistorisches Museum houses several distinct collections of three-dimensional art and objects. Most of the European sculpture and decorative art is from approximately the same period as the paintings (from the 15th to the 18th centuries), but there is also a fine display of medieval objects, while exhibits on show in the Egyptian, Greek and Roman rooms provide an intriguing record of the world's earliest civilizations.

ORIENTAL AND EGYPTIAN ANTIQUITIES

FOUR SPECIALLY decorated rooms adorned with Egyptian friezes and motifs provide the perfect setting for the bulk of the museum's collection of Egyptian and Near Eastern antiquities. The

Blue ceramic hippopotamus from Middle Kingdom Egypt (around 2000 BC)

nucleus of the collection was formed under the earlier Habsburg monarchs. Most of the items were either bought in the 19th century, after Napoleon's Egyptian expedition had increased interest in the area, or added early this century, when Austrian archaeologists excavated at Giza; an outstanding example is the so-called *Reserve Head* (around 26th century BC). The entire 5th-dynasty Tomb Chapel of Ka-Ni-Nisut, from the Pyramid district of Giza, and its well-preserved hieroglyphics (from around 2400 BC) are on display in Room II.

The remarkable collection of objects and sculpture spans a wide chronological period from the Pre-Dynastic era until Roman times. There is a bust of King Thutmosis III *(see p123)* as well as portraits of Egyptian gods and goddesses. In Rooms I and V, where the decorative scheme incorporates Egyptian columns from Aswan, there are items associated with the mortuary cult in Ancient Egypt, including sarcophagi, canopic jars (which used to contain the entrails of mummified corpses), scarabs, mummy cases and papyrus books of the dead. In Room VIII there is a small blue ceramic statue of a hippopotamus. These were often found in Middle Kingdom tombs, as hippopotamus hunting was a royal privilege given to citizens who had won the king's favour. Many of the small-scale

sculptures on display were made to contain deceased souls. Other rooms house mummified animals, Egyptian scripts and artifacts such as pots, clothing and jewellery.

Also shown are a glazed brick relief of a lion from Babylon, and items from Arabia.

GREEK AND ROMAN ANTIQUITIES

ONLY PART OF the museum's Greek and Roman collection is housed in the main building; the finds from Ephesus and Samothrace are displayed in the Neue Burg *(see p95)* in the Hofburg.

If you approach the collection from the Egyptian galleries, the first room you come to (Room X) is devoted to early Greek sculpture. Rooms K6–7 house the Austria Romana collection which includes a statue of the *Youth from Magdalensberg*, a 16th-century cast of a lost Roman statue, found buried in an Austrian field. The main gallery (Room XI), decorated in the style of an imperial Roman villa, includes a mosaic of Theseus and the Minotaur, a Roman marble statue of Isis, Greek sculpture and a sarcophagus with fine relief decoration. Rooms XII and XIII house numerous portrait heads.

The collection also boasts figurines and bronzes from Greece and Rome, vases from Tanagra (a town in Ancient Greece) and a large collection of Roman cameos, jewellery,

Room I from the Egyptian galleries, with papyrus stalk columns from Aswan (around 1410 BC)

busts of Roman Emperors and Roman glass. Etruscan and Cypriot art are in rooms K1–3. Coptic, Byzantine and Germanic items are shown in the rest of the rooms, where pride of place goes to the Treasure of Nagyszentmiklós, a late 9th-century collection of golden vessels found in Romania in 1799.

Medal of Ulrich II Molitor (1581)

SCULPTURE AND DECORATIVE ARTS

THE COLLECTION CONSISTS OF many treasures bought or commissioned by Habsburg connoisseurs, particularly Rudolf II and Archduke Leopold William, for their *Kunstkammern*, or chambers of art and marvels housed in their Habsburg residences. In addition to sculpture, these princely treasuries contained precious items of high craftsmanship, exotic, highly unusual novelties, and scientific instruments. Among the most intriguing are some intricate automata, including a musical box in the form of a ship, and a moving clock. Some of the royal patrons worked in the studio themselves; on display is some glass blown by the Archduke Ferdinand II and embroidery sewn by Maria Theresa.

Virgin with Child (about 1495) by Tilman Riemenschneider

As in the Picture Gallery, the main emphasis is on the Renaissance and Baroque, although there is a great display of medieval items. These include fine, late Gothic religious carved statues by artists such as Tilman Riemenschneider, some medieval ivories, drinking horns and communion vessels. The highlights of the Italian Renaissance rooms are a marble bust of a laughing boy by Desiderio da Settignano, a marble relief of Bacchus and Ariadne and a fine bronze and gilt figurine called Venus Felix after an antique marble statue. Included in the large German Renaissance collection are early playing cards and a table centrepiece, incorporating "vipers' tongues" (in fact, fossilized sharks' teeth), said to ward off poison. Other gems include Benvenuto Cellini's Salt Cellar *(see p122)*, made for the French king François I (stolen from the museum in 2003), and some statuettes by Giambologna. This section is closed for restoration until 2007 but the Italian Renaissance items can be seen in the Italian Renaissance paintings rooms (first floor).

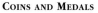

Youth from Magdalensberg, 16th century, cast after a Roman original

COINS AND MEDALS

TUCKED AWAY on the second floor is one of the most extensive coin and medal collections in the world. For those with a special interest in the area it is exceptional. Once again, the nucleus of the collection came from the former possessions of the Habsburgs, but it has been added to by modern curators and now includes many 20th-century items. Only a fraction of the museum's 500,000 pieces can be seen in the three exhibition rooms.

Room I gives an overview of the development of money. It includes coins from Ancient Greece and Rome, examples of Egyptian, Celtic and Byzantine money, and medieval, Renaissance and European coins, as well as the whole range of Austrian currency.

Also on display is a collection of primitive forms of money such as stone currency from Yap Island in Micronesia.

Rooms II and III house an extensive collection of 19th- and 20th-century medals. The portrait medallions are often miniature works of art in themselves. Particularly noteworthy are the unusual silver and gilt medals belonging to Ulrich Molitor, the Abbot of Heiligenkreuz, and the silver medallion which was engraved by Bertrand Andrieu and minted to commemorate the baptism of Napoleon's son. This shows the emperor as a proud father, lifting aloft his baby, the King of Rome *(see p175)*.

Natural History Museum ⓫

Skull from Upper Paleolithic period

ALMOST THE MIRROR image of the Kunsthistorisches Museum, the Natural History Museum was designed by the same architects, and opened in 1889. Its carefully devised interior decoration reflects the nature of the collections. These are quite wide ranging and include archaeological, anthropological, mineralogical, zoological and geological displays. There are casts of dinosaur skeletons, the world's largest display of skulls illustrating the history of man, one of Europe's most comprehensive collections of gems, prehistoric sculpture, Bronze Age items, and extinct birds and mammals.

★ Hallstatt Archaeological Finds
This reconstructed chariot from the Bycis Kala cave in Moravia dates from the early Iron Age.

Children's centre   Aquariu

Lecture Hall

★ Venus of Willendorf
This ancient fertility figure (see p20) found in Lower Austria is around 24,000 years old.

KEY

- ☐ Mineralogy
- ☐ Geology, Paleontology
- ☐ Archaeology
- ☐ Anthropology
- ☐ Zoology
- ☐ Temporary exhibition space
- ☐ Non-exhibition space

Main entrance from Maria-Theresia-Platz

STAR SIGHTS

★ Hallstatt Archaeological Finds

★ Venus of Willendorf

★ Cast of *Iguanodon bernissartensis*

★ Cast of *Iguanodon bernissartensis*
This is just one of several dinosaur skeletons and casts on show in the paleontology department.

The central cupola was designed by Johannes Benk around 1881. It is crowned by a bronze statue of the Greek god Helios.

First floor

Micro-theatre

Ground floor

Zigzag Herons
Part of the Birds of the World display, this pair came from Brazil 150 years ago. Today they are extremely rare.

MUSEUM GUIDE
The museum displays range over two floors. To the right of the entrance on the ground floor are the rooms that are devoted to gemstones and mineralogy; to the left are the rooms housing the displays that chart the evolution of humans and also contain the prehistoric collections. On the first floor are the zoological rooms and temporary exhibitions.

Portrait of Kaiser Francis I *(1773)*
This portrait by Franz Messmer and Ludwig Kohl is of the Natural History Museum's founder and hangs on the stairs.

Caryatid Symbolizing Iron
This allegorical figure forms part of the decorative scheme of the mineralogy room. It represents the metal iron.

MARIA-THERESIA-PLATZ

This square separates the Kunsthistorisches Museum from the Natural History Museum and focuses around an 1888 statue of Maria Theresa *(see p27)* by Kaspar von Zumbusch. It shows the Empress clasping the Pragmatic Sanction of 1713, which made it possible for a woman to succeed to the throne. Below, her generals are portrayed setting forth on horseback from four spurs projecting from the base of the statue, while further back against the plinth stand her principal nobles and advisors, including her doctor van Swieten.

Neues Rathaus ⑫

Friedrich-Schmidt-Platz 1. **Map** 1 B5
& 5 A2. 52550. Rathaus. for
1pm Mon, Wed & Fri & through
phone bookings for groups.

THE NEW TOWN HALL is the
seat of the Vienna City and
Provincial Assembly. Built from
1872 to 1883 to replace the
Altes Rathaus *(see p85)*, it is
unashamedly Neo-Gothic in
style. The architect, Friedrich
von Schmidt, was chosen by
the authorities in a competition
for the best design.

A huge central tower, topped
by the 3-m (11-ft) statue of a
knight in armour with a lance,
dominates the front façade.
Known affectionately as the
Rathausmann, it was designed
by Franz Gastell and made by
the wrought-iron craftsman
Alexander Nehr. The most
attractive feature of the façade is
the lofty loggia with its delicate
tracery and curved balconies.

The building has seven courtyards and summer concerts are
held in the Arkadenhof courtyard. At the top of the first of
the two grand staircases is the
Festsaal, a ceremonial hall that
stretches the length of the
building. Round all four sides
are Neo-Gothic arcades and
statues of Austrian worthies,
including prominent Habsburgs.

Beneath the town hall is the
Wiener Rathauskeller, a popular
restaurant *(see p215)*.

Dreifaltigkeits-kirche ⑬

Alser Strasse 17. **Map** 1 B4.
4057225. Rathaus.
8–11:30am Mon–Sat, 8am–noon
Sun. entrance on
Schlösselgasse for services.

BUILT BETWEEN 1685 and 1727,
the church of the Holy
Trinity contains an altarpiece
(1708) in the north aisle by the

**16th-century crucifix by Veit
Stoss, in the Dreifaltigkeitskirche**

painter Martino Altomonte,
and a graphic crucifix in the
south aisle from the workshop
of Veit Stoss. It was to this
church that Beethoven's body
was brought after he died in
1827. Following the funeral
service which was attended by
many of his contemporaries,
including Schubert and the
poet Franz Grillparzer, the
cortege bore his coffin to the
cemetery at Währing on the
city outskirts.

University ⑭

Dr-Karl-Lueger-Ring 1. **Map** 1 C4 &
5 A2. 42770. Schottentor.
6:30am–8:30pm Mon–Fri, 8am–
1pm Sat.

FOUNDED IN 1365 by Duke
Rudolf IV, the University of
Vienna now has approximately
50,000 students. The versatile
architect Heinrich Ferstel
designed its present home
in 1883, adopting an Italian
Renaissance style.

From the entrance hall, huge
staircases lead up to the
university's ceremonial halls. In
1895 Gustav Klimt was
commissioned to decorate the
hall with frescoes, but the
degree of nudity portrayed in
some panels proved
unacceptable to the authorities.
Eventually, when no
agreement could be reached,
Klimt returned his fee to the
government and took back the
paintings; they were destroyed
during World War II.

**Front elevation of the Neues Rathaus showing the Rathausmann on his
tower some 98 m (320 ft) above the ground**

A spacious arcaded courtyard, lined with busts of the university's most distinguished professors, is located in the centre of the building. Among the figures on display include the founder of psychoanalysis, Sigmund Freud *(see p110),* and the philosopher Franz Brentano. Nearby are the smoke-filled and poster-daubed corridors of today's university students.

Café Landtmann **⑮**

Dr-Karl-Lueger-Ring 4. **Map** 1 C5 & 5 B2. 24100. Schottentor, Volkstheater. 8am–midnight daily.

IF THE CAFE CENTRAL *(see p58)* was, and perhaps still is, the coffee house of Vienna's intelligentsia, this café *(see p58)* is undoubtedly the coffee house of the affluent middle classes. With mirrors and elegant panelling, it is an exceedingly comfortable place. Established in 1873 by coffee-maker Franz Landtmann, it is still a popular café. It was Sigmund Freud's *(see p110)* favourite coffee house.

The attractive Dreimäderlhaus *(left)* on Schreyvogelgasse

Dreimäderlhaus **⑯**

Schreyvogelgasse 10. **Map** 1 C5 & 5 B2. Schottentor.

A DELIGHTFUL REMNANT of Biedermeier Vienna is found in the houses on one side of the cobbled Schreyvogelgasse. The prettiest is the Dreimäderlhaus (1803). There is a legend that Schubert had three sweethearts *(drei Mäderl)* ensconced here, but it is more likely that the house was named after the 1920s' operetta, *Dreimäderlhaus,* which uses his melodies.

One of the arcades surrounding the University courtyard

Mölker-Bastei **⑰**

Map 1 C5 & 5 B2. Schottentor.

A FEW PACES AWAY from the bustling Schottentor, a quiet street has been built on to a former bastion of the city walls. It boasts some beautiful late 18th-century houses. Beethoven lived here, and the Emperor Franz Joseph nearly met his death on the bastion in 1853 when a tailor attempted to assassinate him. No. 10 is the house where the Belgian Prince Charles de Ligne lived during the Congress of Vienna in 1815 *(see p30).* De Ligne, an elderly aristocrat, wrote a number of cynical commentaries on the various activities of the crowned heads of Europe who came to Vienna at that time. A ladies' man, he caught a fatal chill while waiting for an assignation on the bastion.

Plaque on the front of the Pasqualati Haus

Pasqualati Haus **⑱**

Mölker-Bastei 8. **Map** 1 C5 & 5 B2. 5358905. Schottentor. **Museum** 9am–12:15pm & 1–4:30pm Tue–Sun.

THE PASQUALATI HAUS is no different in appearance from any of the other houses along this lane, but it is the most famous of more than 30 places where Ludwig van Beethoven resided in Vienna. Named after its original owner, Baron Johann von Pasqualati, it was Beethoven's home between 1804 and 1808, and 1810 and 1815. He composed many of his best-loved works here, including the Symphonies 4, 5, 7 and 8, the opera *Fidelio,* the Piano Concerto No. 4, and string quartets. Today, the rooms on the fourth floor which the composer occupied house a small museum. Various memorabilia, such as a lock of Beethoven's hair, a photograph of his grave at Währing cemetery, a deathbed engraving and early editions of his scores are on display. The museum also contains busts and paintings of Beethoven and his patron Prince Rasumofsky, the Russian ambassador to Vienna.

Liebenberg monument (1890) below the Mölker-Bastei

The Burgtheater ⓲

THE BURGTHEATER IS THE most prestigious stage in the German-speaking world *(see also p230)*. The original theatre built in Maria Theresa's reign was replaced in 1888 by today's Italian Renaissance-style building by Karl von Hasenauer and Gottfried Semper. It closed for refurbishment in 1897 after the discovery that the auditorium had several seats with no view of the stage. Forty-eight years later a bomb devastated the building, leaving only the side wings containing the Grand Staircases intact. Subsequent restoration was so successful that today its extent is hard to assess.

JOHANN
NESTROY
1801 – 1862

Two statues of the muses of music and dramatic art adorn the roof.

Busts of playwrights
Lining the walls of the Grand Staircases are busts of playwrights whose works are still performed here, including this one of Johann Nestroy by Hans Knesl.

Ceiling frescoes by the Klimt brothers and Franz Matsch cover the north and south wings.

Entrance for tours

Candelabra lining the staircase

★ Grand Staircases in North and South Wings
Two imposing gala staircases lead up from the side entrances to the foyer. Each is a mirror image of the other.

Main entrance on Dr Karl-Lueger-Ring

STAR FEATURES

★ **Grand Staircases in North and South Wings**

★ **Der Thespiskarren by Gustav Klimt**

Foyer
The 60-m long (200-ft) curving foyer serves as a waiting area during intervals. Portraits of famous actors and actresses line its walls.

Auditorium
The central part of the Burgtheater was rebuilt in 1952–5 after war damage, but the auditorium is still decorated in the imperial colours of cream, red and gold.

★ Der Thespiskarren
This ceiling fresco (1886–8) by Gustav Klimt, part of the series The History of the Theatre, depicts Thespis, the first performer of a Greek Tragedy.

Sculpted cherubs on the balustrade (1880–83)

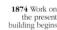

Front Façade
A statue of Apollo (about 1883) seated between Melpomene and Thalia presides over a frieze of Bacchus and Ariadne by Rudolf Weyr.

TIMELINE

1741 Maria Theresa founds the Burgtheater in an empty ballroom at the Hofburg

1776 Joseph II reorganizes the theatre and promotes it to the status of a national theatre

The Old Burgtheater in the mid-18th century

1874 Work on the present building begins

1888 The Burgtheater opens on 14 October in the presence of the Emperor Franz Joseph and his family

1897 The auditorium is adapted

1945 World War II fire destroys the auditorium

1955 Theatre reopens with Grillparzer's King Ottokar

1750	1850	1900	1950

OPERA AND NASCHMARKT

**Relief on the façade
of the Secession Building**

THIS IS AN AREA of huge contrasts, ranging from the stateliness of the Opera House and the opulence of the Opernring shops to the raucous modernity of Mariahilfer Strasse. This long street is lined with cinemas and department stores, drawing shoppers not just from Vienna but from much of eastern Europe. The other major thoroughfare in our area is the Linke Wienzeile, which runs parallel to the Rechte Wienzeile. Both roads stretch from just beyond the Ringstrasse to the city outskirts, following the curving and sometimes subterranean River Wien. Between these roads is the bustling Naschmarkt, which is overlooked by Otto Wagner's Jugendstil apartments on the Linke Wienzeile. Visitors wanting to escape the crowds should visit the celebrated Café Museum, located near the three great cultural institutions of the area – the Academy of Fine Arts, the Opera House and the Secession Building.

SIGHTS AT A GLANCE

Streets and Squares
Mariahilfer Strasse ❽

Historic Buildings
Hotel Sacher ❷
Opera House pp140–1 ❶
Theater an der Wien ❺
Wagner Apartments ❼

Museums and Galleries
Academy of Fine Arts ❸
Haydn Museum ❿
Kaiserliches Hofmobilien-
depot ❾
Secession Building ❹

Markets
Naschmarkt ❻

GETTING THERE
This area is served by Zieglergasse (line U3), Neubaugasse (line U3) and MuseumsQuartier (line U2) U-Bahn stations. Bus 13A runs from Josefstädter Strasse to Mariahilfer Strasse and to the southern end of the Linke Wienzeile. Bus 57A travels the length of Gumpendorfer Strasse.

KEY

▦	Street-by-Street map See pp136–7
Ⓤ	U-Bahn station
🅿	Parking

◁ **Main staircase and hallway at the Opera House**

Street-by-Street: Opernring

BETWEEN THE OPERA HOUSE and the Karlskirche, two of the great landmarks of Vienna, lies an area that typifies the varied cultural vitality of the city as a whole. Here are an 18th-century theatre, a 19th-century art academy, and the Secession Building. Mixed in with these cultural monuments are emblems of the Viennese devotion to good living: the Hotel Sacher, as sumptuous today as it was a century ago; the Café Museum *(see p58)*, still as popular as it was in the 1900s; and the hurly-burly of the colourful Naschmarkt, where you can buy everything from oysters and exotic fruits to second-hand clothes.

★ **Academy of Fine Arts**
This Italianate building is home to one of the best collections of old masters in Vienna ❸

The Goethe Statue was designed by Edmund Hellmer in 1890.

The Schiller Statue dominates the park in front of the Academy of Fine Arts.

★ **Secession Building**
This delightful structure, built in 1898 as a showroom for the Secession artists, houses Gustav Klimt's (see p56) Beethoven Frieze ❹

Theater an der Wien
Today this 18th-century theatre is used for major musicals. It was the venue for many premieres including Beethoven's Fidelio ❺

SCHILLERPLATZ

ELIS

NIBELU

MAKARTGASSE

GETREIDEMARKT

MILLÖCKERGASSE

LINKE WIENZEILE

Naschmarkt
This market sells everything from fresh farm produce to bric-a-brac. It is liveliest on Saturday mornings ❻

Hotel Sacher
The famous Sacher-torte (see p209) originated here ❷

To Albertinaplatz

GOETHEGASSE

OPERNRING

OPERNGASSE

ETHSTRASSE

NGASSE

RIEDRICHSTRASSE

MUSEUM AND TOWNHALL QUARTER   HOFBURG QUARTER

OPERA AND NASCHMARKT

LOCATOR MAP
See Street Finder, maps 3, 4 & 5

To Kärntner Strasse

0 metres   50
0 yards   50

★ **Opera House**
This stately building, opened on this site in 1869, is still the hub of Vienna's glorious cultural life ❶

CAFE   MUSEUM   CAFE

The Café Museum, built in 1899, once boasted a stylish interior by Adolf Loos *(see p92).* Loos's interior is long gone but the café is still popular with students and artists.

The Mark Anthony Statue
(1899) alongside the Secession Building is a gloriously decadent bronze statue by Arthur Strasser.

STAR SIGHTS

★ **Secession Building**

★ **Academy of Fine Arts**

★ **Opera House**

KEY

- - - Suggested route

Opera House ❶

See pp140–141.

Hotel Sacher ❷

Philharmonikerstrasse 4. **Map** 4 D1 &
5 C5. 📞 514560. 🚇 Karlsplatz.
🕐 6:30am–midnight daily. 📷 ♿
🌐 www.sacher.com

Founded by the son of Franz
Sacher, who, according to
some, was the creator of the
Sachertorte in 1840 *(see p209)*,
this hotel *(see p200)* came into
its own under Anna Sacher.
The cigar-smoking daughter-in-
law of the founder ran the hotel
from 1892 until her death in
1930. During her time the Sacher
became a venue for the extra-
marital affairs of the rich and
noble. It is still a discreetly
sumptuous hotel.

Academy of Fine Arts ❸

Schillerplatz 3. **Map** 4 D2 & 5 B5. 📞
58816225. 🚇 Karlsplatz. 🕐 10am–
6pm Tue–Sun & public hols. ⬤ 1 Jan,
1 May, Corpus Christi and following
Fri, 1 & 2 Nov, 24, 25 & 31 Dec. 📷
📷 ♿ 🌐 www.akademiegalerie.at

Theophil Hansen built the
Academy of Fine Arts in
Italian Renaissance style from
1872 to 1876. In 1907 Adolf
Hitler was barred from entrance

Façade of the Secession Building

on the grounds that he lacked
talent. Today the Academy acts
as an arts college and has a
gallery showing changing
exhibitions. These include late
Gothic and early Renaissance
works, some Rubens' pieces,
17th-century Dutch and Flemish
landscapes, as well as a 19th-
century Austrian collection.

Secession Building ❹

Friedrichstrasse 12. **Map** 4 D2. 📞
5875307. 🚇 Karlsplatz. 🕐 10am–
6pm Tue, Wed, Fri–Sun, 10am–8pm
Thu. 📷 📷 ♿ 🌐 www.secession.at

Joseph maria Olbrich designed
the unusual Secession Building
in Jugendstil style *(see pp54–7)*
as a showcase for the Secession
movement's artists
(see p34). The
almost windowless
building, with its
filigree globe of
entwined laurel
leaves on the roof,
is a squat cube with
four towers. The
motto of the
founders, em-
blazoned in gold on
the façade, states,
*"Der Zeit ibre
Kunst, der Kunst
ibre Freibeit"*,
which translates as:
"To every Age its
Art, to Art its
Freedom".
Alongside the
building stands the
marvellous statue of
Mark Anthony in
his chariot being

Columned entrance to the Theater an der Wien

drawn by lions (1899), by
Arthur Strasser. Gustav Klimt's
Beethoven Frieze is the
Secession's best-known exhibit.
Designed in 1902 as a decora-
tive painting, it covers three
walls and is 34 m (110 ft) long.
It shows interrelated groups of
figures and is thought to be a
commentary on Beethoven's
Ninth Symphony. *(See also p35.)*

Theater an der Wien ❺

Linke Wienzeile 6. **Map** 3 C2.
📞 588300. 🚇 Kettenbrückengasse.
🕐 for performances.
🌐 www.musicalvienna.at

Emanuel schikaneder founded
this theatre *(see p226)* in
1801; a statue above the entrance
show him playing Papageno in
the premiere of Mozart's *The
Magic Flute* in the forerunner
of the present theatre. The
premiere of Beethoven's *Fidelio*
was staged here in 1805.

Typical stall at the Naschmarkt

Naschmarkt ❻

Map 3 C2–C3. 🚇 Kettenbrückengasse. **Market** 🕐 6am–6:30pm Mon–
Fri, 6am–2pm Sat. **Schubert Museum**
🕐 9am–12:15pm, 1–4:30pm Tue–Sun.

The naschmarkt is Vienna's
liveliest market. It has
many well-established shops
and some of the best snack
bars in Vienna *(see pp217–19)*.
As you walk west it gradually
becomes less formal, with flower
vendors', wine producers' and
farmers' stalls spilling out onto
the street and offering meats,
breads and so on. This area in
turn leads into the flea market –
a chaos of makeshift stalls.
    It's also worth going to No. 6
Kettenbrückengasse, by the
U-Bahn, to see the simple flat
where Franz Schubert died in
1828. It displays facsimiles,
prints and a family piano.

The Majolikahaus, one of the Wagner Apartments

Wagner Apartments 🟶

Linke Wienzeile 38 & 40. **Map** 3 C2.
Ⓤ *Kettenbrückengasse.*

L OOKING ONTO THE Nasch-
markt are two remarkable
apartment buildings. Designed
by Otto Wagner in 1899, they
represent the apex of Jugendstil style *(see pp54–7)*. No. 38
has sparkling gilt ornament,
mostly by Kolo Moser. The
façade of No. 40 has subtle
flower patterns in pink, blue
and green. Even the sills are
moulded and decorated.
No. 40, which is called the
Majolikahaus after the glazed
pottery used for the weather-
resistant surface decoration, is
the more striking. No. 42 next
door, in historicist style *(see
pp32–3)*, shows what
Secession architects were
reacting against.

Mariahilfer Strasse 🟶

Map 3 A3 & 5 A5. Ⓤ *Zieglergasse,
Kirchengasse, Babenberger Strasse.*
Stiftkirche ⏰ *7:30am–6pm
Mon–Fri, 7am–11pm Sat, 8:30am–
9:30pm Sun.* **Mariahilfer Kirche** ⏰
8am–7pm Mon–Sat, 8:30am–7pm Sun.

T HIS IS ONE OF Vienna's
busiest shopping streets.
On the corner of Stiftgasse is
the Stiftkirche. The architect is

unknown, but the church
dates from 1739. The façade is
an austere pyramidal structure,
rising to a bulbous steeple. Of
particular interest, there are
some lively Rococo reliefs set
into the walls.
Across the street at No. 45 is
the house where the playwright
Ferdinand Raimund was born
in 1790. Its cobbled courtyard
is lined with shops.
Mariahilfer Kirche is named
after a 16th-century cult of the
Virgin Mary which was
founded at the pilgrimage of
Mariahilfer Kirche at Passau.
The Viennese church is in
the Baroque style and is
dominated by two towers with
bulbous steeples.

Kaiserliches Hof- mobiliendepot 🟶

Andreasgasse 7. **Map** 3 A2.
📞 52433570.
Ⓤ *Zieglergasse.*
⏰ *10am–6pm Tue–Sun.* 📷

T HE IMPERIAL furniture
collection, founded
by Maria Theresa in
1747, gives an intimate
portrait of the Habsburg
way of life, as well as a
detailed historical record of
Viennese interior decoration
and cabinet-making in the 18th
and 19th centuries. Also
included in the collection are

pieces created by artists and
designers of the early 20th
century. Room after room
is filled with outstanding
furnishings and royal domestic
objects, ranging from a faithful
re-creation of Empress
Elisabeth's Schönbrunn Palace
apartments to a simple folding
throne that was used while
travelling. The exhibits, which
range from the mundane to
the priceless and often
eccentric, provide a fascinating
and evocative insight into
the everyday lives of the
imperial family.

Haydn Museum 🟶

Haydngasse 19. **Map** 3 A3.
📞 *5961307.* Ⓤ *Zieglergasse.* ⏰
9am–12:15pm & 1–4:30pm Tue–Sun.
● *1 Jan, 1 May, 25 Dec.* 📷 📷

A S WITH MANY of the museums
dedicated to composers,
the Haydn Museum does not
have a very comprehensive
collection of exhibits: only a
few copies of documents and
scores, a piano and clavichord.
Haydn built this house in
what was then a new suburb
of Vienna with money he had
earned from his successful
visits to London which had
taken place between 1791 and
1795. He lived in the house
from 1797 until his death in
1809 and it was here that he
composed many of his major
works, including *The Creation*
and *The Seasons.* There is also
a room that contains some
furniture and
mementoes
belonging to
Johannes
Brahms.

**Antique wheelchair in the
Kaiserliches Hofmobiliendepot.**

The Opera House ❶

Gustav Mahler by Rodin

V IENNA'S STATE OPERA HOUSE, or Staatsoper, was the first of the grand Ringstrasse buildings to be completed *(see pp32–3)*; it opened on 25 May 1869 to the strains of Mozart's *Don Giovanni*. Built in Neo-Renaissance style, it initially failed to impress the Viennese. Yet when it was hit by a bomb in 1945 and largely destroyed, the event was seen as a symbolic blow to the city. With a brand new auditorium and stage incorporating the latest technology, the Opera House reopened on 5 November 1955 with a performance of Beethoven's *Fidelio*.

Reliefs of Opera and Ballet *(1861–9)* *Painted allegorical lunettes by Johann Preleuthner represent ballet, tragic opera and comic opera. The one here depicts comic opera.*

The Auditorium

★ Grand Staircase
A superb marble staircase sweeps up from the main entrance to the first floor. It is embellished with statues by Josef Gasser of the seven liberal arts (such as Music and Dancing) and reliefs of opera and ballet.

★ Schwind Foyer
The foyer is decorated with scenes from operas painted by Moritz von Schwind. Among the busts of famous composers and conductors is Rodin's bronze bust of Mahler (1909).

Main entrance

One of the five bronze statues by Ernst Julius Hähnel, depicting Heroism, Drama, Fantasy, Humour and Love, standing under the arches of the loggia.

STAR FEATURES

★ Grand Staircase

★ Schwind Foyer

★ Tea Room

★ Tea Room
Franz Joseph and his entourage used to spend the intervals in this graceful room, which is decorated with silk hangings bearing the Emperor's initials.

THE VIENNA OPERA BALL

On the last Thursday of the Vienna Carnival *(see p65)* the stage is extended to cover the seats in the auditorium to create space for the Opera Ball *(see p231).* This is an expensive society event which opens when the cream of the *jeunesse dorée* – well-to-do girls clad in white and their escorts – take to the floor.

VISITORS' CHECKLIST

Opernring 2, A-1010. **Map** 4 D1 & 5 C5. **℡** 514442250. **Ⓤ** Karlsplatz. **🚋** 1, 2, D, J. **◯** for performances. **✉** call 514442606/2421 for details. **♿ 📷 👓 🖥 ♫ Ⓦ** www.wiener-staatsoper.at

The Architects
The architects of the Opera House were August Siccardsburg (right) and Eduard van der Nüll (left).

Fountain
On either side of the Opera House stand two graceful fountains. Designed by Hans Gasser, this one depicts the legendary siren Lorelei supported by figures representing Grief, Love and Vengeance.

***The Magic Flute* Tapestries**
One of the two side salons, the Gustav Mahler Saal, is hung with modern tapestries by Rudolf Eisenmenger illustrating scenes from The Magic Flute.

BELVEDERE QUARTER

THIS IS A GRANDIOSE and extravagant district. From the Karlsplatz, with its gardens and statues, there is a lovely view of Johann Bernhard Fischer von Erlach's Baroque Karlskirche. East of this great church, visitors can see more delights, including the two palaces of the Belvedere, now public galleries, and the Schwarzenberg Palace, now a hotel. These huge palaces and beautiful gardens were designed by Johann Lukas von Hildebrandt,

Statue of Leonardo da Vinci in the Künstlerhaus

following the crucial defeat of the Turks in 1683. Only after the Turkish threat had been removed was it possible for Vienna to expand. The turbulent history of the city is excellently documented in the Historical Museum of the City of Vienna in Karlsplatz. Just a few paces away is the Musikverein, home to the Vienna Philharmonic. There is also the Bestattungsmuseum (undertakers' museum), that chronicles the importance the Viennese attach to pomp and death.

SIGHTS AT A GLANCE

Streets and Squares
Rennweg **9**
Schwarzenbergplatz **7**

Historic Buildings
Imperial Hotel **6**
Karlsplatz Pavilions **4**
Musikverein **3**
Schwarzenberg Palace **8**
Theresianum **13**

Museums and Galleries
Bestattungsmuseum **12**
Historical Museum of the
City of Vienna **2**
Künstlerhaus **5**
*Palaces and Gardens
of the Belvedere
pp152–57* **10**

Parks and Gardens
Botanical Gardens **11**

Churches
Karlskirche pp148–49 **1**

GETTING THERE
This area is served by the Karlsplatz (lines U1, U2, U4) and Taubstummengasse (line U1) U-Bahn stations. Tram 71 runs along Rennweg and Bus 4A goes from Wittelsbachstrasse to Karlsplatz.

KEY
- Street-by-Street map
  See pp144–45
- U-Bahn station
- Badner Bahn station
- P Parking

0 metres 250
0 yards 250

◁ **Botanical Gardens**

Street-by-Street: Karlsplatz

THIS PART OF THE CITY became ripe for development once the threat of Turkish invasion had receded for good in 1683 *(see pp26–7)*. The Ressel Park, at the front of the Karlskirche, gives an unobstructed view of this grandiose church, built on the orders of Karl VI. The park itself is lined with a variety of cultural institutions, notably the Historical Museum of the City of Vienna and, across the road, the Musikverein.

★ Karlsplatz Pavilions
These pavilions were built as part of the underground system of 1899 **4**

Underpass

To Karlsplatz U-Bahn

Ressel Park café

The Technical University
with its Neo-Classical façade (1816) fronts on to Ressel Park, which contains busts and statues of famous 19th-century Austrian scientists and engineers.

Ressel Statue

KARLSPL

STAR SIGHTS

★ **Karlsplatz Pavilions**

★ **Historical Museum of the City of Vienna**

★ **Karlskirche**

Henry Moore's Hill Arches were presented to the City of Vienna by the artist himself in 1978.

Musikverein
This Ringstrasse-style (see p146) concert hall, home of the Vienna Philharmonic Orchestra, is renowned for its superb acoustics **3**

LOCATOR MAP
See Street Finder, map 4

★ Historical Museum of the City of Vienna
This museum houses relics of Roman Vienna, stained glass from the Stephansdom and the reconstructed rooms of celebrated Viennese such as Adolf Loos (see p92) **2**

★ Karlskirche
Promised to the people during the 1713 plague, this is Vienna's finest Baroque church **1**

French Embassy

THE ART NOUVEAU FRENCH EMBASSY

Built in 1904–12 by the French architect Georges Chédanne, the Embassy is typical of French Art Nouveau, resembling houses along Rue Victor Hugo in Paris. Unaccustomed to this foreign style, some thought the building was oriental, giving rise to a rumour that its plans had been mixed up with those of the French Embassy in Istanbul.

Art Nouveau façade of the French Embassy

0 metres 50
0 yards 50

KEY

- - - Suggested route

Karlskirche ❶

See pp148–9.

Historical Museum of the City of Vienna ❷

Karlsplatz. **Map** 4 E2. 🎫 *5058747.* 🚇 *Karlsplatz.* ⏰ *9am–6pm Tue–Sun.* 📷 ♿ 📷 🆆 *www. wienmuseum.at*

THE HISTORICAL MUSEUM of the City of Vienna moved to its current location in 1959. The ground floor usually has Roman and pre-Roman items, as well as exhibits from the Gothic period. These include 14th- and 15th-century gargoyles and figures, and stained glass from the Stephansdom, and carved portraits of early rulers of Vienna. These displays are sometimes moved for visiting exhibitions.

The first-floor 16th- and 17th-century exhibits include prints depicting Turkish sieges from 1529 onwards, as well as a portrait of the Turkish commander Kara Mustafa, captured banners and weapons, and prints of the celebrations after Austria's victory. Here too are Johann Bernhard Fischer von Erlach's original plans for the Schönbrunn Palace *(see pp172–5)*, and the original lantern from No. 6

The monumental, historicist-style façade of the Musikverein

Schönlaterngasse *(see p74)*. On the second floor are a reconstructed 1798 room from the Caprara-Geymüller Palace in Wallnerstrasse, panelled with painted silks, and the apartment of Austria's most famous poet, Franz Grillparzer. There are displays chronicling the popularity of ballet, theatre and operetta.

Exhibits from this century include Richard Gerstl's portrait of Arnold Schönberg *(see p39)* and portraits by Egon Schiele and Gustav Klimt. There is a room (1903) from Adolf Loos's house *(see p92)* in Bösendorferstrasse, silver- and glassware by Josef Hoffmann, designs from the Wiener Werkstätte *(see p56)* and pictures of Vienna over the past hundred years.

Musikverein ❸

Bösendorferstrasse 12. **Map** 4 E2. 🎫 *5058190.* 🚇 *Karlsplatz.* ⏰ *for concerts only.* 📷 ♿ 🆆 *www. musikverein.at*

THE MUSIKVEREIN building – the headquarters of the Society of the Friends of Music – was designed from 1867 to 1869 by Theophil Hansen, in a mixture of styles employing terracotta statues, capitals and balustrades. It is the home of the great Vienna Philharmonic Orchestra *(see p229)*, which gives regular performances here, and forms the orchestra of the Opera House. The concert hall seats almost 2,000. Tickets are sold on a subscription basis to Viennese music lovers, but some are also available on the day of the performance. The most famous annual event here is the New Year's Day concert *(see p65)*.

Karlsplatz Pavilions ❹

Karlsplatz. **Map** 4 D2. 🎫 *5058747.* 🚇 *Karlsplatz.* ⏰ *Apr–Oct: 1:30–4:30pm Tue–Sun.* 📷

OTTO WAGNER *(see pp54–57)* was responsible for designing and engineering many aspects of the early underground system in the late 19th century. Some of these bridges and tunnels are remarkable in themselves, but cannot match his stylish pair of underground railway exit pavilions (1898–9) alongside

Sunflower motifs on the façade of the Karlsplatz Pavilions

The enormous Hochstrahlbrunnen in Schwarzenbergplatz

Imperial Hotel ⑥

Kärntner Ring 16. **Map** 4 E2 & 6 D5.
📞 50110. Ⓤ Karlsplatz. 📷 ♿
🅦 www.luxurycollection.com

ALONG WITH the Hotel Sacher *(see p138)*, this is the best known of the 19th-century hotels. You can sip tea to the sound of a pianist playing in the background or stay in the same room Richard Wagner occupied. Adolf Hitler made the hotel his headquarters after the Anschluss *(see p36)*.

Schwarzenberg-platz ⑦

Map 4 E2. Ⓤ Karlsplatz. **Arnold Schönberg Center** 📞 7121888.

AT THE CENTRE of this grand square is the equestrian statue (1867) of Prince Schwarzenberg, who led the Austrian and allied armies against Napoleon at the Battle of Leipzig (1813). The square combines huge office blocks, the Ringstrasse and the Baroque splendours of the Schwarzenberg and Belvedere palaces. Behind the fountain of Hochstrahlbrunnen (1873), at the intersection of Prinz-Eugen-Strasse and Gusshausstrasse, is the monument commemorating the Red Army's liberation of the city. It is none too popular with older Viennese, who still recall the brutalities endured in the Russian zone until 1955.

The Arnold Schönberg Center, at the eastern end of the square, houses recordings, scores and memorabilia from the famous Viennese composer.

the Karlsplatz, which are among his best-known buildings. The green copper colour of the roofs and the ornamentation complement the Karlskirche beyond. Gilt patterns are stamped onto the white marble cladding and eaves, with repetitions of Wagner's beloved sunflower motif. But the greatest impact is made by the buildings' elegantly curving rooflines. The two pavilions face each other: one is now a café, the other is used for exhibitions.

Künstlerhaus ⑤

Karlsplatz 5. **Map** 4 D2 & 6 D5.
📞 5879663. Ⓤ Karlsplatz.
⏰ 10am–6pm Fri–Wed; 10am–9pm Thu. 🚫 ♿ 🅦 www.k-haus.at

COMMISSIONED BY the Vienna Artists' Society as an exhibition hall for its members, the Künstlerhaus was built in 1868. The society favoured grand,

academic styles of painting in tune with the historicist Ringstrasse architecture. The Künstlerhaus itself is typical of this style, which is named after the Vienna boulevard where the look is most prevalent *(see pp32–3)*. Designed by August Weber (1836–1903) in a Renaissance palazzo style, the Künstlerhaus is now used for temporary art exhibitions.

Palazzo-style façade of the Künstlerhaus (1868)

Karlskirche ❶

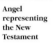

DURING VIENNA'S PLAGUE epidemic in 1713, Emperor Karl VI vowed that as soon as the city was delivered from its plight he would build a church dedicated to St Charles Borromeo (1538–84), a former Archbishop of Milan and a patron saint of the plague. The following year he announced a competition to design the church, which was won by the architect Johann Bernhard Fischer von Erlach. The result was a richly eclectic Baroque masterpiece: the gigantic dome and portico are borrowed from the architecture of ancient Greece and Rome, while there are Oriental echoes in the gatehouses and minaret-like columns. Building took almost 25 years, and the interior was richly embellished with carvings and altarpieces by the foremost artists of the day, including Daniel Gran and Martino Altomonte.

Angel representing the New Testament

The Pulpit
Two putti surmount the canopy of the richly-gilded pulpit, decorated with rocailles and flower garlands.

Stairway (closed to public)

★ High Altar
The high altar features a stucco relief by Albert Camesina showing St Charles Borromeo being assumed into heaven on a cloud laden with angels and putti.

The two gatehouses leading into the side entrances of the church are reminiscent of Chinese pavilions.

Pediment reliefs by Giovanni Stanetti show the suffering of the Viennese during the 1713 plague.

Angel representing the Old Testament

Main entrance

STAR FEATURES

★ High Altar

★ Frescoes in the Cupola

★ The Two Columns

Cupola
Cross

★ **Frescoes in the Cupola**
Johann Michael Rottmayr's fresco, painted between 1725 and 1730, depicts the Apotheosis of St Charles Borromeo. It was the painter's last commission.

JOHANN BERNHARD FISCHER VON ERLACH

Many of Vienna's finest buildings, including the Trautson and Schönbrunn Palaces, were designed by Fischer von Erlach (1656–1723). He died before he finished the Karlskirche and his son completed it in 1737.

★ **The Two Columns**
Inspired by Trajan's Column in Rome, they are decorated with spiralling scenes of St Charles Borromeo's life. Qualities of Steadfastness are illustrated on the left, and Courage on the right.

Visitors
entrance
and tickets

St Charles Borromeo
Lorenzo Mattielli's statue of the patron saint crowns the pediment.

Angel
representing the New
Testament

Schwarzenberg Palace and Joseph Fischer von Ehrlach's fountain

Schwarzenberg Palace **8**

Schwarzenbergplatz 9. **Map** 4 E2.
See **Where to Stay** p201.

THE PALAIS SCHWARZENBERG was built by Johann Lukas von Hildebrandt *(see p152)* in 1697 and then altered by the Fischer von Erlachs *(see p149)* in the 1720s. The main salon has a domed hall with a magnificent chandelier. Behind the palace are the lawns and shady paths of the park, focused around a pool and fountain designed by Joseph Emanuel Fischer von Erlach. Part of the building has now been converted into a luxurious hotel and restaurant, while one wing is now occupied by the Swiss Embassy. It is only open to guests of the hotel, restaurant and embassy.

The present head of the Schwarzenberg family served as an advisor to President Havel after the Velvet Revolution in Czechoslovakia in 1989.

Rennweg **9**

Map 4 E2. **U** *Karlsplatz.*
Gardekirche ◯ *8am–8pm daily.*

RENNWEG RUNS from the Schwarzenbergplatz along the edges of the Belvedere palaces. At No. 3, a house built by Otto Wagner *(see p57)* in 1890 is now the (former) Yugoslav Embassy. Though the façade is in shabby condition, the house remains an interesting example of Wagner's work

just as he was making the transition from Ringstrasse pomp to his later Jugendstil style of architecture.

Next door at No. 5 is where Gustav Mahler *(see p39)* lived from 1898 to 1909. No. 5a is the Gardekirche (1755–63) by Nikolaus Pacassi (1716–99), Maria Theresa's court architect. It was originally built as the church of the Imperial Hospital and since 1897 has been Vienna's Polish church. A huge dome covers the entire interior, which adds to its spaciousness. One feature of interest is the gilt Rococo embellishment over the side chapels and between the ribs of the dome. Just beyond the Belvedere palace gates at No. 6a stands a Baroque mansion, while the forecourt at No. 8 has formed part of the Hoch-

schule für Musik since 1988. At No. 10, behind splendid wrought-iron gates, stands the Salesianerinnenkirche of 1717–30. The Baroque façade is flanked by monastic buildings in the same style. The upper storey has scrolled projections that serve as the base for statues. Like the Gardekirche, this church is domed, its design partly attributed to Joseph Emanuel Fischer von Erlach *(see p149)*. Apart from the pulpit, the interior is of little interest.

At No. 27, the present-day Italian Embassy is the palace where Prince Metternich *(see p30)* lived until he was forced to flee the city in 1848.

Palaces and Gardens of the Belvedere **10**

See pp152–57.

Botanical Gardens **11**

Rennweg 14. **Map** 4 F3. 🕻 4277 54190. 🚃 71. ◯ *Easter–mid-Oct: 9am–dusk daily; also open in winter (weather permitting).* 📷 ♿

THE MAIN ENTRANCE to the Botanical Gardens is on the corner of Prätoriusgasse and Mechelgasse. Other entrances

Detail of the façade of the Salesianerinnenkirche in Rennweg

are on Jacquingasse, and via a small gate at the rear of the Upper Belvedere which leads to the Alpine Garden and the Botanical Gardens. The latter contains more than 9,000 plant species. The Botanical Gardens were created in 1754 by Maria Theresa and her physician van Swieten for cultivating medicinal herbs. Expanded to their present shape in the 19th century, they remain a centre for the study of plant sciences as part of the University of Vienna's Institute of Botany. Of equal interest to amateurs, the gardens offer a quiet spot to sit and relax after sightseeing.

The Botanical Gardens created by Maria Theresa in 1754

Bestattungs-museum ⑫

Goldeggasse 19. **Map** 4 E4. 📞
501954227. Ⓤ Südtiroler Platz. 🕐
noon–3pm Mon–Fri (by appt only). 📷

IN VIENNA, DEATH and pomp have always been allied with one another, and even today the Viennese like to be buried in style. For the clearest insight into this fascinating feature of Viennese life, it's worth making a visit to this undertakers' museum.

One of the more eerie items, shown immediately after you enter, is the wrought-iron grille (1784) that formed the entrance to the Catholic cemetery at Matzleindorf. Its motif is of a crowned skeleton. You can see the various lanterns and staffs and liveries that were part of the pall-bearers' equipment from the 17th century onwards, as well as the special livery decked around the horses that pulled the hearse. In the 19th century, Viennese specialist couturiers provided widow's mourning attire complete with black handbag and black jewellery. Also in the 19th century a bell was often attached to a rope within the coffin, allowing the recently deceased, should he or she unexpectedly reawaken, to signal the alarm. This device became unnecessary if you requested in your will to be stabbed

in the heart before the coffin lid was nailed down, and the stiletto used for this practice is on display. Other displays show how corpses were dressed up and seated on a chair for one last photograph.

The custodian of the museum will also show you one of Joseph II's *(see p28)* more eccentric innovations from the late 18th century: the economy-model coffin with a trapdoor in the bottom which allowed the shrouded corpse to be dumped into the grave and the coffin to be reused. This story partly illustrates why the tireless reformer was not universally loved by his subjects. His attempts at reform were often perceived as doing more harm than good, or as unnecessary. The emperor was soon forced to abandon this unpopular idea.

Theresianum ⑬

Favoritenstrasse 15. **Map** 4 E3.
Ⓤ Taubstummengasse. ● to public.

THE ORIGINAL BUILDINGS of this former imperial summer palace date from the early 17th century, but were

Matzleindorf cemetery grille (1784) in the Bestattungsmuseum

essentially rebuilt after the Turkish siege of 1683 in a Baroque style by the architect and theatre designer Lodovico Burnacini (1636–1707) and others. Known at that time as the Favorita, it became a favourite residence of emperors Leopold I,

Façade of the Theresianum

Joseph I and Karl VI. In 1746 Maria Theresa, who had moved into Schönbrunn *(see pp172–75)*, her summer palace, handed it over to the Jesuits. They established a college here for the education of children from less well-off aristocratic families – the sons of these families were trained to be officials.

Today, the Theresianum is still a school and, since 1964, has also been a college for diplomats and civil servants. In the Theresianum park on Argentinierstrasse stands Radio House. It has a beautiful entrance hall, which was designed by Clemens Holz-meister in 1935.

Palaces and Gardens of the Belvedere ⑩

Statuary on a gate of Lower Belvedere

THE BELVEDERE WAS BUILT BY Johann Lukas von Hildebrandt as the summer residence of Prince Eugene of Savoy, the brilliant military commander whose strategies helped vanquish the Turks in 1683. Situated on a gently sloping hill, the Belvedere consists of two palaces linked by a formal garden laid out in the French style by Dominique Girard. The garden is sited on three levels, each conveying a complicated programme of Classical allusions: the lower part of the garden represents the domain of the Four Elements, the centre is Parnassus and the upper section is Olympus.

★ **Upper Cascade**
Water flows from the upper basin over five shallow steps into the pool below.

Putti on the Steps *(1852)*
Children and cherubs representing the 12 months adorn the steps to the left and right in the middle area of the gardens.

Lower cascade

Bosquet or hedge garden

JOHANN LUKAS VON HILDEBRANDT

Hildebrandt became the court architect in Vienna in 1700 and was one of J B Fischer von Erlach's greatest rivals. In addition to the Belvedere, he designed the Schönborn Palace *(see p110)*, the Kinsky Palace *(see p110)* and the Maria Treu Kirche *(see p116)*.

Statues of the Eight Muses

Lower Belvedere *(see pp156–7)*

Entrance to Lower Belvedere from Rennweg

Coloured etching of the Upper Belvedere and Gardens by Karl Schütz (1784)

Triumphal gate to Lower Belvedere

TIMELINE

1717–19 Dominique Girard landscapes the gardens	1765 Lower Belvedere becomes the barracks for the military guard	1897 Archduke Franz Ferdinand, heir to the throne, moves to the Upper Belvedere	1953 Museum of Medieval Austrian Art opens to the public
1720 Orangery built	1781–1891 Belvedere houses the Imperial Picture Gallery, which opens to the public		

	1750	1800	1850	1900	1950

1721–3 Upper Belvedere built	1752 Habsburgs acquire the Belvedere		1923–9 The Baroque Museum, the 19th-century Gallery and the 20th-century Gallery open to the public	1955 The Austrian State Treaty signed in the Marble Hall
1714–16 Lower Belvedere built	1779 Belvedere gardens open to the public		

Detail on Upper Cascade

★ **Main Gate of the Upper Belvedere**
The Baroque iron gate (1728) by Arnold and Konrad
Küffner, with an "S" for Savoy and the cross of Savoy,
leads to the south façade of the Upper Belvedere.

VISITORS' CHECKLIST

Map 4 F3. *Upper Belvedere*
see pp154–5. **Lower Belvedere**
and Orangery *see pp156–7.*
Gardens ⏱ 6:30am–dusk all
year round. 📷 ♿

★ **Upper Belvedere Façade**
The lively façade dominates
the sweeping entrance to the
palace (see pp154–5)*. The*
domed copper roofs of the
end pavilions resemble the
shape of Turkish tents – an
allusion to Prince Eugene's
victories over the Turks.

Entrance
to Upper
Belvedere
(see pp154–5)
and gardens
from Prinz-
Eugen-Strasse

Statues of Sphinxes
With their lion bodies
and human heads,
the imposing sphinx
statues represent
strength and
intelligence.

Orangery
(see p156)

Stables

Entrance to Orangery

STAR SIGHTS

★ **Upper Cascade**

★ **Main Gate of the**
 Upper Belvedere

★ **Upper Belvedere**
 Façade

Upper Belvedere

STANDING AT THE HIGHEST POINT of the garden, the Upper Belvedere has a more elaborate façade than the Lower Belvedere: it was intended to be a symbolic reflection of Prince Eugene's glory, and was appropriate for the festive occasions for which it was originally used. In addition to the impressive interiors of the Sala Terrena with its sweeping staircase, the chapel and the Marble Hall, the building now houses the collections of 19th- and 20th-century paintings belonging to the Austrian Gallery.

Viewing balcony for chapel

★ Chapel
The centrepiece of this brown, white and gold interior is an altarpiece, The Resurrection, *by Francesco Solimena (1723), set among statues of angels. Prince Eugene could enter the chapel from his apartments.*

Laughing Self-Portrait *(1908)*
This picture is by Richard Gerstl, the Viennese artist who was developing his own Expressionist style when he killed himself in his twenties.

GALLERY GUIDE
The ground floor houses temporary exhibitions. Art from the period around 1900 is on the first floor, along with late 19th-century art. Early 19th-century art is on the second floor, where there is also a Biedermeier collection.

KEY

☐	Neo-Classicism-Romanticism
☐	Biedermeier
☐	Early 20th-century art
☐	Historicism-Realism-Impressionism
☐	Temporary Exhibitions
☐	Non-exhibition space

Main entrance from gardens

★ Sala Terrena
Four Herculean figures by Lorenzo Mattielli support the ceiling vault of the Sala Terrena, while white stuccowork by Santino Bussi covers the walls and ceiling.

★ Gustav Klimt Collection
This marvellous Jugend-stil collection by Gustav Klimt is considered by some to be the Belvedere's highlight. In the work here, Judith I *(1901), Klimt depicts the Old Testament heroine as a Viennese* femme fatale.

VISITORS' CHECKLIST

Prinz-Eugen-Strasse 27, A-1030.
Map 4 F4. 79557. 13A to Prinz-Eugen-Strasse. Süd-bahnhof. 0, 18, D, 71. see p157. see p157. www.belvedere.at

The Tiger Lion *(1926)*
This savage beast from the 20th-century collection was painted by Oskar Kokoschka, a leading figure in Austrian Expressionism.

Second floor

Marble Hall

The Plain of Auvers *(1890)*
Van Gogh's airy landscape from the 20th-century collection captures the colours of summer fields in the south of France.

First floor

Stairs to

STAR SIGHTS

★ Chapel

★ Gustav Klimt Collection

★ Sala Terrena

Ground floor

Corpus Christi Morning *(1857)*
This bright genre scene is typical of the Austrian Biedermeier painter Ferdinand Georg Waldmüller.

Lower Belvedere and Orangery

T HE MUSEUM OF AUSTRIAN BAROQUE ART is housed in the elegant
rooms of the Lower Belvedere, which were used by Prince
Eugene for day-to-day living. Works of art by the
artists and sculptors who shaped the city during
Vienna's Golden Age (approximately 1683–1780)
are gathered together under its roof. There are
paintings by J M Rottmayr, Martino Altomonte,
Daniel Gran and Paul Troger amongst others,
and sculptures by Franz Xaver Messerschmidt and Georg Raphael Donner.

**Exit to
Orangery,
Museum of
Medieval Art
and stables**

**Prince
Eugene's
former
bedroom**

★ Hall of Mirrors
*A statue of Prince Eugene (1721) by Balthasar
Permoser stands in this room, whose walls
are covered with huge gilt-framed mirrors.*

**The Marble
Hall**

Hall of Grotesques
*The hall is decorated
with paintings of
grotesques inspired
by ancient Roman
frescoes of fantastical
creatures. They
were created by the
German painter
Jonas Drentwett.*

KEY

☐ Museum of Baroque Art

☐ Non-exhibition space

THE ORANGERY

Next door to the Lower Belvedere is the handsome
Orangery building, originally used to shelter tender
garden plants in winter. The Museum of Austrian
Medieval Art is housed here, and the gallery contains
masterpieces of Gothic and early Renaissance painting
and sculpture. Notable among the sculptures is the
Romanesque Stammerberg Crucifix from the end of the
12th century, which may be the oldest surviving
example of Tyrolean woodcarving. Seven painted
panels by Rueland Frueauf the Elder (1490–94) show
the Passion taking place in an Austrian setting.

The Orangery and gardens in winter

★ Ecce Homo *(1508)*
*Urban Görtschacher's composition
shows Pontius Pilate below the judgement hall, condemning Christ.*

St Jacob's Victory over the Saracens *(1764)*
Franz Anton Maulbertsch's painting portrays St Jacob's victory at the Battle of Clavigo.

Intentional Jester *(after 1770)*
Franz Xaver Messerschmidt's Character Heads (studies in physiognomy and temperament) are one of the museum's highlights. Their exaggerated expressions represent a departure from idealized portraiture.

GALLERY GUIDE
The Museum of Austrian Baroque Art displays large works of sculpture in the Marble Hall and the Hall of Grotesques, while smaller exhibits are on show in other rooms.

Christ on the Mount of Olives *(around 1750)*
Paul Troger's painting shows Christ deep in prayer on the Mount of Olives after the Last Supper. This detail depicts him being comforted by an angel.

Library

Main entrance

To gardens

STAR SIGHTS

★ **Hall of Mirrors**

★ **Figures from the Providentia Fountain by G R Donner**

★ **Ecce Homo by Urban Görtschacher**

★ **Figures from the Providentia Fountain** *(1739)*
The original lead figures that Georg Raphael Donner made for the Providentia Fountain in the Neuer Markt (see p105) are displayed in the Marble Hall. This central statue represents Providence.

FURTHER AFIELD

OR A CITY of over two million inhabitants, Vienna is suprisingly compact. Nonetheless, some of the most interesting sights are a fair distance from the city centre. At Schönbrunn sprawls the immense palace and gardens so loved by Maria Theresa,

Detail on riding school (1882–6) next to Hermes Villa

and the monastery at Klosterneuburg houses some of Austria's great ecclesiastical art treasures. Many parks and gardens, including the Prater, the Augarten and the Lainzer Tiergarten, all former private Habsburg domaines, are now open to the public.

SIGHTS AT A GLANCE

Historic Buildings
Amalienbad ⑯
Augarten Palace and Park ⑨
Favoriten Water Tower ⑮
Hundertwasser Haus ⑪
Kaiser Pavilion ⑳
Karl Marx Hof ⑦
Schönbrunn Palace and Gardens pp172–75 ⑲
Wagner Villas ①
Werkbundsiedlung ㉑

Churches and Monasteries
Kirche am Steinhof ②
Klosterneuburg ⑥
Wotruba Kirche ㉓

Museums and Galleries
Geymüller Schlössl ③
Heeresgeschichtliches Museum pp166–7 ⑬
Kriminalmuseum ⑩
Technical Museum ⑱

Parks and Gardens
Danube Park ⑧
Lainzer Tiergarten ㉒
Prater pp162–63 ⑫

Historic Districts
Grinzing ④
Kahlenberg ⑤

Monuments
Spinnerin am Kreuz ⑰

Cemeteries
Central Cemetery pp168–9 ⑭

25 kilometres = 15 miles

KEY

	Central Vienna
	Greater Vienna
🚆	Main line railway station
🚌	Coach and bus station
=	Motorway
····	Motorway tunnel
=	Major road
=	Minor road

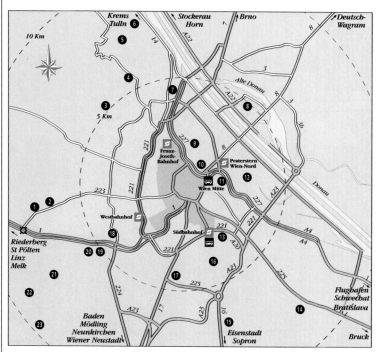

◁ **Part of the façade of the Hundertwasser Haus, built in 1985**

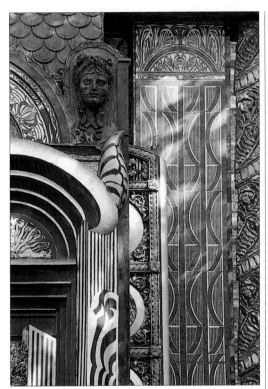

Detail of Ernst Fuchs' Brunnenhaus, next to Wagner Villas

Wagner Villas ❶

Hüttelbergstrasse 26, Penzing.
📞 9148575. Ⓤ Hütteldorf. 🚌 148, 152. ⏰ 10am–5pm Mon–Fri. 📷
📷 🅦 www.ernstfuchs-zentrum.com

THE VILLA Otto Wagner, designed by Wagner from 1886 to 1888 as his own residence, is stylistically midway between his earlier Ringstrasse architecture and the decorative elements of Jugendstil (see pp54–7). The house is built on a grand scale and incorporates classical elements such as Ionic columns, and seems more suitable for a north Italian hillside than for the more austere climate of Austria. The present owner, the painter Ernst Fuchs (see p36), has imposed his own personality on the villa, adding a fertility statue and garish colours.

The simpler villa next door was built more than 20 years later. Completed in 1913, the house is of steel and concrete rather than brick. It is very lightly decorated in a severe geometrical style with deep blue panels and nailhead ornament. The glass ornament is by Kolo Moser (see p57).

Kirche am Steinhof ❷

Baumgartner Höhe 1, Penzing.
📞 9106011201. 🚌 48A. ⏰ phone for opening times. 📷 📷

COMPLETED IN 1907, this astonishing church was Otto Wagner's (see pp54–7) last commission. It is set within the grounds of the Psychiatrisches Krankenhaus, a large mental hospital. The exterior is marble clad with nailhead ornament and has spindly screw-shaped pillars, topped by wreaths, supporting the porch. Four stone columns along the façade are adorned with angels by Othmar Schimkowitz (1864–1947). The statues at each corner of the façade are of St Leopold and St Severin to the left and right respectively. They were designed by Richard Luksch and are seated in chairs by Josef Hoffmann (see pp56–7).

The interior is a single space with shallow side chapels. The main decoration consists of gold and white friezes and square roof panels ornamented with gilt nailhead. Illumination is provided by daylight shining through lovely blue glass windows by Kolo Moser (see p57).

Geymüller Schlössl ❸

Khevenhüllerstrasse 2, Währing.
📞 711360. 🚌 41A. 🚃 41. ⏰ by phone appointment. 📷 📷

THE GEYMÜLLER SCHLÖSSL in Pötzleinsdorf, northwest of the city, is a temple to Biedermeier style (see pp30–31). Dating from 1808, the house was built for Johann Heinrich von Geymüller, a rich banker. Now a branch of the Austrian Museum of Applied Arts (see pp82–3), it has a collection of intricate Biedermeier and Empire furniture, such as an apparently simple desk that combines a writing desk with a water-colour cabinet. Gadgets abound: spittoons, still-lifes painted on porcelain, bowls, and 200 clocks dating from 1780 to about 1850, the heyday of Viennese clock manufacture.

Jugendstil angels by Othmar Schimkowitz adorning the façade of the Kirche am Steinhof

Grinzing ❹

🚇 *Heiligenstadt.*
🚌 *38A.* 🚋 *38.*

GRINZING IS THE most famous *Heuriger* village *(see pp188–9)*, but it is also the least authentic, as many of the inns here cater to very large groups of tourists. It is nonetheless very pretty.

It is divided into the Oberer Ort and Unterer Ort (upper and lower towns), the lower town being where you will find more authentic *Heurige* along such lanes as Sandgasse.

Grinzing was repeatedly destroyed by Turkish troops during the many sieges of Vienna *(see p26–7)*, and was again damaged by Napoleon's forces in 1809 *(see p30)*.

Kahlenberg ❺

🚌 *38A.*

KAHLENBERG, at 484 m (1,585 ft) *(see pp182–3)*, is the highest point of the Vienna Woods. It has a television mast at the top, as well as a church, an observation terrace and a restaurant. The views over the vineyards below and the city beyond are fabulous, with the Danube bridges to the left and the Vienna Woods to the right. The Kahlenberg played a crucial part in the city's history, in 1683 when the Polish king, Jan Sobieski, led his troops down from this spot to the rescue of Viennese forces who were fighting for the city.

Klosterneuburg ❻

Stift Klosterneuburg. 🎔 *022434110.*
🚌 *239, 340.* 🚈 *Franz-Josefs-Bahnhof to Klosterneuburg-Kierling.*
🕐 *May–Oct: 10am–noon 1:30–4:30pm Mon–Sat; Nov–Apr: 10am–noon 1:30–4:30pm Mon–Sat; all year: 10am–noon 1:30–4:30pm Sun & public hols.* 🎫 *daily.* 📷 📷

ABOVE THE DANUBE, 13 km (8 miles) north of Vienna, stands the vast monastery and fortress of Klosterneuburg.

The peach- and salmon-coloured façade of the Karl Marx Hof

Dating originally from the 12th century, it houses the astonishing Verduner Altar, completed in 1181 *(see p23)*. In the 18th century it was expanded by Karl VI, who intended to build a complex on the same grand scale as the Escorial palace near Madrid. The work was halted after his death in 1740.

Statue in Grinzing

Karl Marx Hof ❼

Heiligenstädterstrasse 82–92, Döbling. 🚇 *Heiligenstadt.* 🚋 *D.*
⛔ *to the public.*

THE KARL MARX HOF, dating from 1927 to 1930, is an immense council block which contains 1,382 flats. It is the most celebrated of the municipal housing developments built during the period of Red Vienna *(see p36)*, when 63,000 new dwellings went up across the city between 1919 and 1934. The architect of the Karl Marx Hof was Karl Ehn, a pupil of Otto Wagner *(see p54–7)*.

Danube Park ❽

🚇 *Alte Donau.* 🚌 *20B.* 🕐 *24 hrs daily. Danube Tower* 🎔 *26335720.*
🕐 *9:30am–midnight daily.* 📷 ♿

ADJOINING UNO-CITY *(see p37)*, the complex of United Nations agencies, is the Danube Park. Laid out in 1964, the park has cycle paths, cafés and other amenities. Rising 252 m (827 ft) above the park is the Danube Tower, with two revolving restaurants and an observation platform. The park and surrounding area have been redeveloped as the Danube City housing project, encompassing the Millennium Tower.

View of the Klosterneuburg monastery with its Baroque dome

Prater ⓬

ORIGINALLY AN IMPERIAL HUNTING GROUND, these woods and meadows between the Danube and its canal were opened to the public by Joseph II in 1766. The central avenue, or Hauptallee, was for a long time the preserve of the nobility and their footmen. During the 19th century the western end of the Prater became a massive funfair with booths, sideshows, beer gardens and *Wurst* stands catering for the Viennese workers.

The Miniature Railway
The Liliputbahn travels a 4-km (2½-mile) circuit.

To Praterstern station

Planetarium

Messegelände exhibition centre

Tennisplätze **(Tennis Courts)**

★ **Ferris Wheel**
The huge wheel circulates very slowly at a speed of about 75 cm (2½ ft) per second, allowing riders spectacular views over the park and funfair.

★ **Volksprater Funfair**
An amusement park has existed here since the last century. Today the enormous funfair is full of high-tech rides ranging from dodgem cars to ghost trains.

The Trotting Stadium
Built in 1913, the Krieau Stadium is the scene of exciting regional and international trotting races from September to June (see p231).

(see p231)

STAR SIGHTS
★ **Hauptallee**
★ **Volksprater Funfair**
★ **Ferris Wheel**

SPORTSPIELSPANNUNG

OKTOBER 1993

1.	2.
8.	10.
15.	16.
23	24.
30.	31.

TRABEN - KRIEAU

THE HISTORY OF THE FERRIS WHEEL

One of Vienna's most famous landmarks, the giant Ferris Wheel was immortalized in the film of Graham Greene's *The Third Man*. It was built in 1896 by the English engineer Walter Basset, but it has only half the original number of cabins as fire destroyed many of them in 1945.

VISITORS' CHECKLIST

🚇 🚊 🚆 *Prasterstern.* 🚌 74A.
🚋 *0, 5.* **Funfair** ⬜ *15 Mar–end Sep: 10am–11pm daily.* **Ferris Wheel** ☎ *7295430.* ⬜ *May–Sep: 9am–midnight daily; Oct & Mar–Apr: 10am–10pm daily; Jan–Feb & Nov–Dec: 10am–8pm daily.* ● *24 Dec.* **Planetarium** ⬜ *8pm Wed, 7pm Fri, 3pm, 5pm & 7pm Sat & Sun.* ● *9 Jan–18 Feb, 12 Nov–25 Dec, Aug.* **Miniature railway** ⬜ *15 Mar–mid Oct: 10am–11pm daily.* **Golf course** ⬜ *8am–4pm Mon–Thu.* **Stadionbad** ⬜ *29 Apr–16 Sept: 9am–7pm Mon–Fri, 8am–7pm Sat & Sun.* **Maria Grun Kirche** ⬜ *10am–3pm Sun.* **Lusthaus** ⬜ *noon–6pm Sat, Sun & public hols (Apr–Oct: also noon–11pm Mon–Tue & Thu–Fri).* 📷

0 metres 800

0 yards 800

Stadion (Stadium)

Stadionbad (Swimming pool)

★ Hauptallee
The avenue lined with chestnut trees stretches for 5 km (3 miles) through the centre of the Prater.

Cycle Paths

Maria Grun Kirche

Golfplatz (Golf course)

Lusthaus
The 18th-century octagonal pavilion is a former hunting lodge which now houses a restaurant.

Baroque façade of the Augarten Palace set amid 18th-century parkland

Augarten Palace and Park ❾

Obere Augartenstrasse 1. **Map** 2 E2. 5A. **Ⓤ** Praterstern. 🚋 31, 32. ◯ 6am–dusk daily. **Porcelain Museum** ◯ 9:30am–6pm Mon–Fri, 9:30am–noon Sat. **Ambrosi Museum** ◯ 10am–6pm Tue–Sun. 📷 ♿

THERE HAS BEEN a palace on this site since the days of Leopold I, when it was known as the Alte Favorita, but it was destroyed by the Turks in 1683 and then rebuilt around 1700 to a design attributed to Johann Bernhard Fischer von Erlach *(see p149)*. Since 1948 it has been the home of the Vienna Boys' Choir *(see p39)* and consequently it is inaccessible to the public.

The park was planted in the second half of the 17th century, renewed in 1712, and opened to the public in 1775 by Joseph II. The handsome gates by which the public now enters the gardens were designed by Isidor Canevale in 1775. Mozart, Beethoven, and Johann Strauss I all gave concerts in the park pavilion. The Augarten was also used for royal receptions and gatherings while the Congress of Vienna *(see p30)* was taking place in 1815. The pavilion used to be the imperial porcelain factory, founded in the 18th century, but has been run since the 1920s by the municipal authorities. Its showroom has displays showing the history of Augarten porcelain. Behind the pavilion is the studio of the early 20th-century sculptor Gustinus Ambrosi, open to the public as the Ambrosi Museum.

The Augarten has the oldest Baroque garden in Vienna, with topiary lining long paths shaded by walls of foliage. In the distance, you can see two of the huge and terrifying flakturms that the Viennese are unable to rid themselves of. Built by German forces in 1942 as defense towers and anti-aircraft batteries, these enormous concrete monoliths could house thousands of troops. So thick are their walls that any explosives powerful enough to destroy them would have a similar effect on the surrounding residential areas. There are four other such flakturms still standing in other parts of the city.

Kriminalmuseum ❿

Grosse Sperlgasse 24. **Map** 6 E1. 📞 2144678. **Ⓤ** Nestroyplatz. 5A. 🚋 N, 21. ◯ 10am–5pm Thu–Sun. 📷

SINCE 1991, this house of medieval origin has been the home of Vienna's museum of crime. Once known as the *Seifensiederhaus* (the soap

Hundertwasser Haus ⓫

Löwengasse/ Kegelgasse. **Ⓤ** Landstrasse. 🚋 Hetzgasse. 📷 to the public.

THE HUNDERTWASSER HAUS is a municipal apartment block created in 1985 by the artist Friedensreich Hundertwasser *(see p37)*, who wished to strike a blow against what he saw as soulless modern architecture. The resulting building, with its irregular bands of colour and onion dome cupolas, has been controversial since its construction. While it is loved by some, others think it is more like a stage set than a block of flats.

Apartments delineated by colour

Typically irregular window

Main entrance on Löwengasse

boiler's house), this museum's 20 rooms mostly chronicle violent crime, charting the murderous impulses of Vienna's citizenry from the Middle Ages to the 20th century, and the history of the judicial system.

Many of the exhibits come from the archives of the Viennese police force and are distinctly gruesome; there is a wide selection of murder weapons, mummified heads of executed criminals, death masks and case histories

Painting depicting a 1782 robbery

illustrated with photographs and prints. Many of the more unsettling exhibits give a notion of how the Viennese poor of earlier centuries were involved in crime. Political crimes, such as the lynching of a government minister during the revolution of 1848 (see p30), are also covered.

This interesting museum provides a blend of documentary social history and a chamber of horrors which portrays the darker side of Viennese life with gusto.

Prater ⑫

See pp162–63.

Heeresgeschicht-liches Museum ⑬

See pp166–7.

Central Cemetery ⑭

See pp168–9.

Favoriten Water Tower ⑮

Windtenstrasse 3, Favoriten.
☎ 5995931006. Ⓤ Reumannplatz.
🚊 15A. 🚎 65, 65A, 7A, 15A. ⬜ for guided tours (phone to arrange).

A COMPLEX KNOWN as the Favoriten pumping station was constructed in 1889 by Franz Borkowitz as part of a municipal scheme for the transportation of drinking water from the Alpine foothills to the rapidly-growing city. By 1910 the construction of other installations around Vienna meant that the operations of the complex had to be scaled down, and of the seven original buildings only the highly decorative yellow-and-red-brick

water tower remains. The fascinating feature of this incongruous-looking tower that soars 67 m (220 ft) into the sky is the original pumping equipment which is still in place. Its utilitarian appearance provides a stark contrast to the ornate turrets, pinnacles and tiles of the building's superstructure. In recent years the interior has been restored and guided tours are available to the public. Nearby is the small children's funfair, the Böhmische Prater (see p234).

Favoriten Water Tower

Corner of block with first-floor café and staircase topped by onion dome

Uneven ceramic line

Roof gardens planted with hundreds of trees and shrubs

Heeresgeschichtliches Museum ⓭

THIS IMPRESSIVE MUSEUM of army history is housed in a single block of the military complex known as the Arsenal. It was completed in fortress style in 1856. Theophil Hansen designed the museum itself *(see façade, right)*, which chronicles Austria's military prowess from the 16th century onwards. Exhibits relate to the Turkish siege of 1683, the French Revolution and the Napoleonic wars. Visitors should not miss seeing the car in which Archduke Franz Ferdinand was assassinated, or the modern armaments used in the war that the murder precipitated.

STAR SIGHTS

★ **Hall of the Commanders**

★ **Turkish Standard**

★ **To the Unknown Soldier by A E Lienz**

KEY

☐ Tank park

☐ 16th–19th centuries

☐ 19th and 20th centuries

☐ Non-exhibition space

Ground floor

Sea Power Austria

Republic and Dictatorship 1918–1945

Tank Park

Situated behind the museum are the armoured vehicles used in the Austrian army from 1955 as well as those that belonged to the German army that occupied Austria.

Main entrance from Ghegastrasse

THE ASSASSINATION OF FRANZ FERDINAND

On 28 June 1914 the heir to the throne, Archduke Franz Ferdinand, and his wife Sophie von Hohenberg paid a visit to Sarajevo. Gavrilo Princip, a Serbian nationalist, assassinated the couple, provoking an international crisis that later resulted in World War I. The museum houses the car in which the couple were killed.

MUSEUM GUIDE

The museum is housed on two floors. To view it in chronological order, begin on the first floor on the left, where exhibits relating to the Turkish siege are displayed. Other rooms chronicle the various 18th-century wars and Napoleon's victory over Austria. The 19th and 20th centuries, including heavy artillery used in World War I, are covered on the ground floor. There is also a tank park.

adetzky
848-1866

★ **Hall of the Commanders**
In the entrance hall, 56 life-size marble statues of supreme commanders of the army decorate the piers leading to the staircase.

First floor

VISITORS' CHECKLIST

Arsenal, Ghegastrasse Objekt 18, A-1030. 795610.
13A to Südbahnhof, 69A.
Südbahnhof. 18, O, D.
9am–5pm Mon–Thu, Sat & Sun. 1 Jan, Easter Sun, 1 May, 1 Nov, 24, 25 & 31 Dec.
W www.bmlu.gu.at/hgm

★ **Turkish Standard**
The central part of this banner contains the Islamic creed from the Koran: "There is no god but God, and Mohammed is his prophet." It was captured from the Turks before the siege of 1683 (see p26).

10-Pounder Mortar
This cannon is engraved with the two-headed imperial eagle and the monogram of Karl VI.

Memorabilia of Franz Ferdinand, including his uniform, portrait and the car in which he was assassinated, is exhibited here.

★ **To the Unknown Soldier** *(1916)*
The Tyrolean artist Albin Egger Lienz created a potent symbol of modern mass warfare in this painting.

Central Cemetery ⑭

Headstone of Brahms' grave

AUSTRIA'S LARGEST burial ground, containing two and a half million graves, was opened in 1874 on the city's southern outskirts. The central section includes graves of artists, composers, architects, writers and local politicians. Funerals are usually quite lavish affairs, as the Viennese like to be buried in style, with the pomp appropriate to their station in life. The cemetery contains a vast array of funerary monuments varying from the humble to the bombastic, paying tribute to the city's enduring obsession with death.

★ Dr-Karl-Lueger-Kirche
Max Hegele, a pupil of Otto Wagner, designed this church dedicated to Vienna's mayor in 1907–10.

Arcades around the Dr-Karl-Lueger-Kirche

Presidential Vault
This contains the remains of Dr Karl Renner, the first President of the Austrian Republic after World War II.

Fritz Wotruba's grave *(see p171)*

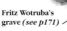

CEMETERY LAYOUT

The cemetery is divided into specific numbered sections: apart from the central garden of honour where VIPs are buried, there are old and new Jewish cemeteries; a Protestant cemetery; a Russian Orthodox section and various war graves and memorials. It is easier to take the circulating bus that covers the whole area than to walk.

The Monument to the Dead of World War I is a powerful depiction of a mother lamenting by Anton Hanak.

Old Jewish cemetery

Islamic area

Protestant area

New Jewish cemetery

Arnold Schönberg's Cube
The grave of the modernist Viennese composer Arnold Schönberg is marked with this bold cube by Fritz Wotruba.

STAR SIGHTS

★ Musicians' Graves

★ Dr-Karl-Lueger-Kirche

Theophil Hansen's Grave
The architect of Vienna's Parliament building (see p121) lies near other artists and architects. Hansen died in 1891.

Monument to Dr Johann Nepomuk Prix by Viktor Tilgner (1894).

VISITORS' CHECKLIST

Simmeringer Hauptstrasse 234,
2 Tor, A-1110. [📞] 760410.
[Ⓢ] Zentralfriedhof, Kledering.
[🚋] 71, 72. [🕐] Nov–Feb: 8am–
5pm daily; Mar, Apr, Sep, Oct:
7am–6pm daily; May–Aug:
7am–7pm daily. [📷] [♿]

The Arcades
Some spectacular monuments are to be found carved in the semi-circular arcades that face the main entrance, including this memorial to the miner August Zang. It shows the entrance to a mine and is dated 1848.

Main Entrance from Simmeringer Hauptstrasse

★ Musicians' Graves
Among the city's musicians buried in this area are Johann Strauss I and II (grave pictured left), Beethoven, Brahms and Schubert. There is a monument to Mozart, who was buried in St Marx cemetery.

Russian Orthodox Chapel
Built in traditional Russian Orthodox style and completed in 1894, this chapel is used by Vienna's Russian community.

Amalienbad 🔟

Reumannplatz 23, Favoriten.
📞 *6074747.* 🔟 *Reumannplatz.* 🚌
7A, 14A, 66A, 67A, 68A. 🚊 *6, 67.*
Swimming pool 🕐 *9am–6pm Tue,
9am–9:30pm Wed & Fri, 7am–9:30pm
Thu, 7am–8pm Sat, 7am–6pm Sun.*
Sauna 🕐 *1–9:30pm Tue, 9am–
9:30pm Wed–Fri, 7am–8pm Sat,
7am–6pm Sun.* 🅿

P**UBLIC BATHS** may not seem
like an obvious tourist
destination, but the Jugendstil
Amalienbad (1923–6) shows
how the municipal administration in the 1920s not only
provided essential public
facilities, but did so with
stylistic vigour and conviction.
The two designers, Otto
Nadel and Karl Schmalhofer,
were employees of the city's
architectural department.

The magnificent main pool
is covered by a glass roof that
can be opened in minutes and
is surrounded by galleries overlooking the pool. Elsewhere
in the building are saunas
and smaller baths and pools
used for therapeutic purposes.
When first opened, the baths
were one of the largest of
their kind in Europe, designed
to accommodate 1,300 people.
The interior is enlivened by
imaginative mosaic and tile
decoration, which is practical
as well as colourful. The
baths were damaged in World
War II but were impeccably
restored in 1986.

Spinnerin am Kreuz

Spinnerin am Kreuz 🔟

Triesterstrasse 10, Meidling.
🔟 *Meidling.* 🚌 *15A, 65A, 7A.* 🚊 *65.*

A **MEDIEVAL COLUMN** marks the
southernmost boundary
of Vienna's inner suburbs.
Built in 1452 and carved on
all sides, it stands on the spot
where, according to legend, a
woman sat spinning for years
awaiting her husband's return
from the Crusades. Known as
the Spinner at the Cross, it was
designed by Hans Puchsbaum.
Pinnacled canopies shelter
groups of statuary, including a
crucifixion and a grotesque
figure placing the crown of
thorns on the head of Christ.

Technical Museum 🔟

Mariahilfer Strasse 212, Penzing.
📞 *899986000.* 🕐 *9am–6pm
Mon–Fri, 10am–6pm Sat, Sun & public
hols.* 📷 🅿 🆆 *www.tmw.ac.at*

F**RANZ JOSEPH** founded the
Technisches Museum Wien
in 1908, using the Habsburgs'
personal collections as core
material; it opened its doors
10 years later. It documents all
aspects of technical progress,
from domestic appliances to
large turbines, and includes
exhibitions on heavy industry,
energy, physics and musical
instruments.

A major new section of the
museum opened in June
1999, featuring displays on
computer technology and oil
and gas drilling and refining,
as well as a reconstruction of
a coal mine.

The Railway Museum forms
an integral part of the
Technical Museum. It houses
an extensive collection of
imperial railway carriages
and engines. One of the prize
exhibits is the imperial
carriage that was used by
Franz Joseph's wife, the
Empress Elisabeth.

Schönbrunn Palace and Gardens 🔟

See pp172–75.

Decorative, geometrically-patterned tiling from the 1920s in the Amalienbad

Kaiser Pavilion ⑳

Schönbrunner Schlosstrasse 13, Hietzing.
🕿 8771571. ⓤ *Hietzing.* 🚌 *51A,
56B, 58B, 156B.* Ⓢ *Westbahnhof to
Penzing.* 🚊 *10, 60, 62.*
⭕ *1:30–4:30pm Tue–Sun.* 📷

OTTO WAGNER *(see p57)*
designed and built this
railway station between
Schönbrunn and Hietzing for
the imperial family and royal
guests in 1899. A lovely
building in the shape of a
white cube with green ironwork and a copper dome, it
has a waiting room panelled
with wood and glass, with a
peach and russet asymmetrical
carpet, and a stylish marble
and brass fireplace. The
cupola is decorated with glass
and gilt flower and leaf motifs.
  Wagner built the pavilion
without a commission from
the emperor in an attempt
to showcase his work.
Unfortunately, Franz Joseph
used the station only twice.

The Jugendstil Kaiser Pavilion

Werkbund-siedlung ㉑

Jagdschlossgasse, Veitingergasse and
Woinovichgasse, Hietzing. 🚌 *54B,
55B.* 🚊 *60.*

IN THE 13TH DISTRICT you can
find the 30 or so fascinating
"model" houses of the
Werkbundsiedlung (housing
estate) built in the early 1930s
for the municipality by some
of Europe's leading architects.
They are neither beautiful nor
lavish, since the idea was to
produce a formula for cheap
housing, with two bedrooms,

Hermes Villa in the grounds of the Lainzer Tiergarten

that was plain and functional.
No. 19 Woinovichgasse is by
Adolf Loos *(see p92)*, and
Nos. 83–5 Veitingergasse are
by Josef Hoffmann *(see p56)*.
Each architect had to design
a single building, placed side
by side with the rest in order
to evaluate the different
qualities of each. Although
intended to be temporary,
they have luckily survived.

Lainzer Tiergarten ㉒

Lainzer Tiergarten, Hietzing. **Tiergarten**
🕿 8041315. 🚌 *60A.* ⭕ *mid-Feb–
mid-Nov: 8am–dusk daily.* 📷 **Hermes
Villa and Garden** 🕿 *8041324.*
⭕ *for exhibitions 10am–6pm
(Apr–Sep), 9am–4:30pm (Oct–Mar)
Tue–Sun & public hols.* 📷

THE LAINZER TIERGARTEN is a
former Habsburg hunting
ground which has been
converted into an immense
nature reserve in the Vienna
Woods *(see p176)*. The Tiergarten was opened to the
public in 1923 and is still
encircled by its 24-km (15-
mile) stone wall, protecting
its herds of deer and wild
boar. From the entrance, a
15-minute walk
along paths
through woods
and meadows
brings you to the
Hermes Villa,
built by Karl von
Hasenauer in
1884. It became a
retreat for the
imperial family,
notably the
Empress

Elisabeth and her husband
Franz Joseph, who had a suite
of rooms on the first floor.
Inside are murals of scenes
from *A Midsummer Night's
Dream*, as well as art and
historical exhibitions.

Wotruba Kirche ㉓

Georgsgasse/Rysergasse, Mauer.
🕿 8886147. 🚌 *60A.* ⭕ *Mar–Oct:
2pm–4pm Thu & Fri, 2pm–8pm Sat,
9am–5pm Sun or* 🕿 *888 5003 for
appointment to see the church.* 📷

BUILT BETWEEN 1965 and 1976
in uncompromisingly
modern style, this church
stands on a hillside very close
to the Vienna Woods. It forms
a pile of uneven rectangular
concrete slabs and glass panels,
some of the latter rising to the
height of the church. They
provide its principal lighting
and views for the congregation
out on to the woods and hills.
The building is raw in style,
but powerful and compact.
Designed by the sculptor Fritz
Wotruba (1907–75), the church
looks different from every
angle and has a strong sculptural quality. It accommodates
a congregation of up to 250.

**The exterior of the Wotruba Kirche by Fritz
Wotruba, not unlike a modern sculpture**

Schönbrunn Palace and Gardens ⑲

THE FORMER SUMMER RESIDENCE of the imperial family takes its name from a beautiful spring that was found on this site. An earlier hunting lodge was destroyed by the Turks, so Leopold I asked Johann Bernhard Fischer von Erlach to design a grand Baroque residence here in 1695. However, it was not until Maria Theresa employed Nikolaus Pacassi that the project was completed in the mid-18th century. The strict symmetry of the architecture is complemented by the gardens with fountains and statues framed by trees and alleyways.

Public swimming pool

Obelisk Cascade

Orangery

Maze
The maze was a favourite element of many European stately gardens. This one at Schönbrunn provides a puzzling detour for visitors.

STAR SIGHTS

★ **Gloriette**

★ **Palm House**

★ **Coach Museum**

Main entrance

Theatre

★ **Coach Museum**
The former Winter Riding School houses the coaches, sleighs and sedan chairs that were used to transport the imperial family.

TIMELINE

1683 First hunting lodge on site destroyed during the Turkish siege	**1705** Jean Trehet lays out the gardens **1730** Palace is completed **1744−9** Nikolaus Pacassi adapts the building for Maria Theresa		**1916** Emperor Franz Joseph dies here, aged 86		**1918** Emperor Karl I abdicates Austrian throne in the Blue Chinese Salon *(p174)*

1650	1700	1750	1800	1850	1900	1950

1696 Leopold I commissions J B Fischer von Erlach to design a new palace *Emperor Leopold I*		**1805 and 1809** Napoleon uses palace as headquarters **1775** Gloriette is built **1752** Maria Theresa's husband, Franz Stephan, founds a menagerie, now the zoo	**1952** Reconstruction is completed after war damage **1882** Palm House is built	

★ Gloriette
This Neo-Classical arcade, designed by Ferdinand von Hohenberg and built in 1775, is the crowning glory of the hill behind the palace.

VISITORS' CHECKLIST

Schönbrunner Schloss Strasse 47, A-1130. ☎ 81113239. Ⓤ Schön-brunn. 🚌 10A. 🚋 10, 58. **Palace** ☐ Apr–Jun: 8:30am–5pm; Jul–Aug: 8:30–7; Sep–Oct: 8:30–5; Nov–Mar: 8:30–4:30 daily. 🎭 ⏚ ♿🖊🎁❚❚☐🎁🎵 **Gardens** ☐ 6am– sunset daily. **Coach Museum** ☐ Apr–Oct: 9am–6pm daily; Nov– Mar: 10am–4pm Tue–Sun. ● public hols. **Zoo** ☎ 877 9294. ☐ daily (times vary). 🅆 www.schoenbrunn.at

Neptune Fountain
This exuberant fountain and basin, at the foot of the hill, was sculpted in 1780 by Franz Anton Zauner.

Schönbrunn Zoo
Founded in 1752 at the order of Franz Stephan, the historic zoo has an octagonal pavilion.

Japanese Gardens

★ Palm House
A vast collection of exotic plants flourishes in the magnificent tropical green-house that was erected in 1882.

Hielzing Gate

Façade of Schönbrunn Palace seen from the gardens

Inside Schönbrunn Palace

THE ROCOCO DECORATIVE SCHEMES devised by Nikolaus Pacassi dominate the Schönbrunn state rooms, where white panelling, often adorned with gilded ornamental framework, tends to prevail. The rooms vary from extremely sumptuous – such as the Millionen-Zimmer, panelled with fig wood inlaid with Persian miniatures – to the quite plain apartments occupied by Franz Joseph and Empress Elisabeth.

★ Round Chinese Cabinet
Maria Theresa used this room for private discussions with her State Chancellor. The walls are adorned with lacquered panels and vases.

★ Great Gallery
Once the venue for imperial banquets, the gallery was used for state receptions as recently as 1994.

Hidden staircase
which leads to the apartment of the State Chancellor on the floor above and was used for access to secret conferences.

Blue Chinese Salon
The room where Karl I abdicated in 1918 has hand-painted wallpaper with blue insets showing Chinese scenes.

Napoleon Room

Millionen-Zimmer

Memorial Room

First Floor

★ Vieux-Lacque Room
During her widowhood, Maria Theresa lived in this room, which is decorated with exquisite oriental lacquered panels.

Main entrance

Large Rosa Room
Landscape scenes of Switzerland and northern Italy by Joseph Rosa give this room its name. The paintings are surrounded by Rococo gilded panels.

Breakfast Room
The imperial family's breakfast room has white wood panelling inlaid with appliqué floral designs worked by Maria Theresa and her daughters.

STAR SIGHTS

★ **Round Chinese Cabinet**

★ **Great Gallery**

★ **Vieux-Lacque Room**

The Blue Staircase (so called due to its original decorative scheme) leads to the entrance for guided tours of state rooms.

ROOM GUIDE
The state rooms open to the public are on the first floor. The suite of rooms to the right of the Blue Staircase were occupied by Franz Joseph and Elisabeth. Two galleries divide these from rooms in the east wing, which include Maria Theresa's bedroom and rooms used by Grand Duke Karl. Two guided tours, the Imperial and the Grand Tour, cover several rooms.

KEY

☐ Franz Joseph's apartments

☐ Empress Elisabeth's apartments

☐ Ceremonial and reception rooms

☐ Maria Theresa's rooms

☐ Grand Duke Karl's rooms

☐ Non-exhibition space

Portrait of Napoleon

Portrait of Maria Louisa

MARIA LOUISA AND THE KING OF ROME

After Napoleon's fall from power, his young son by his Austrian wife Maria Louisa was kept a virtual prisoner in Schönbrunn Palace. In 1832 at the age of 21, after a lonely childhood, he died of consumption in what is known as the Napoleon Room. He was called the Duke of Reichstadt, or the King of Rome, and the Memorial Room contains his portrait as a five-year-old and his effigy. There is also a crested larch under a glass dome; the unhappy boy claimed that he never had a single friend in the palace apart from this bird.

Day Trips from Vienna

WITHIN AN HOUR OR TWO'S JOURNEY from Vienna there is an astonishing range of countryside from Hungarian-style plains to alpine mountains, majestic rivers and idyllic lakes. Vienna is at the centre of Austria's wine-growing country and is surrounded by historic castles and churches, among which nestle picturesque wine-producing towns and villages. All the sights are accessible by bus or train and trips such as Baden and Gumpoldskirchen can easily be combined.

Mayerling and the Vienna Woods ❶

Vienna Sightseeing organizes trips (see p238). 🚌 *365 from Südtiroler Platz to Mayerling and Heiligenkreuz, or 265 to Heiligenkreuz.* **Mayerling Chapel** 🚍 *02258 2275.* ⬜ *1 Apr–1 Oct: 9am–12:30pm, 1:30–6pm Mon–Sat, 10am–12:30pm, 1:30–6pm Sun & public hols; 2 Oct–31 Mar: 9am–12:30pm, 1:30–5pm Mon–Sat, 10am–12:30pm, 1:30–5pm Sun & public hols. Ring bell for attention.* ⬛ *1 Jan, Good Friday, 25 Dec.* **Heiligenkreuz Abbey** 🚍 *02258 8703131. Phone to check opening hours.* 🖐 *obligatory.*

WHERE THE LOWER slopes of the Alps meet the Danube and Vienna Woods there are several interesting sights.

The Mayerling hunting lodge, now the chapel, was the scene in 1889 of the double suicide of Crown Prince Rudolf *(see p32)*, heir to the Austro-Hungarian throne, and his 17-year-old lover Mary Vetsera, daughter of the diplomat Baron Albin Vetsera. Their tragic deaths shook the entire Austro-Hungarian empire and were the subject of the Viennese musical *Elisabeth* by the Hungarian Sylvester Levay. After his son's death, the distraught Emperor Franz Joseph gave the hunting lodge to a Carmelite convent and it was completely rebuilt. Some of Crown Prince Rudolf's furniture remains in the chapel.

A few miles north of Mayerling is the medieval Cistercian abbey of Heiligenkreuz. Much of the abbey was rebuilt in the Baroque period, having been largely destroyed during attacks by the Turks in 1529 and 1683. Inside is a 12th-century nave and a 13th-century chapter house (with Baroque wall paintings). Fine Baroque features include the bell

tower and Trinity Column. The abbey houses the tombs of 13 of the Babenbergs who ruled in Austria during the medieval period *(see pp22–3).*

Baden ❷

🚌 *552, 360W or 1134 (Mariazell) from Wien Mitte.* 🚈 *or* 🚊 *from Südbahnhof.* 🚃 *Badner Bahn (WLB) from Karlsplatz/Oper.* 🚍 *02252 22600600.*

TO THE SOUTH of Vienna are several spas and wine-growing towns in the hills of the southern Vienna Woods. The most famous is Baden, a spa with curative hot springs dating back to Roman times. As well as bathing in sulphurous water and mud to treat rheumatism, you can enjoy hot pools of 36°C (97°F).

In the early 19th century Baden was popular with the Imperial Court of Vienna. Then many elegant Biedermeier

Gumpoldskirchen wine festival

villas, baths, town houses and a square were built, and the gardens of the Kurpark laid out. The park extends from the town centre to the Vienna Woods and has a rose garden and a memorial museum to Beethoven and Mozart. Today you can sample local wines in Baden's restaurants.

SIGHTS AT A GLANCE

Day Trips
Mayerling and the Vienna Woods ❶
Baden ❷
Gumpoldskirchen ❸
Eisenstadt ❹
Rust and Lake Neusiedl ❺
Mariazell ❻
River Trip from Krems to Melk ❼

KEY

⬜ City centre

⬜ Greater Vienna

✈ Airport

▬ Motorway

▬ Major road

═ Minor road

25 kilometres = 15 miles

Gumpoldskirchen ❸

🚈 *or* 🚊 *from Südbahnhof or Baden.* 🚍 *02252 63536.*

TYPICAL WHITE WINES are available from this pretty medieval village, where many 16th-century houses are still in use as *Heurige* (wine taverns). Twice a year, in late June and at the end of August, the main streets are converted into one enormous *Heuriger* for the famous Gumpoldskirchen wine festivals. There are also magnificent walks among the surrounding vineyards.

Eisenstadt ❹

🚌 *566 or 766 from Wien Mitte to Eisenstadt Domplatz.* 🚈 *from Südbahnhof; change at Bruck an der Leitha.* 🚍 *02682 63384.* **Schloss Esterházy** 🚍 *02682 7193000.* ⬜ *Apr–Oct: 9am–5pm daily; Nov–Mar* ⬜ *only.* 9am–5pm Mon–Fri. **Haydn Museum** 🚍 *02682 7193900.* ⬜ *Apr–Oct: 9am–5pm daily; Nov–Mar: by appt only.* **Jewish Museum** 🚍 *02682 65145.* ⬜ *May–Oct: 10am–5pm Tue–Sun; Nov–Apr: by appt only.*

TO THE SOUTHEAST of Vienna lies Burgenland, Austria's easternmost province and part of Hungary until 1918. Here

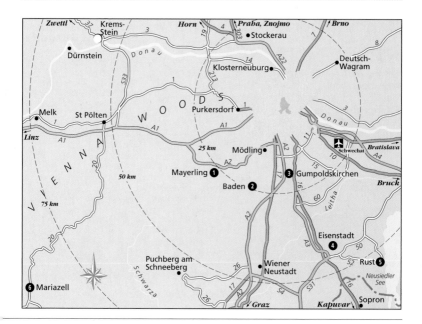

you can see the imposing residence of the Esterházy Princes, who claimed to be descended from Attila. Schloss Esterházy was built for Prince Paul Esterházy in 1663–73 and contains the Haydnsaal, a great hall of state decorated with 18th-century frescoes. Joseph Haydn (see pp38–9) conducted the prince's orchestra here and lived nearby on Haydngasse; his house is now a museum. He is buried in the Bergkirche, west of Schloss Esterházy.

Until World War II, Eisenstadt had a significant Jewish population, and there is a Jewish Museum near the palace.

Rust and Lake Neusiedl 5

566 or 766 from Eisenstadt; 666 from Wien Mitte. 02685 502.

TEN MILES (15 km) east of Eisenstadt lies the 320 sq km (124 sq mile) Lake Neusiedl, part of which is in Hungary. The lake is surrounded by reeds, the home of dozens of species of wild birds. The reeds are used locally for folk crafts from thatching to basketwork. Around the lake are several wine villages and resorts, of which the prettiest is the town of Rust. It is known for the storks which nest on its roofs and towers, and for its wine.

Mariazell 6

552 via Baden or 1150 from Wien Mitte. from Westbahnhof, change at St Pölten to Mariazell alpine railway. 03882 2366. **Basilica** 6am–8pm daily. 0388 22595 for tours. **Steam tram** 0388 23014. Jul–Sep: 10:30am–4:30pm Sat, Sun & hols.

THE JOURNEY to Mariazell from St Pölten is by the Mariazell alpine railway. The town has been Central Europe's main Catholic pilgrim site and a Gothic and Baroque basilica, enlarged in the 17th century, testifies to its religious significance. Inside is a wealth of Baroque stucco, painting and decoration. The treasury also forms part of the church.

A cable car up the mountain leaves every 20 minutes from the town centre. The world's oldest steam tram, built in 1884, runs between Mariazell railway station and a nearby lake.

River Trip from Krems to Melk 7

See pp178–9.

View of Mariazell, where a virgin cult began in 1377

River Trip from Krems to Melk ❼

Some 80 km (50 miles) west of Vienna is one of the most magnificent stretches of river scenery in Europe. Castles, churches and wine-producing villages rise up on either side of the Danube valley and breathtaking views unfold. Redolent with history (it has been settled for over 30,000 years), this stretch from Krems to Melk is called the Wachau. A river trip is the best way to take in the landmarks, either with one of the tours organized by Cityrama, Vienna Line, Vienna Sightseeing or DDSG Shipping *(see p238)*, or independently *(see box)*.

The perfectly-preserved medieval town of Dürnstein ④

Krems to Dürnstein
The beautiful Renaissance town of Stein has in modern times merged into one with Krems, which has a medieval centre ①. At the end of Steinerstrasse is the house of the Baroque artist Kremser Schmidt. Climb one of the narrow hillside streets and look across the Danube for a fine view of Göttweig Abbey ②, an excellent example of Austrian Baroque, and in the 17th century a centre of the Counter-Reformation. You can also see the small town of Mautern ③, which

developed from a 1st-century Roman fortification, and now boasts the gourmet restaurant Bacher in Südtirolerplatz.

Once on board, after about 8 km (5 miles) you will pass the perfectly-preserved medieval town of Dürnstein ④, with a Baroque church overlooked by the ruins of a castle. From 1192 to 1193, after his return from the Third Crusade, England's King Richard the Lionheart was held prisoner in the castle by Duke Leopold V of Babenberg *(see p23)*. He was released only on payment of a huge ransom. Dürnstein has conserved much of its medieval and Baroque character and has splendid river views and side streets leading to charming river walks. A separate visit is advisable if you want to see the town at leisure.

Wine-producing towns from Rossatz to Wösendorf
On the opposite bank to Dürnstein lies Rossatz ⑤, which has been making wine for centuries and was once a busy port. Findings of Neolithic and Roman remains testify to early settlement. In the 10th century it belonged to a Bavarian convent, but passed to the Babenbergs and became part of their

Vineyards at Weissenkirchen ⑥

Das Rote Tor ⑫

1,000-Eimer Berg

Venus of Willendorf

Schönbühel Castle

0 km   **5**

0 miles   **3**

KEY

🚢	River boat boarding point
🚉	Railway station
—	Railway line
〰	River
▭	Major road
▭	Minor road

The church at Weissenkirchen which was fortified to hold off the Turks ⑦

Austrian domain. The Renaissance castle and Gothic church were transformed to Baroque around 1700.

At Weissenkirchen ⑥ the church dates mainly from the 15th and 16th centuries. The town is also renowned for its wine, as are Joching ⑦ and Wösendorf ⑧.

Göttweig Abbey

Churches and ruins

Clearly visible on top of a hill, the fortified Church of St Michael ⑨ was built between 1500 and 1523. An unusual architectural detail is the stone hares on its tower. Local folk-lore tells how, once, so much snow fell here that hares were able to leap onto the roof.

On the same side of the river is a ruined arch on a hill, Das Rote Tor ⑩, a fragment of a 14th-century gate through which the Swedes walked on their way to Spitz in 1645 during the 30 Years War (*see p25*). The town of Mitterarns-dorf ⑪ has Roman remains.

Spitz to Aggsbachdorf

Spitz ⑫ is another pretty wine town and was also a Protestant stronghold during the Reformation. It lies at the foot of the 1,000-Eimer Berg (1,000-Bucket Mountain), so called because it is claimed that in a good year the vine-clad hills can produce enough wine to fill 1,000 buckets.

Further on is a wall-like rocky precipice jutting out from the bank, the Teufelsmauer or Devil's Wall ⑬. It has given rise to a number of legends. One tells how the devil's grandmother wanted to stop pilgrims and crusaders by creating a dam. At Schwallenbach ⑭ the church was rebuilt after the Bohemians dev-astated the village in 1463. Although you cannot see it from the boat, you will pass very close to the village of Willendorf ⑮, famous for the prehistoric findings made nearby, including the statue and fertility symbol Venus of Willendorf (*see pp20 and 128*).

Aggstein ⑯ has a ruined castle high above the river. Georg Scheck von Wald, follower of Duke Albrecht I, rebuilt and enlarged the original castle in 1429. Legend has it that he called a rock, placed at the highest point of the castle, his rose garden. He would force his imprisoned enemies to leap to their deaths if the ransom he demanded failed to arrive. Aggsbachdorf ⑰ was settled by the Romans in the 2nd century and owned by the Kuenringer robber-barons during the Middle Ages.

Schönbühel Castle to Melk

The picturesque castle of Schönbühel ⑱ stands on a rocky outcrop overlooking the Danube. Although it has been on record since the 9th century, its present form dates from the early 19th century. Further

The ruined castle above the river at Aggstein ⑯

The Benedictine abbey of Melk dominates the river and town ⑳

on, at the mouth of the 70-km long (43-mile) River Pielach ⑲, 30 Bronze Age tombs and the foundations of a Roman tower have been excavated.

The high point of the trip is the Benedictine abbey of Melk ⑳. The pretty town has Renaissance houses, romantic little streets, old towers and remnants of a city wall built in the Middle Ages. The Baroque abbey, where Umberto Eco's novel *The Name of the Rose* begins and ends, is a treasure trove of paintings, sculptures and decorative art. The great library contains 2,000 volumes from the 9th to the 15th centuries alone. The church has a magnificent organ, and skeletons dressed in luxurious materials inside glass coffins. Some of the Abbey's treasures are not on permanent view.

TIPS FOR INDEPENDENT TRAVELLERS

Starting points: Krems, Dürnstein, Melk or any river trip boarding point if you have a car. River trip tickets are on sale at these points.
Getting there: Take the national network train from Franz-Josefs-Bahnhof to Krems or Dürnstein. For Melk, depart from Westbahnhof.
Stopping-off points: Dürnstein has a variety of Heurige, restaurants, cafés and shops. Melk Abbey has a restaurant. **Melk Abbey** ■ 02752 5550. ◻ Palm Sunday–1st Sun after All Souls: 9am–5pm (May–Sep: 9am–6pm). ▨ 11am & 2pm throughout year.
Cycling: A cycle path runs along the Danube. Bikes for hire at Krems, Melk, Spitz and Dürnstein train stations (reduction with train ticket), or from river trip boarding points. Take your passport for identification. ▥ www.stiftmelk.at

FOUR GUIDED WALKS

VIENNA IS a comparatively small city, with several main attractions within easy walking distance of each other. All six sightseeing areas in this guide have a suggested short walk marked on a Street-by-Street map. Yet the city's suburbs are also worth exploring on foot. The following guided walks take you through some of the best walking areas in and around the city, all easily accessible by public transport. The first walk takes you through the town itself. Starting in the Stadtpark, it continues past the Karlskirche to the elegant Wagner Apartments and the colourful Naschmarkt on the Linke Wienzeile. The bus journey to the start of our second walk at Kahlenberg

Makart statue *(p182)*

is in itself a pleasure. The bus runs along the scenic Höhenstrasse and through the Vienna Woods. Below Kahlenberg, Nussdorf and Grinzing are a far cry from the imperial splendours of the city centre, and have kept their identities as ancient wine villages. The fourth walk takes you to Grinzing via Heiligenstadt, where there are a number of buildings by well-known 20th-century architects. Hietzing, near Schönbrunn, with its quiet streets lined with Biedermeier and Jugendstil villas, is our third walk. There are also signposted routes through the Vienna Woods and the Prater, marked *Stadtwanderwege.* For details of these walks, phone or write to the Wiener Fremdenverkehrsamt *(see p238).*

A Three-Hour Walk from Kahlenberg to Nussdorf *(see pp184–5)*

A Two-Hour Walk to Grinzing *(see pp188–9)*

The Fillgrader Steps on the City Walk

Heiligenstädter Park, on the way to Grinzing

A 90-Minute Walk Around Hietzing *(see pp186–7)*

A Two-Hour City Walk *(see pp182–3)*

KEY

··· Walk route

0 kilometres   2

0 miles   1

◁ **The winding Kahlenberger Strasse pathway** *(see p184)*

A Two-Hour City Walk

T HIS WALK SKIRTS the southwestern perimeter of the inner city, following part of the course of the River Wien. It begins with a leisurely stroll through the Stadt-park, which was laid out in English landscape style when the Ringstrasse was built *(see p32)*. Continuing past Schwarzenbergplatz and Karlsplatz through the lively Naschmarkt, it ends with a glance at some masterpieces of Jugendstil architecture on the Linke Wienzeile.

Jugendstil portal in the Stadtpark, built in 1903–4 as part of the flood defences along the river ⑪

The Stadtpark

Begin at the entrance to the Stadtpark opposite Weihburg-gasse. Almost facing you is an impressive side entrance ① with sculpted portals which was designed between 1857 and 1862.

On the city side, the park contains many monuments to musicians and artists. The first is the gilded statue of Johann Strauss II *(see p39)* playing his violin (1921) ②. Go left past this mon-ument, and left again, into a paved circular seating area with a fountain dedicated to the Sprite of the Danube ③. Turn right out of this area and you come to an iron bridge across the River Wien, from the middle of which you get a view of the embankments ④.

Walk back to the nearby lake ⑤. On its southern side a statue of the Viennese land-scape painter Emil Jakob Schindler (1895) ⑥ sits in the bushes. Follow the path until

No. 38 Linke Wienzeile ㉑

it peters out into a culvert then go left across the bridge. Turn left again until you come to a monument to Franz Schubert (1872) by Karl Kundmann ⑦. Take the path past the lake and turn right at the clock-tower. The painter Hans Makart, who dominated the visual arts in Vienna in the 1870s and 1880s, strikes a rhetorical pose in Viktor Tilgner's 1898 statue ⑧. Walk on past the entrance to the park. On the right is the

bust of Franz Lehár, composer of *The Merry Widow* ⑨. Walk towards the Kursalon ⑩, which opened for concerts, balls and waltzes in the 1860s. Continue past the Kursalon, leaving the park through one of the Jugendstil portals *(see p57)* ⑪.

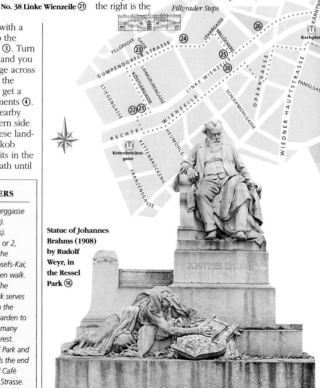

Fillgrader Steps

Statue of Johannes Brahms (1908) by Rudolf Weyr, in the Ressel Park ⑯

Schwarzenbergplatz

Walk straight ahead, crossing the road into Lothringerstrasse. A monument to Beethoven (1880), showing him surrounded by figures alluding to the Ninth Symphony, stands on the right ⑫. Cross the road to the Konzerthaus (1912–13), home to the Vienna Symphony Orchestra (see p228) ⑬.

Cross the busy intersection to get a striking vista of Schwarzenbergplatz to your left, at the end of which is a fountain. It was erected in 1873 to celebrate the city's supply of pure drinking water which comes from the mountains. Behind it is the Memorial to the Red Army which liberated Austria in 1945 ⑭.

The Neo-Renaissance Kursalon ⑩

market and cross the road to look at Otto Wagner's Apartments (see p139) with golden medallions by Kolo Moser at No. 38 ㉑, and the Majolikahaus at No. 40, so called because of its floral tiles ㉒. As you turn into Köstlergasse alongside No. 38 it is worth pausing to admire the entrance.

Confession box, Karlskirche ⑰

KEY

••• Walk route

🔆 Good viewing point

Ⓤ U-Bahn station

Ressel Park

Continue along Lothringerstrasse, pass the Historical Museum of the City of Vienna (see p146) ⑮, into Ressel Park. On the left is a statue of Brahms with his muse at his feet (1908) by Rudolf Weyr ⑯. Look left past Brahms to the Karlskirche (see pp148–9) ⑰. Go on, noting Otto Wagner's pavilions (see p146) at road level ⑱. Pass the Neo-Classical Technical High School ⑲ to leave the park. Cross Wiedner Hauptstrasse, go straight ahead then left into Operngasse, crossing the road. Walk through Bärenmühlendurchgang passage in the building facing you and cross the road into the Naschmarkt ⑳.

Naschmarkt

A lively food market (see p138), originally held in the Karlsplatz, moved here after this part of the river was paved over in the late 19th century. It is a good vantage point from which to admire the elegant 19th-century buildings along the left bank, or Linke Wienzeile. Leave the

Papageno Gate of the Theater an der Wien ㉕

Gumpendorfer Strasse

Turn right at the end of Köstlergasse and walk up Gumpendorfer Strasse. Look left up Fillgradergasse for a glimpse of the Fillgrader Steps ㉓. Continue on to the historic Café Sperl (see p58), once the haunt of the composer Lehár ㉔. Go on and turn right into Millöckergasse to see the famous Papageno Gate of the Theater an der Wien (see p138) ㉕. The sculpture above the entrance shows the theatre's first owner, Emanuel Schikaneder, in the character of Papageno from Mozart's The Magic Flute. Continue down Millöckergasse to the Linke Wienzeile. Bear left, passing the Secession Building (see p138) ㉖, and go on to Karlsplatz U-Bahn.

A Three-Hour Walk from Kahlenberg to Nussdorf

THIS WALKS STARTS at the top of Kahlenberg, a summit of around 500 m (1,600 ft) at the northeastern edge of the Vienna Woods. From here there is a marvellous panorama over the city and its environs. A gradual descent through woods and vineyards leads to the wine village of Nussdorf and the most northern part of Heiligenstadt, an area rich in Beethoven associations, since this is where the composer spent many of his summers. The walk is mainly downhill, though it may be done in reverse.

St Florian

The Schreiberbach, which runs through the village of Nussdorf

Kahlenberg

The walk starts at the summit of Kahlenberg in Am Kahlenberg square ①. Kahlenberg itself was once called Sauberg (Sow Hill) because of the wild boar that roamed here. From the summit café terrace ②, you can admire distant views of the Alps to the south, plains stretching towards Hungary to the east, and the river Danube snaking through the middle. In the square itself at Josefsdorf is the Baroque church of St Joseph ③, where Jan Sobieski, the King of Poland, is said to have celebrated mass before he went into battle to defeat the Turks in 1683. For another view of Vienna you can climb the recently-restored Stefanie Warte ④, or lookout tower.

Kahlenberger Strasse

To the right of the café is the winding path of Kahlenberger Strasse which leads down to the slopes below the summit. After a couple of minutes you reach the small Kahlenberg cemetery ⑤, almost hidden in the woods to your left. It

Kahlenberg cemetery ⑤

contains the grave of Karolina Trauernwieser, said to have been the most beautiful girl in the city at the time of the Congress of Vienna in 1815.

Her tomb bears the admirer's words: "Ye that ere lost an angel, pity me". A few steps on, the trees clear to reveal a stunning view over the Danube plain ⑥ while further along, on the right, is another view over the city ⑦. Kahlenberger Strasse carries on through vineyards ⑧ where grapes for the local *Heurige* are grown.

Nussdorf and Heiligenstadt

After a while, houses along the road announce that you have arrived at the village of Nussdorf. Follow a bend towards the right and then, passing Frimmelgasse, take

View towards Vienna from Kahlenberger Strasse ⑦

the right-hand fork, where the Schreiberbach (Schreiber brook) emerges from underground, to arrive at the Beethoven Ruhe ⑨ (Beethoven's peace); there is a statue of the composer here dating from 1863. Cross the stream by turning left over the bridge, then turn right into Beethovengang. At the end of this street you come to Eroicagasse, named after Beethoven's *(see p38)* Third Symphony. Turn right and then go downhill, crossing Kahlenberger Strasse. The road curves round, leading into Pfarrplatz.

Pfarrplatz
Immediately on your left at No. 2 is a pleasant *Heuriger*, Mayer am Pfarrplatz ⑩ *(see p219)*, where Beethoven is said to have stayed in

1817 while working on his Ninth Symphony. A statue of St Florian in soldier's costume and bearing a standard can be seen in a niche on the corner wall of the *Heuriger*. Also here is the church of St James ⑪, built in the 12th century on a Roman site, but rebuilt after its destruction by the Turks in the 17th century. From Pfarrplatz follow Probusgasse west towards No. 6 at the far end, which is the Heiligenstadt Testament House ⑫. This is where in 1802 Beethoven wrote a long and despairing letter to his brothers, giving a moving

Heiligenstadt Testament House

Beethoven Ruhe memorial ⑨

account of his deafness. Turn right into Armbrustergasse, which curves upwards and passes the new Slovakian Embassy ⑬, until you come to a crossroads. Here,

turn right into Kahlenberger Strasse, which has a pleasant old-world feel to it, especially at its eastern end. No. 26 ⑭, built around 1750 and with a Rococo façade, is where Beethoven stayed on two occasions during the summer of 1817 and in 1824. Further along, on the same side of the road at No. 10, is a pretty *Heuriger* with a figure above its door ⑮ dating from 1636. On the other side of the road, a plaque on the front of Nos. 7–9 ⑯ celebrates 100 years of *Schrammel* music *(see p39)*, a type of Viennese folk song often associated with *Heurige*.

TIPS FOR WALKERS

Starting point: *Kahlenberg summit.*

Length: *3.5 km (2 miles).*

Getting there: *The 38A bus from Heiligenstadt U-Bahn (on the U6 and U4 lines) takes you to the summit. The Schnellbahn at Nussdorf, or the D tram at Schatzgasse takes you back into town.*

Stopping-off points: *The café at the summit of Kahlenberg has a terrace from where you can enjoy the wonderful view of the Danube and the Alps.*

The Mayer am Pfarrplatz Heuriger at Pfarrplatz 2 (see p219) serves wine and meals in a shady courtyard. There is also a restaurant serving full meals in the same square, as well as other Heurige in Probusgasse and Kahlenberger Strasse. At Kahlen-berger Strasse 10, there is a café and Heuriger in the same building. **St Joseph's Church** ☎ *320 3029.* ◯ *9:30am– noon, 1:30–4:30pm daily (ring bell for attention).* **Stefanie Warte Observatory** ◯ *May–Oct: 9am–8pm Sat, Sun & public hols.* **Heiligenstadt Testament House** ☎ *370 5408.* ◯ *9am–12:15pm, 1–4:30pm Tue–Sun.*

Statue of Beethoven

Mayer am Pfarrplatz

Heiligenstadt Testament House

EICHELHOFSTRASSE
NUSSBERGGASSE
H. NIESE-G.
FRIMMELG.
BEETHOVENGANG
KAHLENBERGER STR
Nussdorf
LANGACKERGASSE
SPRINGSIEDELGASSE
ARMBRUSTERGASSE
PROBUSGASSE
SANDGASSE

0 kilometres 1
0 miles 0.5

KEY
∙∙∙ Walk route
�515 Good viewing point
🚉 Bundesbahn station
Ⓢ Schnellbahn station

St James parish church ⑪, rebuilt in the 17th century

A 90-Minute Walk Around Hietzing

THE FORMER VILLAGE of Hietzing runs along the western edge of the extensive grounds of Schönbrunn Palace (see p172–75). In Maria Theresa's time it was a fashionable area where the nobility went to spend their summers; later it became a suburb for the wealthy middle classes. The quiet streets contain a marvellous mix of Biedermeier and Jugendstil villas, while the square around the parish church retains an intimate small-town atmosphere.

From the station to Am Platz
Take the Hadikgasse exit from Hietzing U-Bahn ① and cross the tram tracks and road to Kennedybrücke. Turn right down Hadikgasse and after a minute you arrive at Otto Wagner's Kaiser Pavilion (see p171) ②, a former station designed for the use of the imperial family when they were at Schönbrunn. Retrace

The Kaiserstöckl opposite the Park Hotel, now a post office ⑥

your steps to the U-Bahn and cross the road into Hietzinger Hauptstrasse. Notice the attic of No. 6 with cherubs hugging the columns. The building dates from 1901–2, but the lower storey has been altered to accommodate shops ③. On your left through the railings are long avenues of trees at

the side of Schönbrunn ④. Just across the road is the Park Hotel, its ochre façade echoing that of the palace buildings ⑤. Facing it is the Kaiserstöckl (1770) or Emperor's Pavilion ⑥. Today it is a post office, but it used to be the holiday venue of Maria Theresa's foreign ministers. Continue to Am Platz with its plague column dating from 1730 ⑦. Next door to this is the parish church of Maria Geburt ⑧, originally built in the 13th century, and remodelled in the 17th century. The Baroque interior contains altars by the sculptor Matthias Steindl and ceiling frescoes by Georg Greiner. The church was used by Maria Theresa when she was in residence at Schönbrunn, and her box can be seen in the right-hand wall of the choir. In front of the church stands a statue of Franz Joseph's brother

Façade of the Park Hotel ⑤

Villa Primavesi

```
0 metres            250
0 yards             250
```

KEY

• • • Walk route

Ⓤ U-Bahn station

Elaborate altar by Matthias Steindl in the Maria Geburt Kirche ⑧

TIPS FOR WALKERS

Starting point: *Hietzing U-Bahn.*
Length: *5 km (3 miles).*
Getting there: *the U4 and Tram 58 go to Hietzing.* ***Note:*** *On Sundays you may need to retrace your steps a short distance if the Maxing Gate is locked.*
Stopping-off points: *the BAWAG café in Hietzing's Am Platz is a pleasant place to stop for a coffee.*
Hietzing Heimat Museum
◻ *9am–noon 2–6pm Wed, 2–5pm Sat, 9:30am–noon Sun.*
● *Jul–Aug.* ***Schönbrunn Palace and Park*** *(see pp172–75).*
Villa Primavesi ● *to public.*

Maximilian, the Emperor of Mexico who was executed in 1867 ⑨. Nearby is a Neo-Classical building housing the Hietzing Heimat Museum ⑩, and outside the museum is Vienna's last gas lamp.

Trauttmansdorffgasse and Gloriettegasse

Turn left into Maxingstrasse, named after Maximilian, then right into Altgasse. Almost facing Fasholdgasse is an old *Heuriger*, a Biedermeier building with ochre walls ⑪.

Detail from the majolica façade of the Lebkuchenhaus ⑲

across the road, at No. 27, is the house where the composer Alban Berg *(see p39)* once lived ⑬. Nos. 48 and 50 are contrasting examples of Viennese turn-of-the-century architecture ⑭. More examples of Biedermeier style can be seen at Nos. 54 and 56 ⑮.

At the end of the road, turn right into Gloriette-gasse. On the right at Nos. 14 and 16 is a villa with sculpted figures in the pediments, built in 1913–15 by Josef Hoffmann for the financier Robert Primavesi ⑯. Note the monumental sculpted figures resting in the pediments.

Cross the road to pass a terrace of Biedermeier houses – Nos. 38 and 40 have lunettes above the windows ⑰. No. 21 is the Villa Schopp, designed by Friedrich Ohmann in 1901–2 ⑱. Turn left down Wattmanngasse to see No. 29, the extraordinary Lebkuchen-haus (Gingerbread House) ⑲, so-called because of its dark brown decoration in majolica. It was built in 1914 to designs by a pupil of Otto Wagner *(see pp54–7)*. Turn back into Gloriettegasse. At its southern junction with Wattmann-gasse, at No. 9, is the

house that belonged to Katharina Schratt, the actress and confidante of Emperor Franz Joseph during his later years. It is said that the Emperor was in the habit of arriving here for breakfast ⑳.

Maxing Park and Schönbrunn Park

Walk to the end of Gloriette-gasse, then turn right up Maxingstrasse and cross the road at Maxing Park. If you would like to add another half hour to the walk, Hietzing cemetery, a little further up the hill, contains the graves of Otto Wagner, Gustav Klimt, Kolo Moser and Franz Grillparzer, among others. Alternatively, enter Maxing Park ㉑ and follow the main path upwards towards the right. At the top, go through the gates marked *Zum Tiergarten Schönbrunn*, passing the forestry research institute on your left. Although you are actually in the grounds of Schönbrunn, this heavily wooded area feels very remote from the formal gardens and you may catch a glimpse of deer. At the crossroads in the path turn left, signposted to the Botanical Garden. You soon arrive at a little wooden hut, which was Crown Prince Rudolf's playhouse ㉒.

The path eventually leads to the formally planted Botanical Garden ㉓, which was laid out in 1848 under Emperor Franz I. Take the path through the garden, keeping to the boundary wall with Hietzing. Exit into Maxingstrasse (this gate may be locked on Sundays) and continue north. At No. 18 is the house where Johann Strauss II wrote *Die Fledermaus* in 1874 ㉔. Carry on north along Maxingstrasse and retrace your steps to Hietzing U-Bahn.

NISSELG

KYROWETZG

HADIKGASSE

① ②

Hietzing Ⓤ

NG

③

SCHÖNBRUNNER

Kaiser Pavilion

⑤ ④

⑥

SCHÖNBRUNN PARK

⑨⑧⑦

⑩

Kaiserstöckl

Church of Maria Geburt

FÜRSTENHOF

Plaque on No. 50 Trauttmans-dorffgasse ⑭

Turn down Fasholdgasse into Trautt-mansdorffgasse, a street full of interesting houses. No. 40 is a beautifully-restored, long and low Biedermeier villa ⑫, while

㉒

SECKENDORF-GUDENT WEG

Sculpted figure in a pediment of the Villa Primavesi ⑯

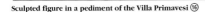

A Two-Hour Walk to Grinzing

THIS WALK THROUGH part of Vienna's 19th district begins at the site of one of the most important monuments of 20th-century Vienna, the public housing development of the Karl Marx Hof. It then takes you through a pretty 19th-century park to the old wine village of Grinzing. Although the village suffered destruction at the hands of the Turks in 1529 and 1683 and from Napoleon's army in 1809, and is now feeling the effects of modern tourism, its pretty main street preserves its charm.

Façade of the 16th-century Reinprecht *Heuriger* ⑮

Karl Marx Hof to Heiligenstädter Park

Facing you as you step out of Heiligenstadt station is the long ochre, terracotta and mauve façade of the Karl Marx Hof (*see p161*), a huge

housing project designed by the city architect Karl Ehn and built from 1927 to 1930 during the Red Vienna period ①. It sprawls for 1.2 km (¾ mile) and has 1,265 flats.

Cross the road and pass through one of the four arches facing you into 12 Februar Platz to see the main façade from the other side. On the keystone of each arch stands a large figure sculpture by Joseph Riedl (1928)

Figure on the Karl Marx Hof ①

② Continue through the square, past a statue (1928) by Otto Hofner of a man sowing seeds ③, and you come to Heiligenstädter Strasse. Turn right, cross the road at the second pedestrian crossing and walk through the square opening in the building facing you. Go up the steps and take the path on the left into Heiligenstädter Park. When you come to a fork, take the left path that winds up a hill, going through woods. Turn right at the top into the formal part of the park ④. From here, you get a good view of the vine-clad slopes of the Kahlenberg ⑤.

Steinfeldgasse

Take the second small path on the right, which descends gradually into Steinfeldgasse, where there is a cluster of houses built by the Secessionist

designer Josef Hoffmann. The first one you come to is the Villa Moser-Moll at Nos. 6–8, designed for Carl Moll and Kolo Moser ⑥. Next to it is the Villa Spitzer ⑦, then the more classical Villa Ast, built in 1909–11 ⑧. Where Steinfeldgasse meets Wollergasse is the Villa Henneberg of 1901 ⑨, and at No. 10 Wollergasse ⑩ is the Moll House II of 1906–7. Its black and white details are charming.

Steinfeldgasse to Grinzinger Strasse

At the point where Steinfeldgasse and Wollergasse meet, there is a path leading down through some woods. Follow this and descend the steps to the Church of St Michael, Heiligenstadt ⑪, which has striking

Trummelhof

modern stained-glass windows. Walk past the church, cross a path leading down to Hohe Warte and go up Grinzinger Strasse. You quickly arrive at No. 70, the house where Albert Einstein stayed from 1927 to 1931 ⑫. On the same side of the road is No. 64, the late 18th-century house where Beethoven and the Viennese playwright Franz Grillparzer lodged during the summer of 1808 while Beethoven was composing the Pastoral Symphony ⑬. Continue up Grinzinger Strasse, passing a number of attractive Biedermeier houses, until you arrive at Grinzinger

Lawns and trees in the Heiligenstädter Park ④

Allee. Turn right past a series of wine gardens and immediately right again to get a quick glimpse of the upper part of Sandgasse, where there are a number of more authentic *Heurige* ⑭.

Grinzing

Turning back on yourself and towards the centre of Grinzing, ascend Cobenzlgasse, the upper fork of Grinzing's main street. The Reinprecht *Heuriger* at No. 22 Cobenzlgasse is a 16th-century house, the façade of

Cobenzlgasse, Grinzing's main street

0 metres 500

0 yards 500

No. 64 Grinzinger Strasse

Courtyard at the Passauer Hof, an old wine press house ⑰

KEY

••• Walk route

☆ Good viewing point

🚋 Tram terminus

Ⓤ U-Bahn station

Ⓢ Schnellbahn station

━ Railway line

TIPS FOR WALKERS

Starting point: Heiligenstadt station.

Length: 3.5 km (2 miles).

Getting there: Heiligenstadt station is served by U-Bahn lines U4 and U6, trains S40 and S45 and buses 10A, 11A, 38A and 39A. Tram D stops on Heiligenstädter Strasse.

Stopping-off points: There are numerous Heurige, coffee shops and restaurants in Grinzing. Avoid the larger Heurige – the smaller ones sell their own wine. Those at the top of Sandgasse tend to be good.

which has a tablet commemorating the composer Robert Stolz ⑮. No. 30 Cobenzlgasse is the Baroque Trummelhof, standing on the site of an 1835 brewery ⑯. Further up on the left, at No. 9, is the Passauer Hof, an old wine press house that contains fragments of a far older, Romanesque building ⑰. On the corner of Cobenzlgasse and Feilergasse is the Altes Presshaus, whose cellar contains an old wine press ⑱.

Turn left into Feilergasse, and you soon come face to face with the impressive white Jugendstil façade of

Nos. 41–3 Himmelstrasse ⑲. Continue down Himmelstrasse to No. 35, another *Heuriger*, Das Alte Haus, which has a charming plaque of the Virgin Mary above its door ⑳. There is another such painting at No. 31, which shows a holy man carrying a cross, bible and a bunch of grapes ㉑. No. 29 ㉒ is another *Heuriger* with a tablet to Sepp Fellner, a *Schrammel* musician *(see p39)* described as "The Schubert of Grinzing". Ironically, at No. 25, a grand building with shields above the doorway, there is a memorial to the real Schubert, described as "The Prince of Song, who loved to tarry in Grinzing" ㉓. Grinzing also has an attractive late Gothic church with a copper cupola and much-restored interior ㉔. Continue down the road to the tram terminus, where the No. 38 tram goes back to town.

Plaque of a holy man on the façade of No. 31 Himmelstrasse ㉑

TRAVELLERS' NEEDS

WHERE TO STAY

WITH MORE THAN 500 hotels and pensions available, Vienna offers accommodation for everyone. From palaces to spartan lodgings, the city has some of the grandest European city hotels as well as numerous small boarding-houses. Hotels are generally larger and better equipped (some also have business facilities), and pensions are always bed and breakfast establishments. From a survey of

different types of accommodation in all price brackets, we have selected 40 of the best. The chart *Choosing a Hotel* on page 197 will help you find a hotel to suit your needs: hotels are listed by area and in order of price category. For more details of facilities and for a short description, turn to the listings on pages 198–201. For further types of accommodation available in and on the outskirts of Vienna, see page 195.

Baroque façade of the Mailberger Hof on Annagasse *(see p199)*

WHERE TO LOOK

ONE OF THE JOYS of visiting Vienna is that you can stay grandly or cheaply right in the city centre. Almost all the famous hotels – the Sacher, the Bristol, the Imperial *(see Listings pp198–201)* – are on or just off the Ringstrasse, as are most of the large chain hotels. In the city centre lie a host of atmospheric and comfortable hotels and many pensions. Most are on fairly quiet side streets. The Townhall and Museum Quarter has a few good small hotels and is the most promising hunting ground for those travelling on a budget. A few hotels in or near the wine villages to the north *(see p201)* are also listed.

The **Österreich Werbung** (Austrian Tourist Board) publishes detailed leaflets listing over 500 hotels and pensions.

HOTEL PRICES

ACCOMMODATION IN Vienna is disproportionately expensive compared to other costs. Many hotels and pensions situated in prime locations are overpriced. There are a number of ways to cut costs. You can expect to pay approximately a fifth to a quarter less for a room in an establishment just outside the Ringstrasse, and less still if you stay further afield.

Most places have rooms at a variety of prices, depending on their size, aspect and, in pensions, whether they have en suite bathrooms. Single rooms tend to be about three-quarters the cost of double rooms. Some places will put an extra bed in the room on request. They may charge for this but it is likely to be a lot less than the cost of a single room. Other hotels have family or triple-bedded rooms.

Vienna's low season runs from November to March (excluding Christmas and New Year) and during July and August (when

Penthouse suite No. 663 in the Bristol Hotel *(see p201)*

residents go on holiday). Few hotels drop their prices in summer, but around half have winter rates up to 25% lower. Most of the large chain hotels reduce the room tariff when they are less busy and offer weekend specials, but even the lower rates compare badly with hotels of the same chain in the United States, for example.

Out of season, it may be worth asking if there's a discount for payment in cash. Many places offer discounts for longer stays (typically over a

Opulent lobby of the Imperial Hotel *(see p201)*

week), and it's possible to find packages such as three nights for the price of two or four nights for the price of three.

The **Österreich Werbung** has offices in the UK, USA, Canada, New Zealand and Australia. They have details of tour operators that provide all-inclusive packages to Vienna, and will be able to advise on the best available prices.

HIDDEN EXTRAS

WITH THE EXCEPTION of most five-star hotels, breakfast is included in the tariff. Rates will always include taxes such as VAT (or MWSt).

Beware if changing money at your hotel: the official exchange rate could well be as much as 10% better.

Parking fees can also mount up. Street parking within the Ringstrasse is restricted to 90 minutes and there are no private garages. Pensions generally leave you to your own devices to find an underground car park, but some hotels have designated spaces. At some hotels a reasonable amount is charged for parking, but at others it can be very expensive: it is a good idea to enquire in advance. Outlying districts do not have such stringent street parking restrictions, and garage parking is cheaper.

If you are cutting costs, try to avoid making phone calls from your room. Most hotels charge a flat rate per unit of time, even though the official rate varies from day-time to night-time and

Statue in the reception area of the Hotel Regina *(see p200)*

week-days to weekends. The surcharge may be up to three and a half times the standard rate, so it is often worth using a public telephone.

Every other Viennese on the street seems to have a four-legged friend in tow, so it's not surprising that many of the hotels allow dogs in the bedrooms. There may be a charge for this.

HOW TO BOOK

EASTER, MAY, June, September, October, Christmas and New Year are considered peak season. During these times, many of the best hotels and pensions in Vienna may be fully booked as early as two months in advance.

Making a reservation direct with any hotel is easy, since most of the staff speak fluent English. If you cancel once

the booking has been made, you may be charged for the room. Check in advance. If you are going to arrive after 6pm, let the hotel know or they may re-let your room to someone else.

The **Wiener Tourismus-verband** (Vienna Tourist Board) office, on the corner of Albertinaplatz, Tegethoffstrasse and Meysedergasse *(see p239)*, can reserve hotel rooms in advance. It is also possible to book accommodation by calling the Tourist Board office on 24555 or visiting www.wien.info

Otherwise, fax, telephone or write direct to the hotel. If the hotel accepts credit cards, a phone call to book will suffice; if not, you may have to send confirmation of the booking in writing. Different hotels in the city have different procedures.

Wrought-iron balconies at the Museum pension *(see p200)*

The Anna Sacher restaurant at the Hotel Sacher *(see p200)*

FACILITIES

HOTELS ARE RATED one to five stars, pensions on a four-star system. As a rough guideline in terms of facilities, a three-star hotel corresponds to a four-star pension. The rating also attempts to cover the quality and ambience of the hotel or pension. Five-star hotels are all reliably smart and well-run. Many four- and three-star hotels proclaim themselves as *Palais*: while this may hold true in the Viennese sense of the word, don't expect anything more than a fine town house. At the cheaper end of the scale, small pensions above two stars are often more friendly and salubrious than cheap hotels. One- or two-star hotels and pensions tend to cater for travellers on a budget and are generally less pleasant.

Usually, only the top hotels have a full range of public rooms: a restaurant, bar, coffee shop and sitting room. In most smaller establishments the lounge is little more than an extension of the reception. Even if there is no bar, you may find that drinks are served. Almost all hotels and pensions have a breakfast room (though all too often it's in a dreary basement). Low-priced pensions provide continental breakfast, while most smart pensions and hotels offer gargantuan buffet feasts, with cheeses, meats, fruit, cakes and cereals.

As most hotels occupy old buildings, it's rare for two bedrooms to be the same. The simplest rooms almost always have a phone, though not necessarily a television. Mid-range hotel rooms often have cable TV and a minibar. Due to size constraints, many bathrooms have only a shower or a truncated tub bath. Many Viennese buildings back on to quiet courtyards, so you can choose between a peaceful room or a room with a view.

In the 19th century there was a restriction on the height of buildings. In order to circumvent the regulation, lower floors were (and still are) called *Hochparterre* and *Mezzanin*. Consequently you may find that the "first floor" is up three flights of stairs. In pensions, a communal lift (usually three-sided and therefore hazardous) serves the whole building.

The quality of service in the best luxury hotels is as good as anywhere in the world. Wherever you stay, it could be well worth befriending the concierge (by perhaps slipping him or her a tip early on in your stay). He or she can be invaluable in directing you to interesting restaurants and bars, and conjuring out of thin air a ticket to the Winter Riding School or a seat at the opera when they have been sold out for months. Most of the reception staff and many other staff speak English, but the standard of service is variable.

TRAVELLING WITH CHILDREN

ALMOST ALL THE HOTELS and pensions have cots (some charge) and can arrange a babysitter. Some may charge the same rate for putting a child's bed in the parents' room as they would for an adult's bed. Usually only the larger hotels allow children under various ages to stay free in their parents' room.

The handsome yellow exterior of the Hotel Josefshof *(see p200)*

DISABLED TRAVELLERS

INFORMATION about wheelchair access to hotels relies on the hotel's own assessment of their suitability. The **Wiener Tourismusverband** also publishes a detailed leaflet.

HOSTELS

THERE ARE EIGHT youth hostels in the city. The **Wiener Tourismusverband**'s youth hostel and camping brochure lists their facilities. Those with better facilities cost around €10–€15 a night for bed and breakfast. Most hostels expect residents to be in by midnight. You will need an International Youth Hostel Federation membership card, which can be obtained before you go or on the spot from any hostel. Contact **Österreichischer Jugendherbergsverband** for more information.

SAISONHOTELS

ANNUALLY FROM 1 July to 30 September two dozen students' hostels become Saisonhotels or seasonal hotels, rated on a scale of one to three stars. At the three-star level expect fairly

decent rooms. You may make enquiries at any time of the year at two of the main chains, **Academia Hotels** and **Rosen-Hotel**. Try to reserve well in advance and expect to pay up to €75 for a double room in one of the better places.

Elegant lobby at the Kaiserin Elisabeth Hotel (*see p198*)

INFORMATION

Österreich Werbung
Margaretenstrasse 1, A-1040. **Map** 4 D2. **C** 810101818. **FAX** 5886648. **W** www.austria.info

Wiener Tourismusverband
Corner of Albertinaplatz, Tegethoffstrasse and Meysedergasse, A-1010. **Map** 4 D1 & 6 C4. **C** 24555. **FAX** 24555-666. **W** www.wien.info

SAISONHOTELS

Academia Hotels
Pfeilgasse 3a, A-1080. **Map** 1 A5. **C** 4017655. **FAX** 4017620. **W** www.academia-hotels.co.at

Rosen-Hotel
Schelleingasse 36, A-1040. **Map** 4 E4. **C** 501520. **FAX** 50152709. **W** www.rosenhotels.at

YOUTH HOSTELS

Österreichischer Jugendherbergs-verband
Schottenring 28, A-1010.

Map 2 D4. **C** 5335353. **FAX** 5350861. **W** www.oejhv.or.at

CAMPING

Camping und Caravaning Club Austria
Mariahilfer Strasse 180, A-1150. **Map** 3 A3. **C** 89121222. **FAX** 89121274. **W** www.arboe.at

Österreichischer Camping Club
Schubertring 1–3, A-1010. **Map** 4 E2 & 6 D5. **C** 711991272. **FAX** 711993743.

SELF-CATERING

Pego
Kirchgasse 1, A-6700 Bludenz. **C** 05552 65666. **FAX** 05552 63801. **W** www.pego.at

PRIVATE HOMES

Mitwohnzentrale
Laudongasse 7, A-1080. **Map** 1 B4. **C** 4026061. **FAX** 402606111.

CHAIN HOTELS

Austria Hotels Hotel de France
Schottenring 3, A-1010. **Map** 2 D4. **C** 313680. **FAX** 3195969. **W** www.hoteldefrance.at

Austria Trend Parkhotel Schönbrunn
Hietzinger Hauptstrasse 10–20, A-1131. **C** 87804. **FAX** 878043220. **W** www.austria-trend.at

Clima Cityhotel
Theresianumg 21a, A-1040. **Map** 4 E4. **C** 5051696. **FAX** 5043552.

Johann Strauss
Favoritenstrasse 12, A-1040. **Map** 4 D3. **C** 5057624. **FAX** 5057628. **W** www.hotel-johann-strauss.at

Hotel Ibis Wien
Mariahilfer Gürtel 22–24, A-1060. **C** 599980. **FAX** 5979090. **W** www.ibishotel.com

Novotel Wien West
Am Auhof Autobahn-station, A-1140. **C** 97925420. **FAX** 9794140. **W** www.novotel.com

Penta Renaissance Hotel
Ungargasse 60, A-1030. **Map** 4 F1. **C** 711750. **FAX** 711758143. **W** www.renaissancehotels.com

SAS Palais Hotel
Parkring 16, A-1010. **Map** 4 E1 & 6 E4. **C** 515170. **FAX** 5122216. **W** www.radissonsas.com

Hilton Vienna
Am Stadtpark, A-1030. **C** 717000. **FAX** 7130691. **W** www.hilton.com

Sofitel Hotel am Belvedere
Am Heumarkt 35–37, A-1030. **C** 716160. **FAX** 71616844. **W** www.accorhotels.com

Wien Hotel Renaissance
Ullmannstrasse 71, A-1150. **C** 89102. **FAX** 89102300. **W** www.renaissancehotels.com

One of the better chain hotels, the Vienna Marriott *(see p199)*

CAMPING

F IVE WELL-EQUIPPED campsites, one open throughout the year, can be found within a radius of 8–15 km (5–9 miles) from the city centre. Most campsites have kitchen facilities and some may have a supermarket. The **Wiener Tourismusverband** produces a camping and youth hostel brochure which gives more details on sites. **Camping und Caravening Club Austria** and **Österreichischer Camping Club** can also provide more information.

SELF-CATERING

U NFORTUNATELY FOR those who are keen to "go it alone", there are limited opportunities for self-catering in the city. **Pego**, a company

that rents homes throughout Austria, has two apartment blocks and a range of flats spread in and around the city; their brochure will give you all the details. You can book by telephone, by fax or in writing. Some apartments have a combined living and sleeping space and most also have a television and telephone. Expect to pay less per night than the price of a pension.

STAYING IN PRIVATE HOMES

S OME VISITORS CHOOSE to stay in a private home. You can book this type of accommodation through the **Wiener Tourismusverband**, but the booking has to be made in person. **Mitwohnzentrale** is a private company that offers the same service. Normally you need to stay a few nights and should expect to pay around €36 per person per night.

CHAIN HOTELS

C HAIN HOTELS are geared towards business people; rates usually vary according to their level of occupancy, rather than the season. Familiar names include the Inter-Continental Wien *(see p201)*, K+K *(see pp198 and 200)* and the Vienna Marriott *(see p199)* as well as the hotels listed on page 197.

The hotel listings are on pages 198–201.

USING THE LISTINGS

The hotel listings are on pages 198–201. Each hotel is listed according to area and price category. After the address, the telephone and fax numbers are given. A selection of the symbols below are also shown, summarizing the facilities each hotel offers:

🛁 all rooms with bath and/or shower unless otherwise indicated
1️⃣ single-rate rooms available
🛏 rooms for more than 2 people available, as well as those allowing an extra bed in a double room
24 24-hour room service
📺 television in all rooms
🚭 non-smoking rooms available
🏞 rooms with good view available
❄ air conditioning in all rooms
🏋 gym/fitness facilities available in hotel
🏊 swimming pool in hotel
🖥 business facilities: these include message-taking service, fax service, desk and telephone in each room, and meeting room within hotel
🧒 children's facilities; babysitting and cots can be arranged
♿ wheelchair access
🛗 lift
🅿 parking available
🍸 bar
🍴 restaurant
💳 credit and charge cards accepted:
AE American Express
DC Diners Club
MC Mastercard/Access
V Visa
JCB Japanese Credit Bureau

Price categories for a double room with bathroom (with either bath or shower) per night, including tax and service:
€ under €75
€€ €76–€110
€€€ €111–€145
€€€€ €146–€200
€€€€€ over €200

View of a campsite at No. 40 Huttelbergstrasse

Choosing a Hotel

ALL OF THE HOTELS summarized here have been inspected and assessed. This chart shows some of the features that may affect your choice. The hotels are listed alphabetically within their price category. For more details, see pages 198–201.

Hotel	Price	NUMBER OF ROOMS	MOST BEDROOMS LARGE	BUSINESS FACILITIES	CHILDREN'S FACILITIES	RECOMMENDED RESTAURANT	CLOSE TO SHOPS AND RESTAURANTS	QUIET LOCATION	24-HOUR ROOM SERVICE	BEST VALUE FOR MONEY
STEPHANSDOM QUARTER (see pp198–9)										
Am Operneck	€	7	●				●			
Christina	€€	33			●		●	■		
Pension City	€€	19					●			
Amadeus	€€€	30			●		●			
Arenberg	€€€	22			●		●			
Austria	€€€	46	●		●		●	■	●	
Kärntnerhof	€€€	43			●		●	■		■
Wandl	€€€	138	●		●		●			■
Zur Wiener Staatsoper	€€€	22			●		●			
Kaiserin Elisabeth	€€€€	63			●		●	■		
K+K Palais	€€€€	66		■	●			■		
König von Ungarn	€€€€	33	●	■	●	■	●			■
Mailberger Hof	€€€€	35	●		●		●	■		
Am Schubertring	€€€€	39			●		●			
Römischer Kaiser Wien	€€€€€	24			●		●	■		
Vienna Marriott	€€€€€	313	●	■	●		●		●	
HOFBURG QUARTER (see p199)										
Nossek	€€	30	●	■	●					■
Pertschy	€€€	50			●		●	■		
Astoria	€€€€	118	●		●		●			
Ambassador	€€€€€	86	●		●		●	■		
SCHOTTENRING AND ALSERGRUND (see pp199–200)										
Arcotel Boltzmann	€€€€	70					●	■		
Regina	€€€€	127			●		●			
MUSEUM AND TOWNHALL QUARTER (see p200)										
Wild	€	19					●			■
Graf Stadion	€€	40					●			
Museum	€€	15					●			
Altstadt Vienna	€€€	36	●		●		●	■		■
Zipser	€€€	47			●		●			
Josefshof	€€€€	118		■	●		●	■		
K+K Maria Theresia	€€€€	133		■	●		●			
OPERA AND NASCHMARKT (see p200)										
Sacher	€€€€€	109	●	■	●	■	●		●	
BELVEDERE QUARTER (see pp200–201)										
Suzanne	€€	26			●		●			
Bristol	€€€€€	140	●	■	●	■	●		●	
Imperial	€€€€€	138	●	■	●	■	●		●	
Im Palais Schwarzenberg	€€€€€	44		■	●	■		■	●	■
FURTHER AFIELD (see p201)										
Altwienerhof	€€	25				■		■		■
Nordbahn	€€	78		■	●		●			
Gartenhotel Glanzing	€€€	14	●	■	●			■		
Landhaus Fuhrgassl-Huber	€€€	38			●			■		■
Inter-Continental Wien	€€€€	453		■	●				●	
Mecure Grand Hotel Biedermeier	€€€€	203	●		●		●			

STEPHANSDOM QUARTER

Am Operneck

Kärntner Strasse 47, A-1010.
Map 4 D1 & 6 D4. [5129310.
FAX 512931020. **Rooms:** 7. 🛏
1 ⊞ TV 🏊 🛐 🖉 MC, V. €

This tiny pension opposite the
tourist office on Kärntner Strasse
is in the centre of the city. All but
one of the bedrooms are large,
comfortable and resolutely un-
stylish. The bathrooms, which have
showers, are somewhat cramped.
You can find quieter rooms
towards the back. Continental
breakfast is served in your room.

Christina

Hafnersteig 7, A-1010.
Map 2 E5 & 6 E2. [5332961.
FAX 533296111. **Rooms:** 33. 🛏
1 ⊞ TV 🏊 🛐 🖉 DC, MC, V.
€€ w www.pertschy.com

The Christina is an unassuming
pension on a quiet, cobbled side
street just within the Stephansdom
Quarter. Though neither old nor
fashionable, it's the kind of place
where you'll be offered a cup of
coffee on arrival. It has been
renovated in Art Deco style and
larger rooms have proper baths.

Pension City

Bauernmarkt 10, A-1010. **Map** 2 E5
& 6 D3. [5339521. FAX 5355216.
Rooms: 19. 🛏 1 ⊞ TV 🖛 🗴
🛐 ▮▮ 🖉 AE, DC, MC, V. €€
w www.citypension.com

This small, friendly hotel is
housed in a late 19th-century
building in the centre of Vienna,
within easy walking distance of
Stephansdom and Hoher Markt.
It is also close to shops, bars and
restaurants. Some of the bedrooms
have good views but the quieter
rooms are away from the street.

Amadeus

Wildpretmarkt 5, A-1010.
Map 2 E5 & 6 D3. [5338738.
FAX 533873838. **Rooms:** 30. 🛏 1
TV 🏊 🛐 🖉 DC, MC, V. €€€
w www.hotel-amadeus.at

This spruce, modern hotel could
have been better named, as other
famous musicians such as Brahms
and Schubert used to frequent a
tavern on this site. But the hotel's
décor matches Mozart's era: the red
carpets, upholstery and lampshades
are complemented by chandeliers
and murals on the stairs. The
Amadeus is located close to the
Stephansdom on a handsome,
wide street with fashionable shops.

Arenberg

Stubenring 2, A-1010.
Map 2 F5 & 6 F3. [5125291.
FAX 5139356. **Rooms:** 22. 🛏 1
⊞ TV 🏃 🛐 🖉 AE, DC, MC, V.
€€€ w www.arenberg.at

A seemingly dull office building
on the northeast corner of the
Ring houses one of the city's most
civilized and friendly pensions. An
honesty bar (help yourself and mark
your drinks down on a tab) sets the
tone. Expect rugs on parquet floors
and bedrooms with antique wallpaper and more prosaic furniture.

Austria

Fleischmarkt 20, A-1010. **Map** 2 E4
& 6 D2. [51523. FAX 51523506.
Rooms: 46. 🛏 42. 1 ⊞ 24 TV
🏃 🛐 P 🖉 AE, DC, MC, V, JCB.
€€€

Up a cul-de-sac and close to the
Old University is the roomy and
somewhat dowdy Austria Hotel.
A plus point is that it is extremely
quiet. Downstairs, there are a
couple of small sitting-rooms and
a breakfast room arranged around
a fountain decorated with shells.
High-ceilinged, spacious bedrooms with modern furniture and
decent, old-fashioned bathrooms
ring a central courtyard.

Kärntnerhof

Grashofgasse 4, A-1011. **Map** 2 E5 &
6 E3. [5121923. FAX 513222839.
Rooms: 43. 🛏 41. 1 ⊞ TV 🏃
🛐 P 🖉 AE, DC, MC, V, JCB.
€€€ w www.karntnerhof.com

A couple of cafés adjoin this well-
run and affordable cul-de-sac
address: a gate at the end leads to
the lovely Heiligenkreuzerhof (see
p75) where you can park the car.
The 19th-century building's best
feature behind its imposing yellowy
façade is a fine Art Deco lift,
enclosed within a spiral staircase.
The better bedrooms have recently
been renovated. Breakfast is served
in rustic, beamed surroundings.

Wandl

Petersplatz 9, A-1010.
Map 2 D5 & 5 C3. [534550.
FAX 5345577. **Rooms:** 138. 🛏 134.
1 ⊞ TV ⊞ 🏃 🛐 🛐 🖉
🖉 AE, DC, MC, V, JCB. €€€
w www.hotel-wandl.com

Close to the Peterskirche, in the
very centre of the city, is the
characterful, old-fashioned Wandl
Hotel. It has been in the same
family for several generations. Some
of the building's finer features
were wiped out by bombs so only
parts of its stuccoed style remain,
notably in a few bedrooms and in
the covered courtyard that serves

as the breakfast room. Other bedrooms are plainer but generally
large and with parquet floors.

Zur Wiener Staatsoper

Krugerstrasse 11, A-1010.
Map 4 E1 & 6 D5. [5131274. FAX
513127415. **Rooms:** 22. 🛏 1 ⊞
TV 🏃 🛐 🖉 AE, MC, V. €€€
w www.zurwienerstaatsoper.at

A tall, thin 19th-century building
on a pedestrian street off Kärntner
Strasse houses this simple little
hotel. Its façade is great fun:
caryatids show off over the porch
and faces peer out of the plasterwork above. Inside, the breakfast
room, bedrooms and bathrooms
(all with showers) are squeezed
into the limited space available.

Kaiserin Elisabeth

Weihburggasse 3, A-1010.
Map 4 E1 & 6 D4. [51526.
FAX 515267. **Rooms:** 63.
🛏 1 ⊞ TV ⊞ 🛐 P Y
🖉 AE, DC, MC, V, JCB. €€€€
w www.kaiserinelisabeth.at

This rather fetching town house
is located in a side street only
yards from the Stephansdom.
It dates from the 14th century
and in the 1800s played host to
many famous musicians such as
Wagner and Liszt. Persian rugs
lie on parquet floors in the
elegant public rooms. The
fin-de-siècle-style bedrooms are
smart. Smaller double rooms
and singles have showers only
in the bathroom.

K+K Palais

Rudolfsplatz 11, A-1010. **Map** 2 E4 &
6 D1. [5331353. FAX 533135370.
Rooms: 66. 🛏 1 ⊞ TV 🖛 🗴
🛐 P Y 🖉 AE, DC, MC, V.
€€€€ w www.kkhotels.com

Canary yellow walls abound in
this successful modern establishment set within a fine 19th-century
building. An impressive glass-
fronted lobby leads through to a
smart breakfast room cum bar and
up a marble staircase to simple,
fresh bedrooms with white duvets
and wicker chairs. The hotel is
situated in a quiet, grassy square
in a business area.

König von Ungarn

Schulerstrasse 10, A-1010. **Map** 2 E5
& 6 D3. [515840. FAX 515848.
Rooms: 33. 🛏 1 ⊞ TV ▤ 🛐 🗴
🛐 P Y ▮▮ 🖉 AE, DC, MC,
V, JCB. €€€€ w www.kvu.at

Atmospheric and extremely good
value, the König von Ungarn
(The King of Hungary) is highly
recommended. Framed signatures
of famous visitors from past

centuries cover its walls, and Mozart is said to have composed *The Marriage of Figaro* in a part of the building now known as the Figarohaus *(see p72)*. The covered central courtyard with its elegant bar/sitting room is one of the city's loveliest. Well-prepared traditional specialities are served in the vaulted red dining rooms. Most bedrooms are large with appealing rustic furniture; more peaceful rooms are to the rear.

Mailberger Hof

Annagasse 7, A-1010. **Map** 4 E1 & 6 D4. **C** 51206410. **FAX** 512064110.
Rooms: 35. 🛏 34. 1 🎯 TV 🏊
Ⓨ 🔼 P 🍴 🍽 AE, DC, MC, V, JCB.
€€€€ W www.mailbergerhof.at

Virtually opposite the Römischer Kaiser Wien *(see below)*, the Baroque Mailberger Hof is a lovely hotel converted from medieval houses. You can dine in its fine open courtyard under parasols, or in the striking, vaulted restaurant. A wide, stone staircase leads to the bedrooms; most overlook the courtyard, are tastefully furnished and have plenty of space.

Am Schubertring

Schubertring 11, A-1010. **Map** 2 F5 & 6 D5. **C** 717020. **FAX** 7139966.
Rooms: 39. 🛏 1 🎯 TV 🏊 🕴
🔼 🖴 P Ⓨ 🍽 AE, DC, MC, V, JCB. €€€€
W www.schubertring.at

This Ringstrasse-style building contains one of the few Jugendstil hotels in the city. Art Deco prints, murals and lamps decorate the smart bar, breakfast and sitting rooms. The hotel's bedrooms on the sixth floor have thick carpets and high-quality reproduction furniture. Some are furnished in Jugendstil fashion with dark wood, others in lighter Biedermeier style. Quiet rooms at the back are available. Every detail has been carefully considered, and the staff show an equal amount of care.

Römischer Kaiser Wien

Annagasse 16, A-1010.
Map 4 E1 & 6 D4. **C** 51277510.
FAX 512775113. *Rooms:* 24. 🛏 1
🎯 TV 🏊 🕴 🔼 🖴 Ⓨ 🍽 AE, DC, MC, V, JCB. €€€€€
W www.hotelroemischerkaiser.at

This terraced house, a classic example of a Viennese miniature Baroque palace, was built for the Imperial Chancellor in 1684. Stylish public rooms with chandeliers and rugs on tiles occupy the ground floor. Upstairs, the bedrooms are cheerful, creamy concoctions; there are also cheaper attic rooms. Bicycles can be hired at the hotel.

Vienna Marriott

Parkring 12a, A-1010. **Map** 4 D1 & 6 E4. **C** 515180. **FAX** 515186736.
Rooms: 313. 🛏 1 🎯 24 TV
🏊 🕴 🖴 🔼 Ⓨ 🍽 🖴 AE, DC, MC, V, JCB.
€€€€€ W www.marriott.com/vieat

A panoply of shops, cafés, bars and restaurants fills the open-plan atrium of this modern glass hotel on the Ringstrasse. There are fairy lights and waterfalls to try to soothe the frenetic atmosphere. Although the hotel lacks a dedicated business centre, it does have business facilities, and is one of the few establishments in the city with a swimming pool. The bedrooms are generally large, but despite sound-proofing and air-conditioning, those looking on to the Stadtpark can be noisy.

HOFBURG
QUARTER

Nossek

Graben 17, A-1010. **Map** 2 D5 & 5 C3.
C 53370410. **FAX** 5353646. *Rooms:* 30. 🛏 26. 1 🎯 🏊 🕴 🔼 €€
@ reservation@pension-nossek.at

You will need to book months in advance to procure a room with a balcony overlooking the Graben in this elegant, but simple, family-run pension. It is spread over three floors and most bedrooms, though short on facilities and with rudimentary bathrooms, are rather special: rugs cover the parquet floors and period furniture and tasteful paintings abound. Equally attractive are the yellow breakfast room, with its brass chandeliers, and the adjacent sitting room.

Pertschy

Habsburgergasse 5, A-1010.
Map 2 D5 & 5 C3. **C** 534490.
FAX 5344949. *Rooms:* 50. 🛏 1 🎯
TV 🔼 🖴 AE, DC, MC, V, JCB.
€€€ W www.pertschy.com

This pension is an endearing combination of rather dowdy décor and a fine 300-year-old building. You enter a courtyard through ancient gates and ascend a wide, stone staircase. A green, carpeted walkway connects the bedrooms, each newly renovated with Rococo-style furnishings and adorned with crystal chandeliers. The breakfast room is decorated in mahogany in coffee house style. The clip clop of the hooves of *Fiaker* horses *(see p250)* clattering along the street where the hotel is located adds to the atmosphere.

Astoria

Führichgasse 1, A-1015. **Map** 5 C4.
C 515770. **FAX** 5157782.
Rooms: 118. 🛏 1 🎯 TV 🏊
🕴 🔼 🖴 Ⓨ P 🍴 AE, DC, MC, V, JCB. €€€€
W www.austria-trend.at

Perhaps the many opera stars who pop in here for a drink do so not only because it is just a stone's throw away from the auditorium, but also because this cosy turn-of-the-century hotel is less in the limelight than some of the more famous places close by. The panelled Jugendstil foyer leads to a rather grand dining room on the first floor. There are some splendid bedrooms, many with their own brass letterboxes. It is worth paying a little more for the extra space and period furnishings.

Ambassador

Neuer Markt 5, A-1010. **Map** 4 D1 & 6 D4. **C** 96161. **FAX** 5132999.
Rooms: 86. 🛏 1 🎯 TV 🏊 🕴
🔼 🖴 Ⓨ P 🍴 AE, DC, MC, V, JCB. €€€€€
W www.ambassador.at

The city's best-located five-star hotel has a 19th-century, Ringstrasse-style façade looking on to Kärntner Strasse, with an al fresco café terrace. Marble, pillars, tapestries, chandeliers and a superfluity of regal crimson and gold endow the hotel with an ostentatious, dated magnificence. Visiting presidents and princes have stayed in the best bedrooms. Some of these have their own sitting rooms, which are screened behind heavy drapes.

SCHOTTENRING AND
ALSERGRUND

Arcotel Boltzmann

Boltzmanngasse 8, A-1090. **Map** 1 C3. **C** 316120. **FAX** 31612816.
Rooms: 70. 🛏 🎯 TV 🏊 🖴 🕴
P 🖴 DC, MC, V. €€€€
W www.arcotel.at

A small, charming hotel with all the amenities of a four-star establishment, the Boltzmann is situated close to the romantic Strudelhof Steps *(see p54)* immortalized in Heimito von Doderer's novel. Surrounded by gardens and parks and a mere ten-minute walk from the historic centre, the hotel offers cosy rooms full of atmosphere and a private little garden where, in the summer, guests can have their breakfast.

Regina

Rooseveltplatz 15, A-1096.
Map 1 C4 & 5 A1. 📞 404460.
FAX 4088392. **Rooms:** 127. 🛏
1️⃣ TV 🍽 🔌 🛗 ⚓ 🅿 🛎
AE, DC, MC, V, JCB. €€€€
W www.kremslehnerhotels.at

This huge 19th-century building has
enough stature to live comfortably
next to the Votivkirche (see p111).
Inside there's a certain grandeur
too, with brass chandeliers and
classical statues. The building has
been a hotel since 1896 and in the
restaurant there is a photo of its
staff in 1913. Today, the hotel
caters mainly for tourist groups.
The old-fashioned bedrooms are
rather lacking in modern comforts
and are a bit of a let down.

MUSEUM AND TOWNHALL QUARTER

Wild

Lange Gasse 10, A-1080. **Map** 3 B1.
📞 4065174. FAX 4022168. **Rooms:**
19. 1️⃣ 🎫 🔌 ⚓ AE, DC, MC, V.
€ W www.pension-wild.com

This pension, in the heart of the
Josefstadt area, is our cheapest
recommendation by some margin.
It is run by an extremely friendly
woman and her son. The small
bedrooms are all spotlessly clean,
properly furnished and have a
washbasin. A toilet and a shower
are shared between every two or
three rooms. There is a kitchen on
each floor and a breakfast room
by the reception area.

Graf Stadion

Buchfeldgasse 5, A-1080. **Map** 1 B5.
📞 4055284. FAX 4050111.
Rooms: 40. 🛏 1️⃣ 🎫 TV 🛎
🍽 🔌 🅿 ⚓ DC, MC, V. €€€
W www.graf-stadion.com

An unsung Biedermeier building
(see pp30–31) on an atmospheric
backstreet contains the low-key,
inexpensive Graf Stadion hotel.
Some of the house's features are
lovely, such as a vaulted breakfast
room (likewise ground-floor
bedrooms) and a superb Art Deco
lift with an upholstered seat and
frosted glass. The bedrooms are
pleasantly simple, with chrome
bedsteads, but lack mod cons.

Museum

Museumstrasse 3, A-1070. **Map** 3 C1.
📞 5234426. FAX 523442630. **Rooms:**
15. 🛏 1️⃣ 🎫 🅿 TV 🔌 ⚓
AE, DC, MC, V. €€ W www.
tiscover.at/hotelpension-museum

Behind a fine façade coated with
putti and wavy wrought-iron
balconies, and set above a cinema
showing black-and-white movies,
this is a classic Viennese pension.
It is right on the doorstep of the
main museums. The spartan but
massive bedrooms have high
ceilings and wooden floors, and
the sitting and breakfast rooms
have furry chairs, ornate fireplaces
and, of course, chandeliers.

Altstadt Vienna

Kirchengasse 41, A-1070. **Map** 3 B1.
📞 5263999. FAX 5234901. **Rooms:**
36 (11 suites). 🛏 1️⃣ 🍽 🔌 🍽
🛎 🅿 ⚓ AE, DC, MC, V.
€€€ W www.altstadt.at

Situated in an interesting old quarter
just west of the main museums,
the Altstadt, open since 1991, has
already become extremely popular.
Designer lighting, boldly-coloured
walls and striking modern furnishings bring life to the ample rooms
of this 19th-century patrician
house. The polished herringbone-
patterned floors and high ceilings
are very attractive. The bedrooms
at the rear of the hotel couldn't be
more peaceful, while those at the
front overlook a church and tiled
roofs. The buffet breakfast is
good, the service excellent.

Zipser

Lange Gasse 49, A-1080. **Map** 1 B5.
📞 404540. FAX 4045413.
Rooms: 47. 🛏 46. 1️⃣ 🎫 TV 🛎
⚓ 🔌 🅿 ⚓ AE, DC, MC, V,
JCB. €€€ W www.zipser.at

This pension in the Josefstadt area
does not have as much character
as some of the others in Vienna,
but it does have smart modern
carpets and furniture throughout,
and the atmosphere is very
friendly. Ask for one of the larger
bedrooms at the rear of the hotel:
they have excellent bathrooms
and big wooden balconies which
are high up and overlook an
attractive leafy courtyard.
These rooms are quieter too.

Josefshof

Josefsgasse 4-6, A-1080. **Map** 1 B5.
📞 40419. FAX 40419150. **Rooms:** 68.
🛏 1️⃣ 🎫 TV 🛎 🍽 🔌
🅿 ⚓ 🛎 AE, DC, MC, V, JCB.
€€€€ W www.josefshof.com

The handsome yellow façade of
the Biedermeier Josefshof rises to
a bell-shaped flourish. It is just
down the road from Vienna's
English Theatre (see p230) in a
quiet backstreet. A marble and
glass hallway suggests more
grandeur than really exists, but the
breakfast room, opening on to a
garden courtyard, is pleasant. The

bedrooms are smart with high-
quality reproduction furniture
and parquet flooring. The out-of-
season rates are generally better
value than those in high season.

K+K Maria Theresia

Kirchberggasse 6-8, A-1070. **Map** 3 B1.
📞 521230. FAX 5212370. **Rooms:**
133. 🛏 1️⃣ 🎫 TV 🛎 🍽 🔌 ⚓
🔌 🅿 ⚓ 🛎 AE, DC, MC, V, JCB.
€€€€ W www.kkhotels.com

The sister to the K+K Palais (see
p198) is more popular with tourist
groups. The modern building
offers a similar overwhelmingly
yellow experience and has striking
modern furnishings – black
leather, ethnic rugs and abstract
prints. A few of the bedrooms
have balconies; some others have
commanding city views. Avant-
garde furniture shops and galleries
abound in the surrounding streets.

OPERA AND NASCHMARKT

Sacher

Philharmonikerstrasse 4, A-1010.
Map 4 D1 & 5 C5. 📞 51456.
FAX 51456810. **Rooms:** 109. 🛏 1️⃣
🎫 📶 TV 🔌 🍽 🛎 📻 🔌 ⚓
🅿 ⚓ 🛎 AE, DC, MC, V, JCB.
€€€€€ W www.sacher.com

Vienna's most famous hotel, the
Sacher (see p138) has been a haunt
for the regal and wealthy ever
since it opened in 1876. Now its
café is full of tourists thanks to the
eponymous chocolate cake (see
p209). The many-panelled public
rooms, in marble and red velvet,
hung with oil paintings, maintain
an intimate scale. The more expensive bedrooms are equally opulent,
while the standard rooms, though
hardly less comfortable, are less
evocative. Whether you go for a
slice of Torte or stay for a weekend,
you will receive outstanding service.

BELVEDERE QUARTER

Suzanne

Walfischgasse 4, A-1010. **Map** 4 D1
& 6 D5. 📞 5132507. FAX 5132500.
Rooms: 26. 🛏 1️⃣ 🎫 TV 🍽 🔌
🔌 ⚓ AE, DC, MC, V. €€
W www.pension-suzanne.at

This popular pension lies just steps
from Kärntner Strasse and the Opera
House. It is hidden away behind
an ugly concrete block and sited
over a flower shop and a sex shop.
However, the bedrooms, with

paintings and comfortable armchairs, have old-fashioned charm and are spread over a number of floors. The more expensive have kitchenettes.

Bristol

Kärntner Ring 1, A-1015. **Map** 4 D2 & 6 D5. 🅲 515160. 🆏 51516550.
Rooms: 140. 🛏 1 🎯 24 TV ⛄ ⛄ 🟰 🛏 🔧 🗝 🐾 P Y 🍴 🍽 AE, DC, MC, V, JCB. €€€€€ W www.westin.com/bristol

The fin-de-siècle Bristol is a very luxurious hotel. The location is superb: on the Ringstrasse and opposite the opera (though just within the Belvedere Quarter). The style – marble, gilt, antiques and paintings everywhere – is of dignified opulence. Each public room is an institution: the famous Korso restaurant for dining (see p215), the gold-pillared sitting room for afternoon tea. Bedrooms divide into top-floor penthouses, superb business suites, and the rest.

Imperial

Kärntner Ring 16, A-1015. **Map** 4 D2 & 6 D5. 🅲 501100. 🆏 50110410.
Rooms: 138. 🛏 1 🎯 24 TV ⛄ ⛄ 🟰 🛏 🔧 🗝 🐾 P Y 🍴 🍽 AE, DC, MC, V, JCB. €€€€€ W www.luxurycollection.com/imperial

If you stay at the Imperial you may well be sleeping under the same roof as a head of state or two. The grandest of Vienna's top hotels exudes an air of exclusivity in its famous, panelled restaurant and its wonderful café (full of elderly ladies). Its over-the-top Ringstrasse style (see pp32–3) is best displayed in a monumental marble staircase. In the 1950s, two extra floors were added, containing smaller rooms designed in cherry wood.

Im Palais Schwarzenberg

Schwarzenbergplatz 9, A-1030. **Map** 4 E2. 🅲 7984515. 🆏 7984714.
Rooms: 44. 🛏 1 🎯 24 TV ⛄ 🛏 🔧 🗝 🐾 P Y 🍴 🍽 AE, DC, MC, V, JCB. €€€€€ W www.palais-schwarzenberg.com

Occupying a portion of the huge Baroque Schwarzenburg Palace (see p150) in its 18-acre (7.5-ha) landscaped park, this hotel has an undeniably breathtaking setting. Honeymoon territory for some, and a getaway from the hurly-burly of Vienna's busier luxury hotels for others, this hotel is surprisingly intimate. Each of its imaginative vaulted public rooms, including its conservatory dining room, are cosy and relaxing. The main building has the larger, better

bedrooms, with antiques and fine paintings. The adjacent stable block has smaller, more modern rooms.

FURTHER AFIELD

Altwienerhof

Herklotzgasse 6, A-1150. 🅲 8926000. 🆏 89260008. **Rooms:** 25. 🛏 18. 1 🎯 TV 🔧 🗝 🍴 AE, DC, MC, V. €€€ W www.altwienerhof.at

The Kellners' hotel lies some way from the centre but close to an underground stop. Many of the overnight guests are French – understandable when outstanding cuisine is the order of the day. Formal dining takes place in impressive mahogany and tapestry-panelled rooms, a lovely conservatory and, in summer, a tree-lined courtyard; one option for residents is a no-choice half-board meal. Old-fashioned, comfortable bedrooms, ranging from stylish suites to simple rooms with just a basin, offer very good value.

Nordbahn

Praterstrasse 72, A-1020.
🅲 211300. 🆏 2113072. **Rooms:** 78. 🛏 1 🎯 TV 🔧 🗝 P AE, DC, MC, V. €€ W www.hotel-nordbahn.at

The famous Ferris Wheel at the Prater (see pp162–63) and the underground are both about five minutes' walk from the Nordbahn. Situated on the busy, tree-lined Praterstrasse, this rather character-less but roomy hotel boasts a small bar, a terrace of sorts, a free car park and a library. The bedrooms offer comfort rather than style and it is a good idea to ask for a room away from the main road. Max Steiner, who wrote the film scores for Gone With The Wind and Casablanca, was born here on 10 May 1888.

Gartenhotel Glanzing

Glanzinggasse 23, A-1190.
🅲 47042720. 🆏 470427214.
Rooms: 14. 🛏 1 🎯 TV ⛄ 🔧 🗝 P AE, DC, MC, V. €€€ W www.gartenhotel-glanzing.at

Built in the 1930s, this interesting ivy-festooned hotel has a rambling garden and stands in leafy suburbs close to the wine villages. Many of the guests are from the American Embassy nearby. Transport to the centre is a five-minute walk away. A civilized retreat, the hotel has a grand piano in the main room, and big bedrooms which make the most of great views. Some bedrooms are modern, others are

in Biedermeier style. The hotel stresses its conviviality and extends its welcome to children.

Landhaus Fuhrgassl-Huber

Neustift am Walde, Rathstrasse 24, A-1190. 🅲 4403033. 🆏 4402714.
Rooms: 38. 🛏 1 🎯 TV 🔧 🗝 🛏 🔧 🗝 P Y AE, DC, MC, V. €€€ W www.fuhrgassl-huber.at

The accordion tunes and rustic décor of this faultlessly spruce hotel may make a welcome, down-to-earth break from classical music and Baroque frippery. The hotel lies in a typical wine village: there's a Heuriger (see p218) next door, and the hotel owner has his own just up the street. In addition, he owns the vineyards behind the hotel. His daughter and son-in-law are the managers, and the hotel is prettily decked out in pine, with tiled floors and stencilled furniture. A bus to the centre stops virtually outside and the journey takes a little over 30 minutes.

Inter-Continental Wien

Johannesgasse 28, A-1037.
Map 4 E1 & 6 E5. 🅲 711220. 🆏 7134489. **Rooms:** 453. 🛏 1 🎯 24 TV ⛄ 🟰 🛏 🔧 🗝 P Y 🍴 AE, DC, MC, V, JCB. €€€€€ W www.vienna.intercontinental.com

So cosmopolitan is the efficient Inter-Continental that it even offers Japanese dishes for breakfast. Other aspects are more Viennese: a pianist and violinist play nightly in the bar area of the elegant, chandeliered foyer. The hotel is a two-minute walk from the Ringstrasse. The upper-floor bedrooms in this modern block have good views across the Stadtpark.

Mercure Grand Hotel Biedermeier

Landstrasser Hauptstrasse 28, A-1030. **Map** 4 F1. 🅲 716710. 🆏 71671503.
Rooms: 203. 🛏 1 🎯 TV ⛄ 🟰 🛏 🔧 🗝 P Y 🍴 🍽 AE, DC, MC, V, JCB. €€€€ W www.accor.com

This hotel occupies the whole complex of a superbly restored narrow, yellow Biedermeier passage courtyard. It offers guests a Vienna in microcosm: a plank-floored tavern, a Heuriger wine cellar and a traditional coffee house that spreads into a bar and restaurant. The large, spacious bedrooms, almost all looking down on the pedestrianized, cobbled passage, are particularly quiet. The hotel lies off one of Vienna's main shopping streets, less than ten minutes on foot from the Ringstrasse.

For key to symbols see p196

RESTAURANTS, CAFÉS AND BARS

The Viennese know how to eat well. The staples of Vienna's cuisine are assimilated from the cooking styles of the Habsburg Empire, and so include *Schnitzels*, originating as North Italian escalopes; dumplings that are a speciality of Bohemia; Hungarian goulash; and even Balkan grills and sausages (*Cevapcici*). Balkan cuisine is a result of the post-Second World War immigration that has multiplied the ethnic cuisines now available in the city. The range of gastronomy is vast, from gourmet nouvelle cuisine down to the booths (*Würstelstände*) selling sausages and beer on street corners. You can take your choice of atmosphere from old-fashioned sumptuous splendour to tavern gardens or Baroque wine-cellars. Mealtimes are also flexible and in the city centre you will always find somewhere serving hot meals between 11:30 a.m. and midnight. The listings *(see pp 212–17)* are divided by area and by price, with the emphasis being on local cuisine, but there is a generous choice of alternatives as well.

Papier-mâché waitress outside restaurant

TYPES OF EATING PLACE

THE HUMBLE *Würstelstände* sell hot dogs and *Leberkäse* (only for the adventurous) which is somewhat alarmingly described as 'meat remnants worked into an undefined formless mass'. On a slightly higher gastronomic level are the numerous small eateries selling sandwiches, filled rolls, pastries and soft drinks. Mouth-watering open sandwiches are the speciality of **Duran** (several outlets, *see p218*) and the celebrated **Trzesniewski** (*see p219*), with a coffee or a miniature Pfiff ($1/8$ of a litre) of beer to accompany them.

Wine cellar sign

If something a little more sustaining is required, the numerous *Stehbeisln* (stand-up counters) at some butchers' and food stores offer fresh dishes and sometimes a welcome bowl of hot soup on a winter's day. Some upmarket restaurants advertise a *Gabelfrühstück* (fork breakfast) serving hot delicacies mid-morning. Another extra repast discovered by the Viennese is the *Jause*, typically cold meats and cheese eaten outside regular mealtimes. All these options are preferable for the budget-conscious traveller to the museum restaurants and cafés which, however good, tend to be more expensive.

Local musician at the Augustiner-keller *(see p218)*

Self-service restaurants such as **Naschmarkt** (Schottengasse, Schwarzenbergerplatz, *see p219*) which offers a wide selection of cold and hot dishes, including grills made to order, can be recommended. Others can be found in the Ringstrassen shopping mall and in Maysedergasse behind the Oper (Markt-Restaurant Rosenberger). Some close early so are better for a quick lunch, while a bustling coffee-house or wine-cellar might be more appealing in the evenings.

WINE CELLARS AND HEURIGEN

WINE CELLARS represent good value, with cold buffets and a limited range of hot dishes on offer to

Open sandwiches available at Zum Schwarzen Kameel *(see p214)*

accompany local wine from the barrel. The atmosphere is informal, and even more so in the gardens of the *Heurigen* (taverns) in the villages at the periphery of the city at Neustift am Walde, Grinzing, Salmannsdorf, and elsewhere. In theory, *Heurigen* serve only the wine from their own vineyards and of the current vintage. *Heuriger* has two meanings: it refers to the youngest available vintage of the local wine and it also refers to the venues that sell such wines by the glass. According to regulations laid down by Emperor Joseph II, pine twigs placed over or by the door (*ausg'steckt*) remained as long as the vintage lasted, after which they were removed and the tavern closed for the year. You will still see such taverns, but in practice the larger ones are open all year and serve

Garden scene at a *Heuriger* where local wine growers are licensed to sell their own wine

Typical sausage stand (or *Wurst-stand*) in the city centre

an extensive buffet with hot and cold cuts of meat. The wine is mostly white, often a blend of local grapes (the *gemischter Satz*) and is a true *Heuriger* until 11th November of the year after harvest. To sample a genuine local product, look for *Eigenbau* by the entrance.

COFFEE HOUSES AND KONDITOREIEN

Vienna's legendary coffee houses (*see pp58–61*) are culturally specific: politicians favour **Landtmann**, whilst literati swap ideas in **Hawelka** (*see p219*). Coffee is served in different ways depending on the strength and addition of hot milk or water required.

Prices vary according to location and type: a Ringstraßen café is more expensive than a smoke-filled den with a billiard table at the rear, or somewhere like the **Café Ministerium** (*see p218*) patronised by the proverbially parsimonious bureaucrats from the nearby ministries.

While coffee houses serve a small range of simple hot dishes, the *Konditoreien* concentrate on pastries and cakes, though a few also do a good light lunch. The great *Konditoreien* in the centre can be rather a scrum in the tourist season, but the fare is irresistible (diabetics also catered for). Since there is a complicated nomenclature for the *Konditoreien* themselves, it is best to go to the display counter and point to the item you want. A cheaper alternative is the Aida chain found throughout Vienna, with less comfortable seating but lower prices, even for the *Sachertorte*.

THE VIENNESE BEISL

What the trattoria is to Italy the *Beisl* is to Vienna, a simple restaurant offering local specialities in an agreeably informal atmosphere. The name is thought to be of Jewish origin (in the 18th century,

many inn-keepers were Jewish). Unfortunately many *Beisln* have gone up-market and their prices have lifted accordingly. All of them serve typical Viennese specialities like *Tafelspitz* (boiled beef), *Vanillirostbraten* (pot roast with garlic), *Kalbsbeuschel* (calf's lung and heart) and of course *Schnitzel*, together with enticingly named desserts: *Powidltascherln* (pasta envelopes with plum jam) or *Zwetschkenknödel* (plums in potato dumpling). Viennese cooking is strong in the soup department, one of the more popular soups being *Eierschwammerlsuppe* made with chanterelle mushrooms. Huge portions of *Wiener Schnitzel* are served at Figlmüller (*see p212*).

The most aspiring *Beisln* should have just as good food as a mid-priced restaurant.

A trendy city bar, the Tunnel (*see p219*), on Florianigasse

Do & Co restaurant *(see p214)* overlooking the Stephansdom

MID-PRICED AND ETHNIC RESTAURANTS

THE TOP END OF the *Beisln* merge with what Austrians somewhat misleadingly call *'gutbürgerliche Küche'*, or 'good plain cooking', since at many places so identified such as **Zum Herkner** in outlying Hernals *(see p216)*, the food is more than good and rather sophisticated. Establishments like **Kern's Beisl** *(see p212)* and **Restaurant Sperl** *(see p216)* offer extremely good value, as do many of the ethnic restaurants throughout the city: **Beim Czaak** *(see p212)* with its roots in Bohemian cuisine, or the Hungarian **Ilona Stüberl** *(see p214)* in the Bräunerstraße. Some restaurants offer great value because they only accept cash. The authentic Greek restaurants tend also to be inexpensive, less so the

Japanese restaurants and *sushi* bars that have enjoyed a boom over the last few years. Pizza and pasta establishments are ubiquitous, but many of the genuine Italian restaurants tend to be found at the luxury end of the market.

Vegetarian restaurants are slowly on the increase, and one of the longest established is **Wrenkh** *(see p212)*.

One of the city's many *Café-Konditoreien*

LUXURY RESTAURANTS

GOURMET EATING in Vienna generally retains a local flavour. Seriously good cuisines may be found at luxury hotels like the Hotel Sacher *(see p200)* or the Palais Schwarzenberg *(see p201)*. Vienna's most prestigious restaurant for sea food is the **Kervansaray-Hummerbar** *(see p216)*, where lobster can be had at a price. Now located in the leafy surroundings of the Stadtpark, **Steirereck** *(see p217)* is still considered one of the best gourmet restaurants in the country, while the **Trattoria Martinelli** *(see p215)* serves traditional Tuscan specialities, which can be enjoyed in the Baroque ambience of the Harrach Palace.

READING THE MENU

THE THREE MAIN divisions of the menu are *Kalte* or *Warme Vorspeisen* (cold or hot hors d'oeuvres), *Hauptspeisen* (main courses) and *Mehlspeisen* (desserts). There may be separate entries for soups (*Suppen*), fish (*Fische*), beef (*Rindfleisch*) and pork (*Schweinefleisch*). Many restaurants have a children's menu and usually a selection of vegetarian dishes. The specials are always good value as well as the individual dishes of the day or *Tagesangebot*. You may also see the phrase *Fertige Speisen* for dishes that are not on the fixed-price menu. A specifically Austrian phrase frequently encountered is *Schmankerln*, which implies regional delicacies. Portions tend to be on the generous side, although there is a trend to lighter eating in the more up-market establishments offering nouvelle cuisine.

The house wines are usually served in glasses which hold exactly a quarter of a litre, though smaller glasses may also be served, and half a litre may come in a carafe. Most restaurants, at least in the city centre, have menus in English.

HOW MUCH TO PAY

Vienna's restaurants generally represent good value for money. However over-indulgence in tempting little delicacies (*Leckerbissen*) can make a big dent in the wallet; small items like coffee are also relatively expensive and a cup in one of the congenial old coffee houses or *Konditoreien* costs around €2.5 to €3. Snack meals provide adequate sustenance at around €5, while double that should buy a modest meal in one of the self-service restaurants or less touristy wine cellars. A reasonably priced *Beisl* might cost €20 a head with a glass of wine, but sticking to the fixed-price menu will probably reduce that significantly. There is a large middle swathe of restaurants where you might expect a bill of up to €36, while luxury and gourmet establishments have prices that accelerate well beyond the €40 mark. Prices can be more expensive in the evening.

Most restaurants with a regular international clientele take credit cards, but many of the *Beisln* and standard Viennese restaurants may only take cash.

Traditional Austrian musicians in a garden restaurant

Krah Krah bar sign

BOOKING AND SERVICE

Always telephone and confirm any special requests especially wheelchair access and facilities for the disabled, if non-smoking seats are available and whether children are catered for. Facilities may be limited and some of the older establishments may have narrow corridors or steps. Booking a day ahead or even on the day is usually sufficient. Even a simple *Beisl* can have a faithful local clientele and you may be disappointed if you wander in and expect to find a free table. Assiduous service is the hallmark of many Viennese restaurants. Tips are traditionally 10% and are mandatory everywhere except in the few places where you may find that the service is included.

USING THE LISTINGS

The restaurant listings are on pages 212–17. Symbols after the address summarize facilities the restaurant offers. Accepted credit cards do change. It is recommended you check in advance if you want to use a particular card. The café and bar listings are on pages 218–219.

|🍴| fixed-price menu
|👶| caters for children
|♿| wheelchair access
|🎵| Live music
|★| highly recommended
|💳| credit cards accepted:
AE American Express
DC Diners Club
MC Mastercard/Access
V Visa
JCB Japanese Credit Bureau

Price categories for a three-course meal for one, including a ¼ litre of house wine, tax and service:

€ under €20
€€ €21–€30
€€€ €31–€40
€€€€ above €40

Restaurant in the Altwienerhof Hotel on Herklotzgasse

What to Eat: Savoury Foods

VIENNESE COOKING is surprisingly varied, a reflection of imperial days when culinary traditions from many parts of Europe influenced the city's cooks. *Schnitzel* may have come to Austria via Milan, which was once under Austrian control. Soups are rich and flavoursome, and often include *Knödel* (dumplings).

Vollkorn Bauernbrot

In winter, roast goose and duck appear on many menus as well as game dishes such as *Rehrücken* (saddle of venison). Seasonal vegetarian specialities include *Eierschwammerl* (chanterelle mushrooms) in autumn and *Spargel* (asparagus) in the summer months.

Salzstangerl (right)

Siebenkorn-brot (left)

Hausbrot (right)

Kaiser-semmel (left)

Frankfurter mit Senf
Frankfurters are one of the many types of sausage sold throughout the city. They are often served with mustard.

Leberknödelsuppe
This clear beef broth includes small dumplings made with liver, seasoned with parsley and marjoram.

Frittatensuppe
Thin strips of lightly seasoned pancakes are added to a clear beef soup.

Eierspeise
Served in the pan, this is like a scrambled omelette.

Smoked ham   Roast pork

Sauerkraut with juniper

Eierschwammerl
Chanterelle mushrooms are picked in autumn and may be served in a salad.

Bauernschmaus
This simple country platter of hot meats can be found in many Viennese restaurants and is usually served with dumplings. The meats include frankfurters, a selection of ham, smoked pork, and roast pork or pork cutlet.

Rindsgulasch
Originally from Hungary, this paprika-spiced beef stew comes with dumplings.

Gefüllte Kalbsbrust
Breast of veal is filled with a variety of meat or vegetable stuffings.

Erdäpfelgulasch
This potato goulash often includes frankfurter sausages.

Wiener Schnitzel
The breaded veal escalope is fried until golden.

Tafelspitz

G'röste

Sauce

Tafelspitz mit G'röste
The top corner of silverside of beef is thickly sliced, boiled and served with fried grated potatoes and an apple and horseradish sauce. It is a typical lunchtime dish and was allegedly eaten every day by the Emperor Franz Joseph.

Gemischter Salat
Mixed salad ingredients are often arranged side by side.

Beef and rice stuffing

Tomato sauce

Heringsalat
Herring is traditional on Ash Wednesday and served year round. In salads it is pickled.

Gefüllte Paprika
Green peppers are stuffed with minced beef and rice and cooked in a tomato sauce.

What to Eat: Sweet Foods

Few cities in the world can rival Vienna's devotion to all things sweet. The Viennese enjoy cakes mid morning or afternoon, and set time aside for between-meal snacks – the afternoon coffee break is known as *Jause*. The finest *Torten* (gâteaux), pastries and cakes such as *Bischofsbrot* (Bishop's bread, which is sponge cake filled with nuts, raisins, glacé fruit and chocolate pieces) tend to be found in *Konditoreien (see p217)* and are usually consumed with a cup of coffee. Traditional Viennese puddings can be found in all good Viennese restaurants *(see pp213–16)* and are typically rich. Some innovative chefs have created their own versions.

Many *Konditoreien* offer cakes baked on the premises

DESSERTS

From sweet *Topfentascherl* (curd cheese envelopes) to *Kastanienreis* (chestnut purée), Vienna's dessert cuisine incorporates rich and varied ingredients. Some recipes are simple, others very extravagant. Fruits such as plums and apples fill featherlight dumplings, pancakes, fritters or strudels, and although *Mehlspeisen* (puddings) translates literally as "dishes with flour", ground almonds or hazelnuts can replace the flour. As well as the selection here there are less obvious choices such as sweet "pasta" served with poppyseeds to create *Mohnnudeln*.

Apfelstrudel
Apple and raisins are encased in a light strudel pastry dusted with icing sugar. The strudel is served warm or cold.

Palatschinken
Thicker than a French crêpe, the Austrian pancake is filled with fruit, curd cheese, chocolate sauce – or simply jam, as here.

Reisauflauf mit Äpfeln
Reisauflauf is a rich rice soufflé. It can be cooked in a creamy and light style, or as a heartier dessert. Here it includes apple and is served with raspberry syrup.

Mohr im Hemd
This rich chocolate pudding is steamed and served with hot chocolate sauce. Chilled whipped cream, usually scented with vanilla sugar, is added just before serving.

Topfenknödel
Light curd cheese dumplings are coated with breadcrumbs (or ground walnuts) which have been fried crisply in butter, and served hot with a fruit compôte or purée.

CAKES AND PASTRIES

Sachertorte is the best-known Viennese *Torte* but there are dozens of others, such as *Dobostorte*, a sponge cake sandwiched together with chocolate butter cream. Many cakes and pastries include chocolate, coffee or cream, while others use fresh fruit and wafer-thin strudel pastry. *Linzertorte* is a classic almond and jam pastry and *Guglhupf* is traditionally made with yeast, though there are many variations. The hollow centre may be filled with flowers for birthdays. *Faschingskrapfen* are deep-fried apricot doughnuts made in the pre-Lenten Carnival time known as *Fasching (see p65).*

Dobostorte
Invented by pâtissier Josef Dobos in Hungary in 1887, this rich cake alternates equal layers of sponge and chocolate butter cream and is glazed with caramel. Doboschnitten *are exactly the same but sold in individual rectangles.*

Linzertorte
A sweet almond pastry case is filled with raspberry, apricot or redcurrant jam and decorated with a pastry criss-cross pattern.

Sachertorte
The famous Sachertorte *has a layer of apricot jam beneath the thick, smooth chocolate coating.*

Mohnstrudel
The sweet, moist, yeast-based dough is spread with ground poppy seeds and raisins and folded over into a roulade.

Guglhupf
Baked in a fluted ring mould, variations on Guglhupf *include this marbelized chocolate version,* Marmorguglhupf.

Rehrücken
Shaped like the saddle of venison after which it is named, this chocolate cake is studded with almonds.

Esterházytorte
Available as a round cake or in rectangular slices, this sweetest of gâteaux is coated with feathered icing.

ORIGINAL SACHERTORTE

This celebrated chocolate gâteau was invented in 1832 by Prince Metternich's pastry chef, Franz Sacher. It has always been available from the Hotel Sacher shop in Kärntner Strasse, which sells it in a variety of sizes and packings. When the nearby Demel Konditorei claimed their *Sachertorte* was authentic on the grounds that a member of the Sacher family had sold them the recipe, the assertion provoked a protracted court case. Sacher won the right to the term "original *Sachertorte*" but was not able to stop the cake from being imitated in Vienna and all over the world.

What to Drink in Vienna

AUSTRIA is a source of excellent wine and good rich beers. Vienna itself is a wine-growing region. It is surrounded by vineyards which supply the *Heurige (see p218)* in villages on the edge of the city with young local wines. Fine Austrian wines are found in good restaurants *(see* Choosing a Restaurant, *p212)*. Home-produced wine is mainly white. Local red wines are improving, especially those from the Burgenland and Carnuntum districts. Sweet *Eiswein* is made from grapes left on the vines until the first frosts. Some first-class brandies are also produced – fruit brandies and schnaps are typical national beverages.

Beyond the villages north and west of Vienna lie vineyards producing *Heurige* wines

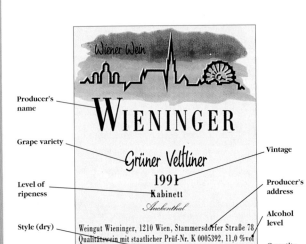

Chardonnay from Styria and sparkling wine from Lower Austria

AUSTRIAN WINES

THE MOST popular wine in Austria is Grüner Veltliner *(see below)*. Other wines include superb dry Rieslings, especially from the Wachau, and rich Weissburgunder (Pinot Blanc) from Burgenland. Red wines tend to be soft and lush – robust reds come from the Blaufränkisch grape *(see below)*. Among recent vintages, 1999, 2000, 2002 and 2003 were good.

Riesling from the Wachau can be light, or full bodied like the Smaragd style.

St Laurent is a soft red wine; at its best it is rich and stylish.

Producer's name

Grape variety

Level of ripeness

Style (dry)

WIENINGER

Grüner Veltliner

1991

Kabinett

Auckenthal

Weingut Wieninger, 1210 Wien, Stammersdorfer Straße 78

Qualitätswein mit staatlicher Prüf-Nr. K 0005392, 11,0 %vol

ÖSTERREICH   trocken   ℮ 0,75ℓ

Vintage

Producer's address

Alcohol level

Quantity

Grüner Veltliner is a fresh, fruity white wine. It is widely grown in Austria and is usually made in a dry style. It also makes excellent *Eiswein*.

Blaufränkisch is a quality local red – the best comes from Burgenland.

Krügel or ½ litre
tankard

Seidl or standard
⅓ litre measure

Krügel or ½
litre of pale beer

Pfiff or ⅛ litre
beer glass

AUSTRIAN BEERS

V IENNA HAS BEEN producing good malty beers
for more than 150 years. Viennese lagers
are bronze in colour and sweet in flavour.
They make an excellent accompaniment to
the hearty soups and stews found in *Beisln*
(see p203). The local Ottakring brewery's *Gold*
Fassl is typical of the style, although lighter
Bavarian-type beers such as *Weizengold* are
also commonly available. One of Austria's
most popular beers is *Gösser*, produced in
Styria and found in the pubs and restaurants
of Vienna. Speciality beers include the Styrian
Eggenberger Urbock, one of the strongest beers
in the world. It is made by the Schloss Eggen-
berg brewery founded in the 17th century.

Kaiser beer,
a light beer

Weizengold
wheat beer

Gösser Spezial
is rich

Bierhof beer mat
advertising a pub
in the Haarhof.

Null Komma Josef
is a local alcohol-
free beer.

OTHER AUSTRIAN DRINKS

Austria offers a good range of non-alcoholic
fruit juices such as *Himbeersaft* (raspberry
syrup) or *Johannisbeersaft* (blackcurrant
juice). Fruit is also the basis of many types
of schnaps (sometimes called *Brand*).
This powerful eau de vie is distilled from
berries such as juniper and
rowan as well as apricots
(Marillen) and quince
(Quitten). It's worth
paying the extra to
sample the exquisite fruit
schnaps produced by the
dedicated specialists.
Almdudler (herbal
lemonade) is also a
speciality. For a few
weeks in autumn,
fermenting grape
juice, *Sturm*, is
available. Milky in
colour and quite
sweet, it is more
alcoholic than its
grape flavour
suggests.

Apricot
schnaps

The Wiener Rathauskeller *(see p215)* is a popular
restaurant serving a number of beers

Choosing a Restaurant

THE RESTAURANTS in this guide have been selected across a wide range of price categories for their good value, exceptional food and interesting locations. The chart below lists restaurants in Vienna by area; entries are alphabetical within each price category. Information on cafés and bars can be found on pages 218–219.

		CREDIT CARDS	VEGETARIAN DISHES	GOOD WINE LIST	VIENNESE CUISINE

STEPHANSDOM QUARTER

BEIM CZAAK   €   DC   ●
Postgasse 15 / Corner Fleischmarkt. **Map** 2 E5 & 6 E3. **◖** 513 72 15.
In the same family's possession since 1920, this is a delightfully informal place offering standards of Viennese cuisine, but also some dishes in the Czech tradition. Pleasing atmosphere of the old-style *Beisl* with few concessions to comfort in the seating, but friendly service. ● *Sun, hols.* 🔥

BETTELSTUDENT   €   AE   ●   ●
Johannesgasse 12. **Map** 4 E1 & 6 D4. **◖** 513 20 44.   DC
More than a fuelling station for hungry students (although it is that), this lively   MC
restaurant with its house beers, speciality breads, good quality steaks and spare   V
ribs also has occasional live music and stays open to the early hours. |●| *lunch.*

KERN'S BEISL   €   ●   ■
Kleeblattgasse 4 (corner Tuchlauben). **Map** 2 D5 & 5 C3. **◖** 533 91 88.
Hard to praise this busy friendly *Beisl* too highly. Austrian regional and Viennese dishes, with a large selection of Austrian wines and spirits. Superb value, no doubt partly because it's cash only. Seasonal items include game (venison stew or cutlets) and vegetarian specialities. ● *Sat, Sun.* |●| *lunch.* 🧍 ★

LUSTIG ESSEN Map 2 E5 & 6 D2   €   AE   ●
Salvatorgasse 4–6 (corner Marc Aurelstraße). **Map** 2 E5 & 6 D2. **◖** 533 30 38.   MC
Don't be phased by the clashing modernist styles of the decor and the rather laçonic service: the food is excellent, and served only in small portions individually cooked to order (so give yourself time). Seasonal Austrian and Viennese cooking is combined with dishes from the WOK and a few Greek and Italian standards are thrown in for good measure. 🧍 🔥

PFUDL   €   AE   ●   ●
Bäckerstraße 22. **Map** 2 E5 & 6 E3. **◖** 512 67 05.   DC
The wood-panelled interior of Pfudl is picturesque enough and the   MC
excellent cooking of Viennese specialities distracts attention from the   V
discomfort of the equally picturesque, rustic chairs. Seasonal dishes and a famous "*Pfudlstrudl*" plus wines from Pfudl's own vineyards. 🧍

EAST TO WEST   € €   AE   ●   ■
Seilerstätte 14. **Map** 4 E1 & 6 D4. **◖** 512 91 49.   DC
In an attractively understated modern interior enjoy tongue-tingling Chinese,   MC
Japanese and Thai dishes with enticing names ("*Geisha Bathing behind the*   V
Rushes", "*Inner Harmony of a Samurai*"). The food is light and aromatic, and   JCB
they've tried hard with the appropriate wines. |●| 🈺 *(only over 10 euros)*

FIGLMÜLLER   € €   ■
Wollzeile. **Map** 2 E5 & 6 D3. **◖** 512 61 77.
Cosy restaurant famous for its huge *Wiener Schnitzels* and the ironic wit of the formally dressed waiters. Touristy, but not simply a "tourist trap"; a good place to experiment with wines by the glass. No beer. ● *Aug and 25/26 Dec.*

MAK-CAFÉ   € €   ●   ●
Stubenring 3–5 (in MAK, the Museum of Applied Arts.) **Map** 4 F1 & 6 F3. **◖** 714 01 21.
With two gleaming bars, frescoed ceiling and a tranquil oasis in the courtyard for eating out in summer, the MAK Café appeals to the fashionable arty crowd. Austrian and international cooking with a light touch, menu changes daily to satisfy its regulars. No credit cards. ● *Mon.* |●| *lunch.* 🧍 *(especially Sun).* ★

TOKO-RI   € €   AE   ●
Salztorgasse 4. **Map** 2 E4 & 6 D2. **◖** 532 77 77.   DC
The interior (on two floors) exudes a slick modern Japanese minimalism and   MC
boasts a *sushi* counter doubling as an aquarium. There are now four outlets   V
of the extremely professional Toko-Ri chain, and this is perhaps the best place to start for devotees of Japanese fish dishes. Besides *sushi*, there is *sashimi, maki, tempura, teriyaki* and *teppanyaki*.

	CREDIT CARDS	VEGETARIAN DISHES	GOOD WINE LIST	VIENNESE CUISINE

Price categories for a three-course meal for one, excluding drinks, but including all unavoidable extra charges such as cover, service and tax:
€ under €20
€€ €21–€30
€€€ €31–€40
€€€€ €41–€50.

CREDIT CARDS
Indicates which credit cards are accepted: AE American Express; DC Diners Club; MC Master Card/Access; V Visa; JCB Japanese Credit Bureau.

VEGETARIAN DISHES
The menu includes dishes suitable for vegetarians.

GOOD WINE LIST
Denotes a wide range of good wines, or a more specialized selection of local wines.

VIENNESE CUISINE
Typical Viennese dishes are offered on the menu.

WEIBELS WIRTSHAUS　　€€　　AE MC V
Kumpfgasse 2. **Map** 4 E1 & 6 E3. 512 39 86.
An intimate interior with cosy little sitting niches, elegant table culture, sophisticated but understated service and above all some excellent Austrian wines by the glass. Austrian cooking at a very high level. Enjoy. ● *Sun.* ❙●❙ ★

WRENKH　　€€　　AE DC MC V
Bauernmarkt 10. **Map** 2 E5 & 6 D3. 533 15 26.
One of the best vegetarian restaurants in Vienna, Wrenkh also runs a fast-food outlet at Rauhensteingasse 12. Noodles laced with sheep's cheese in white wine sauce, potato and leek in mustard sauce, Florentine zucchini and polenta – dishes such as these could tempt the most unregenerate carnivore. ♿ ♿

ZU DEN DREI HACKEN　　€€　　AE DC MC V
Singerstraße 28. **Map** 4 E1 & 6 E4. 512 58 95.
Crammed into a couple of small, plain rooms, this intimate, somewhat old-fashioned restaurant offers excellent traditional Viennese cooking. The Viennese emphasis does not preclude regional Austrian dishes. The offal is good, as is the "walnut pudding". Laid back service. ● *Sun and hols.* ❙●❙ ♿

ENOTECA CINQUE TERRE　　€€€
Marc-Aurel-Straße 10. **Map** 2 E5 & 6 D2. 533 82 65.
Watching your meal being cooked in this tiny corridor of a restaurant is part of the experience. The chef makes insouciant use of cream in wonderful pasta dishes like ravioli with chopped pears and gorgonzola. The fish is mouth-wateringly prepared. The wines (vintage Italian, Spanish and Austrian served as 1/10 of a litre per glass) are seriously good. ● *Sat lunch, Sun, hols.* ★

FADINGER　　€€€
Wipplingerstraße 29. **Map** 2 D4 & 5 C2. 533 43 41.
Fadinger's marvellous cooking gives Viennese cuisine a subtle extra élan by means of original sauces and seasonings. Foodies will enjoy the creative flair of the *hors d'oeuvres* and desserts. Salmon *au gratin* with creamed garlic on leaf spinach with saffron rice, paprika salad and soja, pumpkin soup with croûtons are a few of the dishes on offer. ● *Sat, Sun, hols.* ❙●❙ *lunch.* ♿ ♿

OFENLOCH　　€€€　　DC MC V
Kurrentgasse 8. **Map** 5 C2. 533 88 44.
This historic restaurant serves an imaginative range of classic Viennese dishes, prepared using only the very best local products, largely organically farmed. The fine cooking is matched by the well-kept *Wirtshaus* interior. Weather permitting, diners can eat outside, under towering Baroque houses, on one of Vienna's oldest streets. ● *Sun, Mon.* ❙●❙ *Tue–Fri lunch.* ♿ ♿ ★

PLACHUTTA　　€€€　　DC MC V JCB
Wollzeile 38. **Map** 2 E5 & 6 E3. 512 15 77.
The branch of the family that runs the famous Hietzinger Bräu (*see p. 000*) has opened this trendy and now expanding establishment, brightly decorated in green and yellow. It serves superbly tender Styrian meat. Probably the best place in the city centre for serious carnivores. ♿

SALUT　　€€€　　AE DC MC V
Wildpretmarkt 3. **Map** 2 D5 & 6 D3. 533 13 22.
There are notably few French restaurants in Vienna, however Salut, offering classic French dishes, does something to restore the balance. The decor attempts to transplant a little of Paris to the Danube shore. Fish is a speciality, including *bouillabaisse*. ● *Mon, Sun, hols, two weeks in Aug.*

SALZAMT　　€€€　　V
Ruprechtsplatz 1. **Map** 2 E5 & 6 D2. 533 53 32.
This place opened in the 1980's and rapidly became a favourite watering hole of sophisticates and wannabes, who linger into the night at the stylish modern bar. Excellent meat dishes and desserts. No name on the outside – you are supposed to know where it is. ● *lunch in winter.*

For key to symbols *see p205*

<table>
<tr><td colspan="2">

Price categories for a three-course meal for one, excluding drinks, but including all unavoidable extra charges such as cover, service and tax:
€ under 20
€€ 21– 30
€€€ 31– 40
€€€€ 41– 50.

CREDIT CARDS
Indicates which credit cards are accepted: AE American Express; DC Diners Club; MC Master Card/Access; V Visa; JCB Japanese Credit Bureau.

VEGETARIAN DISHES
The menu includes dishes suitable for vegetarians.

GOOD WINE LIST
Denotes a wide range of good wines, or a more specialized selection of local wines.

VIENNESE CUISINE
Typical Viennese dishes are offered on the menu.

</td></tr>
</table>

	CREDIT CARDS	VEGETARIAN DISHES	GOOD WINE LIST	VIENNESE CUISINE

CANTINETTA ANTINORI   €€€€ | AE DC MC V JCB | ● | ■ |
Jasomirgottstraße 3–5. **Map** 2 D5 & 6 D3. ☏ 533 77 22.
The Tuscan delicacies here come at a price, but it is certainly worth paying. The ambience has a discreet Italian stylishness that is replicated in the service. Try for a table at the rear, which is more intimate than the front. Pasta and fish specialities to accompany that peerless Antinori wine. 🏃 ★

DO & CO   €€€€ | V | ● | | ●
Haas-Haus 7th Floor/ Stephansplatz 12 **Map** 2 E5 & 6 D3 ☏ 535 39 69
Do & Co is something of a Viennese institution, part of a catering empire that stretches from casinos to airlines. This is the jewel in the crown, a restaurant with Vienna's most sought after view of the Stephansdom. International seafood specialities jostle for attention with perfect *Schnitzels*. ♿

ZUM SCHWARZEN KAMEEL   €€€€ | AE DC MC V | ● | ■ |
Bognergasse 5. **Map** 2 D5 & 5 C3. ☏ 533 81 25.
If money is no object, dine in the splendid Jugendstil restaurant adjoining the large lobby with its bar and sandwich counter. Here, classics like *Tafelspitz* are slowly being infiltrated with lighter dishes. The ham sandwiches out front may be the most expensive in town, but they are also the best. ● *Sun & hols.*

HOFBURG QUARTER

ILONA STÜBERL   € | AE DC MC V | | |
Bräunerstraße 2. **Map** 2 D5 & 5 C3. ☏ 533 90 29.
Massive helpings of traditional Hungarian fare like stuffed cabbage, paprika chicken and goulash are on offer at reasonable prices. Pleasant area to sit out on a pedestrian-only street and watch the goings-on of the Graben. 🏃

REINTHALER   € | | | | ●
Gluckgasse 5. **Map** 4 D1 & 5 C4. ☏ 512 33 66.
One of the very few *Beisln* that has preserved its character and mixed clientele from workers in overalls to officials with briefcases. Goodies like calves' livers with hearts and kidneys. Still astonishingly cheap. ● *Sat, Sun.* 🍴 🏃

BEI MAX   €€ | AE DC MC V JCB | ● | |
Landhausgasse 2/Herrengasse. **Map** 2 D5 & 5 B3. ☏ 533 73 59.
Atmospheric restaurant patronised *inter alia* by actors from the nearby Burgtheater, Bohemian types and what the Viennese so picturesquely call "*Promis*" (celebrities). Try the Carinthian noodle dishes. ● *Sat, Sun & public hols.* 🍴 🏃

PALMENHAUS   €€ | AE DC MC V JCB | ● | ■ |
Burggarten /Albertina Entrance. **Map** 4 D1 & 5 B4. ☏ 533 10 33.
This relatively recent arrival on the Viennese scene combines a delightful environment (inside the Palm House and next to the Butterfly House in the Burggarten) with Mediterranean-style cooking. The menu and the choice of wines change monthly. However service can be slow. 🏃 ● *Nov–Mar: Mon, Tue.*

STADTBEISL   €€ | V | | | ●
Naglergasse 21. **Map** 2 D5 & 5 C3. ☏ 533 33 23.
With its pretty Baroque facade and cosy panelled interiors, plus summer tables on the historic street of the nailmakers, the Stadtbeisl is popular with locals and tourists alike. The meaty Viennese cooking is solid rather than inspired, and the service friendly. Good pancakes with fruit and other fillings.

YUGETSU   €€ | AE DC MC V JCB | ● | |
Führichgasse 10. **Map** 4 D1 & 5 C4. ☏ 512 27 20.
In an ultra-modern interior, top quality Japanese food is served (the number of Japanese patrons inspires confidence in the authenticity of the fare). *Sushi* bar on the ground floor and *teppanyaki* on the first floor. Some say this is the best Japanese restaurant in the city. 🍴 🏃

EPHESUS   €€€ | MC V | ● | |
Bräunerstraße 8. **Map** 2 D5 & 5 C3. ☏ 533 90 91.
In the arched interior of Ephesus, with its elegant wall friezes in imitation of the Ephesos ruins, Turkish food returns to the traditions of the Ottoman kitchen. Apart from the levantine dishes on offer, there are Turko-Greek standbys such as *tsatsiki* and *moussaka* The wines are Austrian and Italian. 🏃

NOVELLI BACARO CON CUCINA €€€€ | AE DC MC V
Bräunerstraße 11. **Map** 5 C3. 513 42 00.
Fine Italian restaurant located in the Palais Pallavicini. Classic Italian cooking
with homemade pasta and an excellent wine list; if that isn't enough, the
colourful conversion of the palace in interior will delight the eye. ● *Sun.* &

SCHOTTENRING AND ALSERGRUND

REMBETIKO €€ | V
Porzellangasse 38. **Map** 1 C3. 317 64 93.
For those who hanker after Greek lamb and grilled fish, this may be the
place to restore spirits. The homely interior in Grecian blue and white, and
friendly service, has attracted plenty of regulars while a major plus is the
considerable choice of Greek wines. Informal, fun and very good value. ⛉ &

STOMACH €€
Seegasse 26. **Map** 1 C3. 310 20 99.
The choice of food here is eclectic and large (as are the portions). Claims
to change the menu weekly, but there is always a mixture of Viennese and
seasonal dishes. Located in an attractive Biedermeier house, the courtyard
of which is one of the most attractive in Vienna for summer eating. It's popular
with locals, so booking is obligatory. ● *Wed–Sat lunch, Mon, Tue, hols.* ⛉ &

TRATTORIA MARTINELLI €€€ | AE DC MC V JCB
Freyung 3, Palais Harrach. **Map** 2 D5 & 5 B2. 533 67 21.
The Trattoria Martinelli's priority is to offer authentic Tuscan cuisine in a
genuinely elegant Italian ambience. Among their specialities are the celebrated *osso
buco* and well-kept secrets such as wild duck *ravioli.* ● *Sun (Jan–Mar).* &

MUSEUM AND TOWNHALL QUARTER

SPATZENNEST € | MC V
St.-Ulrichs-Platz 1. **Map** 3 B1. 526 16 59.
Delightful place in a pleasant location near St Ulrich's church and close to
the lively Spittelberg pedestrian area with its eateries and stalls. Appetising,
traditional Viennese fare such as smoked pork dumplings and cauliflower
cheese. Dishes of the day are excellent value. ● *Fri, Sat.* ⛉ &

LUX-GASTHAUS-CAFÉ-BAR €€€ | AE DC MC V
Schrankgasse 4/Spittelberggasse 3 (Pedestrian Zone). **Map** 3 B1. 526 94 91.
With its choice of seating areas (glass atrium, Gasthaus, bistro with red leather
benches), this is excellent value. Seasonal dishes, five salads, wonderful fish; or
just pick at a seductive *hors d'oeuvre* like sheep's cheese and mascarpone
mousse with salad and olive crostinis. First rate wines. ¶❶ & ★

SCHNATTL €€€ | AE DC
Lange Gasse 40. **Map** 1 B5. 405 34 00.
The green-panelled interior of this restaurant in the heart of Josefstadt is
spruced up in post-modern style, with a pleasant courtyard for summer eating.
An effort is made to offer organic produce and the accompanying Austrian
vintages are knowledgeably chosen. The refined menu with seasonal offerings
includes rabbit strudel or char (*Saibling*) with a melange of gherkins.
● *Sat, Sun, hols, week after Easter and second half of August.* ¶❶ *lunch.* ⛉★

ZU EBENER ERDE UND ERSTER STOCK €€€ | AE V
Burggasse 13. **Map** 3 B1. 523 62 54.
Enjoy first rate Viennese cooking in the romantic ambience of this charming
Biedermeier house. The ground floor resembles a traditional *Beisl* and offers
cheaper fare, while on the floor above you can dine in greater elegance.
Intimate and friendly, offering terrine of pike-perch and tomatoes wrapped
in bacon with herb sauce and leaf salad; roulade of catfish fillet with estragon
and balsamic sauce and lentils. Must book. ● *Mon, Sun, hols.* ¶❶ ★

OPERA AND NASCHMARKT

HUNGERKÜNSTLER € | MC V
Gumpendorfer Straße 48. **Map** 3 B3. 587 92 10.
Simple neighbourhood *Beisl*, a bit more versatile than it appears at first
glance, pulling international dishes and good wines out of the hat from
time to time. Nice interior with antique chandeliers. ¶❶ *lunch.* ⛉ & ● *Sun.*

KOSTAS €
Friedrichstraße 6. **Map** 4 D2. 586 37 29.
This little Greek restaurant close to the Secession building and the
Naschmarkt has been winning laurels for its authentic fare (the lamb dishes
are particularly good). Better value than many overpriced and less genuine
rivals. ● *Sun.* ¶❶ *lunch.* ⛉ &

For key to symbols *see p205*

> **Price categories** for a three-course meal for one, excluding drinks, but including all unavoidable extra charges such as cover, service and tax:
> € under 20
> €€ 21– 30
> €€€ 31– 40
> €€€€ 41– 50.

CREDIT CARDS
Indicates which credit cards are accepted: AE American Express; DC Diners Club; MC Master Card/Access; V Visa; JCB Japanese Credit Bureau.

VEGETARIAN DISHES
The menu includes dishes suitable for vegetarians.

GOOD WINE LIST
Denotes a wide range of good wines, or a more specialized selection of local wines.

VIENNESE CUISINE
Typical Viennese dishes are offered on the menu.

	CREDIT CARDS	VEGETARIAN DISHES	GOOD WINE LIST	VIENNESE CUISINE
BELVEDERE QUARTER				
SALM BRÄU €	V	●		●
OSTERIA VENEXIANA DA PABLO €€	DC MC V	●	◼	
RESTAURANT SPERL €€	MC V	●		●
KERVANSARAY–HUMMERBAR €€€€	AE DC MC V JCB			
KORSO BEI DER OPER IM HOTEL BRISTOL €€€	AE DC MC V JCB	●	◼	
FURTHER AFIELD				
GASTHAUS SEIDL €€	DC V		◼	●
GMOA-KELLER €€	AE DC MC V	●	◼	●
SILBERWIRT €€	V	●	◼	●

BELVEDERE QUARTER

SALM BRÄU
Rennweg 8, im Salesianer Kloster. **Map** 4 F3. ☏ 799 59 92.
Busy and friendly atmosphere in this excellent value beer-cellar in the former stables of the Salesian cloister. The *Surstelze* (joint of smoked pork) for two is a speciality (take home what you cannot eat). Beers brewed on the premises as well as numerous beer specialities and unrivalled raspberry *Schnaps*. Booking advisable at mealtimes. †☺† ★

OSTERIA VENEXIANA DA PABLO
Rennweg 11 – Corner Marokkanergasse. **Map** 4 F2. ☏ 714 60 03.
The decor of the *osteria* on the ground floor, and the *trattoria* on the first, conjure a Venetian atmosphere. Nor does the food fail to maintain the illusion – swordfish, veal in marsala and lemon, seafood pasta and a choice of 70 Italian wines, many from the Veneto. ⬤ *Sat lunch, Sun.* †☺† *lunch.* ⬇

RESTAURANT SPERL
Karolinengasse 13 **Map** 4 E4. ☏ 504 73 34.
The extensive menu features Viennese and Austrian specialities, liberally interpreted. Sperl's spinach dumplings are highly recommended. Despite maintaining prices at the level of a gentrified *Beisl*, Sperl's discreetly elegant interior and sophisticated service would not disgrace a far more expensive place. ⬤ *Sat, Sun, second half of July.* †☺† ♿ ★

KERVANSARAY–HUMMERBAR
Mahlerstraße 9. **Map** 4 E1 & 6 D5. ☏ 512 88 43.
A long-standing and distinguished restaurant, specializing in lobster on the splendid first floor (Hummerbar) and serving Turkish gastronomic delights on the ground floor. Competition from other seafood restaurants has made the Hummerbar seem less exotic in recent years, and there may be a stronger case for trying the Turkish section. ⬤ *Sun (Kervansaray), Sun & hols (Hummerbar).*

KORSO BEI DER OPER IM HOTEL BRISTOL
Mahlerstraße 2 (in Hotel Bristol). **Map** 4 D1 & 5 C5. ☏ 515 16 546.
The cooking here is broadly Austrian, but with much added creative flair. The wine list is formidable, both in terms of quality and price. The ambience is one of comfortable elegance – and wealth. ⬤ *Sat lunch, Sun lunch in July.* ♿

FURTHER AFIELD

GASTHAUS SEIDL
Ungargasse 63. **Off Map** from 4 F1. ☏ 713 17 81.
Concentrating on elegantly prepared light cooking, the cuisine is creative (leek soup with salmon noodles and black bread crostini, linguine with paprika cream and sheep's cheese, chicken breast with cherry filling and red wine shallots). Choice of over 400 Austrian wines and there is excellent draught beer. Decidedly up and coming. ⬤ *Sat, Sun, hols, 24 Dec–6 Jan.* †☺† ⬇ ♿

GMOA-KELLER
Am Heumarkt 25. **Map** 4 E2. ☏ 712 53 10.
Although the two sisters who made it famous (and boasted of having once refused entry to the Federal Chancellor) have died, the restaurant is still going strong and is much favoured by the musical fraternity from the nearby concert halls. Seasonal dishes and good open wines. Live piano and jazz evenings. Cosy and fun. ⬤ *Sun, hols, Aug.* ♫ *varies.* ⬇

SILBERWIRT
Schlossgasse 21. **Map** 3 C4. ☏ 544 49 07.
Silberwirt is part of a complex of eateries built on the site of Schloss Margareten, which was devastated by the Turks during the 1683 siege of Vienna'. Time-hallowed Viennese dishes are cooked with care and flair, and served in a relaxed ambience. The fixed-price menu is excellent value and there is a well-chosen range of Austrian wines. †☺† *Mon–Sat lunch.* ⬇

STADTWIRT
€€ · AE DC MC V

Untere Viaduktgasse 45. **(** 713 38 28.
This bustling restaurant, with cosy corner seats and tables for groups, offers superb Viennese cooking at budget prices. The sliced kidneys are the best in town. House wines and draught beer are excellent. Also available are brandies and cigars. Booking essential. ● *Sat lunch, Sun from 4 pm, 24–27 Dec.* 🏃 ★

ZU DEN DREI BUCHTELN
€€

Wehrgasse 9. **Map** 3 C3. **(** 587 83 65.
The ambience here lives up to its Bohemian/Moravian culinary aspirations. Try *svickova* (beef with seasoned cream sauce) and *brimsenhaluska* (sheep's cheese dumplings), not to mention the irresistible desserts. Wash it all down with Czech beer or Moravian wine. Must book. ● *Sun, July, Christmas.* 🍴 🏃

ZUM HERKNER
€€ · AE DC MC V

Dornbacher Straße 123. **(** 485 43 86.
The long trek out to Herkner is certainly worth it (and fortunately close to the end stop of the No. 43 tram). Superb "bourgeois Viennese fare" at moderate prices in a rustic and unstuffy ambience. The seasonal menu is strong on veal dishes, chanterelle mushrooms and carp. Must book. ● *Sat, Sun.* 🏃 ♿

ECKEL
€€€ · AE DC V

Sieveringer Straße 46. **(** 320 32 18.
Charming traditional restaurant for intimate enjoyment in the cosy *Gaststube* in winter, or in the agreeable summer garden. Viennese cooking at its best, with specialities like lobster and crayfish thrown in for good measure, and a superb list of vintage wines (mostly Austrian). Must book. ● *Sun, Mon.* 🏃 ★

GREEN COTTAGE
€€€ · V

Kettenbrückengasse 3. **Map** 3 C3. **(** 586 65 81.
Jugendstil meets the Orient (the interior) and *nouvelle cuisine* goes Chinese (the menu)! The fare ranges from a *Sichuan* version of Mongolian lamb and seasoned grilled fish to deliciously light, rice-based desserts. Some dishes may be salty for the average taste. Attentive service. ● *Sun and lunchtimes.*

STEIRER STUB'N
€€€

Wiedner Hauptstraße 111. **Map** 3 C5. **(** 544 43 49.
The menu includes Alpine lamb, char (*Saibling*) in wild garlic (*Bärlauch*) sauce and carp *gelée*. Excellent desserts, such as orange and Grand Marnier pancakes; superb service and Austrian wines by the glass. Rather far out (take tram 65 from Oper); book ahead. ● *Sun, hols, Sat in July, Aug.* 🍴 🏃 ★

VIKERL'S LOKAL
€€€

Würffelgasse 4. **(** 894 34 30.
Family-run, offering refined Viennese cooking amiably served. Look out for the quail, calf's liver or pig's trotter (but the menu changes daily). Don't be deterred by the dreary location near the Westbahnhof. This and the cash only policy keep the prices astonishingly moderate. ● *Mon, Sun eve.* 🍴 ♿ ★

ALTWIENERHOF
€€€€ · AE DC MC V

Herklotzgasse 6. **(** 892 60 00.
The founder of this sumptuous restaurant worked in some of the finest restaurants in the world before going it alone. The cellar of French wines is certainly the best in Austria. The garden in a Biedermeier courtyard makes the aesthetic experience even more enjoyable. ● *Sun, Sat lunch.* 🍴

HIETZINGER BRÄU
€€€€ · AE DC MC V

Auhofstraße 1. **(** 877 70 87.
In the western suburbs (U4 to Hietzing/Schönbrunn Zoo) is a residential area once inhabited by imperial officials. Imperial too is the Hietzinger Bräu's *Tafelspitz* (boiled beef) speciality. The place, strictly for carnivores, is in a class of its own as far as meat quality goes. Pleasant, if formal, ambience. 🏃

STEIRERECK
€€€€ · AE DC MC V

Meierei im Stadtpark. **Map** 6 F4. **(** 713 31 68.
With its atmospheric location, fabulous service and culinary artistry, Steirereck bids fair to be the best restaurant in the city. Menus of stunning flair show regional and international influences. If you appreciate a meal that is staged as a performance (the sommelier alone should carry off several Oscars), this is the place for you. ● *Sat, Sun.* 🍴

VINCENT
€€€€ · AE DC MC V

Große Pfarrgasse 7. **Map** 2 E3. **(** 214 15 16.
The name bespeaks the owner's passion for modern art, specimens of which adorn the walls. The excellent organic fare is a *nouvelle cuisine* influenced version of Viennese, and decidedly creative – mussels in Muscatel sauce and veal kidneys cooked in port wine and honey with a leek risotto. ● *lunch, Sun, first two weeks of Aug.* 🍴 *business lunch to special order.*

Cafés and Bars

THIS SECTION LISTS a broad cross-section of Viennese cafés, wine cellars, sandwich/self-service bars and *Konditoreien* (*see pp202-3*). The list includes both the traditonal and the new and fashionable, providing an overview of the different types of places available. Individual bars are not listed, although some of the places featured do have lively bars.

	Konditoreien/Coffee house	Szene	Wine Bar/Cellar	Heurige	Outdoor Tables	Live Music
STEPHANSDOM QUARTER						
CAFÉ MINISTERIUM Georg-Coch-Platz 4. **Map** 2 F5 & 6 F3. ☎ 512 92 25. Moderately priced home-cooking (also vegetarian) can be had at this café. Card and chess tables; piano music twice a week. ○ *8am–midnight Mon–Fri.*	●				●	▪
CAFÉ-RESTAURANT DIGLAS Wollzeile 10. **Map** 2 E5 & 6 E3. ☎ 512 57 65-0. Agreeable café offering light food with some vegetarian dishes; also fixed price menu. ○ *7am–midnight daily.* ♫ *Mon, Tue, Fri and Sat piano music from 8.30pm.*	●				●	▪
DURAN SANDWICHES Rotenturmstraße 11. **Map** 2 E5 & 6 D3. ☎ 533 52 35. No frills eat-in and takeaway offering open sandwiches that are virtually as good as Trzesniewski (see below). ○ *11am–7pm Mon–Fri, 11am–1pm Sat.*						
È TRICAFFÈ Rotenturmstraße 25. **Map** 2 E5 & 6 E2. ☎ 533 89 90. All the cafés of this trendy chain (see also Am Hof 2/Corner Bognergasse) serve excellent Italian-style specialities, wines and coffee. ○ *8am–2am daily.*	●				●	
GERSTNER – K.&K. HOFZUCKERBÄCKER Kärntner Straße 13–15. **Map** 4 D1 & 6 D4. ☎ 512 49 63-77. One of the great "Imperial and Royal" *konditoreien* with a marvellous selection of pastries. ○ *8:30am–8pm (in summer to 10pm) Mon–Sat, 10am–6pm Sun & hols.*	●				●	
KONDITOREI HEINER Wollzeile 9. **Map** 2 E5 & 6 D3. ☎ 512 23 43. Heiner offers warm desserts and diabetic cakes and pastries. Their premises overlooking Kärntner Straße 21–23 are nice, but this neo-Biedermeier café is absolutely enchanting. ○ *8:30am–7pm Mon–Sat, 10am–7pm Sun.*	●					
MA PITOM Seitenstettengasse 5. **Map** 2 E5 & 6 D2. ☎ 535 43 13. Cornucopia of good things to eat, large or small dishes, cocktails and wide selection of beers. ○ *5pm–3am Mon–Thur, Sun; 5pm–4am Fri, Sat.*		▪			●	
VIS À VIS Wollzeile 5 (in the passage, opposite Figlmüller). **Map** 2 E5 & 6 D3. ☎ 512 93 50. Light bites mixed delicacies accompany the 350 wines on offer. An essential pit stop for the wine connoisseur at large. ○ *3pm–10:30pm Mon–Fri.* ● *Sat, Sun, hols.*			●			
ZWÖLF-APOSTELKELLER Sonnenfelsgasse 3. **Map** 2 E5 & 6 E3. ☎ 512 67 77. Descend the two floors of catacombs to the Baroque cellar and the Medieval one below it. Plates of cold cuts and other specialities accompany excellent wines. Favoured by young people and students. ○ *4:30pm–midnight daily.*			●			
HOFBURG QUARTER						
AUGUSTINER-KELLER Augustinerstraße 1. **Map** 4 D1 & 5 C4. ☎ 533 10 26. Atmospheric cellar, whose origins go back at least to Baroque times. Viennese cooking, plus (from 6:30 pm) typical *Heurigen* fare and music. Popular with tourists. ○ *11am–midnight daily, Sat till 1am.*			●		●	▪
CAFÉ BRÄUNERHOF Stallburggasse 2. **Map** 4 D1 & 5 C3. ☎ 512 38 93. Old-fashioned café with warm food (lunchtime); Music on weekends and holidays. The favourite café of Austria's most celebrated and curmudgeonly author, Thomas Bernhard. ○ *7:30am–9pm Mon–Fri, 7:30am–7pm Sat, 10am–7pm Sun.*	●				●	▪
CAFÉ HAWELKA Dorotheergasse 6. **Map** 2 D5 & 5 C3. ☎ 512 82 30. A Viennese institution, the preferred café of the city's Bohemians and their dogs. Spartan interior, breakfast until 11am, and Buchteln (warm yeast buns filled with jam) after 10pm. ○ *8am–2am Mon, Wed–Sat; 4pm–2am Sun & hols.*	●	▪				

KONDITOREIEN/COFFEE HOUSE
Establishment offering coffee, cakes and pastries.

SZENE
Type of bar, often with live music, usually open late.

WINE BAR/CELLAR
Simple snacks served alongside an outstanding range of wine.

HEURIGE
Venue serving the youngest available vintage of the local wine.

OUTDOOR TABLES
Facilites for eating and drinking outside, such as a terrace or garden.

LIVE MUSIC
Regular live entertainment.

	KONDITOREIEN/COFFEE HOUSE	SZENE	WINE BAR/CELLAR	HEURIGE	OUTDOOR TABLES	LIVE MUSIC
K&K HOFZUCKERBÄCKEREI DEMEL Kohlmarkt 14. **Map** 2 D5 & 5 C3. (535 17 17. The famous "Royal and Imperial" confectioners offers a light lunch and a huge selection of pastries. Many tourists found munching in the elegant, Neo-Classical interior. Most credit cards accepted. ☐ 10am–7pm daily.	●				●	
KONDITOREI OBERLAA STADTHAUS Neuer Markt 16. **Map** 4 D1 & 5 C4. (513 29 36. Lunch with daily changing specialities and pastries to rival Gerstner and Heiner, including very good Strudel. ☐ 8am–8pm daily, in summer till 9pm.	●				●	
TRZESNIEWSKI Dorotheergasse 1. **Map** 2 D5 & 5 C3. (512 32 91. Famously pokey stand-up eatery with mouth-watering open sandwiches Fillings made from organic produce. ☐ 8:30am–7:30pm Mon–Fri, 9am–5pm Sat.						

SCHOTTENRING AND ALSERGRUND

	KONDITOREIEN/COFFEE HOUSE	SZENE	WINE BAR/CELLAR	HEURIGE	OUTDOOR TABLES	LIVE MUSIC
TUNNEL Florianigasse 39. **Map** 1 A5. (947 57 20 (or 405 34 65 for recorded message). Three-storey eatery (also art gallery) in Josefstadt with warm food available and a cheap breakfast buffet from 9am to 11am. The international cuisine (including pizzas) is generally budget-priced. ☐ 9am–2am daily.		■			●	■

MUSEUM AND TOWN HALL QUARTER

	KONDITOREIEN/COFFEE HOUSE	SZENE	WINE BAR/CELLAR	HEURIGE	OUTDOOR TABLES	LIVE MUSIC
CAFÉ LANDTMANN Dr.-Karl-Lueger-Ring 4. **Map** 1 C5 & 5 B2. (24100. Coffee-house once patronised by Sigmund Freud. Press conferences are frequently held here and it's always crowded in an evening. Extensive menu, homemade desserts and pastries. Quite expensive. ☐ 7:30am–midnight daily.	●				●	
SLUKA Rathausplatz 8. **Map** 1 C5 & 5 A3. (405 71 72. Tucked under the arches of the Neo-Gothic Town Hall, offering a light lunch and buffet of *hors d'oeuvres*, plus (some say) the best *konditoreien* in town. Extensive choice for diabetics. ☐ 8am–7pm Mon–Fri, 8am–5:30pm Sat.	●				●	

BELVEDERE

	KONDITOREIEN/COFFEE HOUSE	SZENE	WINE BAR/CELLAR	HEURIGE	OUTDOOR TABLES	LIVE MUSIC
NASCHMARKT Schwarzenbergplatz 16. **Map** 4 E2 & 6 D5. (505 31 15. The biggest and best of this self-service chain (another branch at Schottengasse 1) offering an extensive menu with dishes cooked while you wait. ☐ 6:30am–10:30pm Mon–Fri, 9am–10-30pm Sat, Sun and hols.					●	

FURTHER AFIELD

	KONDITOREIEN/COFFEE HOUSE	SZENE	WINE BAR/CELLAR	HEURIGE	OUTDOOR TABLES	LIVE MUSIC
MAYER AM PFARRPLATZ Pfarrplatz 2, Heiligenstadt. (370 12 87. In the enchanting village where Beethoven wrote his "testament" is this tavern with extensive rooms, attractive courtyard and garden. Substantial hot and cold buffet. ☐ 4pm–midnight Mon–Sat, 11am–midnight Sun and hols.				■	●	■
WEINGUT-HEURIGER REINPRECHT Cobenzlgasse 22. (320 14 71-0. Marvellous situation in former monastery. Buffet with vegetarian options and picturesque garden reaching into the vinyard. Specialist for Grüner Veltliner (own production). ☐ 3pm–midnight daily.				■	●	■
ZIMMERMANN Armbrustergasse 3–5. (370 22 11. Labyrinthine and fashionable *Heurige* of great character offering a range of Viennese warm dishes as well as the typical *Heurigen* buffet in a friendly atmosphere. ☐ 5pm–midnight Mon–Sat, 4pm–midnight Sun and hols.				■	●	

For key to symbols *see p205*

SHOPS AND MARKETS

Since Vienna is a compact city, it is a pleasant place to shop. The main shopping area is pedestrianized and full of pretty cafés, and although it is not in the same league as London, Paris and New York when it comes to international stores, you can browse around at a more leisurely pace. Austrian-made glassware, food and traditional crafts all make for good buys. However, the shops tend to cater for comparatively conventional and mature tastes and purses. Vienna has a range of markets selling a variety of produce and wares from exotic fruit to old trinkets. The pedestrian shopping areas of Kärntner Strasse, the Graben, and Kohlmarkt house the more expensive shops and are pleasant to wander around. For more details of shops and markets see the *Directory* on page 225.

Augarten porcelain Lipizzaner

BEST BUYS

Many of the best buys in Vienna are small and readily transportable: coffee addicts shouldn't forget to buy freshly ground coffee – the city imports some of the best.

If you have a sweet tooth, you couldn't be in a more appropriate city. It is justly famous for its cakes, pastries and *Torten (see p208–9)* and any good *Café-Konditorei* (cake shop and café) will post cakes back home for you. In November and December, try the buttery Advent *Stollen* available from **Julius Meinl am Graben** *(see p223)* or any good baker. Stuffed with fruit and nuts and dusted with icing sugar, it is a tasty Christmas loaf. Alternatively, buy some prettily-packaged *Sachertorte (see p209)*, available year round. The specialist chocolate shops *(see p223)* are worth a visit, both for the unusual packaging and the chocolate itself.

Sweet *Eiswein* (so-called because the grapes are left on the vines until the first frosts) is an unusual and delicious dessert wine. **Zum Schwarzen Kameel** *(see p223)* sells the rarer red version as well.

Other Austrian-made goods include clothes manufactured in the felt-like woollen fabric known as *Loden (see p223)*. If you feel like treating yourself and have space in your car or suitcase, buy custom-made sheets or high-quality down pillows or duvets made in Austria *(see p222)*. Petit point embroidery, which adorns anything from powder compacts to handbags, is a Viennese speciality *(see p222)*.

Glassware – including superb chandeliers – and **Augarten** porcelain *(see p222)* tend to be highly original, although expensive. Many people collect crystal ornaments made by Swarovski. **Rasper & Söhne** *(see p222)* is a good glass and porcelain shop for such items.

Trachten (Austrian costume) shops *(see p223)* are fun; they have a wide selection of hats, children's dresses, jackets and blouses. **Gilhofer** *(see p223)* stocks old prints and maps. Early editions of works by writers such as Freud, Kraus or Rilke can be found in Vienna's antique bookshops *(see p223)*.

Chest of drawers chocolate box from Altmann & Kühne *(see p223)*

OPENING HOURS

Shops usually open at 8:30 or 9 in the morning and close at 6 or 7 in the evening. Some of the smaller shops close for an hour at lunch time. Traditionally stores were required to close at noon on Saturday, though most now stay open until 5pm. Shops are still closed on Sundays and public holidays, although you can buy items such as groceries, flowers, camera film, books and newspapers at the major railway stations. The supermarket at the airport is open seven days a week.

J & L Lobmeyr's glass shop on Kärntner Strasse *(see p222)*

How to Pay

VIENNA IS NOW more credit card-orientated, with many shops accepting the major cards. Some also take Euro-cheques (with a card), but it is still wise to carry some cash as an alternative.

Where to Shop

THE PEDESTRIAN SHOPPING areas of Graben, Kohlmarkt and Kärntner Strasse have many of the most well-known and expensive shops in Vienna.

The more cheaply priced area is along Mariahilfer Strasse, with department stores selling household goods, and well-known chain stores such as H & M.

View down Kohlmarkt, one of Vienna's pedestrian shopping streets

Rights and Services

IF A PURCHASE is defective you are usually entitled to a refund, provided you have proof of purchase. This is not always the case with goods bought in the sales – inspect them carefully before you buy. Many shops in Vienna will pack goods for you – and often gift-wrap them at no extra charge – and send them anywhere in the world.

VAT Exemption

VAT (VALUE ADDED TAX) or MWSt (Mehrwertsteuer) is normally charged at 20%. If you reside outside the European Union (EU), you are entitled to claim back the VAT on goods purchased in Austria. This is only the case, however, if the total purchase price (this can include the total cost of several items from one shop) exceeds €73. Take along your passport when shopping and ask the shopkeeper to complete Form U34 at the time of sale. This should also bear the shop's stamp and have the receipt attached. You may have the refund credited to your credit card account, have it posted home, or pick it up at the airport.

Purchased goods must not be used prior to exportation. If you leave Vienna by air, present the form at Customs

before checking in, and have it stamped as proof of export. You may also have to show your purchases at Customs, so pack them somewhere accessible. Then post the stamped form to the Austrian shopkeeper or collect the refund at the airport (there is a handling fee). If leaving by car or train, present the form to Customs at the border, where you can also claim a refund. If you are not dis-embarking the train at the border, there is sometimes a customs official on the train to stamp your form.

When you have goods sent directly to your home outside the EU, VAT is deducted at the time of purchase.

One of the famous *Loden* coats from Resi Hammerer *(see p223)*

Since Austria joined the EU in 1995, EU citizens can no longer claim back VAT.

Sales

THE BI-ANNUAL SALES are held in January and July. The best bargains can usually be found in fashions. Electrical and household goods are also much reduced.

Shopping Centres

SHOPPING CENTRES are a fairly recent innovation in Vienna. The most modern are the **Ringstrassen Galerien**, the splendid **Haas Haus** and the spruced-up **Generali Centre**. Built in the same style as the Café Central *(see pp58–61)*, **Freyung Passage** is an arcade of elegant shops in the Palais Ferstel *(see pp108 and 110)*.

Addresses

Generali Centre
Mariahilfer Strasse 77–79. **Map** 3 A3.

Haas Haus
Stock-im-Eisen-Platz 4.
Map 2 D5 & 5 C3.

Freyung Passage
Palais Ferstel 1, Freyung 2.
Map 2 D5 & 5 B2.

Ringstrassen Galerien
Kärntner Ring 5–7. **Map** 6 D5.

Shops and Boutiques

EVEN IF VIENNA DOES NOT BOAST the wide range of shops you find in many other European capitals, it does offer certain goods that are hard to beat elsewhere. Austrian glassware is justly famous and cut-glass gifts are of a high quality. A few shops, such as **Knize** (in the Graben), designed by Adolf Loos, are in themselves worth a visit simply to admire the Jugendstil architecture. It's best to speak English in shops unless you are fluent in German – you will probably receive quicker service!

SPECIALITY SHOPS

VIENNA STILL manufactures leather goods, although nowadays a lot are imported from Italy. **Novotny** have their own workshops as well as firms working exclusively for them. **Robert Horn** designs and manufactures leather travel cases and accessories. He maintains that even he has been unable to improve on the design of a briefcase carried by Metternich at the Congress of Vienna, which he has only slightly modernized.

Petit point embroidery is another Viennese speciality. Some of the most attractive can be found at **Petit Point** (where even the shop's door handle is embroidered) and at **Maria Stransky**.

A marvellous place for party tricks, and much beloved by practical jokers, is **Zauber-klingl. Kober** (see p232) is a "serious" toy shop which sells well-made dolls and toys. Or combine a visit to the novelty and joke shop called **Witte** with a trip to the Naschmarkt. Witte stocks masks, fancy dress outfits, and beautiful old-fashioned paper decorations that are ideal for festivals. **Metzger**, a shop specializing in beeswax, sells its own candles and candlesticks. It also stocks certain gift items, such as honey cakes and boxes of chocolates.

MUSIC

AS YOU WOULD expect in "the City of Music", the range of recordings available is rich and varied. The shops with the widest range of classical CDs are **EMI** and **Gramola**; **Arcadia** specializes particularly in opera and operetta. Shop staff are usually very knowledgeable. For pop music, the **Virgin Megastore** on Mariahilfer Strasse is well stocked, although CDs and tapes are more expensive here than in other countries in Europe. **Doblinger** is excellent for sheet music; it also has a second-hand department and CD shop.

JEWELLERY

VIENNESE JEWELLERS have long been famous for their fine workmanship. Fruit and flower brooches carved in semi-precious stones and sometimes studded with diamonds, are a more recent Austrian innovation. **Juwel** always has a good selection in a wide price range. Both **Köchert** and **Heldwein** were jewellers to the Imperial Court and still produce beautiful jewellery in their own workshops today. Köchert also sells antique pieces and Heldwein are known for their multi-coloured chains of semi-precious stones. A few years ago, one of the pieces designed by **Schullin** won the prestigious Diamonds International award organized by De Beers for innovative design. Their small window usually attracts a crowd of admirers to view their latest creations. Don't let that put you off – prices start at a reasonable level.

GLASSWARE

THE CHANDELIERS at Vienna's Opera House and the Metropolitan Opera in New York are by **J & L Lobmeyr**, as are the chandeliers in numerous palaces throughout the world – including the Kremlin. This company – now run by a fifth generation of the same family – has produced beautiful glasses and crystal chandeliers since the early 19th century, often commissioning famous artists. One range of glasses still in production today was designed by Josef Hoffmann (see p56) in Jugendstil style. Its famous *Musselinglas*, a type of glass so fine that it almost bends to the touch, is exquisite. There is a small but superb glass museum on the first floor and, apart from its own glassware, Lobmeyr also sells select items of Hungarian Herend porcelain.

INTERIORS

VIENNA'S PORCELAIN makers, **Augarten**, are the second oldest in Europe. The company was founded in 1718 and taken over by the House of Habsburg in 1744. Ever since, its products have been marked with their banded shield coat of arms. Each piece of porcelain at **Schloss Augarten** is still hand finished and painted: patterns and shapes are based on original models from the Baroque, Rococo, Biedermeier and Art Deco periods and on designs created by present-day artists. The Schloss Augarten factory is open to visitors. **Rasper & Söhne** stocks glass and porcelain as well as kitchen-ware, and is good for gifts.

Founded in 1849, **Back-hausen** is known for its exclusive furnishing fabrics, woven in the original Jugend-stil patterns, and for its silk scarves and matching velvet handbags. In addition it has a good selection of duvets and household linens. Quality bedding and linens are available at **Gans**, which conveniently has a shop at Vienna's Schwechat airport for last-minute purchases. **Gunkel** stocks household linen and bath robes, and for generations the Viennese have patronized **Zur Schwäb-ischen Jungfrau**, founded in 1720, where fine linens can be made to order as well as purchased ready-made.

FOOD AND WINE

ONE OF VIENNA's most renowned and almost revered food and wine shops, **Zum Schwarzen Kameel** *(see p214)*, sells mouth-watering produce. **Julius Meinl am Graben** food hall, on the pedestrianized Graben, also offers a wide selection of delicacies. Enter via its Lukullus Bar *(see p219)* in Naglergasse if you would like to stop for a snack and a drink.

There is also a good chain of wine merchants called **Wein & Co**, one of which is situated on the Jasomirgottstrasse.

Altmann & Kühne is famous for its tiny, handmade chocolates sold in beautiful boxes shaped like miniature chests of drawers, books, horses and angels.

GIFTS

SUCCESSOR OF THE famous Wiener Werkstätten, the outfit called **Österreichische Werkstätten** has a selection of almost exclusively Austrian goods. In stock are a range of enamelled jewellery designed by Michaela Frey, ceramics, mouth-blown glass, candles and, from late autumn onwards, Christmas tree decorations. The arts and crafts markets *(see p224)* are also good hunting-grounds for picking up knick-knacks.

BOOKS

LOCATED IN the Museums-Quartier, **Prachner** stocks an extensive selection of books on art and architecture. It also has a good selection of books in English, as does the **British Bookshop** and **Shakespeare & Co**. For music books in English, visit **Doblinger** *(see p222)*. Rare old books – as well as new ones – can be purchased at **Heck**. Old prints and maps are available at the specialist **Gilhofer**. **Taschenbuchladen** bookshop stocks a range of paperbacks.

NEWSPAPERS AND PERIODICALS

MOST NEWSPAPER kiosks located within the Ringstrasse stock foreign newspapers – and so do the best coffee houses, where they can be read free of charge. There is no English-language Viennese newspaper. **Morawa** sells a variety of newspapers and periodicals in practically any language.

CLOTHES AND ACCESSORIES

VIENNESE CLOTHES are well-made and tend to be quite formal. **Resi Hammerer** is famous for jackets, coats and capes made from *Loden*. This is a warm, felt-like fabric traditionally in dark green or grey, but now produced in a range of colours.

Tostmann is best known for traditional Austrian costumes or *Trachten*: its *Dirndl* (dresses) are made from a variety of fabrics including beautiful brocades. Its clothes for children are particularly delightful. **Fürnkranz** has several branches throughout Vienna, but its main shop providing elegant day and evening wear is in Kärntner Strasse, with the shop at Neuer Markt stocking more sporty styles. **Flamm** can always be relied upon for simply-tailored dresses and suits in silk and fine wool.

An old-established Viennese name is **Knize**.

In imperial times this was a famous tailoring establishment, but the shop now stocks ready-to-wear clothes for men and women. It also sells its own scent. **Kettner** – almost hidden down a nearby side street – stocks casual daywear for both men and women at all its branches.

All the shoes at **Bellezza** are imported from Italy; the quality, as you would expect, is excellent. **D'Ambrosio**, which has several branches located in the first district, stocks trendy, up-market Italian-style shoes for both men and women at moderate prices. For young, fashionable styles, try **Stephan Kelian**: it has a good selection of Kelian shoes made in France. **Kurt Denkstein** is another shoe retailer with stock at reasonable prices.

Younger, trendier shoppers should head straight to Judengasse – this street has plenty of reasonably priced boutiques with styles to suit every taste. For menswear in particular, **D G Linnerth** stocks informal and sporty clothes designed for teenagers upwards. The branch of the trendy clothes chain **H & M**, on Graben, is worth a visit if only to view the gilded birdcage of a lift.

An optician called **Erich Hartmann** bought a shop with a large stock of horn and tortoiseshell back in 1980. Today he sells a range of hand-made spectacles, combs and chains, all made from horn. His shop looks like a coffee house and is well-known in the city.

SIZE CHART

For Australian sizes follow British and American convention.

Women's clothes

Austrian	36	38	40	42	44	46	48	50
British	10	12	14	16	18	20	22	24
American	8	10	12	14	16	18	20	22

Shoes

Austrian	36	37	38	39	40	41	42	43
British	3½	4	5	5½	6½	7½	8	9
American	5	5½	6½	7	8	9	9½	10½

Men's shirts

Austrian	44	46	48	50	52	54
British	34	36	38	40	42	44
American	S	M	M	L	XL	XL

Antiques, Auctions and Markets

MANY DISTRICTS in Vienna have their own markets – and a few have several – where you can buy arts and crafts, food, flowers and imported and second-hand goods. The city is also known for its Christmas markets, popular with locals in the evenings. If you are interested in antiques and bric-a-brac, it is worth looking in both the specialist antique shops and the main auction house. Alternatively, enjoy browsing round the bustling ethnic stalls and mix of cultures in the Naschmarkt, Vienna's main food market.

ANTIQUES

VIENNA IS JUSTLY FAMOUS for its antique shops. Most are located in the Stephansdom Quarter as well as along Schönbrunner Strasse, where stock ranges from valuable antiques to simply second-hand. The **Dorotheum** (see Auctions), the **Kunst und Antikmarkt** and the Flohmarkt (see Artisan Markets) should not be missed. Jewellery and antique paintings can be particularly good finds. One of the best shops for antique jewellery is the **Galerie Rauhenstein**. It stocks rare and beautiful pieces up to and including the 1940s.

If you are interested in old jewellery and silver and other antiques, **Herbert Asenbaum** is worth a visit. For larger pieces and shops on a larger scale, try **Subal & Subal** on Spiegelgasse or **Reinhold Hofstätter** on Bräunerstrasse. They are both well established and have a good selection of fine antique furniture.

AUCTIONS

OPENED IN 1707 as a pawn-brokers for the "new poor", and appropriately called the Armen Haus (poor house), Vienna's **Dorotheum** is now the city's most important auction house. In 1788 it moved to the site of a former convent called the Dorotheerkirche, which had an altar-piece of St Dorothea in it – hence the name. This is an interesting place to browse around, and since buying is not restricted to auction times, you can often purchase items over the counter. It has other branches dotted around the city.

FOOD MARKETS

BETWEEN the Linke and Rechte Wienzeile, the **Naschmarkt** (see p138) is worth visiting even if you don't buy anything. Exotic fruit and vegetables, notably Greek, Turkish and Asian specialities, crowd the stalls and are piled high in the shops. It is a fascinating place to wander around and observe life. Open all year round, it acts as a meeting point for people of different nationalities who come to buy and sell fruit and vegetables, tea, herbs and spices. The section near the Karlsplatz contains the more expensive Viennese-run stalls. These gradually give way to stands run by colourful Turkish stallholders as you move further towards the flea market.

In addition to the exotic food stalls, you will see Czechs selling hand puppets, Russians selling Babushka dolls and Turks with stalls piled high with eastern clothes. The market is also a good spot for late-night revellers to feast on highly-spiced fish snacks in the early hours of the morning.

Food-lovers should not miss the farmers' market known as the **Bauernmarkt**. From March until the end of October on Tuesdays and Thursdays, a whole range of organic and other country produce is on sale here.

ARTISAN MARKETS

ANTIQUE MARKETS and arts and crafts markets are fairly new to Vienna, but the Flohmarkt (flea market) at the end of the **Naschmarkt** (see p138) and the **Kunst und Antikmarkt** are established hunting grounds for second-hand goods and antiques. The price quoted is probably not the price that you are expected to pay – it's usually assumed that you will bargain.

For the better quality hand-crafted goods, head to the Spittelberg market (see p117) near the Volkstheater. Here artists and craftspeople sell their own products rather than mass-produced factory goods. This is a fashionable and attractive part of Vienna and, although the market is small, you are likely to find gifts of good quality. There are also small galleries and cafés where artists exhibit their works.

The **Heiligenkreuzerhof** (see p75) art market is in a quiet, secluded courtyard where a small, select group of exhibitors is on hand should you wish to discuss the work. The stalls sell jewellery, ceramics and other hand-made goods. Further entertainment and atmosphere is provided by an Austrian folk singer dressed in traditional clothes playing his accordion.

FESTIVE MARKETS

CHRISTMAS MARKETS in Vienna are very special, the most famous of all being the **Christkindlmarkt** (see p64) held in front of the Rathaus. Attractions vary from year to year, but there are always sideshows, decorated trees, performances on a temporary stage and lots of stalls, as well as a workshop for making Christmas presents and baking goodies. Items for sale include honey cakes, bees-wax candles, Christmas decorations and various crafts, although the main attraction is the joyous atmosphere. It is especially magical at night when everything is lit up.

The **Alt Wiener Christ-kindlmarkt** (see p64) at the Freyung is a smaller affair. Two weeks before Easter there is an Easter market here with a large selection of blown and hand-painted eggs. Four other Christmas markets take place in the Spittelberg area, in front of Schloss Schönbrunn, at Karlskirche and at the Heiligenkreuzerhof.

MASTERPIECE

Anatomy of a classic

Vienna's Quiet Standout

The Secession building is a chaste temple of the arts

By Richard B. Woodward

AS A SHOCKING monument against conventional taste, the Secession building by Joseph Maria Olbrich in Vienna has sustained its contrary reputation shockingly well. Nose-thumbing gestures by brash architects are not always appreciated—or even explicable—years later as impassioned motives behind a rebellion cool and anneal into orthodoxy.

But this white-walled temple to the arts, erected in 1898 as an exhibition space for young artists and designers Gustav Klimt, Koloman Moser, Max Kurzweil, Josef Hoffmann, Alfred Roller, Egon Schiele, and others unhappy with the stuffiness of Viennese academia, continues to stand out from its peers, and to do so quietly.

Indeed, the chaste exterior and modest scale were among the most outrageous elements of Olbrich's scheme. The white stucco distinguished the place at a glance from the looming, gray institutions of stone that went up in the last half of the 19th century along the Ringstrasse in this former capital of Austria-Hungary—the empire "on which the sun never rises," as

Olbrich was merely 30 when commissioned for the Secession buil...

against. They just weren't be-
holden to the weighty hand of tradition. "We haven't ...
one," claimed th...
first is...

...rbis

EET JOURNAL.

WSJ.com

journey.wsj.com/stevenlevitt

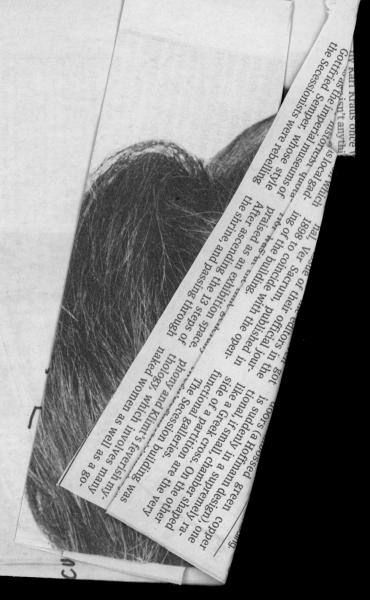

by Karl Kraus once

Gottfried as ... isn't anythi...
the historic is local gad-
nal. issue of which
1898 ver of sacrum ing
ing to coincide with the
of the editors in got
is suddenly pub-
tional jour- like a Greek cross
like a Hoffmann green
side of a supremely ra-
functional partition. On the
The Secession galleries are the other
phony and Klimt's feverish my-
naked women as well as a go-

praised as an ex-
the ascending exhibition spaces,
the shrine and passing through
of praised as an art-
building with the open-
published in
the secessionists' quota-
the imperial is local gad-
the historic is local gad-
the secessionists were rebelling
of the building
praised as an
After an ex-
and passing through
the 13 steps of
shrine and passing through
phony and Klimt's feverish my-
naked women as well as a go-

CU

DIRECTORY

SPECIALITY SHOPS

Kober
Graben 14–15. **Map** 2 D5
& 5 C3. 53360180.

Maria Stransky
Hofburg Passage 2.
Map 5 C4. 5336098.

Metzger
Stephansplatz 7. **Map** 2 E5
& 6 D3. 5123433.
One of two branches.

Novotny
Spiegelgasse 6. **Map** 4 D1
& 5 C4. 5122336.

Petit Point
Kärntner Strasse 16.
Map 4 D1 & 6 D4.
5124886.

Robert Horn
Bräunerstrasse 7.
Map 5 C4. 5138294.

Witte
Linke Wienzeile 16.
Map 3 A4. 58643050.

Zauberklingl
Führichgasse 4. **Map** 5 C4.
5126868.

MUSIC

Arcadia
Kärntner Strasse 40.
Map 4 D2 & 5 C5.
5139568.

Doblinger
Dorotheergasse 10. **Map** 5
C3. 515030.

EMI
Kärntner Str 30. **Map** 4 D1
& 6 D4. 51236750.

Gramola
Graben 16. **Map** 2 D5 &
5 C3. 5335034.

Virgin Megastore
Mariahilfer Strasse 37–9.
Map 3 B2. 5972710.

JEWELLERY

Heldwein
Graben 13.
Map 5 C3. 5125781.

Juwel
Kohlmarkt 1. **Map** 2 D5 &
5 C3. 5336021.

Köchert
Neuer Markt 15.
Map 5 C4. 51258280.

Schullin
Kohlmarkt 7. **Map** 2 D5 &
5 C3. 53390070.

GLASSWARE

J & L Lobmeyr
Kärntner Str 26. **Map** 2 D5
& 6 D4. 5120508.

INTERIORS

Augarten
Stock-im-Eisen-Platz 3–4.
Map 2 D5 & 5 C3.
5121494. *One of
several branches.*

Backhausen
Kärntner Strasse 33.
Map 4 D1 & 6 D4.
514040.

Gans
Brandstätte 1–3. **Map** 4 D1
& 6 D3. 5333560.
One of several branches.

Gunkel
Tuchlauben 11. **Map** 2 D5
& 5 C3. 53363010.

Rasper & Söhne
Graben 15. **Map** 2 D5 &
5 C3. 534330.

Schloss Augarten
Obere Augartenstrasse 1.
Map 2 E2. 211240.

**Zur Schwäbischen
Jungfrau**
Graben 26. **Map** 2 D5 &
5 C3. 5355356.

FOOD AND WINE

Altmann & Kühne
Graben 30. **Map** 2 D5 &
5 C3. 5330927.
One of two branches.

**Julius Meinl am
Graben**
Graben 19. **Map** 2 D5 &
5 C3. 5323334.

Wein & Co
Jasomirgottstrasse 3–5.
Map 6 D3. 5330916.

**Zum Schwarzen
Kameel**
Bognergasse 5.
Map 5 C3. 5338125.

GIFTS

**Österreichische
Werkstätten**
Kärntner Str 6. **Map** 4 D1
& 6 D4. 5122418.

BOOKS

British Bookshop
Weihburggasse 24–6.
Map 6 D4. 5121945.

Mariahilfer Strasse 4.
Map 3 C2. 5226730.

Gilhofer
Bognergasse 2. **Map** 5 C3.
5334285.

Heck
Kärntner Ring 14. **Map**
4 E2 & 6 D5. 5055152.

Prachner
MuseumsQuartier. **Map** 5
A5. 51285880.

Shakespeare & Co
Sterngasse 2. **Map** 2 E5 &
6 D2. 5355053.

NEWSPAPERS AND PERIODICALS

Morawa
Wollzeile 11. **Map** 2 E5 &
6 D3. 515620.

CLOTHES AND ACCESSORIES

Bellezza
Kärntner Str 45. **Map** 4 D1
& 5 C5. 5121953.

D'Ambrosio
Bauernmarkt 1a.
Map 6 D2. 53326880.

Erich Hartmann
Corner of Lilieng.
Map 6 D3. 5121489.

Flamm
Neuer Markt 12.
Map 5 C4. 5122889.

Fürnkranz
Kärntner Str 39. **Map** 6 D4
& 5 C5. 4884426.
One of several branches.

H & M
Graben 8. **Map** 2 D5 &
5 C3. 5125505. *One
of several branches.*

Kettner
Seilergasse 12. **Map** 5 C4.
51322390. *One of
several branches.*

Knize
Graben 13. **Map** 2 D5 &
5 C3. 51221190.

Kurt Denkstein
Bauernmarkt 8. **Map** 6
D2. 5330460.

D G Linnerth
Lugeck 1–2. **Map** 6 D3.
5125888.

Resi Hammerer
Kärntner Str 29–31. **Map**
4 D1 & 5 C5. 5126952.

Tostmann
Schottengasse 3a.
Map 5 B2. 53353310.

ANTIQUES

Galerie Rauhenstein
Rauhensteingasse 3.
Map 6 D4. 5133009.

Herbert Asenbaum
Kärntner Str 28. **Map** 4 D1
& 6 D4. 5122847.

Reinhold Hofstätter
Bräunerstrasse 12. **Map**
5 C4. 5335069.

Subal & Subal
Spiegelgasse 8. **Map** 4 D1
& 5 C4. 5131349.

AUCTIONS

Dorotheum
Dorotheergasse 17. **Map**
4 D1 & 5 C4. 51560.

MARKETS

**Alt Wiener
Christkindlmarkt**
Freyung. **Map** 2 D5 &
5 B2. Dec: 9:30am–
7:30pm daily.

Bauernmarkt
Freyung. **Map** 2 D5 & 5 B2.
Mar–end Oct: 10am–
6:30pm Tue & Thu.

Christkindlmarkt
At the Neues Rathaus.
Map 1 C5 & 5 A2.
Mid-Nov–24 Dec:
2–6:30pm Mon–Fri,
10am–6:30pm Sat & Sun.

Heiligenkreuzerhof
Map 2 E5 & 6 E3.
Apr–Sep: first Sat &
Sun of each month; end
Nov–19 Dec: 10am–7pm
Sat, 10am–6pm Sun.

**Kunst und
Antikmarkt**
Donaukanal-Promenade.
Map 6 F2. May–end
Sep: 2–8pm Sat,
10am–8pm Sun.

Naschmarkt
Map 3 C2. 6am–
6:30pm Mon–Fri,
6am–2pm Sat.

ENTERTAINMENT IN VIENNA

IENNA OFFERS a wide range of entertainment, particularly of the musical variety. There is grand opera at the Opera House – Staatsoper *(see pp140–1)* – or the latest musical at the Theater an der Wien *(see p138)*. Dignified orchestral concerts and elegant Viennese waltzes take place at the great balls during the Carnival season, and waltzes are played in the relaxed atmosphere of the Stadtpark. Even the famous Lipizzaner horses perform to Viennese music and no visit to the city is complete without a trip to the

Pipo at the Ronacher (see p226)

Winter Riding School *(see pp98–9)*. Vienna also has excellent theatres, two of which perform in English, and several cinemas which specialize in classic films. Restaurants close early, but you can still be entertained around the clock at one of Vienna's many nightspots. Within the Ringstrasse, the city buzzes with late-night revellers enjoying jazz clubs, such as the Roter Engel, discos, casinos and bars with live music. Or you can end your day sipping coffee and nibbling pastries at a latenight café *(see also pp217–19)*.

The stage of the Theater in der Josefstadt *(see p116)*

PRACTICAL INFORMATION

A MONTHLY GUIDE to Vienna is issued free by the Wiener Tourismusverband (main Vienna Tourist Office – *see p238*). Posters which list the weekly programmes for the opera houses and theatres are pasted on billboard columns and displayed in most hotel lobbies. They also list casts for all the performances. Each day the four main newspapers in the city, *Die Presse, Kronenzeitung, Standard* and *Kurier (see p239)* publish programme listings. All four also give details of daily cinema performances and concerts as well as the main sporting events.

BOOKING TICKETS

Y OU CAN BUY tickets direct from the appropriate box office (check opening hours, since these vary), or reserve them on the telephone. The phone numbers and addresses for the booking offices are listed in the Music, Theatre and Cinema directories *(see pp229–30)*. The four state theatres, the Burgtheater *(see p132)*, the **Akademietheater** *(see p230)*, the Opera House *(see pp140–1)* and the **Wiener Volksoper** *(see p229)*, all have

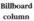

Billboard column

one central booking office, the **Bundestheaterkassen** *(see p229)*. However, tickets for performances at any of these four theatres can also be purchased at the box office of the Wiener Volksoper and the Burgtheater.

Tickets usually go on sale a week before the performance. Tickets for the Vienna State Opera are sold from one month in advance. However, bear in mind that tickets for September performances are sold during the month of June.

Phone reservations for credit-card holders can be made from six days in advance. Written applications for tickets for the state theatre must reach the Vienna State Opera ticket office (address as Bundestheaterkassen) no later than three weeks before the date of the performance.

Standing-room tickets are sold at the evening box office one hour before the start of the performance.

Tickets for the state theatres, the Theater an der Wien *(see p138)* and **Raimund Theater** *(see p229)* can be used on public transport for two hours before, and six hours after, all performances. Agencies are reliable, try **Reisebüro Mondial** *(see p229)*, and hotel staff may be able to obtain tickets, if at higher prices. Otherwise try the box office for returns.

AT THE THEATRE

I F YOU VISIT THE theatre in person, you will be able to see the seating plan and make your choice accordingly. The monthly programme for the state theatres also contains individual seating plans and it is a good idea to have them in front of you when booking your tickets by telephone. Most hotel porters will also have copies of seating plans for the principal venues.

If you book by telephone remember that *Parkett* (stalls) are in front and are usually the most expensive. In some theatres the front rows of the stalls are known as *Orchestersitze*. The *Parterre* (back stalls) are cheaper and the dress circle (the grand or royal circle) is called *Erster Rang*, followed by the *Zweiter Rang* (balcony). At the Burgtheater and Opera House, there are two extra levels called the *Balkon* and *Galerie*. The higher you go, the cheaper the seats are.

Casino Wien in Esterházy Palace

Boxes are known as *Logen* and the back seats are always cheaper than the front seats.

At the **Wiener Volksoper** (*see p229*) they still have *Säulensitze*, seats where the view is partly obscured by a column. These cheap tickets are bought by music lovers who come to listen rather than to view. There are four tiers of boxes at the Volksoper, known in ascending order as *Parterre, Balkon, Erster Rang* and *Zweiter Rang*.

Buffets at Vienna's principal theatres provide alcoholic and non-alcoholic drinks, and tasty snacks which range from open sandwiches at the **Akademietheater** (*see p230*) and Volksoper to the more elaborate

Busker beneath the Pestsäule

concoctions at the Opera House and Burgtheater. Small open sandwiches with caviar, egg, smoked salmon, cheese and salami on Vienna roll-style bread are also common. Glasses of *Sekt*, a sparkling wine, are always available.

Buffets are usually open for up to one hour before the start of a performance and are often fairly empty. They are an ideal place for relaxing with a snack and a drink, and the coffee is extremely good.

It is not usual to tip ushers at theatres, unless you are being shown to a box, but you may round up the price of a theatre programme.

Coats and hats have to be left in the cloakroom before you go to your seat. There is usually no fixed charge, and tipping is at your discretion.

FACILITIES FOR THE DISABLED

A NUMBER OF VENUES offer wheelchair access or help for those with hearing difficulties. Be sure to make your needs very clear when booking tickets.

A booklet, *Wien für Gäste mit Handicaps* (Vienna for handicapped guests), is published by the Wiener Tourismusverband (*see p238*) and provides information on facilities at entertainment venues, museums, hotels, restaurants, cafés, cinemas, post offices and so on.

TRANSPORT

B USES AND TRAMS run until around 11pm, while the underground continues until about midnight (*see Getting Around Vienna, pp250–55*). Night buses are a popular method of transport, with eight routes operating around the city and into the suburbs. They start at 12:30am from Schwedenplatz and continue every half hour until 4am. Tickets usually cost around one euro and are sold on the bus (*see p255*).

You can phone for a taxi from your venue, or take one from outside. Taxis usually line up outside theatres after a performance, otherwise you can go to one of the many taxi ranks which are found on most street corners. Taxis which do not stop when hailed are already booked.

CASINOS

C ASINOS AUSTRIA has become the hallmark for superbly run casinos all over the world (you will even find them aboard luxury liners), but **Casino Wien** is a showcase. It is set in the Baroque Esterházy Palace (*see p80*) and you can play French or American roulette, baccarat and poker there. The complex includes a bar, a restaurant and the **Jackpot Café**, which is a typically Viennese addition.

Casino Wien
Kärntner Strasse 41. **Map** 4 D1.
Casino ⏰ 3pm–4am daily.
Jackpot Café ⏰ 10am–1am daily.
📞 5124836.

Dancing at the grand Opera Ball (*see p141*)

Music in Vienna

THE VIENNA OPERA HOUSE *(see pp140–41)* is one of the greatest of its kind in the world and, like all four state theatres, is heavily subsidised. The acoustics are excellent – the world-famous conductor Arturo Toscanini advised on the rebuilding of the theatre after it was destroyed at the end of the last war. The house orchestra, the Vienna Philharmonic, performs while the Opera House is open from September until June. Most operas are sung in the original language. The city supports two principal orchestras, the Vienna Philharmonic and the Wiener Symphoniker. There are also a number of chamber music ensembles, such as the Alban Berg Quartet, and visiting artists. Church music is often of concert quality. You can hear more informal music in the Stadtpark, where a small orchestra regularly plays waltzes in summer. Live rock music is popular in discos, and there is an annual jazz festival *(see p63)*.

OPERA AND OPERETTA

SEAT PRICES AT the Vienna Opera House range from €4 to €145. Tickets are sold one week in advance of a performance, except standing-room tickets, which are on sale one hour before the performance starts. These are good value, since the most expensive ticket is around €2, but because of this there is usually a long queue. After buying your ticket, if you find a spot near a side rail, you can mark your space by tying a scarf round it – leaving you free to wander around. The New Year's Eve performance is always *Die Fledermaus*, and famous guests sometimes make surprise appearances during the second act.

The **Wiener Volksoper** is renowned for its superb operetta productions of works by composers ranging from Strauss, Millöcker and Ziehrer to Lehár and Kálmán. There are also performances of musicals and light opera by Mozart, Puccini and Bizet, sung in German. The same singers also appear at the Opera House and vice versa – often singing the same role. Prices can range from €3 to €58, and the season is exactly the same as the Opera House.

Concealed in a small side street in the Stephansdom Quarter is one of Vienna's great little opera houses the **Wiener Kammeroper**.

Many international singers such as Waldemar Kmentt, Eberhard Waechter and Walter Berry started their careers here. You can expect anything to be peformed here from the early works of Rossini to classic operetta, as well as rock versions of familiar operas such as *Tales of Hoffmann* and *Carmen*, and opera parodies.

The historic Theater an der Wien *(see p138)* and the large **Raimund Theater** are part of the Vereinigte Bühnen Wien, the City's own theatres. Both of these specialize in putting on performances of grand and lavish musicals. The Wiener Festwochen *(see p62)* is held in May and June, and includes productions by guest companies, which are staged at these two theatres as part of the festival programme.

From mid-July until mid-August the Wiener Kammeroper also play at the **Soirée bei Prinz Orlofsky** festival at the Schönbrunner Schlosstheater *(see p63)*. The festival **Seefestspiele Mörbisch** *(see p63)* takes place every weekend in July and August on a stage projecting on to Lake Neusiedl.

CLASSICAL CONCERTS

THE PRINCIPAL VENUES for classical concerts are the **Musikverein** (including the Brahmssaal and the new halls of Gläserner Saal and Steinerner Saal) and the concert halls of the **Konzerthaus**.

Performances are also held in places such as Schubert's birthplace in Nussdorf *(see p185)* and in many historic palaces.

The New Year's Concert *(see p65)* is televised live from the Grosser Musikvereinsaal in the Musikverein every year. You can apply for tickets by writing direct to the **Wiener Philharmoniker**. However, applications must be received on 2 January (not before, not after) for the next year's concert. You can order from abroad by telegram.

Waltz concerts and operetta, which include stars from the Vienna Volksoper, can be heard at the Musikverein, the Neue Burg *(see p95)* and the Konzerthaus on Tuesdays, Thursdays and Saturdays from April until October. Mozart and Strauss concerts are performed on Wednesdays at the Neue Burg. All tickets are the same price, so the best thing to do is to get there early if you want to make sure of getting the best seat. The **Klangbogen Wien** music festival, which includes opera performances and concerts, is held from July to August.

CHURCH MUSIC

DETAILS OF the many church concerts performed in Vienna are published in all the daily newspapers. Look out particularly for details of Sunday mass at the following places: Augustinerkirche *(see p102)*, Minoritenkirche *(see p103)*, the Karlskirche *(see p148)*, Stephansdom *(see p76)* and Michaelerkirche *(see p92)*. In July and August, many other churches hold organ recitals.

The Vienna Boys' Choir *(see p39)* can be heard during mass at the Burgkapelle *(see p103)* every Sunday and religious holiday at 9:15am except from July to mid-September. (Tickets are available from the Burgkapelle; the box office is open the Friday before). You can also hear them at the **Konzerthaus** every Friday at 3:30pm in May, June, September and October. Buy tickets from hotel porters and from **Reisebüro Mondial**. Book well in advance.

INFORMAL MUSIC

THE DESCRIPTION just outside **Konzert-Café Schmid Hansl** reads, "the home of Viennese song". The original owner of this small café, which serves hot food until it closes, was Hansl Schmid, a very fine singer and musician. Guests would often visit the café just to hear him sing, and sometimes a famous artist might join him in a duet or give a solo performance. The present owner, Hansl Schmid's son, once a member of the Vienna Boys' Choir, has kept up this tradition, and you may well encounter opera stars coming in to perform unexpectedly.

Another Viennese favourite is the **Wiener Kursalon**. Dinner and waltz evenings with the Johann Strauss Salonorchester are held daily throughout the year along with classical ballet performances. Concerts take place in the Stadtpark during the summer months.

ROCK, POP AND JAZZ

WHAT IS POPULAR one week in Vienna's lively music scene may very well be out of fashion the next. Many discos have live music on certain nights or for a limited period.

U4 disco has a different style every night (from industrial to flower power) and Thursday is gay night. **Tanzcafé** and **Volksgarten Club Disco** are the oldest in town with house to hip-hop and salsa. Also still popular is **Take Five**. **Roter Engel** in the Bermuda Triangle has live music every night and there is a midnight show at **Nachtwerk**.

Live concerts are held at the **Café Szene**, **Jazzland**, and on Sundays at **Chelsea**. Popular among artistic circles is the **Broadway Piano Bar** which has live music every night. Monday is Jazz night and Saturday is Night Line featuring renowned performers.

A must for jazz fans is **Porgy & Bess**, with live music and dancing, and the **Jazzfest** held in the first two weeks of July, with concerts in various venues such as the Opera House *(see pp140–41)*, the Volkstheater *(p230)* and the Neues Rathaus *(p130)* as well as many open-air events. All styles, electro and house as well as alternative music can be found at **Café Leopold**, **Schikaneder Bar** and **Flex**.

Theatre and Cinema

V IENNA HAS A GOOD CHOICE of theatres, with an eclectic
mix of styles ranging from classical drama to the
avant-garde. Some places, like the Theater in der Josefstadt *(see p116)* or the recently restored Ronacher, are
well worth visiting for their architecture alone. You can
see productions in English at the English Theatre or, if
you understand German, you can go and watch one of
the many fringe performances. Some cinemas screen
films in their original language. The classic film which
is usually showing somewhere in the city is *The Third
Man*, set in Vienna during the Allied occupation.

THEATRES

V IENNESE THEATRE is some of
the best in Europe and
the Burgtheater *(see p132)*,
one of the City's four state
theatres, is the most important
venue. Classic and modern
plays are performed here and
even if your understanding of
German is limited, you will
still enjoy a new production
(which can often be avant-
garde) of a Shakespeare play.
For classic and modern plays
go to the **Akademietheater**,
part of the Burgtheater.

The Josefstadt Theater *(see
p116)* is worth a visit for the
interior alone. As the house
lights slowly dim, the crystal
chandeliers float gently to the
ceiling. It offers excellent
productions of Austrian plays
as well as classics from other
countries, and the occasional
musical. **Kammerspiele** is
the Josefstadt's "little house".
The old and well-established
Volkstheater offers more
modern plays as well as the
occasional classic and some
operetta performances.

Vienna has a wide range of
fringe theatre from one-man
shows to *Kabarett* – these are
satirical shows not cabarets –
but fairly fluent German is
needed to appreciate them.
German-speakers will also
enjoy the highly recom-
mended **Kabarett Simpl**,
which has recently reopened.

Theatres that give performances in English include the
English Theatre and the
very small **International
Theater**. Plays at the English

Theatre only run for a short
period, but often feature
famous international stars.

The **Ronacher** was once
Vienna's most glamorous
theatre. It became a variety
theatre where the music-hall
star Josephine Baker appeared
among other entertainers. Stall
seats were then replaced with
tables and it became a restaurant. When the Burgtheater
was destroyed in World War
II, performances took place at
the Ronacher until the Burgtheater was rebuilt. Recently
restored, the Ronacher is
once more a variety theatre.

CINEMAS

A CINEMA THAT SCREENS the
latest films in their
original language is the **Burg
Kino**, while the **Haydn
Cinema** and the **Artis
International** show new
releases in English only.
Cinemas that specialize in
showing old and new classics
as well as the more unusual
films are the **Österreichisches Filmmuseum**, **Filmhaus Stöbergasse**,
Filmcasino, and **Votiv-Kino**
(which has a special cinema
breakfast on Sundays). The
Apollo Center is a modern
complex and has the largest
cinema screen in Austria.

DIRECTORY

THEATRES

Akademietheater
Lisztstrasse 1, A-1010.
Map 4 E2.
Ticket Office: Hanuschgasse
3. **Map** 5 C4.
C 514440.

Burgtheater
Dr Karl-Lueger-Ring,
A-1014. **Map** 1 C5 &
5 A2. C 514444140.

English Theatre
Josefsgasse 12, A-1080.
Map 1 B5. C 4021260.

**International
Theater**
Porzellangasse 8, A-1090.
Map 1 C3.
C 3196272.

Kabarett Simpl
Wollzeile 36,
A-1010.
Map 2 E5 & 6 E3.
C 5124742.

Kammerspiele
Rotenturmstrasse 20,
A-1010.
Map 2 E5 & 6 E2
C 42700300.

Ronacher
Seilerstätte 9,
A-1010.
Map 4 E1 & 6 D4.
C 58885.

Volkstheater
Neustiftgasse 1,
A-1070.
Map 3 B1.
C 5247263.

CINEMAS

Apollo Center
Gumpendorfer Strasse 63.
Map 3 A4 & 5 B5.
C 5879651.

Artis International
Schulgasse 5,
A-1010.
Map 1 A2.
C 5356570.

Burg Kino
Opernring 19.
Map 4 D1 & 5 B5.
C 5878406.

Filmcasino
Margaretenstrasse 78.
Map 3 C3.
C 5879062.

**Filmhaus
Stöbergasse**
Stöbergasse 11–15.
Map 3 B5.
C 5466630.

Haydn Cinema
Mariahilfer Strasse 57.
Map 3 B2.
C 5872262.

**Österreichisches
Filmmuseum**
Augustinerstrasse 1.
Map 4 D1 & 5 C4.
C 5337054.

Votiv-Kino
Währinger Strasse 12.
Map 1 C4
C 3173571.

Sport and Dance

OUTDOOR ACTIVITIES ARE extremely popular. Football is followed by many locals – especially since the pre-war victories of the famous "Wonder Team". Visitors who enjoy swimming can take advantage of the pools the city has to offer. Horse racing and ice-skating also attract many locals. Flat racing takes place at the Freudenau in the Prater. The well-equipped **Stadthalle** is ideal for spectator sports like boxing and wrestling and houses its own pool, bowling alleys and ice rink. Many of Vienna's dance schools hold special waltz classes during the Carnival season (see p65).

ICE-SKATING

OUTDOOR ICE-SKATING is very popular in Vienna. Locals make good use of the open-air rinks at the Eislaufanlage Engelmann and the Wiener Eislaufverein (see p234).

SWIMMING

VIENNA CAN BE very warm in summer and has many outdoor pools, including the **Schönbrunner Bad** in the Schönbrunn Palace park (see pp172–73). The **Krapfenwaldbad** has wonderful views over Vienna, and the **Schafbergbad** holds underwater gymnastics every Tuesday and Thursday. The **Thermalbad Oberlaa** has three open-air pools and an indoor pool. The Kinderfreibad Augarten (see p234) is popular with children,

and they can be left at the Kinderfreibad to be watched by the attendants. Beach huts on the Alte Donau coast can be hired daily from **Strandbad Gänsehäufel** or **Strandbad Alte Donau**, where you can also hire boats. Strandbad Gänsehäufel has a beach, a heated pool, table tennis and Punch and Judy shows. For relaxing beaches, the world's longest water slide, barbecues and a night bus at weekends, visit **Donauinsel**.

FOOTBALL

THE VIENNESE ARE enthusiastic football fans, and there are two huge covered football stadiums in the city. The **Ernst Happel Stadion** (which seats 48,000) is in the Prater and the **Hanappi Stadion** (which seats 20,000) is at Hütteldorf.

HORSE RACING

THE PRATER OFFERS a wide range of activities (see pp162–63), including trotting races at the **Krieau**.

DANCING AND DANCE SCHOOLS

DURING THE Carnival season (see p65) many balls, and some fancy dress dances, are held in Vienna. Venues include the Hofburg, the Neues Rathaus (see p130) and the Musikverein (see p229). The grandest event is the Opera Ball (see p141), which takes place on the Thursday before Ash Wednesday. The opening ceremony includes a performance by the Opera House ballet. An invitation is not needed, you just buy a ticket. The Kaiserball is held at the Neue Burg on New Year's Eve (see pp65 and 95). A special ball calendar is issued by the Wiener Tourismusverband – Vienna Tourist Office (see p238).

The Summer Dance Festival (see p63) runs from July to August. You can learn a range of dances, including rock 'n' roll, at some dance schools in the city. During the Carnival season, some schools hold Viennese waltz classes. The **Elmayer-Vestenbrugg** also teaches etiquette.

CHILDREN'S VIENNA

TRADITIONALLY, the Viennese have a reputation for preferring dogs to children. But negative attitudes towards children are gradually disappearing as the number of families has increased since the 1960s baby boom. Most restaurants serve children's portions, and in some of the more expensive places they can eat Sunday lunch at half price. Eating out at a *Heuriger* is less formal, and you can sit outside in summer. Vienna has many playgrounds and almost all museums offer tours that cater for children. Further out there are large parks, a zoo, swimming pools and ice rinks. Various children's activities are organized throughout the year.

Children pay half price on trams

PRACTICAL ADVICE

TRAFFIC IN VIENNA can be fast and drivers are not automatically obliged to stop at pelican crossings. Always cross the road at traffic lights, and watch out for speeding cyclists in the bicycle lanes.

Children up to the age of six can travel for free on public transport. Those between the ages of six and 14 must buy a half-price ticket. During the summer holidays (the end of June to the end of August) children under 18 can travel free provided they can show some form of identification when buying a ticket.

It is a good idea to carry some small change, as you will need it to use public lavatories. These are usually clean. In shops, the assistants may offer children boiled sweets, but do not feel obliged to accept these.

The concierges at many hotels, particularly the larger establishments, can arrange for a baby-sitter. If they cannot, they may be able to suggest a reliable local agency. If you get back from an evening out after about 10 or 11pm, you may have to pay for the baby-sitter's taxi home.

CHILDREN'S SHOPS

TRADITIONAL Austrian clothing, which is still worn by some children in Vienna, can be purchased from **Lanz Trachtenmoden** on Kärntner Strasse. Traditional dress includes *Lederhosen*, leather shorts, for boys and the *Dirndl*, a traditional dress, for girls. The *Dirndl* is worn with a white lace blouse and an apron. A little bag is sometimes carried as well. Lanz Trachtenmoden also stocks a range of beautiful knitwear in a myriad of colours and designs. Children will particularly like the fine embroidered woollen slippers made in the Tyrol.

Dohnal sells Austrian-made clothes for children up to the age of 16, and the large international chains such as **012 Benetton**, **Jacadi** and **H & M** stock a wide selection of good-quality children's clothes.

Haas & Haas sells delightful craft-like presents, including wooden toys and puppets. Their conservatory-style tea house is an ideal place to treat your children to lunch, or a delicious cake or *palatschinken* (see *pp208–9*).

Children on a day out visiting Josefsplatz in the Hofburg

The **Wiener Spielzeugschachtel** sells imaginative wooden toys and children's books, while a more conventional toy shop is **Kober** on the Graben. Kober stocks a superb selection of toys and games, but at high prices.

Dressing up at the Maxim Kinderfest, part of Fasching (see p65)

012 Benetton
Goldschmiedgasse 9. **Map** 5 C3.
[5339005.

Dohnal
Kärntner Strasse 12. **Map** 4 D1 & 6 D4. [5127311.

H & M
Kärntner Strasse 11–15. **Map** 4 D1.

Haas & Haas
Teehandlung, Stephansplatz 4.
Map 2 E3 & 6 D3. [5129770.

Jacadi
Trattnerhof 1. **Map** 5 C3. [5358866.

Kober
Graben 14–15. **Map** 2 D5 & 5 C3.
[5336019.

Lanz Trachtenmoden
Kärntner Strasse 10.
Map 4 D1 & 6 D4. [5122456.

Wiener Spielzeugschachtel
Rauhensteingasse 5. **Map** 6 D4.
[5124494.

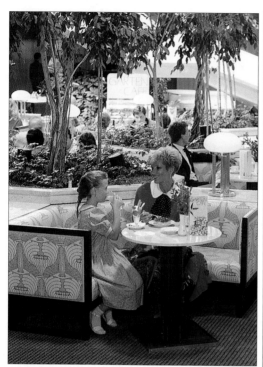

The Vienna Marriott offers special Sunday lunch deals for families

McDonald's

Singerstrasse 4. **Map** 4 E1 & 6 D3.
📞 5139279.
One of several branches.

Pizza Hut

Schottengasse 2.
Map 5 B2. 📞 5331810.

SAS Palais Hotel

Parkring 16. **Map** 4 E1 & 6 E4.
📞 515170.

Wienerwald

Annagasse 3.
Map 4 D1 & 6 D4. 📞 5123766.
Freyung 5, Schottenkeller.
Map 2 D5 & 5 B2. 📞 5331420.
Two of several branches.

SIGHTSEEING WITH CHILDREN

VIENNA HAS A WEALTH of attractions that will appeal to children, including funfairs, museums, sports and the zoo.
It costs around half the adult entrance fee for children to get into museums. If children touch or get too close to the exhibits, the museum attendants are likely to make a fuss.
Vienna has plenty of parks, but some are designed more for admiring from the pathways than running around in. Watch out for signs warning *Bitte nicht betreten*, which means "Please don't walk on the grass". Details of some of the more child-friendly parks and nature reserves are given on page 234.
Children's playgrounds in Vienna are generally safe and well equipped. However, it is advisable to avoid the Karlsplatz play area, which is rather seedy and downmarket.

EATING OUT

RESTAURANTS in Vienna are not as tolerant of noisy or boisterous children as establishments in many other cities, but there are still plenty of places where children are welcome. Some of the more expensive hotel restaurants offer special Sunday lunch deals for families. The best is probably the Vienna Marriott *(see p199)*, where children under six eat free and six to 12-year-olds eat for half price. There is also a playroom with a child minder. The **SAS Palais Hotel** offers a similar deal without the playroom.
Heurige, where you can sit outside in summer, are usually less formal. The best time for families is from 4pm, when most of them open, as they are less crowded. Heuriger Zimmermann *(see p219)* has a small zoo where children can stroke the animals.
There are also a number of fast-food restaurants, including **McDonald's** and **Pizza Hut**. Most of these have special children's menus and some offer free gifts for children, especially on their birthdays. The **Wienerwald** Viennese chicken restaurants also have a children's menu. They are more formal indoors, but some, like the branch in the Freyung, have a garden. Open until 11:30pm, **Lustig Essen** also caters for children.

Lustig Essen

Salvatorgasse 6. **Map** 2 E5 & 6 D2.
📞 5333037.

Family out cycling, a familiar sight at the Prater

Elephants at Tiergarten Schönbrunn in the palace gardens *(see pp172–73)*

THE ZOO, PARKS AND NATURE RESERVES

Situated in Schönbrunn Palace gardens *(see pp172–73)*, this fine zoo *(Tiergarten)* combines historic features with a thoroughly up-to-date layout and the benefit of spacious reserves for the animals. The zoo contains many Baroque animal houses which accommodate elephants and the like. The garden also has a superb maze which was laid out between 1698 and 1740, as well as a labyrinth with various games and riddles. With its frescoed ceilings, the central octagonal pavilion now serves as a charming cafe.

In the Vienna Woods, the Lainzer Tiergarten *(see p171)*, is a nature reserve where children can see deer, wild boar and horses. There are playgrounds and a pond. An easy walk takes you to Hermes Villa hunting lodge, with its café and nature-based exhibitions.

FUNFAIRS

An ideal venue for a family outing is the atmospheric Prater *(see pp162–63)*. Its big wheel is magical at night, and noisier and busier than by day. The Prater park has sandpits, playgrounds, ponds, streams, and a vast area for children to run and play.

The **Böhmische Prater**, a smaller funfair in the Laaerwald, has ponds, birdlife, meadows and playgrounds.

Böhmische Prater
Laaerwald, Favoriten. **(** 6898193.

CHILDREN'S SPORTS

Vienna has some excellent swimming baths, free for children under six, such as the Dianabad *(see p231)*. The **Kinderfreibad Augarten** is a shallow pool and free for children between the ages of six and 15. However, it is not open to anyone else, except accompanying adults. The **Stadionbad** has three children's pools and a water slide and is free to children under 15 on Wednesdays.

In summer, you can swim in the Donau Insel coves. During winter, you can bathe in the hot geysers at Thermalbad Oberlaa *(see p231)*.

Between October and March you can go ice-skating at **Wiener Eislaufverein** or at **Eislaufanlage Engelmann**. Then enjoy hot chocolate in a Ringstrasse coffee house like Café Prückel *(see pp58–61)* or Café Schwarzenberg *(see pp60–61)* on Kärntner Ring.

ICE-SKATING

Eislaufanlage Engelmann
Syringgasse 6–8. **(** 4051425.
○ *3rd week Oct–1st week Mar: 9am–6pm Mon, 9am–9:30pm Tue, Thu, Fri, 9am–7pm Wed, Sat, Sun.*

Wiener Eislaufverein
Lothringerstrasse 28. **Map** 4 E2.
(71363530. **○** *Oct–Mar: 9am–9pm Tue, Thu, Fri, 9am–8pm Sat–Mon, 9am–10pm Wed.*

SWIMMING

Kinderfreibad Augarten
Karl-Meissl-Gasse entrance,

Ice-skating at Wiener Eislaufverein

Augarten Park. **Map** 2 E1.
(3324258.
○ *10am–6pm Mon–Fri.*

Stadionbad
Prater, Krieau. **(** 7202102.
○ *May–Oct: 10am–6pm daily.*

The big wheel forms a familiar landmark in the Prater park *(see pp162–63)*

ENTERTAINMENT

ALTHOUGH MOST THEATRE is performed in German, the **Märchenbühne der Apfelbaum** marionette theatre sometimes puts on shows in English of favourite fairy tales. Fairy stories with music and song can also be seen at the **Lilarum** puppet theatre. The **Wiener Konzerthaus** holds concerts *Für Kinder und Kenner* (children and experts) six times a year on Saturday or Sunday afternoons. In January, watch out for the Maxim Kinderfest, part of Fasching *(see p65)*, when children can dress up in costume. In November and December the Opera House *(see pp140–41)* and the Wiener Volksoper *(see p229)* have traditional children's programmes *(Kinderzyklus)*. Productions include Mozart's *The Magic Flute* and Engelbert Humperdink's *Hansel and Gretel.*

Several cinemas in Vienna show films in the original languages – look in the *Standard* newspaper's foreign films section. See also *Entertainment in Vienna* on pp226–31.

Lilarum
Göllnergasse 8. **C** 7102666.

Märchenbühne der Apfelbaum
Kirchengasse 41.
Map 3 B1.
C 523172920.

Wiener Konzerthaus
Lothringerstrasse 20.
Map 4 E2 & 6 E5.
C 242002.

SPECIAL ACTIVITIES AND WORKSHOPS

THE RATHAUS *(see p130)* has children's activities once a month (details from the town hall), and from mid-November there is a Christmas market *(see pp224–5)* which includes a children's train, pony rides and stalls selling toys, chestnuts and winter woollens. A Christmas workshop is held at the Volkshalle in the Rathaus from 9am to 6pm (7pm at weekends). The activities include baking, silk painting and making decorations.

A Christmas market stall in front of the Rathaus *(see p130)*

MUSEUMS

VIENNA HAS A range of museums for children to enjoy. The Natural History Museum *(see pp128–9)* boasts an impressive collection of fossils. The **Haus des Meeres** (Vienna Aquarium) contains over 3,000 sea creatures, including piranhas, crocodiles and sharks. Feeding time is 3pm.

Popular exhibits at the Völkerkundemuseum *(see p95)* include exotic musical instruments and Montezuma's treasures. Children aged 13 and under are allowed to enter the **Kunsthaus Wien** free. Designed by Friedensreich Hundertwasser, this colourful private gallery has undulating floors and bright paintings. The **Wiener Strassenbahnmuseum** (Vienna Tram Museum) houses the largest collection of vintage trams and buses in the world. Details of tours are available from information offices at Karlsplatz and Westbahnhof *(see p238)*.

Attacus atlas at the Natural History Museum *(see pp128–9)*

The Heeresgeschichtliches Museum *(see pp166–7)* contains a range of war memorabilia and the ZOOM Kindermuseum *(see p120)* offers interactive exhibits. Other options include the Doll and Toy Museum *(see p86)*, the **Zirkus und Clownmuseum**, dressing up events at the Sisi Museum in the Hofburg and at Schönbrunn Palace, experimenting with sight and sound at the

Haus der Musik *(see p80)* and learning about the mechanics of theatre on a back stage tour at the Theatre museum *(see p104)*.

A doll's house (about 1920) from the Doll and Toy Museum *(see p86)*

Haus des Meeres
Esterházypark. **Map** 3 B2.
C 5871417. ⏰ *9am–6pm daily.*

Kunsthaus Wien
Untere Weissgerberstrasse 13.
C 7120491. ⏰ *10am–7pm daily.*

Wiener Strassenbahnmuseum
Erdbergstrasse 109. **C** 7909 44903.
⏰ *May–beginning Oct: 9am–4pm Sat, Sun & public hols. (For tours see p237).*

Zirkus und Clownmuseum
Karmelitergasse 9. **Map** 2 E4 & 6 E1.
C 2110602127. ⏰ *5:30–7pm Wed, 2:30–5pm Sat, 10am–noon Sun.*

Montezuma's headdress in the Völkerkundemuseum *(see p95)*

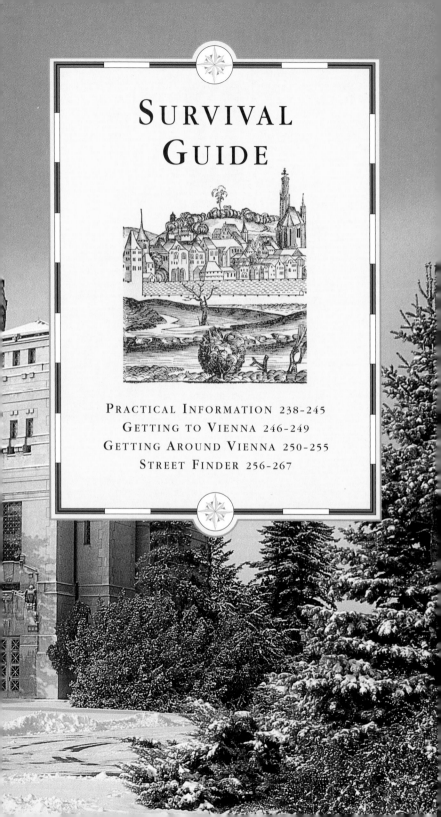

SURVIVAL
GUIDE

PRACTICAL INFORMATION

The best way to get around the centre of Vienna is on foot because many of the sights are in close proximity to each other. Museums and galleries are often crowded at weekends, so it might be a good idea to plan your visits during the week if possible. Sights are sometimes being refurbished, so it is a good

Sign for tourist information

idea to check in advance that they are open before visiting. Tourist offices have a useful free museums leaflet containing up-to-date information. Most shops in the centre are open Monday to Friday 8am to 6pm, and are open until 5pm on Saturdays. Banks are shut all weekend. Embassy details are listed on page 239.

CUSTOMS INFORMATION

NATIONALS FROM most European and many overseas countries do not need a visa to enter Austria, but it is advisable to check your requirements before travelling. Dogs and cats require a rabies vaccination certificate with a German translation. Motorists need a Green Card as proof of third-party insurance. For information on tax-free goods, *see p221*.

TOURIST INFORMATION

YOU CAN plan your trip to Vienna by getting in touch with travel agencies and the representatives of **Österreich Werbung** (the Austrian National Tourist Office) in your own country, or you can approach the **Wiener Tourismusverband** (Vienna Tourist Board) directly. The office is located on Albertinaplatz.

For assistance in organizing day trips from Vienna (*see p176–7*), contact the Österreich Werbung. Tourist information is also available from the offices of Austrian

Airlines (*see p247*). There is also an information office at **Westbahnhof** station, from where you can make hotel reservations. The arrivals hall at Schwechat Airport has a tourist information office where you can reserve rooms and pick up a city map that contains diagrams of the public transport network (*also see inside back cover*).

For cheaper accommodation and information about youth hostels or tickets for pop concerts, the multilingual team at **Jugendinformation Wien** provides assistance and leaflets in various languages.

TOURS AND EXCURSIONS

THE MAIN GUIDED tour operators are **Vienna Sightseeing** and **Cityrama**. Trams are a great way of seeing the 19th-century buildings in the Ringstrasse because, with the right ticket, you can choose where to get on and off (*see p252*). Tours in a 1920s tram (visiting the world's largest tram museum) are organized by **Oldtimer Tram** and leave from Otto Wagner's Pavilions on Karlsplatz (*see p146–7*).

The **DDSG-Blue Danube** organizes tours on the Danube and Danube Canal to sights such as Otto Wagner's Nussdorf locks. In the summer there are a lot of guided walking tours, in English, French or Italian, with a variety of themes. From May to

A guided walking tour around the Hofburg (see pp96–101)

September, cycling enthusiasts can book tours through **Vienna Bike** or **Pedal Power** (*see p252*). Tours are run in German or English, but Italian or French can also be arranged.

SIGHTSEEING TIPS

ENTRANCE PRICES vary considerably between museums. Any major exhibitions put on by museums will involve an extra charge. Children pay roughly half price and there are also reductions for senior citizens and students with identity cards. The only day on which the entrance fee is reduced or free is 26 October – the Austrian National Day. Many museums are closed on a Monday, but it is wise to check opening times, and if you are still in doubt, ring the museum itself. For information on booking theatre and musical perfomances *see pp224–9*.

One of the information offices in central Vienna

DISABLED VISITORS

SERVICES FOR the disabled are poor, but if you contact museums in advance they will help with wheelchairs. Most of the main sights are quite close together and accessible by wheelchair. Just plan your route carefully. A useful book, *Wien für Gäste mit handicaps* (Vienna for Handicapped Guests), is available from tourist offices *(see p239)*. Trams and buses cannot accommodate wheelchairs. At train stations, ask about lifts when you get your ticket. Facilities vary at underground stations, so check first.

STUDENT INFORMATION

VIENNA'S MAIN theatres offer cheap standing-room and unsold tickets at the evening box office prior to the performance. For popular shows you may need to queue for several hours. A university identity card as well as an international

student card also entitles students to a variety of discounts.

Tourist offices will provide information about the cheaper hotels and pensions as well as a list of Vienna's youth hostels *(see p195)*.

RADIO AND NEWSPAPERS

AUSTRIA HAS two main radio stations. Ö1 plays classical music and transmits the news daily at 8am and in English, French and German on the weekends. Ö3 plays popular music and transmits regular traffic bulletins. Radio FM4 transmits in English from 1am to 2pm daily on 103.8 MHz. Vienna Cable Radio transmits on FM 100.8.

The main listings magazine is *Falter*, but the two chief newspapers, *Die Presse* and *Standard*, list films daily. You can buy papers in a *Tabak*

Foreign newspapers are on sale at central kiosks

Trafik (newsagent), a kiosk or, on Sundays, on street corners. Foreign film cinemas include Artis International, Burg Kino and Haydn *(see p228)*.

Many foreign newspapers are available from kiosks. There are also several English-language bookshops, such as the **British Bookshop**, and **Shakespeare & Co**.

ELECTRICAL ADAPTORS

THE VOLTAGE in Austria is 220V AC. Plugs have two small round pins. It is a good idea to buy a multi-adaptor before coming to Vienna.

DIRECTORY			

TOURIST OFFICES

Jugendinformation Wien
Babenbergerstrasse 1
A-1010.
Map 3 C1 & 5 B5.
[*1799.*

Österreich Werbung
Rilkeplatz 5. [*588660.*

Schwechat Airport
Arrivals Hall.
[*70072828 or 70072875.*

Wiener Tourismusverband
Corner of Albertinaplatz,
Tegethoffstrasse and
Meysedergasse.
Map 4 D1 & 6 C4.
[*24555 or 211140.*
[w] *www.wien.info*

Westbahnhof
[*8923392.*

FOREIGN AUSTRIAN TOURIST OFFICES

London
30 St George Street,
London
W1R 0AL.
[*071 629 0461.*

New York
500 Fifth Avenue,
Suite 2009–2022,
New York
NY 10110.
[*212 944 6880.*

Sydney
36 Carrington Street,
1st floor,
Sydney
NSW 2000.
[*02 299 3621.*

Toronto
2 Bloor Street East,
Suite 3330,
Toronto,
Ontario
M4W 1A8.
[*416 967 3381.*

TOUR OPERATORS

Cityrama
Börsegasse 1.
Map 2 D4 & 5 B1.
[*534130.*

DDSG-Blue Danube
Handelskai 265.
[*7268123.*

Vienna Sightseeing
Stelzhamergasse 4–11.
Map 4 F1 & 6 F3.
[*7124683.*

Oldtimer Tram
Schwendergasse 51.
[*7909100.*

EMBASSIES & CONSULATES

Australia
Mattiellistrasse 2–4.
Map 4 E2.
[*506740.*

Canada
Laurenzerberg 2.
Map 6 E2.
[*531383000.*

Ireland
Rotenturmstrasse 16–18.
Map 6 D3.
[*7154246.*

New Zealand
Springsiedlg 28.
[*3188505.*

United Kingdom
Jaurèsgasse 12.
Map 4 F2.
[*716130.*

United States of America
Boltzmanngasse 16.
Map 1 C3.
[*31339.*

INTERNATIONAL BOOKSHOPS

British Bookshop
Weihburggasse 24–6.
Map 4 E1 & 6 D4.
[*5121945.*

Shakespeare & Co
Sterngasse 2.
Map 2 E5 & 6 D2.
[*5355053.*

Personal Security and Health

Pharmacy sign

Although tourists are unlikely to encounter any violence in Vienna, it is always advisable to take care when out walking. The police and emergency services are easy to contact if need be. Pharmacists are respected and their advice is often sought by locals. A visit to the pharmacy, unless the problem is serious, is the easiest choice. Specialist services available include Befrienders, a telephone helpline for English speakers who may be feeling lonely, an AIDS Helpline and an English-speaking Alcoholics Anonymous group.

SOS sign on U-Bahn platforms

EMERGENCY NUMBERS

AIDS Helpline
☎ 599370.

Alcoholics Anonymous
☎ 7995599.
Ask for English language AA.

Befrienders
☎ 7133374.

Dentist
☎ 5122078.
Night and weekend line.

Ambulance
☎ 144.

Doctor on Call
☎ 141.

Fire
☎ 122.

Police
☎ 133.

Vienna Medical Emergency Service
☎ 40144.

Motorway Breakdown
☎ 120.

PERSONAL SECURITY AND PROPERTY

There are a few places to steer clear of in Vienna. The underground is generally safe by day and night. Karlsplatz station, however, which is renowned as a drug centre, is quite unsavoury, particularly at night when it is best avoided. There may be some upsetting sights, although you are unlikely to be bothered. Last trains can be very crowded and the passengers a bit unruly. All under-ground stations have SOS points for emergencies from which you can call the station supervisor or halt trains. In the Prater, care should be taken at night as it is known for pickpocketing and for fights. Areas around the main railway stations can be unpleasant, though not really dangerous. The red light district is on the Gürtel between the West-bahnhof and the Südbahnhof.

Red Cross sign

Recent years have seen an increase in pickpocketing throughout the city so take care of your property and do not go out with a lot of cash (travellers' cheques are the safest way of carrying large sums of money). Care should also be taken when with-drawing money at cash point machines. For robbery, assault or missing persons, visit the nearest police station. Contact your consulate if you lose your passport.

MEDICAL TREATMENT AND INSURANCE

Tick-borne encephalitis is a possible danger wherever there are deciduous trees in Austria and most Austrians and foreign residents are inoculated against it. Inoculation is done in stages, but is not usually recommended for tourists. Only a tiny proportion of ticks carry the disease, which may cause brain damage and in some cases lead to death. The risk is minimal, but to be on the safe side, if you are bitten you should not remove the tick but go to an outpatients department. The Lobau, the Lainzer Tiergarten and Vienna Woods are tick areas, so it is a good idea to wear a hat and long shirt sleeves here.

Britain has a reciprocal arrangement with Austria whereby emergency hospital treatment is free upon presentation of a British passport. In theory, visits to doctors, dentists or

Police motorcycle

Policeman

Fire engine

Police car

Ambulance

DIRECTORY

CRISIS INFORMATION

Lost Property Bureau
Bastiengasse 36.
(40008091.
○ 8am–3:30pm Mon–Fri.

**Pharmacy
Information Line**
(1550.

**Vienna General
Hospital**
Währinger Gürtel 18–20.
Map 1 C4 & 5 A1. **(** 40400.

PHARMACIES

**Internationale
Apotheke**
Kärntner Ring 17. **Map** 4 E2 &
6 D5. **(** 5122825.

**Schweden-Apotheke,
Pharmacie-
Internationale**
Schwedenplatz 2.
Map 2 E2 & 6 E2. **(** 53329110.

Zum Heiligen Geist
Operngasse 16. **Map** 4 D2.
(5877367.

Zur Universität
Universitätsstrasse 10.
Map 1 C4 & 5 A1.
(40252980.

Façade of pharmacy

outpatient departments are also free, but obtaining free treatment can involve a lot of bureaucracy. It is best to take out full health insurance which will also cover flights home

for medical reasons. There are several private hospitals in Vienna, but the main hospital (and the largest in Europe) is the Vienna General Hospital in the ninth district *(see p245)*. In the case of a medical emergency, call an ambulance *(Rettungsdienst)* or the local **Doctor on Call**.

PHARMACIES

IF YOU ARE NOT in an emergency, go to an *Apotheke* (pharmacy) for advice on medicines and treatment. They all display a red "A" sign and operate a night rota system. Any closed pharmacies will display the address of the nearest one open, and the **Pharmacy Information Line** also has details of some which are open. If the problem is serious, call **Vienna Medical Emergency Service**.

LOST PROPERTY

GO TO THE nearest police station in the first instance. If they do not restore your property within seven days (and you are still in Vienna), then try the lost property bureau. For property lost on the railways and the Schnell-bahn, ask at the Westbahnhof, which is open from 8am to 3pm Monday to Friday. You have to go there in person.

Policewoman   **Fireman**

Banking and Local Currency

Bank Austria Creditanstalt

Bank Austria logo

IN THE PAST TEN years, Viennese financial systems have become more accessible. There are now several money-changing machines *(see Directory)*, and you can take any amount of euros or foreign currency in or out of the country. Cash tends to be used rather than credit cards.

BANKING AND EXCHANGE

THE BEST PLACE to change money is at a bank. Although you can use travel agents, bureaux de change *(Wechselstuben)* and hotels, banks offer a better rate. Exchanging a large amount of money at one time can save on commission because there is often a minimum charge or a handling fee of around €3.60. You can also exchange foreign bank notes for euros at one of the automatic money-changing machines (Change-o-mats).

Most banks stay open from 8am to 12:30pm and from 1:30 to 3pm (5:30pm on Thursdays). A few of them (for example, the main Bank Austria-Creditanstalt bank on Schottengasse) do not close for lunch. Some banks, generally those at the main railway stations and at airports *(see Directory)*, stay open longer than usual.

CREDIT CARDS

YOU CAN PAY for items with major credit cards, such as VISA, MasterCard, American Express and Diners Club, in most hotels, shops and major restaurants. However, credit cards are not used as frequently as, for instance,

in the UK or France, so it is a good idea to carry some cash on you at all times. If you are planning to use a credit card, make sure it is accepted first, especially if you carry MasterCard or Euro-Card. Be aware that some establishments also set a minimum expenditure that can be paid for by credit card.

Austrian banks operate a large network of money dispensers, many of which take foreign credit cards with PIN codes. This facility will be clearly stated on the front of the machine; just look for the logo of your card. Cash machines give instructions in German, English and French, and some may also have instructions in Italian, Swedish and Spanish.

Be sure to report lost or stolen cards to your own or the nearest Austrian bank.

TRAVELLER'S CHEQUES

TRAVELLER'S CHEQUES are the safest way to carry large sums of money, with the advantage that you can change as much or as little as you need at any one time. Choose a well-known name such as American Express, Visa, Travelex or cheques issued through a bank. Traveller's cheques can be

changed for cash in most Austrian banks and are useful for paying for your room at many of the larger hotels. There is, however, a minimum commission charge, which may make changing small sums of money uneconomical. It is worth checking the exchange rates before you travel to decide whether sterling, dollar or euro cheques are the most appropriate for your trip.

DIRECTORY

AFTER-HOURS EXCHANGE COUNTERS

City Air Terminal (Hilton Centre)
Map 4 F1 & 6 F4. 🕐 *8am–12:30pm, 2–6:30pm daily.*

Opera-Karlsplatz Passage
Map 4 D1 & 5 C5.
🕐 *8am–7pm daily.*

Schwechat Airport
🕐 *6am–9pm daily.*

Südbahnhof
Map 4 F4.
🕐 *7am–9pm daily.*

Westbahnhof
🕐 *7am–10pm daily.*

AUTOMATIC MONEY-CHANGING MACHINES

Die Erste Bank, Graben 21.
Map 2 D5 & 5 C3.

Bank Austria-Creditanstalt, Kärntner Ring 1.
Map 4 D2 & 6 C1.

Bank Austria-Creditanstalt, Mariahilfer Strasse 54.
Map 3 B2.

Bank Austria, Stephansplatz 2.
Map 1 D5 & 6 D3.

FOREIGN CREDIT CARD MACHINES

Bank Austria-Creditanstalt, Schottengasse 6.
Map 1 C4 & 5 B2.

Bank Austria-Creditanstalt, Schubertring 14.
Map 4 E2 & 6 D5.

AMERICAN EXPRESS

Kärntner Strasse 21–3.
Map 4 D1 & 6 D4. 🄲 *515670.*

Autobank automatic money-dispensing machine

Currency conversion machine which accepts foreign banknotes

The Euro

Twelve countries have replaced their traditional currencies, such as the Austrian Schilling, with the euro. Austria, Belgium, Finland, France, Germany, Greece, Ireland, Italy, Luxembourg, Netherlands, Portugal and Spain chose to join the new currency: the UK, Denmark and Sweden stayed out, with an option to review their situation. The euro was introduced on 1 January 1999, but only for banking purposes. Notes and coins came into circulation on 1 January 2002. A transition period allowed euros and schillings to be used simultaneously, and the schilling was phased out by the middle of 2002. All euro notes and coins can be used anywhere inside the participating member states.

Bank Notes

Euro bank notes have seven denominations. The €5 note (grey in colour) is the smallest, followed by the €10 note (pink), €20 note (blue), €50 note (orange), €100 note (green), €200 note (yellow) and €500 note (purple). All notes show the stars of the European Union.

5 euros

10 euros

20 euros

50 euros

100 euros

200 euros

500 euros

2 euros   1 euro   50 cents   20 cents   10 cents

Coins

The euro has eight coin denominations: €1 and €2; 50 cents, 20 cents, 10 cents, 5 cents, 2 cents and 1 cent. The €2 and €1 coins are both silver and gold in colour. The 50-, 20- and 10-cent coins are gold. The 5-, 2- and 1-cent coins are bronze.

5 cents   2 cents   1 cent

Communications

AUSTRIA'S TELECOMMUNICATIONS network and postal service are now run by two separate companies. The many post offices are easily identified by the yellow post office sign. Phoning abroad at peak times can be problematic as there are not enough telephone lines, although the number is being increased. Many phone numbers have been changed as a result, so if you cannot get through ring directory enquiries *(see below)*. To phone outside Austria, try using a telephone booth at a post office. You do not need change as you pay at the counter.

Emergency phone sign

Coin-operated phone   **Sign for cardphone**

USING THE TELEPHONE

TELEPHONES ARE mainly push-button, and most of them have instructions in four languages: German, English, French and Italian. Austria has one of the most expensive telephone systems in Europe, so make sure you have plenty of change or take a phone-card with you. The coin-operated telephones take 10 cent, 20 cent, 50 cent, €1 and €2 coins.

Phonecards can be purchased from any post office or from newsagents. For international calls, it is best to avoid hotels as they tend to add a hefty surcharge on top of the cost of the call.

Cheap rate calling times from Vienna are between 6pm and 8am Monday to Friday and all day on Saturday, Sunday and public holidays. To make a reverse charge call, for which a fee is payable, go to the nearest post office.

Telephone boxes
There are telephone booths at every post office. Yellow-striped public telephone boxes take coins or phonecards and are found throughout the city. Directories are usually available in telephone boxes, but can be too tatty to use. If you need to find a number, post offices always have legible directories available or contact directory enquiries.

USING A CARD PHONE

1 Lift the receiver.

2 Insert the card in the direction of the arrow and wait for dialling tone.

3 Key in the telephone number required.

4 Replace the receiver at the end of the call and withdraw the card.

USING A COIN-OPERATED PHONE

1 Lift the receiver.

2 Insert coins (10 cent minimum, no change given). Wait for dialling tone.

3 Key in the telephone number required. When the subscriber answers, speak at once.

4 Replace the receiver at the end of the call and collect any unused coins. A display shows how much money is left.

REACHING THE RIGHT NUMBER

- For directory enquiries in Austria, the EU and neighbouring countries, dial 118877.
- For international information, dial 0900 118877.
- All directory enquiries cost €1.35 per minute.
- For international or national telegrams, dial 0800 100190.
- For wake-up service, dial 0900 100100.
- To ring the **USA,** dial 001 followed by the number.

- To ring the **UK**, dial 0044 followed by the number (omit the 0 from the area code).
- To ring **Australia**, dial 0061 followed by the number.
- To ring **New Zealand**, dial 0064 followed by the number.
- To ring the **Irish Republic**, dial 00353 followed by the number.
- The front pages of the A–Z telephone directory list codes for each country. The cost of calls is available at post offices.

Mail and Postal Services

Decorative stamp

THE POST OFFICE provides postage stamps *(Briefmarken)*, telegrams and registered letters, as well as arranging the delivery of packages. There is also an express delivery *(Eilbriefe)* service, but this is a lot more expensive and may only be a day quicker. In addition, the post office sells phonecards and collectors' stamps. You can collect correspondence marked *Post Restante* or *Postlagernd* (to be called for) but you will need proof of identity, such as a passport. You can cash travellers' cheques and giro cheques up to a maximum of €180 per cheque. Main post offices will also change foreign currency into euros and vice versa. Many post offices also have fax machines.

Post office sign

vehicle country code (for example, "D" for Germany) before the post code.

E-MAIL AND THE INTERNET

VIENNA NOW HAS a variety of new internet cafés, where you can collect your email in relative comfort, often with a cup of coffee or a snack. Charges are most reasonable during off-peak times.

SENDING A LETTER

THE AUSTRIAN POSTAL system is reliable, verging on the pedantic, and posting a letter can take some time. Each

Display showing pick up times

Yellow letter box

individual letter is carefully weighed and every size and shape coded separately. Very few letters are sent at the set European rate of 55 cents.

Most post offices in Vienna are open between 8am and noon and 2pm and 6pm from Monday to Friday (but there

are no financial dealings after 5pm). Precise opening times are displayed at every post office. The main post office in each of the city's 23 urban districts *(Bezirke)* is open from 8am to 10am on Saturdays (but not for financial dealings). The **Central Post Office** in the first district is open 24 hours, and those at **Westbahnhof** and **Südbahnhof** open daily from 6am to 11pm and 7am to 10pm respectively, but not all services are available after normal opening hours. The airport post office is open from 7am to 8pm daily.

You can buy postage stamps at newsagents or post offices, which also have stamp-vending machines. Letters for Europe weighing up to 20 g cost 55 cents, as do postcards. Registered letters cost €2.03. You should add the standard

USEFUL ADDRESSES

Central Post Office
Fleischmarkt 19. **Map** 2 E5 & 6 D2.
515090.

Südbahnhof
Wiedner Gürtel 10. **Map** 4 F4.
501810.

Westbahnhof
Gasgasse 2.
8923260.

8921020 (for general information).
W www.post.at

Surfland Internet Café
Krugerstrasse 10.
10am–11pm daily.

Vienna's Districts

Vienna is divided into 23 urban districts or Bezirke, as shown on this map. The district number is incorporated into the Vienna postcode. For example, the 23rd district is written as A-1230. The inset area shows the part of Vienna covered by our Street Finder maps 1–4 (see pp262–5).

GETTING TO VIENNA

A S A POPULAR tourist destination and a major link between Eastern and Western Europe, Vienna is well served by air and rail. There are direct flights from every major European city as well as from North America, Canada, Japan and Australia. However, visitors from New Zealand need to change planes at London or Frankfurt and visitors from Ireland must transit at London or Munich. Vienna

Austrian Airlines aeroplane

also has coach and rail links with the rest of Europe, but this usually involves overnight travel. If you are not eligible for student or special rates, travelling by train is not significantly cheaper. Vienna has good motorway routes to the rest of Europe, but if you are arriving from Germany, do not forget that the Austrian motorway speed limit is only 130 km (80 miles) per hour.

ARRIVING BY AIR

THERE ARE several flights a day between London's Gatwick and Heathrow airports and Vienna's airport at Schwechat. British Airways is the main British airline

with regular flights to Vienna, and the main Austrian carrier is Austrian Airlines.

If you fly from the United States, there are direct flights with Delta from New York and Orlando. Lauda Air, founded by former Formula 1

world-racing champion Niki Lauda, runs flights from Los Angeles and Austrian Airlines from Chicago. There are also direct flights from Sydney and Toronto.

It is not necessary to pay full price for a scheduled

USING SCHWECHAT AIRPORT

Schwechat International Airport is one of the most modern in Europe. A major rebuilding schedule in the early 1990s added an extra boarding pier. Facilities within the airport include restaurants, a supermarket, duty-free shops, banks and tourist information offices. Easily accessed by road, the airport lies 19 km (12 miles) southeast of Vienna.

KEY

☐ Terminal 1
☐ Terminal 2
☐ Transit
☐ Airport services
☐ Customs and passports
☐ Shops

Gates C51–C62

DEPARTURE LEVEL

Gates A1–A8

Access to Gates D, domestic arrival and departure

Duty-free shops

Duty-free shops

Up to restaurant level

ARRIVAL LEVEL

Entrances

Gates B29–B43

Non-duty-free shops

Gates D, domestic departure

Gates D, domestic arrival

Medical centre

Trains to Wien Mitte

Car hire

Lost and found

Trains to Wien Mitte

CAT–City Airport Train & Schnellbahn

AIRPORT COMPLEX

B9 to Vienna

A4 to Vienna

Taxis

Luggage collection

Shuttle buses to Vienna

The modern exterior of Schwechat International Airport

ticket. There are good deals if you shop around the discount agencies; you can get APEX tickets if you book two weeks in advance; and charter flights are available at very competitive prices. Weekend package offers, including the price of two nights at a good Viennese hotel, can also prove to be excellent value, sometimes costing less than the economy-class ticket price.

Schwechat International Airport transit area

SCHWECHAT AIRPORT

VIENNA HAS ONE airport, Schwechat International. It is 19 km (12 miles) from the city centre and is about a 20–25 minute bus ride from the City Air Terminal, which is located in the same building as the Vienna Hilton, and is also easily accessible by train. This modern airport is very easy and quick to use.

The airport supermarket is often used by Viennese caught out by the restricted shopping times in the city and is open 7 days a week from 7:30am until 7pm including holidays.

GETTING INTO TOWN

THE SIMPLEST way to get to the city centre is by taxi or by the CAT-City Airport Train. When you come out of customs you will see signs for taxis and the CAT. There are always plenty of taxis available and they take about 20 minutes to reach the centre of Vienna. The CAT train runs between the airport and Wien Mitte and costs €9 each way. It departs from the basement level of the airport. Further information on the CAT can be obtained by calling 25250 or visiting www.cityairport train.com

There are buses running from 8:10am to 6:40pm, every 30 minutes, to the Südbahnhof and the West-bahnhof stations. Between these times they run roughly every hour, but exact timings can vary somewhat.

The fare for the buses is around €8, including baggage, which you pay the driver

when you get on. The Schnell-bahn train, which also departs from the basement level of the airport, is the cheapest option, but only goes every half hour. This train takes about 30 minutes to connect with Wien Mitte and stops at Praterstern-Wien Nord.

Shopping mall at Schwechat International Airport

ARRIVING BY RAIL

L IKE LONDON and Paris, Vienna has several mainline railway stations, three of which serve international connections.

Most Eurocity services charge a supplement if you buy your ticket less than 72 hours before departure. Many of the train services to Vienna are overnight and, for a small fee, it is possible to reserve a seat or a bed up to two months before travelling. Often there are no buffet facilities on overnight trains, but snacks are sometimes sold by the steward.

Generally, the Westbahnhof handles trains from the west and includes some Budapest services. Southern and eastern

Rail route into Vienna with abbey at Melk *(see p179)* in the background

Sign at Westbahnhof showing how to get to the exit, Regionalbahn, Schnellbahn, ticket machines and Regionalbus station

Travel agency (*Reisebüro*) at Westbahnhof

areas are served by the Südbahnhof, and trains from the north arrive at Franz-Josefs-Bahnhof *(see* Major Rail and Coach Stations *opposite).*

Westbahnhof has interchanges with the U3 and U6 underground lines, the Schnell-

bahn and several tram and bus routes. The Südbahnhof is linked to the Schnellbahn and several tram and bus lines, while Franz-Josefs-Bahnhof is served by the Schnellbahn and the cross-city D tram, which goes directly to the Ringstrasse. All the stations have taxi ranks.

The travel agency *(Reisebüro)* at Westbahnhof is open from 8am to 7pm on weekdays and from 8am to 1pm on Saturdays and can provide information as well as helping with booking hotel rooms.

The travel agency at the Südbahnhof, which is open from 8am to 7pm on weekdays and from 8am to 1pm on Saturdays (with shorter hours from November to April), offers a similar service. In Vienna there is a telephone number for obtaining railway information in English.

Railway information
☎ 051717.

Austrian Federal Railways
☎ 93000.
🖳 www.oebb.at

ARRIVING BY COACH

S ERVICES RUN TO Vienna's main coach station, Wien Mitte, from Eastern European cities such as Bratislava and Budapest, along with domestic routes from eastern Austria *(see p255).* Eurolines run coaches from London Victoria

Eurolines coach

to Wien Mitte. Südbahnhof coach station handles routes from southern and southwestern Austria *(see p255).*

ARRIVING BY ROAD

A LL DRIVERS IN AUSTRIA must carry their driver's licence, car registration document and insurance papers. Visitors need to carry an overseas extension of their annual insurance, such as a Green Card. An international driver's licence is required for people whose language is written in a script other than Roman. Wearing

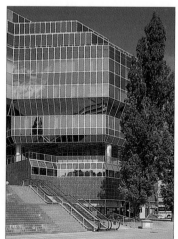

Exterior view of the Franz-Josefs-Bahnhof, which services trains from Prague and northern Austria

seatbelts is compulsory, and children up to the age of 12 or under 1.5 m (5 ft) may not sit on front seats unless with special child seats or seat belts. To travel on motorways in Austria you must have a

Sign on the Gürtel indicating the direction of the city centre

vignette sticker, available at petrol stations and tobacconists, attached to the inside of your windscreen. *Vignettes* are available for 10 days (€7.6), two months (€22) or one year (€72.6). All rented cars will have a *vignette* provided. Visitors arriving by road from the south arrive on the A2 and A23 southern motorways (Südautobahn), from the north on the A22 Danube motorway (Donauuferautobahn), from the west on the A1 western motorway

(Westautobahn) and from the east (including Schwechat International Airport) on the A4 eastern motorway (Ostautobahn). The city centre is marked Zentrum. The motorways converge on the outer ring road (Gürtel), sections of which are quite seedy. A *Parkscheine* is needed to park on inner-city streets and is available from tobacconists.

ARRIVING BY BOAT

FROM APRIL TO October you can arrive by boat along the Danube from Bratislava, the Wachau and Budapest. The

Sign showing direction to the ferry terminal

boat docks at the Donaudampfschiffsgesellschaft (DDSG-Blue Danube) shipping line's landing station at the Reichsbrücke bridge *(see p238)*. It is close to the Vorgartenstrasse U-Bahn station on the U1 line. There is a DDSG-Blue Danube information counter at the dock which can provide city maps.

DDSG-Blue Danube ferry arriving in Vienna from eastern Europe

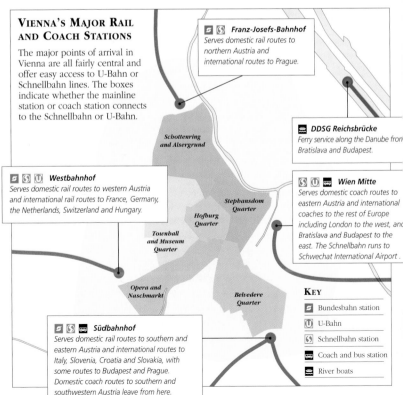

VIENNA'S MAJOR RAIL AND COACH STATIONS

The major points of arrival in Vienna are all fairly central and offer easy access to U-Bahn or Schnellbahn lines. The boxes indicate whether the mainline station or coach station connects to the Schnellbahn or U-Bahn.

Franz-Josefs-Bahnhof
Serves domestic rail routes to northern Austria and international routes to Prague.

DDSG Reichsbrücke
Ferry service along the Danube from Bratislava and Budapest.

Westbahnhof
Serves domestic rail routes to western Austria and international rail routes to France, Germany, the Netherlands, Switzerland and Hungary.

Wien Mitte
Serves domestic coach routes to eastern Austria and international coaches to the rest of Europe including London to the west, and Bratislava and Budapest to the east. The Schnellbahn runs to Schwechat International Airport .

Südbahnhof
Serves domestic rail routes to southern and eastern Austria and international routes to Italy, Slovenia, Croatia and Slovakia, with some routes to Budapest and Prague. Domestic coach routes to southern and southwestern Austria leave from here.

Schottenring and Alsergrund

Stephansdom Quarter

Hofburg Quarter

Townhall and Museum Quarter

Opera and Naschmarkt

Belvedere Quarter

KEY

	Bundesbahn station
	U-Bahn
	Schnellbahn station
	Coach and bus station
	River boats

GETTING AROUND VIENNA

WALKING IS GENERALLY the easiest and most enjoyable way to get around the compact centre of Vienna. There is so much to see, and when you feel tired or hungry there is always a café or *Konditorei* just a few steps away. The good news for pedestrians is that the normally assertive Viennese drivers are dissuaded from driving through the city centre by a complicated and frustrating one-way system, pedestrian zones and

Viennese Fiaker

strict parking limits. If you would rather not walk around the main sights, a network of minibuses crisscrosses the city centre. The public transport system is clean, efficient and easy to use. Run by the City of Vienna Transport Authority, it consists of a tram, bus and underground network. All the services operate from 5am to 12:30am, but it is best to check individual timetables, which are very reliable, before travelling.

WALKING IN VIENNA

WALKING IS AN excellent way to see the city, but there are a few points to remember. Traffic rarely stops at pedestrian crossings so you should proceed with care. British and Australian visitors should remember that motorists drive on the right. On the Ringstrasse, trams run against the traffic, so it is necessary to look both ways. Try to use subways or crossings where there are signals. If you ignore the red figure meaning "Do not cross" you could be fined on the spot by a policeman, even if there is no sign of traffic at the time. Other Viennese pedestrians will also voice annoyance, as jay-walking is regarded as irresponsible. In addition, keep an eye out for cyclists; they share the pavement with pedestrians and, if they are travelling at some speed, may not have time to stop if you stray onto their section of the pavement.

Do not cross

Cross

There are at least 50 guided walking tours in and around Vienna on offer throughout the summer months. They explore themes such as Biedermeier, Baroque or Vienna 1900 and are available in German, English, French

and Italian. For a variety of information on walking tours, contact the Wiener Touris-musverband *(see p238)*.

THE CITY BY FIAKER

TRADITIONAL horse-drawn open carriages or *Fiakers*, many driven by a crusty, bowler-hatted and bewhiskered coachman, are a novel and relaxing way to get around. Take into account that part of the route is on the busy Ringstrasse. You can hire a *Fiaker* at Stephansplatz, Heldenplatz and Albertinaplatz, but to avoid an unpleasant surprise agree the terms (price and length of trip) before you set off. Even a short trip can be costly.

Traffic signal for cyclists

Cycle lane

VIENNA BY BICYCLE

VIENNA IS great for cyclists, as long as you avoid the main roads and tramlines by sticking to the cycle paths. A 7-km (4-mile) cycle path round the Ringstrasse takes you past many sights and there are bike paths to the Hundert-wasser Haus *(see p164)* and to the Prater *(see pp162–63)*. A booklet called *Rad Wege* shows all Vienna's cycle routes and is available from bookshops. Bikes can be hired at some train stations and discounts are given with a train ticket. You will need to leave identification. City cycle tours run during summer at from under the Salztor Bridge *(see p238)*. Pedal Power's 3-hour city tours leave from the Prater Ferris wheel at 10am daily.

Cycling along bicycle lanes in the Prater

| **Beginning of no-parking zone** | **End of no-parking zone** |

| **Priority to traffic on the right cancelled** | **Priority to traffic on the right restored** |

Driving in Vienna

Drivers are aggressive in Vienna, so you will need to be alert as cars race and cut in front of you as a matter of course. Priority is always to the right unless a "yellow diamond" indicates otherwise. You must give way to trams, buses, police cars, fire engines and ambulances. It is useful to belong to an internationally affiliated automobile association or you will be charged by the ÖAMTC (the Austrian motoring association) for breakdowns or repairs. Traffic news is on radio station Ö3, and Blue Danube Radio broadcasts traffic news in English. The speed limit in Vienna is 50 km (30 miles) per hour. Police carry out checks with infra-red guns and can fine you on the spot. The limit for alcohol is 0.5 mg per ml of blood (about 1/3 litre of beer or 1–2 glasses of wine). There are spot checks and you could be fined a considerable sum and have your licence confiscated if you exceed the limit.

Only lead-free petrol and diesel are widely available. A few garages take credit cards, but tend to prefer cash.

Parking Places

Apart from Sundays, when shops are closed, finding a parking spot in Vienna is frustrating and time-consuming. *Anfang* and *Ende* signs can be seen everywhere. You

are not allowed to park between them. Do look carefully as the *Ende* sign may be around a corner or facing the wrong way. If your car is clamped or towed away, telephone or go to the police, who will tell you which of the city's two pounds to go to. The City of Vienna operates a daytime park and pay scheme in districts 1 to 9 *(see p245)*. You can buy parking disks from newsagents *(Tabak Trafiken)*, some banks and petrol stations. Usually, a maximum of two hours is allowed in any space. In other districts, a blue line by the kerb indicates a pay and display scheme. Car parks in Vienna tend to be expensive.

Car park sign

Car Hire

To hire a car, you will need your passport and a driver's licence that has been issued for at least one year. International licences are required for languages in a script other than Roman.

Major car hire firms have outlets at the airport and in the city centre. Car hire is more expensive at the airport, but it is the only place where you will be able to hire a car late at night or at weekends.

Taxis

You can recognize a taxi by the TAXI sign on the roof. They are usually saloon cars, often Mercedes. If a taxi is for hire, the sign on its roof will be illuminated. In the centre of Vienna it is easier to get a taxi at one of the city's ranks, rather than by hailing one in the street. Alternatively you can call one of three numbers (31300, 40100 or 60160) to order a taxi, which will usually come in a few minutes. The operator tells you when to expect it and you should be waiting, as it may drive off if you are not there. A short trip costs from €5 to €10. There are additional costs for more than one passenger, luggage, and late-night and weekend journeys. A trip to the airport costs up to €30. It is usual to tip about 10% of the fare, rounding up the sum to the nearest euro.

Taxi meter

Basic fare / **Supplement fare**

Vienna's taxis are usually saloon cars, often Mercedes

TICKETS AND TRAVEL CARDS

FINDING YOUR WAY around Vienna's transport system is fairly simple, but buying the right ticket at the right price can be a bit more confusing. It is easiest to buy your tickets in advance, either from a newsagent *(Tabak Trafik)*, from a ticket machine or over the counter at an underground or Schnellbahn booking office. A standard ticket covers all areas of Vienna (zone 100). With this you can change trains and lines as often as you like, and even change from the underground to a tram or a bus, but you are not allowed to break your journey.

A weekly season ticket is valid for all areas of Vienna (zone 100) and from Monday to Sunday. This is a good buy if you plan to use public transport for more than four days. One advantage of this ticket

24-hour ticket

72-hour ticket

Wochenkarte
W 08/1999

Weekly season ticket

***Streifenkarte*,
or strip ticket,
valid for four
journeys**

***8-Tage-Karte*
valid for eight days'
travel or for up to
eight people on
the same day**

is that it need not be used just by the person who bought it. More useful for parties of visitors are the green *8-Tage-Karte*. Each card consists of eight strips which, when stamped, are valid for a day on Vienna's public transport. This ticket is good for several people travelling together as up to

eight people may stamp the same ticket. It is important that you start with strip one – stamping strip eight first will invalidate the other seven. Also available are 24-hour tickets and 72-hour tickets, as well as a strip ticket for four rides. All tickets are valid for all public transport including night buses.

1 Use the touch screen to change the language and to select your ticket type.

2 Follow the instructions and insert coins, notes or a credit card to pay for your ticket.

Fahrkarten *(auch Wochenkarten und Monatskarten)*

Vienna Transport Authority ticket machine

Insert your ticket in the direction of the arrow. Wait for the pinging noise to confirm that your ticket has been validated.

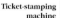

Ticket-stamping machine

Travelling by Underground

station symbol

CONSTRUCTION OF VIENNA'S underground, or U-Bahn, system, one of the most modern in Europe, began in 1969 and continues to the present day. Though Vienna is a compact city and many of the major sights can be reached on foot or by tram and bus, the U-Bahn is a clean, fast and reliable way of crossing the city. It is also useful for travelling further afield. The U-Bahn currently comprises five lines, with line U2 running in a circle that corresponds to the outer edge of the Ringstrasse.

manually and you will need to pull hard as they are stiff and heavy. The U-Bahn is generally safe (*see p240*), but in case of emergencies there are help points on most platforms. You are not allowed to smoke on U-Bahn platforms or on the trains (smoking is also forbidden on trams and buses).

THE UNDERGROUND SYSTEM

DISPLAYS ABOVE the train doors show stations and connections, and a recorded voice announces stops and also connections to trams and buses. Be aware, though, that this announcement may be a station behind. Prams can be stored by the doors; a picture of a pram indicates where. Bicycles are also allowed, but only on a few carriages and at set times. Doors are opened

Emergency help point on a Vienna U-Bahn platform

MAKING A JOURNEY BY UNDERGROUND

1 To determine which line to take, travellers should look for their destination on a U-Bahn map. The five lines are distinguished by colour and number. Simply trace the line to your destination, making a note of where you need to change lines. Connections to other forms of transport are also shown.

Pull handle to open door

The door opens out to the side

2 Tickets can be bought from a newsagent, ticket vending machines or ticket offices. To get to the trains, insert your ticket into the ticket-stamping machine in the direction of the arrow. Wait for the ping indicating that it is validated, and pass through the barrier. Follow the signs (with the number and colour of the line) to your platform.

3 On the platform, check the direction and destination of the train on an electronic destination indicator.

Sign showing stops on line 3 of the U-Bahn, including connecting stops

4 Stops along the line are shown on a plan. A red arrow in the corner shows the direction in which the train enters the station.

5 At your destination follow the *Ausgang* signs to reach street level.

6 At stations with more than one exit, use the map of the city to check which street or square you will come out at.

Viennese tram

Travelling by Tram

THE CITY'S RED AND WHITE trams are a familiar sight, and the Viennese know winter has arrived when tram drivers put up their leather screens against the icy wind that blows through the doors. Sadly many lines are being pulled up to make way for cars, and development of the U-Bahn means that some lines are no longer needed. A visit to Vienna would not be complete without a tram ride, as it offers not only an excellent view of the city, but a nostalgic journey into Vienna's past.

USING A TRAM

USING VIENNA'S TRAMS is a delightful way to get around the city. There are still some old-style trams in use with wooden seats and old-fashioned interiors. A recorded voice announces the stops (as on the underground and buses), and each tram has its route clearly displayed with all the stops marked. The doors are opened by pressing the button beside them. Single-journey tickets can be bought from machines at the front of the tram, but regular passengers tend to use passes or

Tram stop

strip tickets *(see p252)*, which work out cheaper and are more convenient.

Tram exit button

Tram entrance button

SIGHTSEEING BY TRAM

A GOOD WAY to see the parade of handsome 19th-century public buildings on the Ringstrasse is on the tram network. A trip on tram lines 1 and 2 will take you

Trams in a busy Vienna street

past buildings ranging in style from Greek Neo-Classical to Jugendstil *(see p54–7)*. The Tram Museum gives organized tours of Vienna in a 1920s tram (including a visit to Vienna's Tram Museum itself). The meeting point is at Otto Wagner's Karlsplatz Pavilions *(see p146)*, and prospectuses are available from information offices. Private groups may also hire a vintage tram (built between 1913 and 1958) to take them to the Prater or a *Heuriger* or simply to tour the city.

Tram Museum
790944903.

USEFUL TRAM ROUTES

All the main sights round the Ringstrasse can be reached easily by lines 1 and 2. Some lines which go further out run part of the way around the Ringstrasse, while others start from interchanges located around the edge of the Ringstrasse.

Theater in der Josefstadt

Maria Treu Kirche

Franz-Josefs-Bahnhof *(for Museum of Modern Art)*

Parlament

Rathausplatz/ Burgtheater

Burgring

Schottentor Universität *(for Votivkirche)*

Natural History and Kunsthistorisches museums

Resselgasse

Oper

Karlskirche

Schwarzenbergplatz

Weihburggasse

Schloss Belvedere

Unteres Belvedere

Stubentor

Austrian Museum of Applied Arts

Belvedere

Stadtpark Portals

KEY

● Tram stop
○ Interchange stop
— Lines 1 and 2
— Line D
— Lines 62 and 65
— Line J
— Line 71

Travelling by Bus

Bus stop

LITTLE HOPPER BUSES serve the centre of Vienna and larger buses go from the inner suburbs, Ringstrasse and Prater to the outer suburbs. Some buses run along old tram routes, and they are the same municipal red and white colour as the trams. Bus stops are also in the same red and white colours as tram stops.

Route number

Destination

Viennese hopper bus

BUS TICKETS

TICKETS FOR buses, like tram tickets, can be purchased when you get on, but it is more advisable to buy a pass or a strip ticket from Schnellbahn or U-Bahn stations, or from a newsagent, beforehand *(see p252)*. Ticket machines on trams and buses are identical. Tickets other than those bought on the bus or tram need to be stamped in the blue ticket-stamping machine in order to validate them. If you have already made part of your journey by tram or U-Bahn, there is no need to stamp your ticket again. Limited services run on holidays and Christmas Day. On New Year's Eve, buses and other forms of public transport run all night.

2 Insert money in the slot

1 Choose your ticket

3 Collect your ticket and change here

Bus ticket machine

buses *(Bundesbusse)* that run to a variety of destinations in eastern Austria. Coaches to other regions of Austria depart from the Südbahnhof *(see p248)*. The main coach companies that organize excursions and tours in and around Vienna are Cityrama and Vienna Sightseeing *(see p238)*, and their buses and coaches, full of tourists, are a common sight on the roads of central Vienna, especially during the summer months.

COACHES

VIENNA'S MAIN coach station is Wien Mitte *(see p248)*, where you can board one of the orange-coloured federal

NIGHT BUSES

NIGHT BUSES operate every night of the week starting at half past midnight and then at 30-minute intervals until 4am in the morning. There is some variation between the service operating on weekday nights (Sunday night through to Thursday night) and that operating at the weekend and on public holidays. All night buses in Vienna start from Schwedenplatz and travel to most suburbs of the city. All types of bus tickets are valid for travel on the city's night buses.

If you are staying some distance from a night bus route, it is possible to arrange for a taxi to pick you up from your destination stop. Taxis can be booked through the Transport Office in Schwedenplatz.

Travelling by Train

Schnellbahn logo

Bundesbahn logo

THE AUSTRIAN Federal Railways or Bundesbahn, with its familiar red and white logo, has about 5,800 km (3,600 miles) of railways, and offers frequent direct connections to all European countries *(see p248)*. Within Austria, it offers good connections to tourist destinations such as Salzburg and Innsbruck. Further afield destinations *(see pp158–79)* can be reached by Schnellbahn or Bundesbahn lines.

in order to distinguish it from national routes. Timetable information is available from station information offices and is displayed on station departures and arrivals boards.

THE SCHNELLBAHN (known as the S-Bahn for short), with its distinctive blue and white logo, is really a commuter service. It has stops in the centre of Vienna interconnecting with mainline railway stations

(see p249), but is of most use as a means of getting to sights that are further afield. The local Bundesbahn is also a commuter service, when it is sometimes called the Regionalbahn on maps and timetables

Schnellbahn train

STREET FINDER

THE MAP REFERENCES all for of the sights, hotels, restaurants, bars, shops and entertainment venues described in this book refer to the maps in this section. A complete index of street names and all the places of interest marked on the maps can be found on the following pages. The key map *(right)* shows the area of Vienna covered by the *Street Finder*. This map includes sightseeing areas as well as districts for hotels, restaurants and entertainment venues.

All the street names in the index and on the *Street Finder* are in German – *Strasse* translating as street and *Gasse* meaning lane. *Platz* or *Hof* indicate squares or courtyards. Throughout this guide, the numbers of the houses follow the street names, in the same way that you will find them in Vienna.

View of Vienna's roof tops from Am Hof (see p87)

KEY TO STREET FINDER

☐	Major sight
☐	Places of interest
☐	Other building
Ⓤ	U-Bahn station
🚆	Bundesbahn station
🚊	Badner Bahn stop
Ⓢ	Schnellbahn station
🚌	Bus and coach station
P	Parking
ℹ	Tourist information office
✚	Hospital with casualty unit
🚔	Police station
✝	Church
✡	Synagogue
⊠	Post office
=	Railway line
-	One-way street
-	Pedestrian street

SCALE OF MAPS
1–4 & 5–6 RESPECTIVELY

0 metres	250	
		1:12,000
0 yards	250	

0 metres	125	
		1:7,000
0 yards	125	

Section of the Austria fountain (1846) by Schwanthaler (left) and side view of the Schottenkirche (see p110)

0 kilometres	1

0 miles	0.5

1

2

GENTZGASSE

GÜRTEL

WÄHRINGER

RAUSCHERSTRASSE

STRASSE

NORDBAHNSTRASSE

*Schottenring
and Alsergrund*

5

DOBLE

TABOR

6

ALIASTRASSE

*Museum and
Townhall
Quarter*

*Stephansdom
Quarter*

LENZGASSE

3

*Hofburg
Quarter*

4

STRASSE

BERSTRASSE

MARIAHILFER

STRASSE

RENNWEG

*Opera and
Naschmarkt*

MARGARETEN STRASSE

*Belvedere
Quarter*

WIENER GÜRTEL

MARGARETENGÜRTEL

Gateway leading to
the Burggarten from
Albertinaplatz in the
Hofburg Quarter

Generals on horseback
guard the statue of Maria
Theresa (1888) in Maria-
Theresia-Platz, Museum
and Townhall Quarter

Street Finder Index

V IENNA'S STREET and place names are generally spelt as one word; -platz, -strasse or -kirche are put at the end of the name, as in Essiggasse for example. Occasionally they are treated as separate words, for instance Alser Strasse. Abbreviations used in this index are Dr as in Doctor-Ignaz-Seipel-Platz, and St as in Sankt Josef Kirche. Some entries have two map references. The first refers to the smaller scale map that covers the whole of central Vienna, the second refers to the large-scale inset map that covers the Stephansdom and Hofburg Quarters.

USEFUL WORDS	
Gasse	street
Strasse	road
Platz	square
Hof	court
Kirche	church
Kapelle	chapel
Dom	cathedral
Denkmal	monument
Markt	market
(often the sight of an old market)	
Brücke	bridge

General Index

Acknowledgments

DORLING KINDERSLEY wishes to thank the following people who contributed to the preparation of this book.

MAIN CONTRIBUTOR
Stephen Brook was born in London and educated at Cambridge. After working as an editor in Boston, Massachusetts, and in London, he became a full-time writer in 1982. Among his many books are *New York Days, New York Nights*; *The Double Eagle*; *Prague* and *L.A. Lore*. He has also written books on wine and contributes articles on wine and travel to many newspapers and periodicals.

ADDITIONAL CONTRIBUTORS
Gretel Beer, Caroline Bugler, Dierdre Coffey, Fred Mawer, Nicholas Parsons.

PROOF READER
Diana Vowles.

DESIGN AND EDITORIAL
MANAGING EDITOR Carolyn Ryden
MANAGING ART EDITOR Steve Knowlden
SENIOR EDITOR Georgina Matthews
SENIOR ART EDITOR Vanessa Courtier
EDITORIAL DIRECTOR David Lamb
ART DIRECTOR Anne-Marie Bulat
CONSULTANT Robert Avery
LANGUAGE CONSULTANT Barbara Eichberger
Ros Angus, Tessa Bindloss, Chris Clouter, Carey Combe, Lucinda Cooke, Maggie Crowley, Gadi Farfour, Fay Franklin, Sally Gordon, Emily Green, Alistair Gunn, Elaine Harries, Melanie Hartzell, Paul Hines, Joanne Lenney, Helen Partington, Alice Peebles, Robert Purnell, Ella Milroy, Nicki Rawson, Sands Publishing Solutions, Simon Ryder, Andrew Szudek, Samia Tadros, Lynda Warrington, Susannah Wolley Dod.

EDITORIAL ASSISTANCE
Marianne Petrou, Sadie Smith

ADDITIONAL ILLUSTRATIONS
Kevin Jones, Gilly Newman, John Woodcock, Martin Woodward.

CARTOGRAPHY
Peter Winfield, James Mills-Hicks (Dorling Kindersley Cartography)
Colourmap Scanning Limited, Contour Publishing, Cosmographics, European Map Graphics, Street Finder maps: ERA Maptec Ltd (Dublin).
MAP CO-ORDINATORS Simon Farbrother, David Pugh
CARTOGRAPHIC RESEARCH Jan Clark, Caroline Bowie, Claudine Zante.

ADDITIONAL PHOTOGRAPHY
DK Studio/Steve Gorton, Poppy, Steve Shott, Clive Streeter.

FACT CHECKER
Melanie Nicholson-Hartzell

SPECIAL ASSISTANCE
Marion Telsnig and Ingrid Pollheimer-Stadtlober at the Austrian Tourist Board, London; Frau Preller at the Heeresgeschichtliches Museum; Frau Wegscheider at the Kunsthistorisches Museum; Frau Stillfried and Mag Czap at the Hofburg; Herr Fehlinger at the Museen der Stadt Wien; Mag Schmid at the Natural History Museum; Mag Dvorak at the Österreichischer Bundestheaterverband; Dr Michael Krapf and Mag Grabner at the Österreichische Galerie; Robert Tidmarsh and Mag Weber-Kainz at Schloss Schönbrunn; Frau Zonschits at the Tourismusverband.

PHOTOGRAPHY PERMISSIONS
DORLING KINDERSLEY would like to thank the following for their kind permission to photograph at their establishments:

Alte Backstube, Bestattungsmuseum, Schloss Belvedere, Bundesbaudirektion, Deutschordenskirche and Treasury, Dom und Diözesanmuseum, Sigmund Freud Gesellschaft, Josephinum Institut für Geschichte der Medzin der Universität Wien, Kapuzinerkirche, Pfarramt St. Karl, Stift Klosterneuburg, Wiener Kriminalmuseum, Niederösterreichisches Landesmuseum, Österreichischer Bundestheaterverband, Österreichische Postsparkasse (P. S. K.), Puppen- und Spielzeugmuseum, Dombausekretariat Sankt Stephan, Spanische Reitschule, Österreichisches Tabakmuseum and Museum für Volkskunde. Dorling Kindersley would also like to thank all the shops, restaurants, cafés, hotels, churches and public services who aided us with photography. These are too numerous to thank individually.

PICTURE CREDITS
t = top; tl = top left; tc = top centre; tr = top right; cla = centre left above; ca = centre above; cra = centre right above; cl = centre left; c = centre; cr = centre right; clb = centre left below; cb = centre below; crb = centre right below; bl = bottom left; b = bottom; bc = bottom centre; br = bottom right; d = detail.

Works of art have been reproduced with the permission of the following copyright holders:
© DACS 1994: 34cbr, 90c, 105c, 155t; © THE HENRY MOORE FOUNDATION: 144b.

The Publishers are grateful to the following individuals, companies and picture libraries for permission to reproduce their photographs:

GRAPHIC SAMMLUNG ALBERTINA, Wien: 26–7; ANCIENT ART AND ARCHITECTURE COLLECTION: 24b(d), 25t, 29ca; ARCHIV FÜR KÜNST UND GESCHICHTE, Berlin: 8–9, 16(d), 17t, 19tc(d), 19br(d), 21b, 22–3, 24t, 24–5, 25cb, 25bl, 26ca, 26br(d), 27t, 28t, 28c, 28br(d), 29t, 28–9, 29cl, 29bl, 30t(d), 30cl, 32cl, 32br, 33b, 34br, 36tl, 38br, 55b(d), 67 inset, 87b(d), 98cla, 110b(d), 149ca, 152cb, 172b, 237 inset; Erich Lessing 38cb, 39cr, 98cla; AUSTRIAN AIRLINES: 246t; AUSTRIAN ARCHIVES: 35tl.

BILDARCHIV PREUSSISCHER KULTURBESITZ, Berlin: 23bl, 35cbl, 92t; CASA EDITRICE BONECHI, Firenze: 167ca; CHRISTIAN BRANDSTÄTTER VERLAG, Wien: 20ca, 31c(d), 33tl, 34bl, 83t, 99c; BRIDGEMAN ART LIBRARY, London: 133b(d); Albertina, Wien 46br; Bonhams, London 24ca; British Library, London 4t(d), 19bl(d); Kunsthistorisches Museum, Wien 19tr(d), 46cr; Museum der Stadt Wien 33tr, 38car(d), 38bcl, 39cl; Österreichische Galerie 35tr;

HOTEL BRISTOL: 192cr; ©1999 BUNDESGÄRTEN, Wien: 172tl ; BUNDESMINISTERIUM FÜR FINANZEN: 27cb(d); BURGHAUPTMANNSCHAFT IN WIEN: 101ca, 101cb, 101b.

COURTESY OF CAFÉ MUSEUM: 58BR; ARCHÄOLOGISCHER PARK CARNUNTUM: 21tr; CASINOS AUSTRIA: 227c; CEPHAS PICTURE LIBRARY: Mick Rock 161b, 210tl; Wine Magazine 240br; CONTRAST PHOTO: Milenko Badzic 65t; Franz Hausner 166b; Michael Himml /Transglobe 152tr, 176; Hinterleitner 227b; Peter Kurz 63b, 141tl, 233b; Boris Mizaikoffl/Transglobe 63t; Tappeiner/Transglobe 234c; H Valencak 178b.

DDSG-DONAUREISEN GMBH: 249c; ET ARCHIVE, London: 38br; Museum für Gestaltung, Zurich 34cl; Museum der Stadt Wien 26bl, 31tl, 38cal; EUROLINES (UK) Ltd: 248cb; EUROPEAN COMMISSION: 243; MARY EVANS PICTURE LIBRARY, London: 18tl, 18bl, 18br, 19tl, 22c, 25br, 27br, 30cr, 30bl, 30br, 32t, 35b, 38t, 39t, 76tr, 175b, 191 inset.

F. A. HERBIG VERLAGSBUCHHANDLUNG GMBH, München: 98bl, 98br, 99bl, 99br.

ROBERT HARDING PICTURE LIBRARY: Larsen Collinge International 42cb, 232t; Adam Woolfitt 62t, 137t, 150t, 178t, 256tl; HEERESGESCHICHTLICHES MUSEUM, Wien: 47b, 166t, 166b, 167t, 167cb, 167b; HEINZ HEIDER, VOR: 252cl; HISTORISCHES MUSEUM DER STADT WIEN: 17b, 20t, 21ca, 21cbr, 26t, 28cb, 32cr, 32bl, 33ca, 33cb, 43t, 47tl, 49c, 141tc, 141tr, 145ca, 169t; HULTON-DEUTSCH COLLECTION: 28bl, 36tr(d), 38bcr(d), 168ca; HUTCHISON LIBRARY: John G Egan 202t.

THE IMAGE BANK, London: GSO Images 11b; Fotoworld 41bl; HOTEL IMPERIAL: 192b.

JOSEFSTADT THEATRE: 226c.

WILHELM KLEIN: 23t, 26cb; KUNSTHAUS WIEN: Peter Strobel 48t; KUNSTHISTORISCHES MUSEUM, Wien: 24cb, 41cbr, 46cl, 48b, 56c, 95t, 95b, 99t, 100 all, 122–3 all, 124–5 all, 126–7 all, 175tl.

J & L LOBMEYR, Wien: 49t; LEOPOLD MUSEUM-PRIVATSTIFTUNG: *Selbstbildnis*, 1910, by Egon Schiele 46bla, *Hockender Weiblicher Akt*, 1910, by Egon Schiele 120tr, *Self Portrait with Chinese Lantern*, 1912, by Egon Schiele 118t, *Die Schnitter*, 1922 by Egger-Lienz 120t; MAGNUM PHOTOS: Erich Lessing 18tr, 20c, 20bl, 20br, 21tl, 21cbl, 22cb, 23cal, 26c, 29br, 30–1, 31b; MANSELL COLLECTION, London: 9 inset; MARRIOTT HOTELS: 196t, 233t; MUSEUM JUDENPLATZ: Votava/PID 86tl; MUSEUMSQUARTIER, WIEN: Rupert Steiner MQ E+B

GesmbH 41br, 119t, Martin Gendt MQ E+B GesmbH 119bl; MUMOK, MUSEUM OF MODERN ART LUDWIG FOUNDATION VIENNA: *Homme accroupi*, 1907, by André Derain, © ADAGP, Paris & DACS 2002, 119br; *The Red Horseman*, 1974 by Roy Lichtenstein, © Estate of Roy Lichtenstein/DACS 2002, 120b. NARODNI MUSEUM, Praha: 18bc; NATURHISTORISCHES MUSEUM, Wien: 46t, 128–9 except 129br, 235cb.

ÖSTERREICHISCHE BUNDESBAHNEN: 248t, 255b; ÖSTERREICHISCHE GALERIE, Wien: 47ca, 47cb, 154c, 155 all, 156bl, 157 all; ÖSTERREICHISCHES MUSEUM FÜR ANGEWANDTE KUNST, Wien: 28ca, 47tl, 56t, 57c, 82–3 all except 83t; ÖSTERREICHISCHE NATIONALBANK: 243cal, 243cac; ÖSTERREICHISCHE NATIONAL-BIBLIOTHEK, Wien: 20cb, 22t, 23cb, 36c; ÖSTERREICH WERBUNG: 5bl, 27ca, 31tc, 31tr, 34ca, 44b, 98cbl, 101t, 140b, 163cb, 163b, 172t, 179b, 205t, 232cr.

POPPERFOTO: 37tc; RAIFFEISENBANK WIEN: Gerald Zugman 34cr; RETROGRAPH ARCHIVE, London: Martin Ranicar-Breese 193br; REX FEATURES, London: Action Press 36bl, Adolfo Franzo 37tl, Sipa Press 121b, Sokol/Sipa Press 121b; GEORG RIHA: 77t; RONACHER VARIETY THEATRE/CMM: Velo Weger 226t.

HOTEL SACHER: 194t; SCHLOSS SCHÖNBRUNN KULTUR- UND BETRIEBS GESMBH, Wien: Professor Gerhard Trumler 172c, 173 all except 173b, 174 all, 175tr; SCHLOß SCHÖNBRUNN KULTUR-UND BETRIEBSGES.M.B.H. 1999: Wolfgang Voglhuber 139b; SCIENCE PHOTO LIBRARY, London: Geospace 10t; SYGMA: Habans/Orban 37tr, Viennareport 37ca; TRAVEL LIBRARY: Philip Entiknapp 66–7, 221t, 250t.

WERNER FORMAN ARCHIVE: Museum der Stadt Wien 60c; St Stephens Cathedral Museum 23car; WIENER LINIEN GMBH & CO KG: 252 cl; WIENER SÄNGERKNABEN: 5cbr, 39b, 64b; WIENER STADT- UND LANDESBIBLIO-THEK, Wien: 36tc, 36bl; WIGAST AG: 196c, 196b.

VIENNASLIDE: Harald A Jahn 232b; Karl Luymair 230cl; MUSEUM FÜR VÖLKERKUNDE, Wien: 49b, 235b; VOTAVA, Wien: 163t; ZEFA: 153c; Anatol 98–9; Damm 248b; G Gro-Bauer 179t; Havlickek 177b; Sibelberbauer 62b; Streichan 37cb; Studio Mike 208t; V Wentzel 41cbc.

JACKET: Front - DK PICTURE LIBRARY: Peter Wilson bc, cl; POWERSTOCK: Rossenbach main image; V. Wentzel cr. Back - DK PICTURE LIBRARY: Peter Wilson t, b. Spine - POWERSTOCK: Rossenbach

All other images © Dorling Kindersley. For further information see: www.dkimages.com

DORLING KINDERSLEY SPECIAL EDITIONS

Dorling Kindersley books can be purchased in bulk quantities at discounted prices for use in promotions or as premiums. We are also able to offer special editions and personalized jackets, corporate imprints, and excerpts from all of our books, tailored specifically to meet your own needs.

To find out more, please contact: (in the United Kingdom) – Sarah.Burgess@dk.com or SPECIAL SALES, DORLING KINDERSLEY LIMITED, 80 STRAND, LONDON WC2R 0RL;

(in the United States) – SPECIAL MARKETS DEPARTMENT, DK PUBLISHING, INC., 375 HUDSON STREET, NEW YORK, NEW YORK 10014.

Phrase Book

IN EMERGENCY

Help!	**Hilfe!**	**hilf**-er
Stop!	**Halt!**	**hult**
Call a doctor	**Holen Sie einen Arzt**	**hole**'n zee **ine**'n **artst**
Call an ambulance	**Holen Sie einen Krankenwagen**	**hole**'n zee **ine**'n **krank**'n-**varg**'n
Call the police	**Holen Sie die Polizei**	**hole**'n zee dee pol-its-**eye**
Call the fire brigade	**Holen Sie die Feuerwehr**	**hole**'n zee dee **foy**-er-vair
Where is the nearest telephone?	**Wo finde ich ein Telefon in der Nähe?**	voh **fin**-der ish ine tel-e-fone in dair **nay**-er?
Where is the nearest hospital?	**Wo ist das nächstgelegene Krankenhaus?**	voh ist duss next-g'**lay**-g'ner **krunk**'n-hows?

COMMUNICATION ESSENTIALS

Yes	**Ja**	**yah**
No	**Nein**	**nine**
Please	**Bitte**	**bitt**-er
Thank you	**Danke vielmals**	dunk-er **feel**-malse
Excuse me	**Gestatten**	g'**shtatt**'n
Hello	**Grüss Gott**	groos got
Goodbye	**Auf Wiedersehen**	owf **veed**-er-zay-ern
Goodnight	**Gute Nacht**	goot-er **nukht**
morning	**Vormittag**	**for**-mit-targ
afternoon	**Nachmittag**	**nakh**-mit-targ
evening	**Abend**	**ah**b'nt
yesterday	**Gestern**	**gest**'n
today	**Heute**	**hoyt**-er
tomorrow	**Morgen**	**morg**'n
here	**hier**	**hear**
there	**dort**	**dort**
What?	**Was?**	**vuss?**
When?	**Wann?**	**vunn?**
Why?	**Warum?**	var-**room?**
Where?	**Wo/Wohin?**	**voh**/vo-**hin?**

USEFUL PHRASES

How are you?	**Wie geht es Ihnen?**	vee **gayt** ess **een**'n?
Very well, thank you	**Sehr gut, danke**	**zair** goot, dunk-er
Pleased to meet you	**Es freut mich sehr, Sie kennenzulernen**	ess **froyt** mish zair, zee **ken**'n-tsoo-lairn'n
See you soon	**Bis bald/bis gleich**	bis bult/bis **gleyesh**
That's fine	**Sehr gut**	**zair** goot
Where is...?	**Wo befindet sich...?**	voe b'**find**'t zish...?
Where are...?	**Wo befinden sich...?**	voe b'**find**'n zish...?
How far is it to...?	**Wie weit ist...?**	vee **vite** ist...?
Which way to...?	**Wie komme ich zu...?**	vee **komma** ish tsoo...?
Do you speak English?	**Sprechen Sie englisch?**	**shpresh**'n zee **eng**-glish?
I don't understand	**Ich verstehe nicht**	ish fair-**shtay**-er nisht
Could you please speak slowly?	**Bitte sprechen Sie etwas langsamer?**	bitt-er **shpresh**'n zee et-vuss **lung**-zam-er?
I'm sorry	**Es tut mir leid/Verzeihung**	es toot meer lyte/fair-**tseye**-oong

USEFUL WORDS

big	**gross**	**grohss**
small	**klein**	**kline**
hot	**heiss**	**hyce**
cold	**kalt**	**kult**
good	**gut**	**goot**
bad	**schlecht**	**shlesh t**
enough	**genug**	g'**nook**
well	**gut**	**goot**
open	**auf/offen**	**owf/off**'n
closed	**zu/geschlossen**	tsoo/g's**hloss**'n
left	**links**	**links**
right	**rechts**	**reshts**
straight on	**geradeaus**	g'**rah**-der-**owss**
near	**in der Nähe**	in dair **nay**-er
far	**weit**	**vyte**
up	**auf, oben**	**owf, obe**'n
down	**ab, unten**	**up, oont**'n
early	**früh**	**froo**
late	**spät**	**shpate**

entrance	**Eingang/Einfahrt**	**ine**-gung/**ine**-fart
exit	**Ausgang/Ausfahrt**	**ows**-gung/**ows**-fart
toilet	**WC/Toilette**	vay-**say**/toy-**lett**-er
free/unoccupied	**frei**	**fry**
free/no charge	**frei/gratis**	**fry**/**grah**-tis

MAKING A TELEPHONE CALL

I'd like to place a long-distance call	**Ich möchte ein Ferngespräch machen**	ish **mer**-shter ine **fairn**-g'shpresh mukh'n
I'd like to call collect	**Ich möchte ein Rückgespräch (Collectgespräch) machen**	ish **mer**-shter ine **rook**-g'shpresh (**coll**-ect-g'shpresh) mukh'n
local call	**Ortsgespräch**	**orts**-g'shpresh
I'll try again later	**Ich versuche es noch einmal etwas später**	ish fair-**zookh**-er ess nokh ine-mull **ett**-vuss shpay-ter
Can I leave a message?	**Kann ich etwas ausrichten?**	kunn ish **ett**-vuss **ows**-rikht'n?
Hold on	**Haben Sie etwas Geduld**	harb'n zee **ett**-vuss g'**doolt**
Could you speak up a little please?	**Bitte sprechen Sie etwas lauter?**	bitt-er **shpresh**'n zee et-vuss **lowt**-er?

STAYING IN A HOTEL

Do you have a vacant room?	**Haben Sie ein Zimmer frei?**	**harb**'n zee ine **tsimm**-er fry?
double room with double bed	**ein Doppelzimmer mit Doppelbett**	ine **dopp**'l-tsimm-er mitt **dopp**'l-bet
twin room	**ein Doppelzimmer**	ine **dopp**'l-tsimm-er
single room	**ein Einzelzimmer**	ine **ine**-ts'l-tsimm-er
room with a bath/shower	**Zimmer mit Bad/Dusche**	**tsimm**-er mitt **bart/doosh**-er
porter	**Gepäckträger/Concierge**	g'**peck**-tray-ger/kon-see-**airsh**
key	**Schlüssel**	shlooss'l
I have a reservation	**Ich habe ein Zimmer reserviert**	ish **harb**-er ine **tsimm**-er rezz-er-**veert**

SIGHTSEEING

bus	**der Bus**	dair **booss**
tram	**die Strassenbahn**	dee **stra**-sen-barn
train	**der Zug**	dair tsoog
art gallery	**Galerie**	gall-er-**ee**
bus station	**Busbahnhof**	**booss**-**barn**-hofe
bus (tram) stop	**die Haltestelle**	dee **hal**-te-shtel-er
castle	**Schloss, Burg**	**shloss**, **boorg**
palace	**Schloss, Palais**	**shloss**, pall-**ay**
post office	**das Postamt**	dee **pohs**-taamt
cathedral	**Dom**	**dome**
church	**Kirche**	**keersh**-er
garden	**Garten, Park**	**gart**'n, **park**
library	**Bibliothek**	bib-leo-**tek**
museum	**Museum**	moo-**zay**-oom
information (office)	**Information (-büro)**	in-for-mut-**see-on** (-zboo-roe)
closed for public holiday	**Feiertags geschlossen**	**fire**-targz g'**shloss**'n

SHOPPING

How much does this cost?	**Wieviel kostet das?**	vee-**feel kost**'t duss?
I would like...	**Ich hätte gern...**	ish **hett**-er gairn...
Do you have...?	**Haben Sie...?**	**harb**'n zee...?
I'm just looking	**Ich schaue nur an**	ish **shau**-er noor un
Do you take credit cards?	**Kann ich mit einer Kreditkarte bezahlen?**	kunn ish mitt ine-er kred-it-**kar**-ter b'**tsahl**'n?
What time do you open?	**Wann machen Sie auf?**	vunn **mukh**'n zee owf?
What time do you close?	**Wann schliessen Sie?**	vunn **shlees**'n zee?
This one	**dieses**	**deez**'z
expensive	**teuer**	**toy**-er
cheap	**billig**	**bill**-igg
size	**Grösse**	**grers**-er
white	**weiss**	**vyce**
black	**schwarz**	**shvarts**
red	**rot**	**roht**
yellow	**gelb**	**gelp**
green	**grün**	**groon**
blue	**blau**	**blau**

TYPES OF SHOP

antique shop	**Antiquitäten-geschäft**	un-tick-vi-**tayt**'n-g'**sheft**
bakery	**Bäckerei**	beck-er-**eye**
bank	**Bank**	bunk
book shop	**Buchladen/Buchhandlung**	bookh-lard'n/bookh-hant-loong
butcher	**Fleischerei**	fly-sher-**eye**
cake shop	**Konditorei**	kon-ditt-or-**eye**
chemist		
(for prescriptions)	**Apotheke**	App-o-**tay**-ker
(for cosmetics)	**Drogerie**	droog-er-**ree**
department store	**Warenhaus, Warengeschäft**	**vahr**'n-hows, **vahr**'n-g'**sheft**
delicatessen	**Feinkost (geschäft)**	**fine**-kost (g'**sheft**)
fishmonger	**Fischgeschäft**	fish-g'**sheft**
gift shop	**Geschenke(laden)**	g'**shenk**-er(**lahd**'n)
greengrocer	**Obst und Gemüse**	**ohbst** oont g'**moo**-zer
grocery	**Lebensmittel-geschäft**	**layb**'nz-mitt'l-g'**sheft**
hairdresser	**Friseur/Frisör**	freezz-**er**/freezz-**er**
market	**Markt**	**markt**
newsagent/tobacconist	**Tabak Trafik**	tab-**ack** tra-feek
travel agent	**Reisebüro**	**rye-z**er-boo-roe
café	**Cafe, Kaffeehaus**	kaff-**ay**, kaff-**ay**-hows

EATING OUT

Have you got a table for... people?	**Haben Sie einen Tisch für... Personen?**	harb'n zee ine'n tish foor... pair-**sohn**'n?
I want to reserve a table	**Ich möchte einen Tisch bestellen**	ish **mer**-shter ine'n tish b'**shtell**'n
The bill please	**Zahlen, bitte**	**tsarl**'n **bitt**-er
I am a vegetarian	**Ich bin Vegetarier**	ish bin vegg-er-**tah**-ree-er
Waitress/waiter	**Fräulein/Herr Ober**	**froy**-line/hair **oh**-bare
menu	**die Speisekarte**	dee **shpize**-er-kart-er
fixed price menu	**das Menü**	duss men-**oo**
cover charge	**Couvert/Gedeck**	**koo**-vair/g'**deck**
wine list	**Weinkarte**	**vine**-kart-er
glass	**Glas**	**glars**
bottle	**Flasche**	**flush**-er
knife	**Messer**	**mess**-er
fork	**Gabel**	**garb**'l
spoon	**Löffel**	**lerff**'l
breakfast	**Frühstück**	**froo**-shtook
lunch	**Mittagessen**	**mit**-targ-ess'n
dinner	**Abendessen/Dinner**	**arb**'nt-ess'n/dee-**nay**
main course	**Hauptspeise**	**howpt**-shpize-er
starter, first course	**Vorspeise**	**for**-shpize-er
dish of the day	**Tageskarte**	**targ**-erz-kart-er
wine garden(s)	**Heuriger (Heurige)**	**hoy**-rigg-er (-e)
rare	**englisch**	**eng**-glish
medium	**medium**	**may**-dee-oom
well done	**durch**	**doorsh**

MENU DECODER

See also pp204–9.

Apfel	**upf**'l	apple
Almdudler	ahlm-**dood**-ler	herbal lemonade
Banane	bar-**nar**-ner	banana
Ei	**eye**	egg
Eis	**ice**	ice cream
Fisch	**fish**	fish
Fisolen	fee-**soul**'n	green beans (haricot)
Fleisch	**flysh**	meat
Garnelen	**gar**-nayl'n	prawns
gebacken	g'**buck**'n	baked/fried
gebraten	g'**brart**'n	roast
gekocht	g'**kokht**	boiled
Gemüse	g'**mooz**-er	vegetables
vom Grill	fom **grill**	grilled
Gulasch	**goo**-lush	stew
Hendl/Hahn/Huhn	**hend**'l/**harn**/**hoon**	chicken
Kaffee	kaf-**fay**	coffee
Kartoffel/Erdäpfel	kar-**toff**l/**air**-dupf'l	potatoes
Käse	**kayz**-er	cheese
Knoblauch	k'**nob**-lowkh	garlic
Knödel	k'**nerd**'l	dumpling
Kotelett	kot-**lett**	chop
Lamm	**lumm**	lamb
Marillen	mah-**ril**'n	apricot
Meeresfrüchte	**mair**-erz-froosh-ter	seafood
Mehlspeise	**mayl**-shpize-er	dessert
Milch	**milhk**	milk
Mineralwasser	minn-er-**arl**-vuss-er	mineral water
Obst	**ohbst**	fresh fruit
Öl	**erl**	oil
Oliven	o-**leev**'n	olives
Orange	o-**ronsh**-er	orange
frischgepresster Orangensaft	**frish**-g'press-ter o-**ronsh**'n-zuft	fresh orange juice
Paradeissalat	pa-ra-**dice**-sa-lahd	tomato salad
Pfeffer	**pfeff**-er	pepper
pochiert	posh-**eert**	poached
Pommes frites	pomm-**fritt**	chips
Reis	**rice**	rice
Rind	**rint**	beef
Rostbraten	rohst-**brart**'n	steak
Rotwein	**roht**-vine	red wine
Salz	**zults**	salt
Sauce/Saft	**zohss**-er/zuft	sauce
Schalentiere	**sharl**'n-tee-rer	shellfish
Schinken/Speck	**shink**'n/shpeck	ham
Schlag	**shlahgg**	cream
Schnecken	**shnek**'n	snails
Schokolade	shock-o-**lard**-er	chocolate
Schwein	**shvine**	pork
Semmel	**zem**'l	roll
Senf	**zenf**	mustard
Serviettenknödel	ser-vee-**ert**'n-k'**nerd**'l	sliced dumpling
Sulz	**zoolts**	brawn
Suppe	**zoop**-er	soup
Tee	**tay**	tea
Topfenkuchen	**topf**'n-kookh'n	cheesecake
Torte	**tort**-er	cake
Wasser	**vuss**-er	water
Weinessig	**vine**-ess-igg	vinegar
Weisswein	**vyce**-vine	white wine
Wurst	**voorst**	sausage (fresh)
Zucker	**tsook**-er	sugar
Zwetschge	**tsvertsh**-ger	plum
Zwiebel	**tsveeb**'l	onions

NUMBERS

0	**null**	**nool**
1	**eins**	**eye**'ns
2	**zwei**	**tsvy**
3	**drei**	**dry**
4	**vier**	**feer**
5	**fünf**	**foonf**
6	**sechs**	**zex**
7	**sieben**	**zeeb**'n
8	**acht**	**uhkht**
9	**neun**	**noyn**
10	**zehn**	**tsayn**
11	**elf**	**elf**
12	**zwölf**	**tsverlf**
13	**dreizehn**	**dry**-tsayn
14	**vierzehn**	**feer**-tsayn
15	**fünfzehn**	**foonf**-tsayn
16	**sechszehn**	**zex**-tsayn
17	**siebzehn**	**zeep**-tsayn
18	**achtzehn**	**uhkht**-tsayn
19	**neunzehn**	**noyn**-tsayn
20	**zwanzig**	**tsvunn**-tsig
21	**einundzwanzig**	**ine**-oont-tsvunn-tsig
22	**zweiundzwanzig**	**tsvy**-oont-tsvunn-tsig
30	**dreissig**	**dry**-sig
40	**vierzig**	**feer**-tsig
50	**fünfzig**	**foonf**-tsig
60	**sechzig**	**zesh**-tsig
70	**siebzig**	**zeep**-tsig
80	**achtzig**	**uhkht**-tsig
90	**neunzig**	**noyn**-tsig
100	**einhundert**	ine **hoond**'t
1000	**eintausend**	ine **towz**'nt

TIME

one minute	**eine Minute**	**ine**-er min-**oot**-er
one hour	**eine Stunde**	**ine**-er **shtoond**-er
half an hour	**eine halbe Stunde**	**ine**-er **hull**-ber shtoond-er
Monday	**Montag**	**mone**-targ
Tuesday	**Dienstag**	**deen**-starg
Wednesday	**Mittwoch**	**mitt**-vokh
Thursday	**Donnerstag**	**donn**-er-starg
Friday	**Freitag**	**fry**-targ
Saturday	**Samstag**	**zum**-starg
Sunday	**Sonntag**	**zon**-targ

The Vienna Transport Network

THERE ARE FIVE U-Bahn lines running across the city, each identified by a number. The Schnellbahn is essentially a commuter service. Bundesbahn trains to the rest of Austria and Europe run from Vienna's mainline stations. The Badner Bahn operates between its terminal opposite the Opera, and Baden. For more details, see *Getting Around Vienna* on pages 250–55.